Issues in
Management
Accounting

Issues in
Management
Accounting

Edited by:

DAVID ASHTON
University of Bristol

TREVOR HOPPER
University of Manchester

ROBERT W. SCAPENS
University of Manchester

PRENTICE HALL
New York • London • Toronto • Sydney • Tokyo • Singapore

First published 1991 by
Prentice Hall
66 Wood Lane End, Hemel Hempstead
Hertfordshire HP2 4RG
A division of
Simon & Schuster International Group

Typeset in 10/12 pt Compugraphic Times
by MHL Typesetting Ltd, Coventry

Printed and bound in Great Britain by
BPCC Wheatons Ltd, Exeter

British Library Cataloguing in Publication Data

Issues in management accounting.
  1. Management accounting
  I. Ashton, David II. Hopper, Trevor III. Scapens, Robert
  W. (Robert William), _1946–_
  658.1511

  ISBN 0-13-505835-X
  ISBN 0-13-505843-0 pbk

1 2 3 4 5 95 94 93 92 91

Library of Congress Cataloging-in-Publication Data

Issues in management accounting/edited by David Ashton,
  Trevor Hopper, Robert Scapens.
      p.   cm.
  Includes bibliographical references.
  ISBN 0-13-505835-X (U.K.) : £34.50
  ISBN 0-13-505843-0 (U.K.) : £14.95
    1. Managerial accounting. I. Ashton, David. II. Hopper,
  Trevor, 1946–.' III. Scapens, Robert William.
  HF5657.4.I87 1990
  658.15'11—dc20   90-281
                                            CIP

Contents

List of Contributors

MIRGHANI N. AHMED, BSc(Hons), MA(Econ), Dip in Development Finance, is a Teaching Assistant in Accounting at the University of Juba, Sudan. At present he is a PhD candidate at the University of Manchester. His research interests are in the field of management accounting. A major current interest is the issue of cost allocation, both from a behavioural and economic viewpoint.

DAVID ASHTON is Professor of Accounting and Finance at the University of Bristol. His research interests are mainly in the area of finance. He is currently working on taxation and financial policy, differential information in markets and performance appraisal and financing decisions.

MAHMOUD EZZAMEL, BCom, MCom, PhD, is the Price Waterhouse Professor of Accounting and Finance at the University of Manchester Institute of Science and Technology (UMIST). His main research interests are the interface between management accounting and organizational behaviour with particular emphasis on divisionalized organizations, financial statement analysis, and accounting systems in not-for-profit organizations.

MILES GIETZMANN is a lecturer in Accounting at the London School of Economics. His major research interests reside in exploring the interface between agency theory and problems of cost allocation and the use of spreadsheets in the teaching of management accounting.

TREVOR HOPPER is the Peat Marwick McLintock Professor of Management Accounting at the University of Manchester. His current research interests lie in management accounting in the public sector, the politics of accounting and accounting methodology.

SYDNEY HOWELL read English at Cambridge and changed to quantitative research and teaching when, after several years in industry, he read for the PhD at Manchester Business School. He now lectures at MBS in Management Accounting and Control. His areas of research and teaching include Forecasting, Applied Multivariate Statistics, Information Systems and Financial Analysis, particularly of banks. He recently completed a two-year secondment at IBM's International Education Centre in Belgium.

CHRISTOPHER HUMPHREY is a lecturer in Accounting in the Department of Accounting and Finance, University of Manchester. His main current research interests are the application of the Financial Management Initiative in the Probation Service in England and Wales, and the 'expectations gap' regarding the role and nature of the limited company audit.

MALCOLM KING, MA, Dip Adv Maths, DPhil, is a senior lecturer in the Department of Management Studies at Loughborough University of Technology. He has a special interest in IT, derived from his background in quantitative analysis. This interest has led to research projects concerned with the reactions of individuals and organizations to computerized information systems. Another current research interest revolves around several projects developing expert systems to assist management decision-making.

BOB LEE, BTech, MSc, is a senior lecturer in Organizational Behaviour in the Department of Management Studies at Loughborough University of Technology and Director of the part-time MBA programme. His research interests include managerial promotion processes, management development and organizational politics. He is Management Development Adviser to the Royal Bank of Scotland.

ANNE LOFT is a lecturer at the Copenhagen Business School. From 1981 to 1986 she wrote her PhD (now published) at the London Business School. Her major research interests are in the role of the accounting profession and in the historical development of accounting seen in its social context.

JIM MACKEY, PhD, CMA, CPA, is an associate professor at California State University, Sacramento. His research interests concern the role of accounting in the manufacturing industries including cost, operational control and capital budgeting. His prior teaching positions were at York University in Canada and the Universities of Wisconsin and Michigan.

PETER MOIZER is the Professor of Accounting at the University of Leeds. Among his diverse research interests are two projects relating to performance appraisal and rewards: an empirical comparison of the work values of US/UK and male/female professional accountants, and a study investigating how UK corporate financial management perceives that its performance is appraised.

MIKE O'HARA, MA(Oxon), FCA, is a lecturer in Accounting at the University of Manchester, where he has special responsibility for computing in the Department of Accounting and Finance. His research interests are in computer auditing and computer education. Previously he worked for Arthur Young, where he was responsible for computer auditing training and computer training for their professional staff.

JOHN PIPER, BA, MSc, is a senior lecturer in Financial Management and Director of the Management Development Centre at Loughborough University of Technology. His research and consultancy interests span management accounting, management control and strategy. His current research interests include non-profit organization, strategic financial management and retail control.

ALISTAIR PRESTON is an assistant professor of Accounting at Boston University in the USA. His research interests are concerned with the origins and impacts of accounting practices in organizations and the development of qualitative research methods. He is currently working on the development of cost accounting in US hospitals.

ROBERT W. SCAPENS is Professor of Accounting at the University of Manchester. He has held visiting positions at the Ohio State University, the University of Cincinnati and Queens University, Ontario. His current research interests are in management accounting and accountability in large business organizations.

JOHN WHITTAKER, BA(Econ), MA(Econ), FCA, is a lecturer in Accounting and Director of the Accounting and Financial Management degree in the Department of Management Studies at Loughborough University of Technology. His research interests are in financial reporting and management accounting.

RICHARD M.S. WILSON is the Professor of Management Control at the Queen's University of Belfast and previously held the Pannell Kerr Forster Chair in Accounting at Nottingham Business School. He has taught in a number of universities both within the UK and overseas as well as having held senior commercial posts. Professor Wilson's main research interests are the determinants of early career success in accounting, the marketing of financial services, and the interface of managerial accounting, marketing and strategy.

Preface

Management accounting textbooks at the undergraduate, professional and managerial levels tend to neglect a series of important theoretical and practical developments in the subject area. Conversely, much of the literature covering these developments is not easily accessible to either students or practitioners. The purpose of this book is to help reduce this schism. Active researchers in the emergent areas have been invited to write about them in a manner appropriate to students and practitioners of management accounting.

The chapters seek to explain advances in a number of theoretical areas which directly impinge on management accounting practice. These include: decision-making; management control; microeconomics, including information economics and agency theory; organization theory; and accounting history. Insights gained from these theoretical advances and also from significant changes in practice are explored through a series of important topics. These include forecasting, model building and the use of micro-computers; the effect of information technology upon the work of management accountants; designing accounting systems that facilitate creativity and change within organizations; strategic management accounting; cost allocation; transfer pricing; performance appraisal and rewards; the effect of new methods of production management (e.g. JIT, MRP) upon accounting control systems; and the use of management accounting in the public sector.

The book is intended to update conventional textbooks and to expand important topic areas which are not normally well covered. The aim of the book is therefore to supplement, rather than to replace, existing second- and third-year undergraduate course texts in management accounting. It is also intended that accounting practitioners interested in accessible expositions of contemporary research in management accounting will find the book useful. Only the reader can judge whether the book is effective in these intentions. We hope that it is.

DAVID ASHTON
TREVOR HOPPER
ROBERT W. SCAPENS

xiii

Acknowledgements

Figures 5.2—5.6 reprinted with permission from L.A. Gordon, *et al.* (1978) 'Strategic decision processes and the design of accounting information systems: conceptual linkages', *Accounting, Organizations and Society*, vol. 3, no. 3/4. Copyright © Pergamon Press plc. All rights reserved.

Figures 5.11 and 5.12 reprinted with permission from p. 37 and p. 86 of *Competitive Advantage* by Michael E. Porter, published by The Free Press. Copyright © 1985 by Michael E. Porter. All rights reserved.

Figure 5.14 reprinted by permission from p. 120 of *Analysis for Strategic Marketing Decisions* by George S. Day. Copyright © 1986 by West Publishing Company. All rights reserved.

Figure 5.15 reprinted with permission from p. 81 of *The PIMS Principles* by Robert D. Buzzell and Bradley T. Gale. Copyright © 1987 by the Free Press. All rights reserved.

Tables 5.1—5.5, data derived from K. Simmonds (1986), 'The accounting assessment of competitive position', *European Journal of Marketing*, vol. 20, no. 1, pp. 16—31. Reprinted with permission.

Chapter 1

Introduction

DAVID ASHTON, TREVOR HOPPER and
ROBERT W. SCAPENS

Post Second World War management accounting in retrospect

In the 1950s and 1960s Western industrialized countries, especially North America and Britain, held strong positions in international markets. Their products were highly regarded, 'they could be sold relatively easily, and competition over price and quantity was relatively low. The assumption of benign and sometimes protected markets had several consequences for management control within companies. Management was concerned primarily with internal matters, especially production capacity. This focus on production meant that management controls were orientated towards manufacturing and internal administration rather than towards strategic and environmental considerations.

This was reflected by management styles within companies. Authority stemming from experience and position rather than professional expertise and qualifications tended to predominate. The emphasis lay on line hierarchies with staff functions playing a secondary, supportive role. Management decision-making was assumed to be highly structured and formal, with readily identifiable objectives and decision alternatives. There was little innovation in products or production processes. Existing products sold well, and existing production processes were well understood.

Paradoxically, given the inwardness and cost orientation of control systems then prevalent, relative efficiency was not high. There was little incentive for firms to minimize manufacturing costs, as increased costs could always be passed on to customers. Consequently, inefficient and poor management practices were common in many industries. This was exemplified by poor industrial relations practices.

Despite the pioneering work of British engineers and accountants in devising cost accounting systems at the turn of the century, the application of such systems had been slow in Britain, compared say to North America. Furthermore, even where cost accounting systems were used, the dissemination of cost information tended to be slight, and its use for management decision-making poorly exploited. In general, cost accounting systems were only loosely integrated with the management planning and control systems. Given that the latter were often very rudimentary, this is not surprising. While it would be unfair to attribute the blame for poor marketing, product development and technological innovation to the cost accounting systems, the focus on routine historical events and the neglect of prospective planning may have contributed to the financial conservatism of British industry and its emphasis on the short run and the status quo. Management accounting systems tended to be reactive, identifying problems and actions only when deviations from the business plan took place. Such systems reflected and reproduced mechanistic rather than innovative styles of management.

Pressures for change

The 1970s brought a considerable decline in the fortunes of British industry, though closer examination shows this to be an acceleration of a trend of relative decline exhibited throughout this century. A world-wide recession, following the oil price shock of 1973, threatened established markets for many British products. This was compounded by a decline in protected markets and increased competition from Europe and newly-emerging industrial nations, especially in the Far East. Accompanying and underpinning this increased competition was rapid technological development. Japan, for instance, was rapidly becoming one of the world's leaders in the use of robotics and computer-controlled processors, whereas much of British industry in the 1970s still used the production processes which had served so well in the 1950s and 1960s. The new technologies, however, reduced costs and improved quality, in many cases with far less labour. This had significant implications for employment and gave rise to social as well as economic consequences.

Technological change not only had an impact on manufacturing processes but it also had substantial effects on information processing within organizations. Developments in computers, and especially the emergence of micro-, or personal, computers, markedly changed the amount of data which can be accessed by managers. Managers can be informed to a far greater extent than ever before about all aspects of their company's operations. The design, maintenance and interpretation of information systems is now of considerable importance for effective management.

Thus the deployment of technology has become crucial for industrial success. As well as its effects on internal operations and controls, increased scientific knowledge has created significant new markets, for example in electronics, and has given added importance to product innovation and development. This in turn requires companies to employ organization structures and styles of management which are flexible and responsive to change. Unfortunately the response of British companies to these technological changes has been disappointing. The reasons are complex; they include factors such as poor education and training, low rates of industrial research and development and, significantly for this text, styles and methods of management that do not foster competitive innovation.

During the 1980s there was a major decline in the size of British manufacturing industry. Some companies failed to meet the new competition and went out of business, while other companies modernized and became more cost effective through the use of new technologies. The latter companies are, in general, now more competitive and more technologically advanced than their predecessors in British industry. Also, through a process of growth and mergers, many of these companies are now much larger and more international. The increase in size, coupled with the need to employ more professional specialists has led to highly differentiated organizations, with greater division of labour and departments. However, the need to co-ordinate these differentiated activities in order to meet environmental challenges has placed a premium on integration and adaptation. The pressures created by the need to simultaneously cope with organizational differentiation and integration has required newer and more sophisticated forms of management. Alongside the decline in manufacturing industry, there has been an increase in service industries. For example, there has been a continuing growth in the commercial sector of the British economy and major increases in the size of industries such as leisure and tourism.

To summarize, as British industry enters the last decade of the twentieth century, it is facing considerable uncertainty in both home and international markets, and unprecedented advances in manufacturing and information-processing technologies. In addition, it must be recognized that service industries (including industries in the commercial sector) form a major and growing part of the British economy, whereas the manufacturing sector has declined quite significantly.

Management accounting knowledge and practice

In its early days management accounting was essentially concerned with such cost accounting issues as the determination of product costs. Production technology was relatively simple, with products going through a series of distinct manufacturing processes. At each stage it was fairly easy to identify labour and material costs. The speed of the manufacturing process was frequently governed by the speed of manual operations. Hence, direct labour provided a natural basis for assigning indirect costs to individual products. It was this manufacturing technology which gave rise to the cost accounting systems which are described in management accounting textbooks even today. During the 1930s the focus on product costs was supplemented by work on budgets and responsibility accounting, and extended to divisional performance measurement and transfer pricing in the 1950s. Such developments stemmed primarily from practical innovations by managers and engineers and were relatively uninformed by academic research. It is interesting to note that researchers such as Johnson and Kaplan (1987), who are trying to address contemporary Western management accounting problems, lay great stress on the need to re-examine the history of management accounting. Such researchers believe that accounting research has become divorced from practice and, because of its domination of managerial education and training, has frustrated rather than facilitated solutions to new problems. Chapter 10, by Mackey, on accounting and operations technology, is illustrative of this emerging line of research.

In contrast to the paucity of academic management accounting research in previous periods, it is probably fair to say that the late 1950s to the mid-1970s were the heyday of management accounting research. Academics believed that they had solutions to the problems faced by practitioners. Numerous papers were published in academic journals, many of which found their way into the professional accounting literature. Much of today's textbook material is derived from research undertaken in that period. This research largely entailed the application of neoclassical economic theory to the problems of business decision-making and control. The models and techniques were attempts to 'programme' the decision-making and control processes. It was assumed that the objective of management decision-making is to maximize the wealth of shareholders, and that there is little uncertainty about either the decision alternatives or the decision outcomes.

By the early 1970s researchers were extending the models developed in the 1960s, primarily to deal with uncertain outcomes and the costs of providing information. There were linear programming models, cost variance investigation models, transfer pricing models, performance evaluation models, opportunity cost models, to name but a few. All these models were extensively researched and the associated decision procedures clearly defined. The objective of this research was to provide managers with a set of decision tools which would help them in their day-to-day work.

Despite pioneering work by Argyris and Simon, and their colleagues, in the 1950s, organizational and behavioural research into management accounting did not begin to flourish until the late 1960s. The 1970s witnessed a considerable amount of research into motivational aspects of management accounting systems. This was followed by contingency theory research, which tried to relate the design of accounting control systems to such organizational factors as size, technology and management styles, and to the type of environment in which they operate. The chapter by Moizer, Chapter 7, is illustrative of some of the issues raised by this research. It emphasizes the role that reward systems play in motivating individuals. The essential message is that accounting systems cannot be designed independently of motivational factors and performance appraisal systems.

During the 1980s, however, rather less management accounting research appeared in the academic journals, and there were few major contributions in the professional press. In general, management accounting researchers became increasingly critical of the existing state of management accounting knowledge. Furthermore, it became apparent that there was a significant gap between the 'theoretical' material contained in management accounting textbooks and the methods used by management accountants in practice. Chapter 3, by Ahmed and Scapens, which examines this gap between theory and practice in the context of overhead allocations, is illustrative of such concerns.

While not all researchers agree upon the existence of such a gap, or even whether it constitutes a problem, management accounting research in the 1980s became increasingly fragmented and moved away from the trends which had emerged in previous research. Some of the more significant changes are described below. First, economic-based management accounting research became less normative and more descriptive in an attempt to more realistically model and interpret managerial behaviour and the role of control systems. Agency theory, which is discussed by Ashton in Chapter 6, became particularly important, as it permits researchers to examine conflicts over control and the contribution of rewards and information. Previously economists had tended to ignore internal organizational control problems. They regarded the firm as essentially a single economic actor. By opening up what was previously regarded as a 'black box', significant new insights into managerial practice could be achieved. This is also noted in Chapter 3, by Ahmed and Scapens, on cost allocation and Chapter 4, by Ezzamel, on transfer pricing.

Second, there was a significant revival of research examining contemporary accounting problems, for example the introduction of new methods of operations management, such as JIT and MRP, and new systems for the control of overheads, such as activity costing. Similarly, the impact of new information technology became an important but still under-researched area. For example, the widespread adoption of spread sheets for financial analysis described in

Chapter 11, by O'Hara, has important ramifications for the role of management accountants. Chapter 14, by King and others, discusses the potential of new information technologies and its impact (or the lack of it) on British companies.

Third, the difficulties of adapting to environmental change have become another important research theme. This theme is addressed in several chapters, albeit in different ways. Gietzmann (Ch. 12) and O'Hara, operating from economic and management science backgrounds, examine the ability of computer models to cope with short-run uncertainties, while Wilson (Ch. 5) is concerned with more general strategic and marketing issues and with how management accounting might become more proactive and externally orientated. In contrast, Preston (Ch. 8) examines how managers make decisions and how decision-making is related to managerial cultures and creativity. In so doing, he questions whether conventional 'rational' depictions of decision-making are appropriate.

Fourth, there has been an increase in the variety of research methods being used. This has led to a major methodological debate amongst accounting researchers regarding how research should be conducted and the philosophical basis which underpins it. The variety in current research methods is illustrated in various chapters; for instance, the mathematical economics of Ashton, the behavioural analysis of Moizer (Ch. 7), the critical perspectives of Loft (Ch. 2), the anthropological emphasis of Preston and the managerial pragmatism of Wilson. Underpinning these various research methods are some fundamental methodological differences about the role and purpose of research. Although these methodological differences remain unresolved, common to all the methods is a significant change brought about by the increased emphasis upon fieldwork and descriptive research. Current research is, in general, directed at understanding practice, where previous research was more concerned with prescribing managerial behaviour and developing normative models.

Finally, there has been a significant evolution of research *on* management accounting, as opposed to research *in* management accounting. The revival of historical research as described by Loft is a notable example. In part, such research may be due to a genuine puzzlement about differences between textbook prescriptions and practice. In addition, there is an increasing interest in the social role of accounting. This has led to a growing number of critical studies seeking to understand the social and political context of management accounting. Chapter 9, by Humphrey, on accounting in the public sector is in this vein. It questions the rhetoric and taken-for-granted assumptions of policy-makers about the effectiveness of accounting controls currently advocated in the public sector.

These various changes in management accounting research are explored in greater detail below.

Management accounting research in the 1980s: addressing the gap?

Developments in economic approaches

Academic concern over the perceived gap between theory and practice has led to major changes in economic-based management accounting research in the 1980s. In general, there has been a drift away from normative research to more descriptive economic approaches which seek to model the complexities of management control and the internal organization of firms. The normative research had resulted in a series of decision models, such as discounted cash flow models and linear programming, which were intended to help managers make optimal decisions. Optimality was taken as synonymous with the maximization of the wealth of the owners or shareholders, and it was tacitly assumed that once appropriate decision rules were identified, the employees would unquestioningly and unselfishly implement them. Any necessary control mechanisms were assumed to be provided through the discipline of market forces. If entrepreneurs and their employees were not wholly efficient, new firms would enter the industry and price-cutting would ensure that inefficient producers were forced out.

In practice, there are many social and economic barriers to perfect competition. Even the briefest acquaintance with industrial and commercial organizations suggests considerable slackness and apparent inefficiency. In principal—agent (PA) analysis, it is accepted that employees are motivated by self-interest rather than altruism and are more likely to pursue personal rather than organizational goals. Moreover, it is impossible to monitor continually the behaviour and actions of employees to prevent them from pursuing their own self-interests. What prevents the organization, in such circumstances, from degenerating into anarchy is a series of binding agreements or contracts between the owners and their employees. These contracts specify the actions to be undertaken by employees as well as designating the rewards that will accrue to them. Thus, in PA analysis the economist is abandoning the view of the firm as an entity with the single purpose of maximizing owners' wealth in favour of a view of the firm as a collection of interlinked contracts.

The chapter by Ashton looks at the mathematical structure of such contracts. He argues that complex mathematics are required to model even quite simple situations. This is clearly a severe restriction on the development of realistic models of the organization. Nevertheless, the idea of the firm being composed of self-interested and economically rational agents yields many insights into the structure and nature of organizations.

A major area of difference between the theory and practice of management accounting is cost allocations. Recently the debate on this subject has been heightened by claims that both the theoretical and practical approaches to cost allocations are not relevant for modern businesses, especially businesses using new computer-based manufacturing technology. In this volume Ahmed and Scapens trace the debate over cost allocations from the discussion of methods of recovering the massive capital costs incurred by the railway companies which were established in the mid-nineteenth century, to the problems of determining the costs of producing individual products in a factory operated by robots at the end of the twentieth century. They point out that many of the technical approaches to the subject rely on concepts and methods derived from economics, whereas in practice cost allocations are influenced by a diverse set of legal, political and social, as well as economic factors. Consequently it is important for researchers to be sensitive to the organizational and social context within which cost allocations are to be used.

The chapter by Ezzamel looks at a specific type of cost allocation in a particular context, namely the transfer prices used within divisionalized businesses to charge for the goods and services exchanged internally. Transfer prices can have a major influence on the allocation of resources between divisions, and on the assessment of the performance of individual divisions and their managers. A transfer price which is 'high' will, other things being equal, result in the selling division appearing to be 'more' profitable and the buying division appearing to be 'less' profitable. This can lead to major shifts in the resources allocated to both divisions with the apparently more profitable division gaining greater access to corporate resources relative to the apparently less profitable division. The success of a transfer pricing system in co-ordinating and guiding the activities of a divisionalized business depends on its ability to capture the relevant organizational and economic factors. Ezzamel illustrates the variety of factors which have to be considered in setting transfer prices. He also points out that many of the theoretical models which have been developed give undue attention to economic factors and fail to capture important organizational and behavioural factors.

Developments in techniques

A recurring theme in several chapters is how developments in computers, especially the availability of cheap personal computers and spreadsheet software, are having a major impact on how managers can conduct analysis. Proponents of spreadsheets argue that their greatest strength lies in their facility for rapidly exploring alternative scenarios. This enables management to cope with uncertainty in decision inputs. In his chapter, Gietzmann mounts a spirited defence of one of the classical techniques of operational research, namely linear programming (LP). He argues that for certain well-structured problems LP remains a powerful tool for planning in the face of uncertainty. He argues that the ability of LP to search through a set of alternative decisions and to identify an optimal decision gives it a considerable advantage over spreadsheets. The difficulty with using spreadsheets to identify optimal decisions is that they do not indicate whether an optimal decision has been achieved, or even which decision alternative looks the most promising. When an optimal solution has been reached using LP, however, parametric sensitivity analysis ensures that optimality is maintained while 'what if' questions are answered.

Forecasting is a prerequisite of any planning technique. Increasing the sophistication of the planning methodology will not necessarily compensate for poor-quality forecasts. Equally, a forecast is of little value unless it can modify intended actions. Hence, it is important to consider both the accuracy of the forecast and the potential consequences of any errors.

In Chapter 13, on forecasting, Howell introduces the main methods of mathematical forecasting. He discusses the forecasting necessary for a specific economic decision in the context of a real organization, where everyone has subjective beliefs, biases and vested interests — including the most 'objectively' trained mathematical forecaster — and where data sets may be distorted in various ways. Throughout the chapter Howell stresses the power of simple models and the need for parsimony in model building. Since the chapter itself uses no algebra (the algebra is confined to the appendix), it should give the non-technical reader an insight into the nature and limitations of popular forecasting methods. Even readers trained in statistics or econometrics may find some new ideas which are not yet widespread in their disciplines.

While, in general, quantitative techniques have struggled to gain acceptance by practising management accountants, the one tool of analysis which has gained overwhelming acceptance is the electronic spreadsheet. Its acceptance undoubtedly owes much to the fact that it automates rather than replaces existing techniques. For many years accountants have used projections of profit-and-loss statements and balance sheets as a means of analysing decisions. The spreadsheet merely emulates this process, albeit with greater speed and accuracy, and facilitates the rapid exploration of many alternative strategies. The chapter by O'Hara traces the growth in the use of spreadsheets, explains their structure and identifies some of the problems which arise in their use.

Finally, and perhaps most obviously, technological innovation is impacting upon accounting practice through improved technologies of information processing. The chapter by King and his colleagues outlines some of the potential contributions such advances can make to management accounting practice. Sadly, their research suggests that British management is responding only slowly to these possibilities.

New technology and environmental adaptation

It can be argued that too often budgets represent the past carried forward, and the emphasis on monitoring performance by the feedback of actuals against budget leads to an over-concern with internal rather than external matters, and past rather than future events; seé Chapters 5, 8 and 10, by Wilson, Preston and Mackey respectively. It may be that this is the only role for management accounting as we know it, but this is not the view held by several of the contributors to this book. The chapter by Wilson seeks to demonstrate how accounting practice can be integrated with strategy formulation and marketing. Wilson argues that cost accounting systems tend to be directed at the operational level, whereas studies of strategy suggest that key success factors lie in strategic choices and monitoring business performance relative to competitors. Hence, strategic management accounting systems are needed to look at the organization holistically and to examine its competitive position. Such systems should look outwards and forwards, and examine, *inter alia*, the relative market share of existing products, their position in the product life cycle, market prospects, the portfolio of products produced, and incorporate costings based on experience curves. The analysis should not be based solely on the individual organization but on its competitive advantages relative to competitors. In addition, it should analyse competitors' past and future costs and their market performance and strategic options.

Wilson examines three operational systems pertinent to strategic management accounting: (1) Porter's contribution to strategy formulation and implementation, (2) the profit impact of market strategy (PIMS) study and (3) Simmond's work on strategic management accounting. While these systems have acknowledged problems and deficiencies, it is strongly argued that they provide the basis for practical developments which management accounting has neglected in the past.

Earlier in this introduction it was argued that cost accounting systems described in textbooks assume relatively simple, labour-intensive production processes, whereas modern production technologies are highly automated, with much continuous processing. The speed of processing is no longer determined by the labour input. This change has profound implications for management accounting, as is discussed in Chapter 10 by Mackey. He traces how manufacturing processes have changed following the adoption of materials requirements planning (MRP), just-in-time manufacturing (JIT) and automated manufacturing. He goes on to examine their impact upon accounting system design, the usefulness of accounting information, its cost and benefits, and the feasibility of measuring costs.

Traditional manufacturing processes use inventories to buffer individual departments against the uncertainties of supply from preceding departments and raw materials suppliers. Such buffering permits departments to be controlled as relatively independent entities through responsibility accounting systems, while co-ordination is achieved through master production schedules. The accounting systems focus on materials and labour costs, with overheads recovered by a system of overhead allocation. In such a system, inventories are accepted as a necessary 'evil'. MRP often produces significant reductions in inventories, but in so doing renders departments far more interdependent. Thus performance measures emphasize meeting due dates, rather than the budget, as individual departments have much less autonomy.

MRP can be seen as an extension of traditional manufacturing methods, whereas JIT represents a very different philosophy. Production departments are restructured into work cells each with a variety of machines. The emphasis is on high quality and inventory reduction. Production is in response to orders upstream rather than being determined by inputs from preceding departments. Such a system requires considerable flexibility and teamwork within departments. Tasks previously carried out by service departments are now usually the responsibility of the work cells. The system emphasizes constant improvement through incremental changes in response to 'failures', sometimes deliberately induced to discover areas requiring improvement. In addition, suppliers' delivery schedules and so on are closely co-ordinated with production.

JIT presents a series of challenges to conventional cost accounting systems. For example, its climate of continual improvement means that standards are constantly changing. Also, adverse variances may not represent 'failures' but rather experiments directed at securing improvements. The performance emphasis switches from maximizing fixed capacity to meeting short-term demand and quality. It is argued that this requires new accounting measures of effectiveness, including measures that reflect a longer time perspective than traditional efficiency measures. Given the team approach, with its flexibility and change, static negotiated budgets become less meaningful. Furthermore, JIT moves many of the traditional overhead functions such as maintenance, work design and quality control, into the work cell; thereby making them direct costs and susceptible to more direct forms of control. Nevertheless, certain indirect costs remain as overheads, hence there continues to be an interest in overhead allocation bases and activity costing.

JIT may well be a precursor to automated manufacturing systems. Such systems require good discipline in submitting data and result in higher fixed costs. It is argued that, in such circumstances, strategic management accounting is needed rather than information for short-run decision-making. While the full implications and effects of major changes in manufacturing processes upon accounting systems are not yet fully understood, it is clear that they are raising a series of problems and challenges which urgently need to be addressed by accountants.

Social behaviour, control and creativity

The current interest in Japanese methods of management reinforces the relevance of behavioural research in management accounting, for it raises a series of issues regarding how social factors, such as groups, cultures and reward systems affect performance. Whilst economic-based researchers have acknowledged the need to model control systems and to incorporate payment systems into their analysis, emphasis upon monetary rewards as the major motivating factor means that their approach is still relatively simplistic.

Alternative theories of motivation are explored in Chapter 7. It examines how accounting controls are related to the systems of performance appraisal and rewards. Accounting systems are frequently integral to performance appraisal; they help define roles and expected levels of performance, and they report achievement to higher levels of management. Moizer examines three major complementary theories of motivation; namely, expectancy theory, equity theory and goal-setting theory. He argues that the design of accounting systems is integrally connected to issues in organizational design. But if organizational goals are not matched to the individual's estimates of what is achievable, they may be rejected and 'poor' performance may result. Thus it is important to recognize individual differences in setting goals.

These ideas are echoed in the chapter by Preston, who argues that the conventional wisdom of budgeting is premised upon a rational model of organizational reality. This rationalist model has become so pervasive in management accounting theory and textbooks that it is taken for granted and rarely questioned. Preston argues that if we wish to understand more about budgeting and how it operates in organizations, it is necessary to explore and critically evaluate the philosophical underpinnings of the traditional budgeting model. If these underpinnings are found to be deficient, then it will be necessary to use alternative perspectives of what organizations are and how human beings behave. This may lead to different conceptualizations of budgets and the budgeting process. He argues that 'rational' models assume that everything, including environments, organizations, organizational process and individual behaviour, belong to a presumed natural order. This natural order is characterized as an objective knowable system of variables and rules governing their relationship. Everything can ultimately be explained if the relevant variables and rules are identified. Budgeting under conditions of high environmental uncertainty is then seen as a process of matching the appropriate organizational system, including the budgeting system, with the conditions experienced in the environment.

Preston's concern is that this rational model of budgeting neglects the role of human beings. If human behaviour is seen as entirely determined by organizational structures and processes, then there is no room within this model for the self-determining actions and creative expression of individuals.

Prescriptions for improving creativity in organizations are relatively rare in the literature. This is due, in part at least, to the failure to recognize that budgets mean different things to different people and that organizations evolve different cultures. Thus it is not possible, nor is it desirable, to construct general prescriptions for budgeting in all organizations. Rather, the designers of budgetary systems should consider the meanings that people attach to budgets and the way in which they may be integrated into, and give shape to, the culture of the organization. Such a process involves the active participation of the organizational members and must allow ample room for improvization and new ideas.

In general, it is suggested that alternative forms of budgeting should create an atmosphere of organized anarchy and promote playful and experimental behaviour. Possible strategies include emphasizing hypothetical scenarios of the future, valuing intuition, decoupling planning from control, breaking away from previous experience and seeing the past as reinterpretable. Finally, it should also be noted that creative potential is evident in organizations, and may be observed in the informal processes through which managers meet and discuss problems and future events. Within traditional management accounting, these informal processes are positively discouraged, thereby stifling any creative potential that may already exist.

Critique and policy

One of the offshoots of the perceived gap between theory and practice and the inadequacies of management accounting, especially with respect to new manufacturing technologies, has been an increased interest in management accounting history, which until recently has been relatively neglected. To understand the present it appears that we need to better understand the past, and it is argued that the resolution of current theoretical controversies may be helped through historical studies.

The chapter by Loft examines recent controversies in management accounting history which have emerged, partly because of the arguments in Johnson and Kaplan's book, *Relevance Lost*. Their argument is that the management accounting systems which developed in the United States in the late nineteenth and early twentieth centuries have lost their relevance due to an over-emphasis on financial accounting and the excessive influence of academics in business schools. The early systems, they maintain, were crucial to the development of large firms, as they provided essential systems for internal co-ordination. However, there have been few developments since the 1930s, they argue, and the effects of obsolete and inappropriate systems are now becoming apparent, particularly with the advent of Japanese competition.

However, as Loft's chapter explains, Johnson and Kaplan's interpretation of history has been challenged, especially by 'critical' accounting researchers. These researchers challenge Johnson and Kaplan's assumptions that the cost accounting systems which emerged along with the technological and economic developments were inevitable and represented a form of social progress. Instead they argue that cost accounting was implicated in the domination and disciplining of labour in the early stages of capitalism and that the emergence of cost accounting was socially governed by the systems of thought then prevalent, the actions of the state and the results of inter-professional disputes between such groups as engineers and accountants. The debate continues and it may never be conclusive. Nevertheless, it is important in that it illustrates how accounting techniques are related to social factors and how accounting did not merely reflect society but also helped shape it.

In the long run such historical work may provide insights into why Anglo-Saxon countries appear to lay greater stress on accounting techniques than the new competitor countries, such as Japan. It may also help to explain why certain expertise claimed by professional accountants in the Anglo-Saxon countries are performed elsewhere by engineers or business economists. The value of historical work is that it can help us question taken-for-granted assumptions about the role and nature of management accounting, and thereby broaden our view of how controls might be reformed, not only from a corporate perspective but also from the broader societal and public-interest perspectives.

Such concerns are central to contemporary debates over the introduction of management accounting techniques and philosophies into the public sector. The chapter by Humphrey expresses concern, *inter alia*, that the methods being promulgated in the public sector are to some extent a simplistic caricature of private sector practice. He shows how the use of accounting measures of efficiency can contribute to lower overall effectiveness and goes on to argue that the individualistic enterprise culture grounded in a market-based philosophy can reduce the strengths of such organizations by weakening commitments to public service and collegial relations.

It may be that the accounting methods used in the public sector are technically deficient. For example, the emphasis on financial efficiency measures related to inputs rather than outputs may not complement the desired effectiveness goals and thereby produce dysfunctional behaviour. In addition, performance assessment based on the costs of individual units may be unreliable due to major interdependencies between units, which in turn may hinder integration in policy formulation and action. Nevertheless, the need to control service costs remains. It may be that the solution lies in improved and/or reformed accounting methods rather than the rejection of accounting *per se*. The chapter by Humphrey questions whether the assumptions and methods of control implied in conventional management accounting systems are appropriate to public-sector organizations with their ethos of public service, their conflicting and complex goals, and their modes of decision-making which stress the accommodation of conflict and the achievement of multiple goals. In this context it is interesting to note that many of the other contributors to this book are expressing various concerns about the efficiency of conventional management accounting systems in the private sector. Such concerns raise broad issues about the introduction of management accounting into the public sector. It is increasingly being recognized that management accounting systems are not value-free and neutral. Nevertheless, accounting systems have been central to a number of very contentious government programmes. In this sense the accounting profession with its professed expertise does not merely follow policy but also helps shape it. In so doing, accounting systems have consequences for the distribution of power and resources not only within organizations but within society more generally. Increasingly, accounting is implicated in issues concerning the provision of public services by private-sector organizations. Thus it is perhaps unsurprising that an increasing volume of management accounting research is questioning the role of accounting in broader socio-economic contexts and examining whether there are alternatives outside the realm of traditional accounting expertise.

Concluding comments

As the above discussion has indicated, there has been an explosion in and fragmentation of management accounting research. However, the various topics and methodologies share a common recognition that the use of accounting by managers and others in organizations, and its role and social significance, is often more subtle and complex than seems to be appreciated in textbooks.

The approaches to management accounting research which are informed on the one hand by economics and on the other hand by behavioural sciences, might appear to be mutually exclusive due to fundamental differences in the philosophy of the social sciences. However, there are signs of a synthesis. For example, the chapters by Ezzamel on transfer pricing and Ahmed and Scapens on cost allocation offer insights derived from both styles of research. However, it would be premature and perhaps naïve to assume that it is yet possible to proffer a single agreed theoretical approach. Indeed, at present the different methodologies are continuing to raise new issues and reinterpretations of accounting theory and practice. Where this will culminate is unclear. However, what is interesting is that the various research approaches are highlighting the complexity of control processes and the conflicts of interest underlying them. We now invite the reader to examine the approaches set out in the following chapters and to consider the issues raised.

Reference

Johnson, H.T. and R.S. Kaplan (1987) *Relevance Lost: The Rise and Fall of Management Accounting*, Boston, Mass.: Harvard Business School Press.

Chapter 2

The history of management accounting: relevance found

ANNE LOFT

The historian E.H. Carr writes, 'The past is intelligible to us only in the light of the present; and we can fully understand the present only in the light of the past.' However, until recently management accountants have shown little awareness of the relevance of historical understanding to current issues. If considered at all, the history of management accounting has tended to be seen as being concerned with how management accounting progressed from meagre beginnings in nineteenth-century factories to an important role in the running of twentieth-century business enterprises. Because the past was viewed as merely the imperfect prelude to the present, then the history was seen as a 'dusty' specialist subject of no relevance to current theory and practice.

During the past decade this attitude has begun to change. Interest in management accounting history has been growing, and it is now stimulating discussion and debate, especially since the publication in 1987 of Johnson and Kaplan's provocatively titled *Relevance Lost: The Rise and Fall of Management Accounting*. This brought together in a coherent form a set of ideas which have been developing over the last two decades. In this chapter they will be referred to as the Johnson and Kaplan school of management accounting history. Their key argument is as follows: corporate management accounting systems used today are inadequate to meet the demands of competition in the modern world. In particular they are inadequate for the effective functioning of new systems of production management (such as flexible manufacturing systems). Others have argued that this is due to a lag in replacing old-style cost and management accounting systems with modern information and accounting systems. According to Johnson and Kaplan this is *not* the case. After a detailed discussion of the history of management accounting in the United States, they concluded that efficient accounting systems for managerial decision-making and control actually were developed in the nineteenth and early twentieth centuries. Unfortunately they have since been distorted and misused and have quite simply 'lost' their 'relevance' (hence their title). In *Relevance Lost* the tone is

17

evangelistic; history is used to argue for change in the *present*, and it is thus brought firmly out of its dusty antiquarian corner of academic life.

A reason why the book has been taken seriously was the 'discovery' around a decade ago that the success of Japanese industry had seemingly occurred *without* the massive commitment to management accounting made by large American corporations. This surprised managers and academics alike, for they had assumed that conventional management accounting systems were a necessity for business survival. It suggested that management accounting was culturally specific; Japanese culture rapidly came under scrutiny in an attempt to identify why they were *more* successful with *less* refined management accounting systems.

The relationship of management accounting to culture has also interested a more critical group of researchers. This perspective stemmed from research of actual management accounting systems which noted that systems in practice did not run as theory would lead us to believe. Management accounting in practice came to be recognized as playing additional and different roles to those depicted in textbooks.

What distinguishes this school of 'critical researchers' (as we can call them) from the Johnson and Kaplan school is their perception of society and the nature and role of management accounting therein. Management accounting is not simply seen as a technique for making organizations more efficient — to the benefit of workers, management and owners alike — but as a way of controlling workers and legitimating systems of control. This is not necessarily beneficial to them, society or the environment. This school argued that to understand the role of management accounting today, it is important to understand its history. In other words, to understand the social pressures which influenced the development of the techniques and the motivations and justifications for their use. But their analysis does not end there; they invert the conventional question by asking how management accounting *itself* has influenced developments in organizations and society. From here onwards the chapter divides naturally: the first part discusses the arguments of the Johnson and Kaplan school, whereas the second section examines the 'critical' developments.

The Johnson and Kaplan school

An important stimuli to the development of ideas concerning the history of management accounting was the work of the business historian Alfred D. Chandler (1962, 1977). Chandler discusses management accounting in its organizational context, which represents an implicit critique of 'traditional' histories of management accounting. These were revealed to be not wrong as such, but overly narrow in their approach.

According to traditional histories, management accounting evolved from the techniques of cost accounting developed in England in the late nineteenth century. Cost accounting developed because the double-entry system of bookkeeping in factories could not provide the owners with relevant information on product costs. This was essential for pricing goods in increasingly competitive markets, especially in periods of trade depression. To get an estimate of production costs, cost accounting was grafted onto bookkeeping systems. At first it just enabled the allocation of labour and materials to units produced. Later systems became more sophisticated, enabling the allocation and apportionment of overheads to be made in a double-entry bookkeeping system integrated with the financial records. The early lead which the United Kingdom had in new ideas and procedures was quickly taken over by the United States after 1900. The key development in cost and management accounting is thus seen as the invention of systems which integrated the cost records with the financial records. The publication, in 1887, of *Factory Accounts* by Emile Garcke and J.M. Fells is regarded as an important first step towards this. The traditional history of management accounting which followed is one of brave pioneers inventing ever more clever techniques and systems: from the distribution of overheads, to techniques to aid decision-making, such as the break-even chart and discounted cash flow analysis. A notable characteristic of this traditional view is that cost accounting is an 'independent variable'; while it passively serves the goals of the organization, it neither shapes nor is shaped by those goals.

Chandler's work revealed the paucity of this perspective. He brought to the fore the importance of management accounting to the development of the giant firm, and *vice versa*. Chandler concluded that modern cost-accounting arose in the United States during the mid-nineteenth century with the advent of the railways, and a little later in the chemical, steel and metal working industries. It arose because of a coupling of the growing size of organizations and complexity of production processes, with oligopolistic markets consisting of a few large producers. These producers needed cost information in order to determine prices, to assess how the different parts of the business were performing and generally to try to outwit their rivals. As giant vertically integrated and later multidivisional corporations developed in the first decades of this century, management accounting became a key factor in the co-ordination of the wide range of activities taking place over a large geographical area.

Chandler's ideas inspired other researchers, amongst them H. Thomas Johnson. In his study of cost accounting at the Lyman Mills Corporation, a cotton textile firm operating in New England in the mid-nineteenth century, Johnson discovered a system far more sophisticated than that which the reader of traditional history, or of Chandler, would have expected and which served different purposes. At Lyman Mills cost accounting was primarily used to solve organizational difficulties through acting as a means of internal control over activities. Johnson writes that:

> All the evidence examined points to the conclusion that Lyman used its elaborate cost system to facilitate control of internal plant operations: for example, to assess the physical productivity of mill operatives; to assess the impact on operations of changes in plant layout; and to control the receipt and use of raw cotton. (1972, p. 474)

Other work by Johnson, and by Willard Stone, seemed to confirm this idea. It is this work, coupled with inspiration from Williamson's transaction cost theory and Kaplan's insights on the lack of relevance of modern management accounting, which merge to give *Relevance Lost* its shape and power as a book.

A uniting strand through *Relevance Lost* is the ideas of Oliver Williamson (1975). Central to his work is the explanation of the origins and evolution of large corporations. This he does through comparing and contrasting the corporate form with the market system, viewing them as alternative ways of ordering the whole process of production and distribution. He argues that corporate management structures, such as management accounting systems, exist because their costs as a means of co-ordinating operations are lower than the alternative of market co-ordination. Imagine a situation where all the employees of IBM were not 'collectivized' under one corporate form but were instead independent operators who were continually contracting through the market with their present colleagues, consumers and producers of the various services. Such a market-based structure of organization might eventually produce a computer, but the total costs of doing so would almost certainly outweigh the costs of the bureaucracy needed to replace the market. These costs of co-ordination (the costs of the bureaucracy and dealing in markets) have become known as 'transaction costs', and the whole approach has become known as 'transaction cost theory'. These ideas can be applied to the development of cost and management accounting as Johnson and Kaplan do accordingly.

Johnson (1983) argues that in the market economy of Western Europe, which developed from around AD1000, the information that the merchant needed to conduct business — to decide what to sell, and at what price — was provided by market prices. The double-entry bookkeeping which developed was merely a way of keeping records of money owing and owed. It did not act as an aid to decision-making and control. The rise of the factory changed all this. Market prices stopped supplying all conceivable information for decision-making and control when merchant-entrepreneurs contrived to administer the work of labourers by gathering them together into a centralized workplace. A prime example of this was the textile industry of northern England (often regarded as representing the birth of industrial capitalism). Here merchants changed from making contracts with workers who made cloth in their homes, to a factory system where employers took over the organization of production for the artisans. Instead of a piece-rate set by the market, where workers were paid for what they produced, there was a wage contract where the employee was paid for his or her time. If there was a piece-rate system in the factory, it was the employer who set this rate.

However, there was a problem: no automatic market signals existed to allow the organizers of the factories to evaluate internal intermediate output, that is products which would be processed further. The question 'how efficient was their production?' required an answer. An especially important cost was wages. The market wage for factory workers only contained partial information about the cost of the intermediate output produced by the worker. The missing information was the workers' productivity during the time they earned their wage. Cost accounting, hypothesize Johnson and Kaplan, was devised by these merchants as an ingenious means of replicating that information. Double-entry cost accounts held the potential to provide information about labour and other conversion costs per unit of output. It is noted how early textile cost accounts match the wages paid to workers with output produced. Comparing this with the cost of outwork gives a simple way of evaluating how efficient the factory is.

More complex cost accounting systems developed as businesses became larger and machinery more complex. The cost of processes could no longer simply be compared with rates outside the factory. Johnson's work on the cost accounts of the Lyman Mills illustrates these points. The conclusion reached is that in the new, large organizations that emerged in the nineteenth century:

> management accounting practices in manufacturing, rail transportation, and distribution firms had one common purpose: to evaluate a company's internal processes. ... In all cases this new accounting information focused on the efficiency with which single-activity firms used resources in their internally managed processes. (Johnson and Kaplan, 1987, p. 42)

The existence of these systems leads them to locate the origins of cost and management accounting earlier than traditional histories. It is also clear that they were produced to aid internal control, rather than the traditional view that they were produced primarily for the pricing of products and the valuation of stock and work-in-progress (for inclusion in the financial accounts). Now we come to a most important point in Johnson and Kaplan's argument, namely that cost and management accounting did not merely arise because the growing organizations needed it, it *facilitated* this growth. It focused attention on the advantages from internally organizing production of parts rather than purchasing them in the market.

Further advances in management accounting systems were associated with the scientific management movement, whose most famous advocate was Frederick Taylor. Started in the United States by engineer-managers (not accountants) during the last two decades of the nineteenth century, the movement's aim was to improve the efficiency of production processes by standardizing jobs and processes as much as possible. In the late nineteenth and early twentieth century engineers and accountants used the information about standards that ensued for three purposes:

1. To analyse the potential efficiency of tasks or processes (this developed directly from Taylor's work).
2. To compare the actual efficiency with this potential (an innovation credited to the management consultants Harrington Emerson and G. Charter Harrison). This was the forerunner of flexible budgeting systems.

From these two usages a new purpose for cost accounting developed; this was to evaluate the *overall profitability of the entire enterprise*. In other words, the newly efficient parts should add up to a profitable whole.

3. To simplify the task of valuing stock and work-in-progress for the yearly financial report (financial accountants discovered that standard cost information could be used in this way).

According to Johnson and Kaplan, usages 1 and 2 in the list were the crucial drive behind the setting up of cost accounting systems; usage 3 was merely a by-product.

A merger wave in the United States around the turn of the century created huge vertically integrated firms. The most successful of these firms developed the unitary, or centralized, form of organization, where the firm's overall operations were broken down into separate departments each with highly specialized activities. Each department was run by its own manager, leaving top management free to co-ordinate activities and to direct strategy and policy. This marked the birth of many of the mammoth US firms we know today, for example General Electric, American Tobacco, National Biscuit and Du Pont. Johnson and Kaplan discuss the management accounting system developed in Du Pont between 1903 and 1915, which remains a model for large and complex business organizations today.

Following Williamson's transaction cost approach, Johnson and Kaplan claim that these firms were created because their owners perceived that there were opportunities to make higher profits in a large well-managed hierarchy, rather than in using market exchange. Management accounting played an important role in ensuring that the costs of administrating the firm did not exceed the gains to be made from its existence. For the very complexity of the organization could lead an integrated firm to sink into a morass of bureaucratic inefficiency, losing all the potential gains. The use of management accounting to control the transaction costs was of crucial importance to the firms and to management accounting.

Two new management accounting techniques were developed to assist this process: budgets (to co-ordinate and balance the internal flow of resources from raw materials to the final consumer), and return on investment (ROI). ROI was an important breakthrough because it focused the attention of managers, for the first time, on the productivity and performance of *capital itself*. Nineteenth-century single-activity firms had tended to ignore how well capital was being used once it had been purchased. Now the efficient management of capital became a driving force in the firm. Just as the calculation through cost accounting systems of such figures as cost per labour-hour drove the search for labour-saving efficiencies, the calculation of ROI drove a search for more productive opportunities to use capital. The chief object of management accounting systems became the assessment of overall profitability in these firms.

When, after the First World War, some of these vertically integrated firms became 'multidivisional', management accounting again played an important role in keeping all of these divisions acting together while working towards goals set by top management. Accounting systems provided data to evaluate the performance of each division, to evaluate company-wide performance and to decide on future company policy. They used management accounting in the same manner as the vertically integrated firm but with one important addition: they used the ROI measure to delegate to division managers the responsibility for using capital efficiency. Then divisional managers could be controlled using this data, be refused more capital or even dismissed if they did not perform effectively. This was an important facility in situations where managers could pursue their own goals instead of those of the owners.

After this period managers came to rely more and more on the *financial numbers themselves* as their basic information source. 'Management by numbers' has become the norm. But these numbers became directed at the third use of costs (according to the schema given earlier), namely that of valuing inventory in financial statements. Product costing in manufacturing firms was replaced by a cost accounting which did *not* attempt to trace each product's consumption of resources for cost management purposes. This is the crux of the problem of the 'lost relevance' of management accounting: the cost information that apparently aids financial reporting is misleading and irrelevant for strategic product decisions.

How did this happen? The responsibility for the use of management accounting for valuing inventory was placed in the hands of auditors anxious to produce objective, auditable, verifiable and 'conservative' inventory figures to satisfy the US capital market's need for reliable financial reporting. On the other hand, Johnson and Kaplan argue that this was not the major reason why firms moved from costing systems that attempted to trace each product's consumption of resources for cost management purposes. Firms moved away because the profits from using managerial costing were not worth the added costs of gathering the information. They use the problems of the systems set up by Alexander Hamilton Church (see Johnson and Kaplan, 1987, p. 64) as evidence to support this argument.

Thus Johnson and Kaplan claim to refute two commonly held ideas: first, that management accounting is a more recent phenomenon than financial accounting, and developed from it; and second, that cost accounting was developed to fill a need generated by financial reporting. In other words, they assert that management accounting has its own long history, and it is not an offshoot of financial accounting. Its use for valuing stock for reporting purposes was merely a by-product of its more important use as a tool of management.

Why did rational managers begin to use this irrelevant information produced by the cost accounting systems directed at inventory valuation? A major part of the blame, they suggest, should be taken by the university departments of accounting (very influential in the United States) which convinced modern managers that management by numbers is best. Provocatively Johnson and Kaplan write that 'academic cost accountants, more than auditors and managers, may have contributed to accounting's lost relevance for cost management, especially since World War II' (p. 145). They end the book by discussing possible management accounting systems which use information-processing capabilities of modern information technology to produce relevant information, which will require the active involvement of engineers and operating managers, not just accountants — 'the task is just too important to be left to accountants'.

Johnson and Kaplan's history is written with a clear message: management accounting had a golden age from the late nineteenth to the early twentieth century; but now it has lost its relevance, it must change if American corporations are to survive in competitive world markets. It is hardly surprising that the content and message of *Relevance Lost* have proved controversial. Its interpretation of history will continue to be debated for the history of management accounting is difficult to study: questions such as 'how can we know how systems operated in practice as opposed to in theory?' and 'are surviving archives representational?' and so on, can always be asked. Other interpretations of these events can be made, some of which are discussed below.

Critical studies of management accounting history

There is, as yet, no *single* management accounting history written from a critical perspective which covers the developments in the way that Kaplan and Johnson do. Some are explicitly critical of the Johnson and Kaplan school, others contain a more implicit critique in that they tackle the history in a very different way. Such critiques can lead to a different and more questioning enquiry into the history of management accounting. Burchell *et al.* (1980) suggest that it is important to open up the debate to examine the following questions:

1. How has accounting come to function as we now know it?
2. What social factors have been involved with its emergence and development?
3. How has it become intertwined with other aspects of social life?
4. What consequences has it had?

While Johnson and Kaplan's work is an agenda for improving practice, the radical agenda involves revealing how accounting systems control and discipline individuals within firms. This involves examining social relationships inside and outside the organization. One of the fundamental issues is that of accounting *change* — accounting systems change over time, but little is known about either the causes or effects of such changes. We need to *actively* examine the underlying forces and processes, and to look at the wider economic and social context of the organization. Accounts do not just reflect the organization, they may play a part in the actual emergence of organizations as we know them. For example, defining the goal of an organization as profit maximization depends on the use of accounting concepts and systems to define and calculate this thing 'profit'.

Underlying traditional descriptions of the history of cost and management accounting systems (prior to Chandler and the Johnson and Kaplan school) lies an assumption that there is a 'perfect' system for a business to be run effectively, or that for each trade there will be an ideal system which is a variation of this general system. The history of cost and management accounting is seen as the recording of the process whereby systems came closer and closer to this ideal. Johnson and Kaplan's work has a more complex model. The organization is seen to exist in an environment which includes factors such as market conditions, the degree of stability in the conditions of trade, and fluctuations in exchange rates. Hence the discussion in *Relevance Lost* of the growth of multidivisional firms in an 'environment' characterized by oligopoly. The 'internal environment' in the firm is also important, for it is essential that the costs of the firm's bureaucracy is less than the cost of trading in the market. The problem of controlling the organization so that costs are minimized and profits maximized is seen as being solved through the *matching* of the characteristics of the environment to those of the control system (management accounting being an essential part of the control system). In other words, the organization will function most profitably when it can control the environment it is in. In this perspective practices tend to appear as inevitable and to be the 'best' because they exist. Multidivisional companies became dominant because the transaction costs of the organizational bureaucracy (including the cost and management accounting system) were less than the costs of using the market. It is argued that they are now out of step with their environment, that their power is waning and that they will 'die out' if they do not adapt to the new global competition. The necessary adaptation is seen as being dependent on developing 'new and more flexible approaches to the design of effective cost accounting, management control, and performance measurement systems' (Johnson and Kaplan 1987, p. 224).

Neimark and Tinker (1986) argue that Johnson and Kaplan's perspective is Social Darwinist: as only systems which fit in with the internal environment survive — and enable the organization itself to survive in the long term (in Darwin's theory of evolution species become extinct because their competitors ate them, or drove them out of their environment). There are, however, problems with such reasoning. The application of Darwin's theories to the *social* (as opposed to the natural) world is very controversial. Humans are sentient beings who can live in co-operative social relationships; the organizations which they create are not the same thing as an animal or a plant. This raises the question of why such analogies are made in the first place. Tinker argues that theories such as transaction cost act to mystify the origins and motivations of theorizing, thereby helping legitimate a status quo where the vast majority of the planet's population are exploited in order that a dominant élite can enjoy the fruits of labour.

Johnson and Kaplan follow Chandler's line of causation: the environment caused large companies to follow certain strategies, which in turn 'caused' the multidivisional company. An opposite line of causation may be just as valid, namely that the large companies' strategy of trying to dominate the market by driving competitors out, or swallowing them up, led to monopoly and oligopoly and in turn to bureaucracy and wastefulness.

Neimark and Tinker (1986) refer to how Johnson and Kaplan's definition of 'the environment' (which caused the strategies which caused the structure) is very limited: it merely consists of neutral and impersonal technological and/or market forces. 'People' are missing because *individuals* in these studies are defined in terms of being human 'atoms'. They are not viewed as belonging to a structure of social relations that is part of the wider society. Individual and collective interests of workers are ignored, for they are regarded as 'atoms' who have entered into individual wage contracts with the firm — and that is the end of their involvement. There is no reason why such corporations should stop producing the CFC gas which is destroying the earth's ozone layer; the environment simply does not come into their calculations — unless it affects their publicity or there is the possibility of compensation claims. The mental and physical health of their staff is also not of interest — unless there is the possibility of compensation claims against the company, or they are all important shareholders.

Tinker and his associates have not produced a fully worked through alternative history of management accounting. They have tended to concern themselves with the relationship between accounting and large-scale social changes, as in Tinker's *Paper Prophets: A Social Critique of Accounting* (1985). This opens with a discussion of controversies over corporate accountability (such as the Slater Walker debacle). This leads to a general critique of accounting as it now is and ends with a plea for a new basis for accounting theory and practice: emancipatory accounting. These ideas could produce an alternative history of management accounting. Some hints are given in their critique of transaction cost theory. As they see it, transaction cost theory lacks a socio-historic perspective on human society. It unrealistically identifies the business firm as emerging from a world of competitive markets and atomistic individuals who can rationally identify the costs and benefits of various forms of organizing production. According to Tinker and Neimark, the system of market exchange and capitalist production was imposed upon the highly developed system of rights and obligations in feudal society. In general, capitalist social and organizational control systems (of which management accounting is just one) are *not* neutral mechanisms for making production more efficient, but are a practical means through which capital exploits labour on a day-to-day basis. The idea that these systems are necessary for 'efficiency' and are not 'political' in any way, is a means through which this exploitation continues to be legitimated.

The development of primitive cost accounting systems into sophisticated management accounting systems must be seen within the history of capitalism. Accounting helps justify how owners of capital exploit those who work for their living. It is the social conflict that pervades capitalist society that provides the source for change. These social relationships are not simply 'outside' of the corporation but are *themselves* shaped by what goes on inside it. Management accounting systems within corporations help to mystify and reify the existence of structural inequality in society.

The Tinker school's perspective is linked to that of the 'labour-process school', the major difference being one of emphasis. While Tinker and associates have tended to work at a rather general level of analysis, the labour-process school is more concerned with examining the detailed processes through which labour is controlled (hence the name 'labour process') and addressing accounting's role in this.

Expressing the essence of the labour-process approach Braverman writes that:

> when the capitalist buys buildings, materials, tools, machinery, etc., he can evaluate with precision their place in the labour process. He knows that a certain proportion of his outlay will be transferred to each unit of production and his accounting practices allocate these in the form of costs or depreciation. But when he buys labour time, the outcome is far from being either so certain or so definite that it can be recognised in this way, with precision and in advance. .... It thus becomes essential for the capitalist that control over the labour process pass from the hands of the worker into his own. This transition presents itself in history as the *progressive alienation of the process of production* from the worker; to the capitalist it presents itself as the problem of *management*. (Braverman 1974, pp. 57–8; original emphasis)

This perspective, by focusing on how management activity, including accounting, routinely expresses and furthers the priorities of capital, brings questions of power and control to the fore (Hopper *et al.* 1987). Understanding changes in the labour process is seen as the key to broader social analysis. Hopper (1988) has used this approach to show how an alternative version of Johnson and Kaplan's history could be created. He argues that the emergence and later development (or, indeed, abandonment) of particular types of cost and management accounting are better explained by the changes in controls over labour processes which changing phases of capitalism invoked. Cost accounting developed in the period of the 'homogenization' of labour from the 1870s. A period where work was reorganized and restructured (facilitated by mechanization and increasing plant size) in such a way that more semi-skilled, as opposed to skilled, labour could be used; workers became more easily substituted for each other. This does not dispute Johnson and Kaplan's assertion that cost accounting in the late nineteenth century evolved primarily for management to evaluate internal processes of companies through product and department costs. *However*, it questions their explanation. Hopper argues that changes in control systems in the period were directed at the power of labour rather than efficiency. The homogenization of labour requires piece-work, record-keeping and technology, and elaborate records were needed in order to get information on what aspects of the work could be speeded up. Applying this to accounting, the growth of cost accounting systems was concomitant with restructuring production tasks to control labour. Following Braverman, it is suggested that the abstraction of knowledge from production labour to management tasks was a factor in subordinating and disciplining labour. Hopper theorizes that early accounting developments were significant in making the finances of operations visible to owners, and the shifting of financial knowledge from labour to capital was a major plank in the homogenization of labour and bore directly upon the distribution of economic rewards.

Under the heading 'Management accounting: managed managers managing', Hopper (1988) looks at the development of management accounting during the present century, writing that Johnson and Kaplan's puzzlement with accounting developments post 1925 (the period in which relevance was 'lost') is due to the inadequacy of their analysis. He brings out the importance of the *control of labour* as the decisive factor here for the introduction of the internal accounting controls that came to dominate American industry in the post Second World War period. The 'push' was the problems with the basic system of control in primary-sector firms, especially the problem of overpowerful foremen. Inspired by Braverman, Hopper writes that the solution adopted was the creation of 'abstract shadow organizations' replicating and monitoring physical production processes. Management itself grew to such an extent that *it* needed managing; accounting, through budgets and related controls, was crucial to this (hence 'managed managers managing'. The ensuing bureaucracy was not an inevitable consequence of efficiency but rather an extension of the separation of knowledge from production, leading to a division of labour between management and production workers. Management accounting controls such as budgets and ROI arose from corporate controls over *managerial labour processes*, and bureaucracies were not sought by capitalists because they were more efficient than market co-ordination (Johnson and Kaplan 1987) but were a cost which they suffered because they needed to control labour processes and gain knowledge of production.

Armstrong (1985, 1987) points out that the labour-process literature tends to be functionalist if read as an explanation of the development by employers of control systems; that is, the techniques for controlling labour (including accounting) appear as the *only* solution to top management's problem of control. The explanation thus suffers from precisely the 'what exists exists because it is best' problem, already identified in the work of Johnson and Kaplan (although in this case what 'exists' is a repressive control system rather than a system for ensuring 'efficient production'). Studies of the labour process in other cultures, most notably the Japanese, illustrate that the Anglo-Saxon 'answer' to the problem of control is certainly not the only one. An additional problem with the labour-process approach is that it tends to relate changes in control strategies to economic crises, while history seems to indicate that the answer is more complex.

Armstrong's answer is to look at the division of labour within management, in particular to competition between management 'professions' such as engineering, personnel management and accountancy. While most of Armstrong's work deals with the United Kingdom (this will be returned to later), he does briefly provide an alternative to Johnson and Kaplan. He writes that the critique which the proponents of scientific management made of traditional supervision, and the answer they provided, namely that the planning department should have total control, was a product of the 'ideology of engineering'. American mechanical engineers had been accustomed to a dominant position in controlling work in factories (either as owners or managers). In the increasingly large and bureaucratic factories of the turn of the century they were losing control to general managers. Through what we can call an 'ideology of engineering', they claimed that scientific management was the answer to the difficulty of controlling labour, and engineers themselves should be in charge. Unfortunately for the engineers this knowledge of job timing, planning and organizing could easily be appropriated by other groups of management workers. Engineers did not become the key managers in the huge corporations, accountants and financial managers did. The origins of this lay in the response to the economic crises of 1920–22. Prior to this date corporations tended to be run by operational managers in a pyramid structure, in which accountants were among the staff advising these managers. After the multidivisional structure pioneered by General Motors it tended to be financial staff and accountants who sat at the top of the organization: for it was they who possessed the tools necessary for making decisions allocating capital between divisions. The growth of large corporations is not by itself enough to explain the growing power of financial staff. It was critical that they were *already* represented in the management hierarchies, as they were in the United States (and the United Kingdom), one of the reasons they were there being the audit requirements imposed by the securities market. This seems to be borne out by the observation that in Germany (where capital was supplied by banks) or Japan (where the government was a major source), such audit requirements were not imposed and accountants have never achieved the same power.

Armstrong's account relates the growth of management accounting to the growth in the influence and numbers of the professional group which practised it. In traditional management accounting history there is a simple line of causation, namely that top management of large corporations realized what a valuable technique management accounting was, therefore follows a growth in the numbers of accountants. Armstrong emphasizes the positive role of accountants in creating work for themselves. Having obtained a role in the hierarchy early on, they were able to move into powerful positions as the multidivisional form was introduced, subsuming under their authority the techniques of cost accounting developed by engineers. With this theory Armstrong is trying to avoid the functionalist trap into which both labour-process writers (and Johnson and Kaplan) tend to fall — namely that accounting seemingly *has* to exist because of the functions of control (labour process) or efficiency (Johnson and Kaplan) it fulfils. Armstrong's theory is more subtle. Accounting and other controls are seen as substitutable, and the extent of use of accounting control systems depends on social and historical factors.

Michel Foucault has inspired a rather different line of thinking in the history of management accounting. This is represented in the works of Miller and O'Leary (1987), Loft (1986, 1988) and Hoskin and Macve (1986, 1988a, 1988b). Whilst Foucault does not write directly about the history of management accounting (nor indeed at any length about the factory), his ideas can be applied to it in a fascinating way, for he emphasizes the importance in the development of modern society of techniques aimed at watching and controlling what individuals do. An importance which he notes has been previously overlooked by scholars.

In his book *Discipline and Punish: The Birth of the Prison* (1977) Foucault uses the history of prisons as an exemplar of a society-wide phenomenon occurring from the late eighteenth century onwards: the growth of 'disciplinary institutions'. Prisons, armies, hospitals, schools, mental institutions and factories all have in common that within them people are arranged and grouped into different categories — for instance, in the school according to their age and ability, in the hospital according to type of illness, and in the factory according to function. Even more importantly, they are arranged so that they can be watched and punished if they do not obey the rules, hence the phrase 'disciplinary institutions', in which 'disciplinary techniques' are practised. The term 'disciplinary techniques' covers a wide variety of methods of watching and controlling, including the recording of people's work, the progression of their illness, and also the architecture of buildings themselves, which gives a clear space in which everything can be seen.

Disciplinary techniques grew in accuracy, extent and importance during the nineteenth century in armies, hospitals, schools, factories and other institutions. In the case of manufacturing, 'great manufacturing spaces' (to quote a contemporary source) were created where production could be organiz%d on a more systematic basis than when conducted by outworkers, or in cramped and dark workshops. In such 'spaces' individual workers could be assigned positions arranged to facilitate their surveillance and the creation of records about their work. These records in turn could enable the comparison of workers and the detailed assessment of their use to the business, i.e. control.

Loft (1988) writes how cost and management accounting can be seen as one of the techniques of surveillance and control of individuals in a business organization. Its peculiar characteristic is that it replicates the production processes and makes them 'visible' on paper (or inside a computer) and in monetary terms. Through this *monetarization* the virtual 'encirclement' of the activity of work by financial measures is achieved. Consider an item being physically produced on an assembly line; the adding to it of brackets, the painting of it, and so on, are procedures which have already been planned in the office and their consequences assessed through financial procedures. After the physical processes are over, the record of the events is again translated into financial terms to be compared with the budget. The line itself, the factory building and the watching supervisor are all disciplinary technologies. The discipline of accounting itself tends to operate further up the organizational hierarchy, enabling the 'managing of managers' (to use Hopper's phrase quoted earlier). However, management accounting is far more than a petty little control over managers. The effects of its discipline are felt from the very bottom of the organization to the uttermost top, the accounting system 'recreates' the activity of the organization in financial terms, enabling its control.

In making certain things visible, other things become 'invisible', such as pollution of the environment and the physical and emotional effects on the employees who have to do repetitive boring jobs. Accounting is the disciplinary technology which enables the prioritizing of the financial above all other considerations. The importance of Foucault's perspective is that it brings into the open and analyses the importance of the 'small' techniques of discipline, such as management accounting, which scholars have tended to ignore. The history of management accounting must be seen as the history of one of the central disciplinary techniques in industrial society.

Foucault was a professor of the *history of systems of thought*. He was concerned with explaining how what we think of as 'true' and our present 'systems of thought' came to have this status. He concentrated on what he called 'the human sciences', the intellectual disciplines concerned with the creation and application of knowledge about 'man'. Thus he worked on such subjects as the changing concepts of madness and its distinction from reason over the last five centuries, and on the emergence of modern medicine. It is *through* the operation of the disciplinary controls that knowledge is created which adds to the knowledge base of the human sciences. Thus it is through the systematic observation of patients in hospital that medical knowledge has been created. It is through the regular observation of work and workers that 'scientific management', 'the social psychology of industry' and so on have been created. Knowledge and power are closely linked, knowledge enables power, and power enables knowledge to be created. Accounting knowledge is a 'truth' about work created through the monetarization of measurements of the process of work. The process of the measuring of work, which is at the basis of accounting, involves the exercise of power; the legitimate knowledge of work becomes that which is in the record, not that in the worker's memory. The knowledge of costs, of variances, and so on, which is created is used in the process of disciplining managers (and possibly back through them to workers), and also in the process of creating the budget which forms the norm for the next period. Knowledge and power are thus tightly linked together.

Foucault aims to help us understand how the world is today by reminding us of how the things we take for granted, and our ways of speaking about them, came into being in the first place (this he calls the 'genealogical' question). It involves challenging the assumptions, the 'truth' of our time, by going back into history and examining the details of the emergence of this 'truth'; not to look for *the* single origin, but the whole complex of dispersed origins. Thus, on this view, in order to understand the current power of management accounting, we should seek the diverse origins of the system of thought 'management accounting' and of its practice. The question of how it relates to other practices and ways of thought must be addressed.

Hoskin and Macve (1986, 1988a, 1988b) have written of the origins of management accounting from a Foucauldian viewpoint, tracing its links back to the development of double-entry bookkeeping. They ask two central questions of the history of accounting. First, why is it that accounting first developed in Europe in the thirteenth and fourteenth centuries? Second, why was it only sporadically used before the nineteenth century?

Most accountants have a vague idea that an Italian called Pacioli invented double-entry bookkeeping in 1494. Hoskin and Macve remind us that accounting history scholars have demonstrated that Pacioli was only the publicizer of what was already done in practice. They hypothesize that accounting was born out of the reading, writing and examining initiated in the medieval universities. This new knowledge formed through processing texts gave power to the learned 'masters' and 'graduates' of the universities. This was connected with the spread of an 'arithmetic mentality' and the growth in the analysis and rewriting in various forms of what had already been written (e.g. commentaries and indexes to the Bible). While in Johnson and Kaplan's view the introduction of double-entry bookkeeping was a rational means of keeping track of what was owing and what was owed in an increasingly complex market economy, Hoskin and Macve see it as a more complex process connected with social movements at the time. It is no mere accident that new systems of accounting coincided with the idea of purgatory where God becomes the great examiner in the sky to whom all are 'accountable' for their actions.

Although by 1400 Italian merchants were using accounting as a tool of management and control, for many centuries the use of accounting hardly spread and there was little technical development. Hoskin and Macve attribute this to there being no 'power-knowledge framework' in which the techniques 'could discover their modern applications'. Crudely put, the world was not yet in such a state that such a development could occur. Accounting tended to be a sporadically updated record of the past; it was not concerned with the future — in other words, the coherent network, in time, of disciplinary techniques which surround work in our society. Planning and budgeting before work was carried out, measurement during the processes, and checking afterwards, were absent. According to Hoskin and Macve, it was only after the development of the giving of 'marks' in educational institutions that the power of education, and thereby accounting, was transformed. In the late eighteenth and early nineteenth centuries a new kind of mathematization was taking place on many fronts, tending to the *quantification* of human qualities, of which the giving of marks for performance is the most crucial. Constant examination and constant marking together create a way of tracing and predicting an individual's performance. This 'marking' fed back into accounting practice through a very specific event: the creation in 1817, at West Point in the United States, of a sophisticated system of marking, surveillance and discipline. Pupils of the system were later crucial to the introduction of the techniques of management and accounting which were to spread throughout American industry.

Hoskin and Macve discuss in detail the West Point/Springfield Armory link. The key person in this link was Daniel Tyler, who as a pupil at West Point experienced an educational system which combined a hierarchical organized *structure* which gave precise times and places for each individual's work, and a *dynamic* system of testing and evaluating done by numbers and applied to every element of cadet life. It was the *examination* at Springfield that brought together the hierarchical structure and judgement with reference to a standard. Tyler introduced at Springfield between 1832 and 1842 systems of human accountability, where it was discovered that accounting knowledge was a powerful technique for harnessing human performance. It could provide a link between the whole *financial* system and the disciplining of work in general. The West Point system had an impact on US industry, first in the US armories at Springfield and Harper's Ferry; and second, through the organization of the first forms of corporate managerialism on the railways. Developments which Chandler has shown to be of crucial significance to the emergence of modern management accounting.

In their search for the origins of management accounting Miller and O'Leary

(1987) focus on the first three decades of the twentieth century, the period when standard costing and budgeting emerged in their modern form. Looking at this development from a Foucauldian standpoint, they see it as a small but important part in the growth of disciplinary power generally. The individual became subject to new forms of discipline within the factory (e.g. through accounting) and outside (e.g. having 'intelligence' and 'healthiness' measured).

At the end of the nineteenth century a new impersonal 'scientific management' was beginning to spread in American industry (as noted earlier). Instead of the personal supervision of the boss, there were norms and standards for work, including how it was to be done. Even mundane tasks, such as shovelling coal, became subject to this discipline. Workers were observed shovelling, measurements made, and this knowledge used to instruct precisely *how* they should shovel in order to be most efficient. After detailed norms and standards were created, the boss needed, theoretically, only to step in when these were not kept to. By planning, recording and checking work through records, discipline came to be seen to reside *not* in the will of the boss, but in the economic machine, the anonymous demands of efficiency. Standard costing and budgeting, an important element in the range of new disciplinary techniques, measured the work of the individual on a daily basis, enabling the 'governing' of their activity. These accounting techniques provided a way of expressing in money terms the contribution of individuals to the collective efficiency of the enterprise.

Beyond the factory, disciplinary power spread. This was a time when efficiency was much debated, the idea being that if all the citizens were more efficient, the nation as a whole would be more efficient. The notion emerged that government should ensure this efficiency through programmes directed at improving the mental and physical health of the population. Programmes put into action included intelligence testing (which would enable individuals to be 'scientifically' allocated to suitable education or work) and sterilizing the mentally retarded to stop them breeding more of their own 'inefficient' kind. Miller and O'Leary discuss the development of management accounting in the context of what they call 'the governable person'. This refers to the idea of the person as having certain attributes which could be measured and through which they could be controlled or 'governed'. In the enterprise, management accounting — along with the scientific management it grew out of and the nascent industrial psychology — helped to make the person 'governable'.

Looking at the same period as Miller and O'Leary, but from a slightly different standpoint, Loft (1986, 1988) examined the history of cost accounting in the United Kingdom during the turbulent period of the First World War and the years immediately following, when the practice of cost accounting spread rapidly. An important part in this appears to have been played by an unforeseen consequence of government actions. From small beginnings in 1914, the scale of the war grew. Five million men entered the armed forces, and the power of the state over individual citizens and business increased tremendously. The scale of war production was enormous. By the end of the war the Ministry of Munitions controlled over 3.5 million workers and it was claimed to be the biggest buying, importing, selling, manufacturing and distributing business in the world. Some factories were taken over by the government, but in most cases it did not fire the existing management and take over the running of the factory itself. Rather it allowed the original owners to run the business while controlling in detail what went on. The problem was, what should manufacturers be paid for the items which the government directed them to make, and for which there was no normal market price? It was solved through a regulation which laid down that the price should be what it *cost* to make plus a margin for profit. Suddenly the measurement of costs became far more important; manufacturers were forced to look more closely at their costing systems, and the government set in process procedures for checking and analysing costs.

Costing techniques do not spread independently of knowledgeable individuals. Chartered and Incorporated accountants working from their professional offices were employed by the government to administer this new law. From being almost entirely occupied with bankruptcy, auditing and financial accounting, professional accountants' expertise came to include cost accounting.

The emphasis on costing gave clerks involved with it a new importance. In the reorganization of job categories in the first population census after the war, one of the new additions was 'costing and estimating clerks'. After the war some of these higher-ranking clerks who had become involved with cost accounting formed an association called the Institute of Cost and Works Accountants, the forerunner of the Chartered Institute of Management Accountants. Their aims were, first, to be accepted as 'professional' accountants like the members of the Chartered and Incorporated bodies that they were excluded from; and second, to further the spread of 'scientific' costing techniques in British industry. Thus here the diverse 'origins' of management accounting are illustrated — 'origins' that include the unintended consequences of the uneasy course which the wartime British government steered between 'business as usual' and a totalitarian command economy. This illustrates how the spread of the discipline (including both the knowledge and the disciplinary technique) of accounting in the twentieth century are not simply to be found in Johnson and Kaplan's rational economic necessity. They have much more complex 'origins' which cannot be separated from the fortunes of the occupational group(s) who carry out the work and who 'market' the techniques to manufacturers and the activities of the state.

Bougen's case study (1989) of accounting in industrial relations is set in approximately the same period as the previous author's, namely the 1920s. He examines in detail how a particular UK company, Hans Renold & Co Ltd, used accounting as an important tool in a strategic management initiative to improve worker—management relations and corporate performance. Renold (the firm was family owned) introduced a complex profit-sharing scheme in 1921 where bonus payments were to be linked to increased efficiency in production. It was not just a simple 'carrot' to get workers to be more efficient but was also a way of 'educating' employees into the harsh realities of the commercial world. To this end a committee of management and employee representatives was set up to monitor the scheme.

Renold was probably surprised when employees began to challenge the technical details of the profit-sharing scheme, especially an item called 'wages of capital'. As time went by labour became more and more dissatisfied, for the scheme failed to generate bonus payments from mid-1921 to early 1923. The savings which labour made seemingly went only to safeguard the 'wages of capital', there being nothing left for them. There was tension, for management continued to attempt to educate employees about the realities of business life through discussing the company's problems and priorities within the accounting framework provided by the profit-sharing scheme. Suspicion grew, and as the employees gained a growing grasp of its intricate mechanics, they began to challenge management decisions arguing, for example, that work done by outside concerns could be done more easily and cheaply within the firm. They also began to argue in a sophisticated manner over the descriptive ability of accounting, and its reconciliation with their own perceptions of factory activities. They recognized the capacity that management had to manipulate data for their own purposes: by mid-1926, the firm was making good profits, but management reformulated the profit-sharing scheme to their own advantage. Eventually the scheme was terminated after a merger of the company in 1930.

Bougen writes that this case demonstrates how personal objectives and expectations, organizational structures and environmental circumstances all influence the emergence of systems of accounting; they do not emerge in an organizational and environmental vacuum. In this case the use of accounting was not simply the result of a single rational line of thought, but of a variety of organizational processes, including the *idea* of its use as an educational tool. In practice it was used to create the agenda and script for management—labour discussions and to attempt to enhance managerial control over workshop activities. As labour challenged the scheme, so management changed the accounting. The development of accounting systems cannot be divorced from the underlying power structure of the organization; the scheme was initiated, designed (and changed) by management. Accounting was 'injected' into the core of the management—labour relations in the factory and became a focal point for the articulation of disagreements and challenges by labour of management's authority. This historic case shows how an appreciation of the emergence, roles and consequences of accounting is impossible without study of the social, economic and political relationships of its context.

Conclusion

This chapter was subtitled 'Relevance Found': from being a dusty, seemingly uninteresting subject, the history of management accounting has become the object of debate. Management accounting's history has been 'opened up' during the last decade. In Johnson and Kaplan's theory, management accounting is placed in its organizational context, giving a richer history than the earlier, narrow technique-based accounts, where cost accounting appears as developed by 'great men' in a virtual organizational and social vacuum. However, Johnson and Kaplan's placing relies ultimately on economic theories with Darwinistic assumptions, which can and have been questioned. The inquisitors include a new group of more radical management accounting historians, who, using insights from theorists such as Marx and Foucault, have analysed accounting as a social and political phenomenon — a set of techniques and a body of knowledge which not only *reflect* the society in which they are found but which have also played an important role in that society's development. In other words, accounting plays a *constitutive* role. Thus management accounting's past is not only considered to be important in explaining management accounting in the present but also in explaining the development of modern industrial society itself.

References

Armstrong, P. (1985) 'Changing management control strategies: the role of competition between accountancy and other organisational professions', *Accounting, Organisations and Society*, vol. 10, no. 2, pp. 129–48.

Armstrong, P. (1987) 'The rise of accounting controls in British capitalist enterprises', *Accounting, Organisations and Society*, vol. 12, no. 5, pp. 415–36.

Bougen, P.D. (1989) 'The emergence, roles and consequences of an accounting–industrial relations interaction', *Accounting, Organisations and Society*, vol. 14, no. 3, pp. 203–34.

Braverman, H. (1974) *Labour and Monopoly Capital*, New York: Monthly Review Press.

Burchell, S., C. Clubb, A. Hopwood, J. Hughes and J. Nahapiet, (1980) 'The roles of accounting in organisations and society', *Accounting, Organisations and Society*, vol. 5, no. 1, pp. 5–27.

Chandler, A.D. (1962) *Strategy and Structure: Chapters in the History of the Industrial Enterprise*, Cambridge, Mass.: MIT Press.

Chandler, A.D. (1977) *The Visible Hand: The Managerial Revolution in American Business*, Cambridge, Mass.: Harvard University Press.

Foucault, M. (1977) *Discipline and Punish: The Birth of the Prison*, Harmondsworth: Penguin.

Garcke, E. and J.M. Fells (1887) *Factory Accounts*, London: Crosby, Lockwood.

Hopper, T. (1988) 'Social transformation and management accounting', in *Proceedings of the Second Interdisciplinary Perspectives in Accounting Conference*, Manchester.

Hopper, T., J. Storey, H. Willmott (1987) 'Accounting for accounting: towards the development of a dialectical view', *Accounting, Organisations and Society*, vol. 12, no. 5, pp. 437—56.

Hoskin, K. and R.H. Macve (1986) 'Accounting and the examination: a genealogy of disciplinary power', *Accounting, Organisations and Society*, vol. 11, no. 2, pp. 105—36.

Hoskin, K. and R.H. Macve (1988a) 'The genesis of accountability: the West Point connections', *Accounting, Organisations and Society*, vol. 13, no. 1, pp. 37—73.

Hoskin, K. and R.H. Macve, (1988b) 'Cost accounting and the genesis of managerialism: the Springfield Armory episode, in *Proceedings of the Second Interdisciplinary Perspectives in Accounting Conference*, Manchester.

Johnson, H.T. (1972) 'Early cost accounting for internal management control: Lyman Mills in the 1850s', *Business History Review*, Winter, pp. 466—74.

Johnson, H. Thomas (1983) 'The search for gain in markets and firms: a review of the historical emergence of management accounting systems, *Accounting, Organisations and Society*, vol. 8, no. 2/3, pp. 139—46.

Johnson, H. Thomas and Robert S. Kaplan (1987) *Relevance Lost: The Rise and Fall of Management Accounting*, Boston: Harvard University Press.

Loft, A. (1986) 'Towards a critical understanding of accounting: the case of cost accounting in the UK, 1914—1925', *Accounting, Organisations and Society*, vol. 11, no. 2, pp. 137—69.

Loft, A. (1988) *Understanding Accounting in Its Social and Historical Context: The Case of Cost Accounting in Britain 1914—1925*, New York: Garland.

Miller, P.B. and T. O'Leary (1987) 'Accounting and the construction of the governable person', *Accounting, Organisations and Society*, vol. 12, no. 3, pp. 235—65.

Neimark, M. and A. Tinker, (1986) 'The social construction of management control systems', *Accounting Organisations and Society*, vol. 11, no. 4/5, pp. 369—95.

Tinker, A.M. (1985) *Paper Prophets: A Social Critique of Accounting*, London: Holt, Rinehart & Winston.

Williamson, O. (1975) *Markets and Hierarchies: Analysis and Antitrust Implications: A Study of the Economics of Internal Organization*, New York: Free Press.

Chapter 3

Cost allocation theory and practice: the continuing debate

MIRGHANI N. AHMED and ROBERT W. SCAPENS

A cost allocation can be defined as the partitioning of a cost among a set of cost objects. For this purpose, the cost object could be production units, machines, groups of machines, individual products or groups of products. Most textbooks distinguish between allocations of two general types of cost: joint costs and common costs.

Joint costs are the costs of a single process, or a series of processes, that simultaneously produce two or more outputs. Joint costs can be found in many industries, including chemical production, food processing and oil refining. The oil industry is a good example, as the crude petroleum that enters an oil refinery is used to produce a vast array of products including gasoline, kerosene, fuel oil, asphalt and so on.

Common costs are the costs of a single intermediate product or service which is provided to two or more users. A good illustration of common costs is a centralized computer facility which services a number of divisions or departments. Other examples of common costs include research and development costs, general administration costs, the costs of centrally produced electricity and the expenditure of maintenance departments.

The principal feature of both joint costs and common costs is a 'block' of costs which has to be divided among a number of products or users. In small or simple businesses it may be possible to attribute costs directly to individual products or users. But as businesses become more complex, it is increasingly difficult to attribute costs in this way. Consequently, it is not surprising to discover that historically interest in cost allocations accompanied the development of large-scale business enterprises.

Historical background

Cost allocation first became an important issue in the latter half of the nineteenth century. At that time businesses were becoming increasingly complex, with large-scale operations replacing small localized activities. With the development of the railways and extractive industries, and especially the huge investments in powered machinery, there was an enormous growth in overhead costs (Solomons 1952, Brummet 1957). Various methods of allocating overhead costs to production units were in use by the 1870s. For instance, a book published in 1878 by Thomas Battersby, a Manchester Public Accountant, contained a list and criticisms of six different methods.

As productive operations became more complex, there was an accompanying increase in the scale of administrative activities, such as supervision, planning, control and co-ordination. This gave rise to additional fixed costs in the form of salaries and incentives to directors, supervisors and foremen. Such costs were regarded as essential for the control of production, and therefore needed to be allocated to products and departments.

The growth of competition in the closing decades of the nineteenth century, and the increasing difficulty in fixing prices, further stimulated interest in overhead allocations and costing in general (Solomons 1952, Brummet 1957). A recognition of the importance of overheads in pricing emerged along with a general belief that cost information is relevant for decision-making. Businessmen were coming to recognize that allocating overheads could aid product pricing. For example, Henry Metcalfe wrote:

> [cost information] enters into the important questions of what we can afford to make at market prices; of what is the lowest selling price; and also into estimates relating to the differences caused by the addition or removal of parts and substitution of processes. (1886, p. 442)

Pricing became a particular problem as governments and other large buyers started to call for competitive tenders for construction contracts, and as quoted prices became more common for machinery (Checkland 1966). In addition, in the railway industry, the huge investments in the permanent way and rolling stock created serious problems in the setting of fare schedules (Wells 1978).

There seemed to be a belief amongst industrial engineers and accounting practitioners at that time, that if prime costs could be associated with units of output or departments, then indirect costs (i.e. overheads) should be dealt with in the same way. A measure of unit costs was needed for various decision-making purposes; including setting prices, competitive bidding, job order costing and assessing the efficiency of production. In 1901 Hamilton Church, an English electrical engineer, promoted his 'scientific machine-hour rate' and 'supplementary rate' systems of allocating overheads as methods of estimating the costs of individual jobs and contracts (Church 1901).

In addition to Church's systems, various other methods were described in books and journals of the time. Among these were: (1) percentage of cost of material, (2) percentage of direct labour costs, (3) percentage of prime cost, (4) a fixed rate per man-hour and (5) a fixed rate per machine-hour. Some of those methods are still described in textbooks today. Others have been refined over the years, but the basic structures remain much the same.

Importance of allocating costs

Despite objections to cost allocations in the academic literature, many textbooks argue that allocations are needed for specific purposes, including cost-based pricing and government contracts (e.g. Hartley 1983, p. 275; Horngren 1982, p. 511; Kaplan 1982, p. 355). Companies that price all or a large part of their output on a cost-plus basis certainly need to include overheads in their cost of production. Similarly companies engaged in defence or other government contracts have an incentive to allocate costs when establishing mutually satisfactory prices. Furthermore, some companies are required by law to allocate costs to products or activities in order to justify the prices they quote to government departments or agencies.

Financial reporting is another reason for allocating costs. For example, published financial statements set the full cost of production against sales revenues, with opening and closing inventories normally valued at full costs. Income reporting for tax purposes provides another, in this case a statutory, justification for cost allocation. In addition, internal management reports frequently use full costs for evaluating the financial performance of individual profit centres.

The use of cost allocation in performance evaluation is, however, a very controversial subject. One view suggests that as overhead costs are a joint responsibility, all sections of the organization should be aware of them. Furthermore, cost allocations can be used to motivate individual managers to exercise a degree of control over their consumption of central services (Zimmerman 1979, p. 5). The alternative view is that such allocations move costs away from where they are incurred (and ought to be controlled), to other parts of the organization where it is more difficult to exercise control.

Although many accounting textbooks discuss these and other purposes for cost allocations, the academic view remains that cost allocation is a useless and wasteful exercise.

The academic view

Probably the best-known analysis of cost allocations was made by Arthur Thomas, who published two monographs (1969 and 1974) in which he claimed that allocations are not only 'unnecessary, but essentially arbitrary and incorrigible' (1974, p. 3). Allocations are arbitrary, he argued, because they are based on subjective judgements and have no defensible theory. They are incorrigible because they are incapable of verification. Thomas based his arguments on the assumption that inputs to production processes interact with each other to generate a joint output which is different from the total of the various inputs. The jointness renders arbitrary any attempt to determine the contributions of the individual inputs. Given this arbitrariness, Thomas argues that no single allocation method can be appropriate for all decision settings. However, he did attempt to set out minimum requirements for a theoretically justifiable allocation scheme (1969, p. 7):

1. It should be unambiguous.
2. It should be additive.
3. It should be possible to defend it theoretically.
4. It should divide up exactly the amount to be allocated.

Although the logic and economic validity of allocations has been debated extensively in the last two decades, economists as long ago as the 1930s recognized the irrelevance and arbitrary nature of cost allocations. Writers, such as Edwards (1952), Baxter (1952) and Coase (1952), argued that overhead allocations are unhelpful and possibly misleading. Edwards, for example, wrote, 'I believe cost accountants have spent too much effort in trying to arrive at total cost by building up complicated and delicate oncost structures which depend on arbitrary assumptions' (1952, p. 101). It was Edwards's contention that cost accountants ought to concentrate on estimating the marginal variations in cost following expansions or contractions in economic activity, rather than attempting to measure average costs.

The academic debate in the 1930s, and also in more recent years, was influenced considerably by economic decision-making perspectives, such as the concepts of opportunity cost and marginal costing. Over the years the academic literature on cost allocation, although emphasizing the notion of arbitrariness, has produced a wide range of quantitative models. Before examining the dominant perspectives and the assumptions underlying these models, a brief discussion of five criteria suggested in the literature for assessing cost allocation schemes will be helpful. However, it should be recognized that these criteria are not used consistently by all writers.

1. *Neutrality.* A cost allocation scheme is neutral if it does not interfere, alter or in any way distort the decision-making process. Any departure from the principle of neutrality is assumed to lead to economic inefficiency. However,

a neutral allocation scheme will lead to decisions that satisfy marginal optimality conditions. It thereby avoids distorting the decision-making process. Unfortunately, an allocation scheme which is neutral with respect to one decision may not be neutral for all other decisions.

2. *Ability to bear*: Costs should be assigned to cost objects in proportion to their ability to bear those costs. Sales revenues, gross profits, total value of assets and total costs are examples of bases used to relate costs to cost objects. The principle involved is that the cost allocation scheme should use some surrogate measure for the size of the cost object. The presumption is that 'larger' cost objects can afford to bear larger shares of overheads costs.

3. *Cause-and-effect relationship*: This criterion requires a meaningful casual relationship between the cost objects and the costs to be allocated. Here the basic principle is to allocate costs to those factors which cause the costs; for example, factory maintenance costs might be allocated among divisions in proportion to the hours of maintenance work performed in each division. The criterion is defensible if casual factors as well as the costs incurred are easily identifiable.

4. *Benefits received*: This criterion is primarily concerned with allocating costs in proportion to the benefit received by each cost object. The premise is that cost objects should be charged for the amount of service they receive. For example, the costs of a power plant might be allocated in proportion to the consumption of power by the different departments or divisions.

5. *Equity or fairness*: This is sometimes regarded as the most desirable characteristic of a cost allocation scheme (e.g. see Young 1985, p. vii). It implies that the scheme should produce an allocation which is just and fair to all parties involved; that is, each party should bear an equitable share of the allocated costs. However, there are differences of opinion as to what constitutes equity. The term is so ambiguous, subjective and broad that other criteria are needed to define what is 'fair' and 'equitable'.

Despite the variety in these five criteria, accounting researchers have given most attention to the search for neutral cost allocation schemes. We will now describe approaches which have been proposed for the two general types of allocation problems, namely allocations of joint costs and allocations of common costs.

Joint cost allocations

As explained earlier, joint costs arise when a production process simultaneously produces two or more outputs. The point at which the joint products become separately identifiable is known as the split-off point, and joint costs are total costs incurred up to that point. All subsequent costs can be separately identified and should be charged to the individual products. Bases for joint cost allocations usually described in textbooks include physical units, sale value, constant gross percentage and net realizable value. An illustration of joint cost allocation using each of these four bases is set out in Tables 3.1, 3.2 and 3.3. As indicated in Table 3.1, three products (X, Y and Z) are jointly produced by a single production process. Products X and Y can be sold either at the split-off point or after further processing, but product Z must be further processed before it is sold.

Table 3.1   Selected data relating to three joint products

Products	Units produced	Sales revenue at the split-off point (£)	Sales revenue after further processing (£)	Additional processing costs (£)
X	12,000	55,000	72,000	15,000
Y	6,000	47,000	60,000	12,000
Z	2,000		28,000	5,000
	20,000		160,000	32,000

Joint costs incurred up to the split-off point = £96,000

The various allocations using the four different bases are set out in Table 3.2. The physical units method allocates the joint costs of £96,000 in proportion to the number of units produced (column 1). For example, using the data in Table 3.1, the joint cost allocated to product X is calculated as follows:

$$\frac{12,000}{20,000} \times £96,000 = \underline{£57,600}$$

Table 3.2   Allocation of joint costs using four different bases

Products	(1) Physical units	(2) Sale Value	(3) Constant percentage	(4) Net realizable value
X	£57,600	£43,200	£42,600	£42,240
Y	28,800	36,000	36,000	36,096
Z	9,600	16,800	17,400	17,664
	£96,000	£96,000	£96,000	£96,000

Similarly, the sale value method assigns the joint costs in proportion to the sales revenue generated by each product (column 2). The constant percentage method (column 3) follows a slightly different approach — joint costs are allocated so that all products report the same gross profit percentage. For example, if the whole production process earns 20 per cent gross profit, then each product is assigned a total cost equal to 80 per cent of its sales revenue. The additional processing costs are deducted from these total costs to determine the allocation of the joint costs; these calculations are set out in Table 3.3.

Table 3.3 Allocation of joint costs using the constant percentage method

Products	(1) Sales revenue	(2) Gross profit (20%)	(3) Total cost (80%)	(4) Additional processing costs	(5) Allocated joint costs
	Table 3.1	col. (1)×0.2	col. (1)×0.8	Table 3.1	col. (3)−col. (4)
X	£72,000	£14,400	£57,600	£15,000	£42,600
Y	60,000	12,000	48,000	12,000	36,000
Z	28,000	5,600	22,400	5,000	17,400
	£160,000	£32,000	£128,000	£32,000	£96,000

Our final method, the net realizable value method (column 4 of Table 3.2), seems to be the most popular in practice. This method allocates joint costs in proportion to the revenue-generating potential of the individual products — as measured by their net realizable value at the split-off point (less any selling and distribution costs). If a product, such as Z, cannot be sold at the split-off point, its net realizable value is its subsequent sales revenue less the cost of further processing, selling and distribution.

Although allocations of joint costs are essential for certain purposes (such as inventory costing, cost-plus pricing, financial and tax reporting) their usefulness for decision-making is highly questionable. Horngren, for example, notes that 'Any method of allocating truly joint costs to various units produced is useful mainly for purposes of inventory costing which, of course, will affect the income statement and balance sheet. Such allocation is useless for cost-planning and control purposes' (1982, p. 532).

The rationale underlying such arguments relies heavily on economic theory. Specifically, given information on cost and demand functions, optimal output and pricing policies can be determined without allocating joint costs. Furthermore, short-run decisions are subject to the constraints implied by existing capacity and the relevant costs for decision-making comprise marginal costs, whereas joint cost allocations generally ignore capacity constraints and reflect average costs.

However, it is recognized that the allocation of joint costs is sometimes necessary in practice. In such circumstances, the academic view is that practitioners should allocate costs in ways which do not distort product profitability. This approach has produced a variety of quantitative models, which attempt to apply an economic approach to decision-making with joint products. Manes and Smith (1965), for example, showed that there is an optimal allocation of joint costs when two products are produced in fixed proportions and some of one product can be sold at a given cost. Similarly, Hartley (1971) suggested a model in which dual prices are used to allocate fixed joint costs in proportion to the value of the scarce resources used in production. Jensen (1974) proposed a non-linear programming model to allocate joint costs to two complementary products. The primary objective of such quantitative models is to ensure that allocations of joint costs do not distort optimal decision-making processes.

Common cost allocations

As indicated earlier, service departments exist to provide services of various kinds to other departments. In some instances, the service departments may even consume part of their services themselves. In general, common cost allocations are more pervasive than joint cost allocations; they arise in almost every organization.

The distinction between fixed and variable common costs is explained in most textbooks. Whereas variable common costs can be attributed to the services actually used, fixed costs must be allocated. Three methods of allocating common costs are usually described in textbooks: the direct method, the step-down method and the reciprocal method.

Table 3.4 Selected data for common cost allocations

| | Producing departments | | Service departments | | |
	A	B	Maintenance	Power	Personnel
Overheads before allocating service departments' cost	£120,000	£150,000	£20,000	£48,000	£40,000
Allocation bases:					
Maintenance hours	80	20	—	40	20
KWH consumed	4	16	2	—	2
Numbers of employees	60	30	30	18	—

Table 3.5 Allocation of common costs using the direct and step-down methods

	Producing departments		Service departments			Total
	A	B	Maintenance	Power	Personnel	
Direct Method:						
Departmental overheads	£120,000	£150,000	£20,000	£48,000	£40,000	£378,000
Allocations:						
Maintenance (based on maintenance-hours)	16,000	4,000	(20,000)			
Power (based on KWH consumed)	9,600	38,400		(48,000)		
Personnel (based on no. of employees)	26,667	13,333			(40,000)	
Total costs allocated	£172,267	£205,733				£378,000
Step-down method:						
Departmental overheads	£120,000	£150,000	£20,000	£48,000	£40,000	£378,000
Allocations:						
Power	8,000 (1/6)	32,000 (2/3)	4,000 (1/12)	(48,000)	4,000 (1/12)	
Personnel	22,000 (1/2)	11,000 (1/4)	11,000 (1/4)		(44,000)	
Maintenance	28,000 (4/5)	7,000 (1/5)	(35,000)			
Total costs allocated	£178,000	£200,000				£378,000

Using the selected data set out in Table 3.4, Table 3.5 illustrates both the direct method and the indirect method. The direct method allocates each service department's total costs directly to the production departments. It ignores any services rendered by one service department to another. The step-down method, however, recognizes the services provided to other service departments using a sequence of reallocations in which service department costs are allocated in turn to production departments and to other service departments. But no further costs are allocated to a service department once its costs have been allocated. Thus, this method ignores the complexity of situations in which two or more service departments simultaneously provide services to each other, as well as to production departments. The textbook method for dealing with such allocations is the reciprocal method. An illustration of common cost allocations using this method is set out in Tables 3.6 and 3.7.

Table 3.6   Data for reciprocal cost allocations

Departments	Overheads before allocating service departments costs	Services consumed	
Producing departments		Maintenance	Power
R	£200,000	40%	70%
S	250,000	40%	25%
Service departments			
Maintenance (*M*)	20,000	—	5%
Power (*P*)	30,000	20%	—
	£500,000	100%	100%

Using linear algebra (with M = total maintenance department costs, and P = total power costs), the data in Table 3.6 can be expressed as follows:

$$M = 20,000 + 0.05P \tag{3.1}$$
$$P = 30,000 + 0.2M \tag{3.2}$$

Substituting equation 3.2 into equation 3.1:

$$M = 20,000 + 0.05 (30,000 + 0.2M)$$
$$= 20,000 + 1,500 + 0.01M$$
$$0.99M = 21,500,$$
$$\text{and } M = \underline{21,717}$$

Now, from equation 3.2: $P = 30,000 + 0.2 (21,717) = \underline{\underline{£34,343}}$

Table 3.7 Allocation of departmental overheads using the reciprocal methods

| | Producing Departments | | Service departments | | Total |
	R	S	Maintenance	Power	overhead costs
Departmental overheads	£200,000	£250,000	£20,000	£30,000	£500,000
Allocations:					
Maintenance (*M*)	8,687	8,687	(21,717)	4,343	
Power (*P*)	24,040	8,586	1,717	(34,343)	
	£232,727	£267,273			£500,000

With these figures for *M* and *P*, we can allocate the service department costs using the services consumed, as set out in Table 3.6. The resulting allocations are shown in Table 3.7.

The common cost allocation literature which developed in the 1960s pointed out the theoretical weaknesses of all three of the above methods. In particular, it was argued that for decision-making purposes the user of a common service should be charged only with the opportunity cost of using that service. However, because allocations using, for example, the direct or the step-down method, involve partitioning total costs, they yield average costs and there is no guarantee that such calculations will reflect the opportunity cost of the service. Nevertheless, the allocation of service department costs do influence decisions concerning the use of the services and consequently, optimal decisions may not be taken.

In addition, academic writers have also been critical of the activity measures used for common cost allocations — for instance, gross investment, sales revenue, total cost and so on. They argue that such measures will not lead to profit-maximizing decisions. As an alternative, a variety of normative models have been constructed. These models attempt to reflect, within the allocation procedures, the opportunity costs of using the services concerned.

Moriarity (1975), for example, proposed an allocation model which was designed to motivate divisional managers to use internally produced services rather than the alternatives available from external sources. Instead of allocating costs directly to divisions, the model allocates the cost savings as an offset to the costs of obtaining services externally. Each division is charged with the cost of obtaining services externally and then credited with a share of the total cost savings from using the common service.

Moriarity claims that his approach provides several advantages over existing allocation models. First, each division's share of common costs will not exceed the cost of its next best alternative. This should motivate divisional managers to use internal services, when it is cheaper for the company as a whole to do so. Second, some portion of common costs is charged to every division. Third, division managers are made aware of the relative costs of internal and external services. Finally, the approach is neutral with respect to decisions on whether two or more divisions should jointly produce the service for themselves.

The Moriarity model, as noted by Louderback (1976), is not without conceptual errors, however. Because of the nature of the model, a division could receive a negative common cost allocation. Louderback suggested a modification to the Moriarity model in which divisions are charged with the incremental costs of providing the service internally, plus a portion of the difference between the incremental costs of buying the service outside and the incremental cost of providing it internally. The result is that the total cost charged to the division is always equal to or greater than the incremental cost of providing the service internally, and less than the incremental cost of acquiring it from outside.

The mathematical approach to cost allocation was further extended towards the end of the 1970s with the use of game-theoretic approaches. Because actions taken by one department can affect the profits earned by others, it was suggested that cost allocation schemes should provide incentives for co-operative actions which preserve the optimal efficiency of all departments and, hence, maximizes company-wide profits. Researchers using game-theoretic concepts proposed allocation schemes based on the properties of neutrality, fairness, co-operative behaviour, and efficiency. However, their schemes required considerable amounts of information and a high level of mathematical sophistication.

Generally, academic approaches, including the use of game-theoretic concepts, lack relevance in practice. As will be discussed below, the empirical evidence suggests that allocation practices differ substantially from the academic prescriptions.

Cost allocation practices

Despite the overwhelming objections to costs allocations in the academic literature, costs continue to be allocated in practice for a whole variety of reasons. We will review evidence concerning cost allocation practices contained in four surveys taken at different times over the last twenty-five years: Baumes (1963), Mautz and Skousen (1968), Fremgen and Liao (1981) and Bourn and Ezzamel (1987).

Baumes (1963) reported the results of a survey of 158 divisionalized companies in the United States. Fifty-three percent indicated that they allocate all central expenses to divisions. An additional 26 per cent reported making partial allocations — mostly charges for specific services. Among the principal reasons for allocating central expenses was that allocations 'serve as a reminder that such expenses exist and that divisional earnings should be sufficient to cover a proportionate share' (p. 1). In addition, it was claimed that allocations help in assessing divisional profitability, aid product pricing, encourage use of central services and act as a check on head office expenses. The study also disclosed that a variety of allocation methods and bases were being used. Approximately 35 per cent of the companies allocated all central expenses using a single basis — a blanket allocation. The ratio of divisional sales to total corporate sales was the most commonly used single basis; others included, forecast sales, cost of sales, number of employees, labour cost and fixed costs. Some companies (20 per cent) allocated separately the individual categories of expense, while the remainder (45 per cent) used individual bases for certain items of expense, but a blanket allocation for the remainder.

Mautz and Skousen (1968) reported the results of another survey undertaken in the United States. Their survey included an intensive investigation of the allocation practices of six companies, as well as a questionnaire study of 412 companies. They found that 306 of these companies allocate common costs to their divisions. The study demonstrated that common costs are often large in proportion to net incomes; in 255 of the companies the common costs exceeded net income. Thus Mautz and Skousen concluded that the choice of an allocation base can significantly affect divisional net income. Furthermore, their survey found substantial variety in the allocation bases used — sales, net taxable income, assets, investment and profits. Almost three-quarters of the companies, however, claimed to use more than one basis.

Fremgen and Liao (1981) reported the findings of a further survey, once again in the United States. It covered 123 large diversified firms, of which 84 per cent indicated that they allocate corporate common costs to their primary profit centres. The main reason given for such allocations was to remind profit centres that indirect costs exist and that profit centre earnings must be adequate to cover a share of those costs. Additional reasons suggested that allocations should reflect the usage of central services, motivate profit centre managers to check on central service costs, encourage the use of central services and minimize state or local taxes.

More recently, Bourn and Ezzamel (1987) conducted an in-depth survey of nine profit and not-for-profit organizations in the United Kingdom. They found that all the organizations engaged in cost allocations, although different practices did exist. When asked about the role of cost allocations in pricing policies, most of the respondents maintained that in situations of high technological and environmental uncertainty, fixed costs constitute a high proportion of total costs and, consequently, have to be recovered in product prices. However, when they examined short-term decisions and performance evaluation, Bourn and Ezzamel found considerable variations in cost allocation practices. In some cases allocations were used to ensure that fixed costs were fully recovered and to monitor divisional use of fixed facilities. In other cases, it was argued that allocations are not used as they would distort decision-making and performance evaluation (although not pricing policies) and possibly lead to harmful intra-organizational conflict.

Generally, there seems to be no doubt that the mathematical cost allocation research documented in academic journals is little used in practice. Simple methods remain a characteristic feature of practice. However, recently these simple methods have come under increasing criticism from writers who favour activity-based cost allocations. The source of this criticism and the nature of the activity-based approach is discussed below.

Activity-based costing

The proponents of activity-based cost allocations argue that traditional overhead allocation systems are obsolete and of little relevance in the context of new production technologies (Miller and Vollmann 1985, Johnson and Kaplan 1987, Cooper and Kaplan 1988). They claim that traditional systems not only provide distorted cost information for important managerial decisions, such as pricing, product mix and cost reduction, but they also fail to control the increasingly significant amount of overhead costs which are incurred in manufacturing industries. Johnson and Loewe argued that:

> Existing management accounting procedures fail to control overhead creep in part because they address symptoms, not causes ... . Because they direct managers' attention toward cost numbers rather than toward resource-consuming activities that eventually cause costs, these procedures do not help managers control activities that consume resources. (1987, p. 26)

Underlying the activity-based approach is the view that the forces which drive overheads, and indeed most organizational costs, arise from specific activities (Miller and Vollmann 1985, p. 144). Thus, overhead control must focus on the management of these activities. For example, the design of a short-cycle product process which minimizes work-in-progress can eliminate activities and costs which arise from handling, storing, inspecting and issuing part-finished jobs.

Some attempts have been made in the United States to relate overhead costs to their underlying activities. Cooper and Kaplan (1988), for example, propose a system which traces overhead costs to specific activities and then from activities to individual products or groups of products. The key to their approach is the idea that all activities exist to support the production and distribution of goods and services, and hence can be classified as product costs.

The design of an activity-based cost system requires an analysis of the demands made by particular products on overheads and indirect resources. Cooper and Kaplan (1988, p. 98) suggest three rules for such an analysis.

1. Examine expensive resources.
2. Examine resources whose consumption differs significantly by product and product type.
3. Examine resources whose demand patterns are uncorrelated with traditional allocation measures, such as direct labour, processing time, and materials.

Rule 1 focuses the analysis on resources that cause significant differences in product costs, and rules 2 and 3 identify those resources which may be distorted by traditional cost allocation systems.

Activity-based costing is said to offer many advantages. As the system provides more accurate cost information about production and support activities, it opens up a range of strategic options, for example dropping unprofitable products, raising or lowering prices, and focusing on profitable operations. Furthermore, activity-based costing can provide information for evaluating new technologies which cannot be properly evaluated without information about existing costs.

Jones and Wright (1987) described the cost classification system used by the Tektronix Group to identify cost reduction opportunities and to support its just-in-time manufacturing strategy. Because the average labour component of the group's total product cost had been decreasing for many years, the management decided to replace its method of absorbing overhead costs on the basis of direct labour. The new costing system, which related overhead costs more directly to activities and products, was specifically designed to increase the standardization of component parts (with fewer and unique part numbers). Standardization was seen as a way of reducing the costs of design and engineering, and, hence, as a means of lowering manufacturing overheads. In addition to improving management information, the new cost system improved co-operation between the accounting staff and the manufacturing departments of the group.

In another study, Johnson and Loewe (1987) described the experience of the Weyerhaeuser Corporation, which developed a procedure, referred to as a charge-back system, to manage its corporate overhead costs. The system charges all overhead costs to users on the basis of the activites which drive the consumption of corporate resources. Departmental managers can choose the amount of resources they want to consume, but they are charged with the costs of those resources. This enables managers to understand the nature and costs of the resources they use.

Although the activity-based approach looks attractive, it is unlikely to be practical to relate *all* overheads to specific activities. Moreover, the approach implicitly assumes a sense of harmony and co-operative behaviour among operating units, and between operating units and service functions. It does not acknowledge the possibility of conflict over the allocation process. Apart from their narrow concern over efficiency and optimal profitability, the proponents of activity-based approaches have not attempted to explain why firms insist on using simple methods of cost allocation. Other accounting researchers, however, have tried to explain their use. As will be discussed below, agency theory offers a conceptual framework for such research.

An agency theory framework

As discussed earlier, accounting researchers generally accept that allocations are unnecessary and should, in theory at least, be avoided. Nevertheless, they argue that if allocations are going to be used, they should be neutral in their effect on managerial decisions. In practice, however, allocations do not appear to be performed in the ways advocated in the research literature.

This situation has encouraged certain accounting researchers to seek explanations for the cost allocations used in practice. For example, Zimmerman argued that 'Accounting researchers typically ignore the positive question of why firms persist in allocating costs in spite of the continual admonitions by educators against doing so and in a different way to the proposed models' (1979, p. 505).

A change of emphasis in cost allocation research emerged with the more positive approach to management accounting research during the 1970s. This approach places greater stress on theories that describe and explain observed management accounting practices. Accounting researchers became more concerned with explaining the reasons for particular practices than with developing normative models (see Scapens 1985). Agency theory has been used by a number of these researchers as a basis for such an approach.

Agency theory models a situation in which a principal (a superior) delegates decision-making authority to an agent (the subordinate) who receives a reward in return for performing some activity on behalf of the principal. The outcome of the agent's action affects the principal's welfare in some way, for example sales revenue, output, or contribution margin. The principal attempts to combine a reward system with an information system, in order to motivate the agent to choose the action which maximizes the principal's welfare. The need to motivate the agent in this way stems from two important features of the model: (1) the unobservability of the agent's actions (because of privately held information) and (2) conflicts in tastes and/or preferences between the agent and principal. If the agent's action were observable, the principal could enter into a contractual relationship with the agent in which the reward is related directly to the action taken.

For cost allocation problems, the unobservability of the agent's action and the possibility of conflict are particularly important where an agent has authority to use a resource or facility (e.g. a power plant or a computer) provided by the principal. The agent may attempt to improve his/her own welfare by using more or less than would be in the principal's best interest. Such a situation may be managed through an information system which includes cost allocations. The agency theory framework has been used to explore the role of cost allocations in such situations. For example, Zimmerman (1979) examined two possible roles for cost allocations: (1) controlling a manager's discretionary spending on perquisites and (2) rationing an internal service.

In the first setting, Zimmerman argued that a fixed overhead allocation may induce divisional managers to reduce spending on perquisites by limiting their discretionary funds. Furthermore, divisional managers may be induced to monitor their superiors' consumption of perquisites because divisional performance will be affected by the allocation of costs incurred at the superior level. Thus cost allocations may control overhead costs by reducing consumption at the divisional level, and by exerting pressure on superiors to control their costs.

In the second setting, Zimmerman argued that cost allocations can act as a proxy for externalities, thus, for example, the costs of delay which are incurred when a user of a shared facility (eg. telephone service) causes others to wait for the service. He argued that as these externalities are difficult and costly to measure accurately, cost allocations might represent an efficient surrogate.

Despite limitations in his analysis, Zimmerman highlighted a number of behavioural and organizational issues associated with cost allocations which had not been considered previously. Another study which attempted to examine cost allocations within the agency framework was provided by Demski (1981). He concluded that no information value arises from the allocation itself, and that if any value does arise, it comes from measuring the activity variables on which the allocations are based.

Baiman (1982), in a review of agency theory research in management accounting, concluded that agency models do not readily provide explanations for cost allocation practices. However, he suggested that a multi-agent framework (i.e. with one principal and several agents) might lead to a possible rationale for cost allocations. He used the example of a firm planning to acquire a central computer service. The head office (the principal) would want to induce divisional managers (the agents) to reveal privately held information about their demands for the computer service. This might be achieved through employment contracts which include a reward system based on allocations of the computer's fixed costs.

It should be recognized, however, that agency theory has its own theoretical and methodological limitations. Its mathematical formulations are generally restricted to a single period, two-person model. The results from such models may not hold in the long run or when there are multiple agents. Problems associated with coalitions amongst agents are suppressed in the two-person analysis. In addition, some researchers (e.g. Williamson, 1975) have argued that organizations are not susceptible to analysis from a contracting point of view, because hierarchies (i.e. business organizations) are created to mediate exchange in conditions where complete contracts cannot be written or enforced. Spicer and Ballew (1983) argued that as firms grow in size and complexity, additional levels of hierarchy and greater spans of controls are added to the extent that the complex interdependencies require considerable co-ordination. They believe that the complexities of modern organizations will defy modelling in the structured way required for agency theory.

Behavioural and political aspects

Although the agency theory framework adds behavioural and motivational factors into the analysis of cost allocations, it continues to rely on economic concepts such as efficiency and utility maximization. Our discussion will now move beyond this purely economic view of cost allocations and focus on social and organizational contexts, with particular emphasis on the implications for management control and performance evaluation, authority and power relations, and regulatory aspects of pricing government contracts.

The social and organizational contexts of cost allocations have been discussed by various writers in recent years. For example, Thomas (1974) argued that allocations may be 'useful' to the preparers of accounting reports in the following situations:

1. when they are required for legal or regulatory purposes;
2. when they are perceived to advance his/her economic or political interests;
3. when they are perceived to facilitate agreement concerning the distribution of resources.

Other writers (e.g. Horngren 1982, and Kaplan 1977) have noted that cost allocation can function as a mechanism for motivating and controlling managers. Horngren (1982) argued that:

> Whether to include uncontrollable or indirect costs is a difficult question which must ultimately be resolved in terms of how the given alternative influences management behaviour in a particular organisation. In one organisation, the allocation may be desirable because it induces the desired behaviour. In another organisation the same allocation procedure may cause an opposite behavioural effect. (p. 508)

Such comments suggest that the usefulness of allocations can be explained, in part at least, by their ability to motivate particular behaviour. Bodnar and Lusk (1977), for example, argued that cost allocations can be used in a university which wants to encourage its academic staff to pursue research and generate publications. They suggested that costs and/or revenues could be allocated in such a way as to favour departments with good publication records. Consequently, the allocations would encourage research publications.

A number of empirical surveys and case studies have suggested behavioural explanations for cost allocations. The following are some of the reasons given for allocating costs: to remind divisional managers that overhead costs exist (Baumes 1963, Fremgen and Liao 1981, Singhvi 1978), to encourage the use of central services (Baumes 1963, Fremgen and Liao 1981), to relate the divisions earnings to total company profits (Fremgen and Liao 1981, Mautz and Skousen 1968) and to act as a check on central services and divisional expenses (Baumes 1963). These are all essentially behavioural in nature. For example, reminding divisional managers of the existence of overheads may induce a sense of cost responsibility. Furthermore, a check on central services and divisional expenses should induce a sense of cost consciousness at both levels.

Such uses of allocations add a new dimension to the issue of cost allocation. In particular, they cast doubt on the academic view that allocations should be avoided if they distort effective control and performance evaluation. Second, they weaken the notions of collective rationality, consensus and goal congruence which have traditionally been assumed by academics. Third, they suggest that the divergent and conflicting interests of organizational participants give rise to mechanisms which discipline, regulate and motivate managers to behave in an organizationally desirable way.

Cost allocations themselves, however, may be a source of conflict. Bourn and Ezzamel (1987) found that in some organizations conflict can lead to elaborate allocation schemes. In addition, there is evidence that cost allocations reflect the power of particular groups. For example, Pfeffer and Salancik (1974) observed that certain university budget allocations can be understood in terms of the relative power of individual departments. Furthermore, powerful groups may also dictate the basis for the allocations.

Negotiating and price setting for government contracts provide another dimension to the allocation problem. In the case of military products, their unique characteristics and the absence of competitive markets have given rise to particular concern over the pricing of contracts. Prices are normally set on the basis of direct costs, plus overheads and a profit margin. Although the whole process of pricing military contracts is complex, the allocation of overheads poses particular difficulty. Consequently, various governments have established accounting rules for the allocation of overheads.

In the United States, Congress established the Cost Accounting Standard Board (CASB) in 1970 to produce uniform cost accounting standards. The allocation of overhead costs for both commercial and defence contracts was a major factor leading to the establishment of this body. Although the CASB no longer exists, its pronouncements continue to have legal effect for federal government contracts.

In the United Kingdom there has also been a concern over the pricing of government contracts. Historically, there have been a number of cases of overpricing on defence contracts and the excessive profits have been widely documented (Flower 1966, Hartley 1964, Loft 1986). The ambiguity of overhead allocations played an important role in these cases. Faced with such problems, the government formulated regulations and accounting standards during the First and Second World Wars to ensure that prices paid for defence products were reasonable and fair (Pears 1952). Among these regulations were rules and standards for allocating overhead costs. As contract prices were often set on the basis of direct cost plus a reasonable profit, the government took the power to verify these costs (Loft 1986). The government first introduced cost accounting standards and then gave government investigators the power to review cost determination and contract prices. In short, the role of cost allocations in negotiating government contracts indicates the historical, legal and political aspects of the subject.

The foregoing discussion demonstrates the wider implications and context of cost allocations. The management control and motivation dimension emphasizes the role of cost allocations in securing particular behaviour. The possibility of conflict over cost allocations indicates the importance of the political and organizational forces which are inherent in the social context of organizations. Finally, the regulation of overheads in government contracts illustrates the legal and political significance of allocations. To summarize, cost allocations are shaped by a diverse set of institutional, economic and social factors.

References

Baiman, S. (1982) 'Agency research in managerial accounting', *Journal of Accounting Literature* (Spring), pp. 154–213.

Battersby, Thomas (1878) *The Perfect Double Entry Bookkeeper*, Manchester, John Heywood.

Baumes, Carl G. (1963) 'Allocating corporate expenses', *Business Policy Study*, No. 108, New York: National Industrial Conference Board.

Baxter, W.T. (1952) 'A note on allocation of oncosts between departments', in D. Solomons (ed.) *Studies in Costing*, London: Sweet & Maxwell, pp. 267–76.

Bodnar, G. and E.J. Lusk (1977) 'Motivational considerations in cost allocation systems: a conditioning theory approach', *The Accounting Review* (October), pp. 857–68.

Bourn, M. and M. Ezzamel (1987) 'Why firms allocate costs?' in R. Scapens, J. Arnold and D. Cooper (eds.) *Management Accounting: British Case Studies* London: CIMA, pp. 315–50.

Brummet, R. Lee (1957) *Overhead Costing*, Michigan Business Studies 13, No. 2, Ann Arbor; Bureau of Business Research, School of Business Administration, University of Michigan, 1957.

Checkland, S.G. (1966) *The Rise of Industrial Society in England 1815–1885*, London: Longman Green.

Church, H.A. (1901) 'The proper distribution of establishment charges', *Engineering Magazine*, July, pp. 508–17.

Coase, R.H. (1952) 'Business organisation and the accountant', in D. Solomons (ed.) *Studies in Costing*, London: Sweet & Maxwell, pp. 105–58.

Cooper, R. and R. Kaplan (1988) 'Measure costs right: make the right decisions', *Harvard Business Review*, September–October, pp. 96–103.

Demski, J.S. (1981) 'Cost allocation games', in S. Moriarity (ed.) *Joint Cost Allocations*, Orman, Oklahoma: Centre for Economic and Management Research, pp. 142–73.

Edwards, R.S. (1952) 'The rationale of cost accounting', in D. Solomons (1952) *Studies in Costing*, London: Sweet & Maxwell, pp. 87–104.

Flower, J.F. (1966) 'The case of the profitable bloodhound', *Journal of Accounting Research*, Spring, pp. 16–36.

Fremgen, J. and S. Liao (1981) *The Allocation of Corporate Indirect Costs*, New York: National Association of Accountants.

Hartley, K. (1964) 'Costing of government defence contracts', *The Accountant*, 30 May, pp. 684–88.

Hartley, R.V. (1971) 'Decision making when joint products are involved', *The Accounting Review*, October, pp. 746–55.

Hartley, R.V. (1983) *Cost and Managerial Accounting*, Boston: Allyn and Bacon.

Horngren, C.T. (1982) *Cost Accounting: A Managerial Emphasis*, 5th edn, Englewood Cliffs, NJ: Prentice Hall.

Jensen, D. (1974) 'The role of cost in pricing joint products: a case of production in fixed proportions', *The Accounting Review*, July, pp. 465–76.

Johnson, T. and A. D. Loewe (1987) 'How Weyerhaeuser manages corporate overhead costs', *Management Accounting*, August, pp. 20–6.

Johnson, T. and R. Kaplan (1987) *Relevance Lost: The Rise and Fall of Management Accounting*, Boston: Harvard Business School Press.

Jones, W.J. and A.M. Wright (1987) 'Material burdening', *Management Accounting*, August, pp. 27–31.

Kaplan, R.S. (1977) 'Application of quantitative models in managerial accounting: a state of the art survey', *Management Accounting: State of the Art*, Robert Beyer Lecture Series, Madison: University of Wisconsin Press, pp. 30–71.

Kaplan, R. (1982) *Advanced Management Accounting*, Englewood Cliffs, NJ: Prentice Hall.

Loft, Anne (1986) 'Towards a critical understanding of accounting: the case of cost accounting in the UK 1914–1925, *Accounting, Organizations and Society*, Vol. 11, No. 2., pp. 137–69.

Louderback, J. (1976) 'Another approach to allocating joint costs: a comment', *The Accounting Review* (July 1976), pp. 683–85.

Manes, R. and V. Smith (1965) 'Economic joint cost theory and accounting practice', *The Accounting Review*, January, pp. 31–5.

Mautz, R. and K. Skousen (1968), 'Common cost allocation in diversified companies', *Financial Executive*, June, pp. 15–25.

Metcalfe, H. (1886) *The Cost of Manufacturers*, New York: John Wiley.

Miller, G.J. and E.T. Vollmann (1985) 'The hidden factory', *Harvard Business Review*, September–October, pp. 142–50.

Moriarity, S. (1975) 'Another approach to allocating joint costs', *The Accounting Review*, October, pp. 791–5.

Pears, J.S. (1952) 'The costing of government contracts', in D. Solomons (ed.) *Studies in Costing*, London: Sweet & Maxwell, pp. 579—94.

Pfeffer, J. and G. Salancik (1974) 'Organizational decision making as a political process: the case of a university budget', *Administrative Science Quarterly*, Vol. 19, No. 1, pp. 135—51.

Scapens, R.W. (1985) *Management Accounting: A Review of Contemporary Developments*, London: Macmillan.

Singhvi, S.S. (1978) 'Corporate budgeting and financial management', *Journal of Accounting, Auditing and Finance*, Spring, pp. 290—3.

Solomons, D. (1952) 'The historical development of costing', in D. Solomons (ed.) *Studies in Costing*, London: Sweet & Maxwell, pp. 1—52.

Spicer, B.H. and V. Ballew (1983) 'Management accounting systems and the economics of internal organization', *Accounting, Organizations and Society*, Vol. 8, No. 1, pp. 73—96.

Thomas, A. (1969) 'The allocation problem in financial accounting theory', *Studies in Accounting Research No. 3*, Sarasota, FL: American Accounting Association.

Thomas, A. (1974) 'The allocation problem: part two', *Studies in Accounting Research No. 9*, Sarasota, FL: American Accounting Association.

Wells, M.C. (1978) *Accounting for Common Costs*, Urbana, Illinois: Centre for International Education and Research in Accounting.

Williamson, O.E. (1975) *Markets and Hierarchies: Analysis and Antitrust Implications*, New York: The Free Press.

Young, P.H. (1985) *Cost Allocation: Methods, Principles, Applications*, Amsterdam: North-Holland.

Zimmerman, J. (1979) 'The cost and benefits of cost allocations', *The Accounting Review*, July, pp. 504—21.

Chapter 4

Transfer pricing

MAHMOUD EZZAMEL

Economic theory and transfer pricing

The early work on transfer pricing was based on traditional economic theory which assumed that firms rely on the pricing mechanism to determine the optimal product mix which maximizes profits. Three main assumptions are usually invoked in arriving at optimal transfer prices. First, the firm has two divisions: an intermediate division (I) which makes and sells an intermediate product, for example, yarn, and a final division (F) which buys the intermediate product and transforms it into another product which is then sold in the outside market, for example lengths of textile. Second, the work technologies of both divisions are independent of each other as are demands for their products. Technological independence means that the operating costs of each division are not affected by the level of operations in the other division. Demand independence implies that additional external sales by either division do not affect the external demand for the products of the other division. Third, divisions have restricted autonomy in running their activities, with the maximization of overall company profit being the overriding criterion to top management. Given these assumptions, optimal transfer prices can be derived under different market situations ranging from perfect competition, through imperfect competition and discriminating monopoly, to complete absence of external markets.

Perfect outside markets

If the intermediate product can be traded in a perfect external market, then the market price will be the optimal transfer price (see Hirshleifer 1956). In this case the market price is established through the interaction of supply and demand in a free and competitive market. Each division should be permitted maximum autonomy in relation to setting its activity level and as to whether it should transact with other divisions in the company or with external customers and suppliers. Acting as a selfish profit-maximizer, each division would determine its optimal activity level as the one at which its marginal cost (MC) equals its marginal revenue (MR). Quite simply, divisions would behave as if they all constitute one entity whose aim is to maximize global profit. Further, in this setting complete decentralization leads to economies in information transmission, since knowledge of the market price obviates the need for vertical flow of detailed information. There are no advantages to be gained from vertical integration between divisions given the presumed absence of transactions costs in external trading.

Imperfect outside markets

In reality, markets exhibit various degrees of imperfection. For example, selling a product in external markets usually involves incurring various costs in the form of advertising, transport, credit terms and debt collection. Further, firms may prefer to rely on internal sources of product supply rather than being completely dependent upon more risky external suppliers. Moreover, there may not be a perfect substitute for the internal product in external markets. These, and similar, imperfections provide strong arguments in favour of internal trading between company divisions since this minimizes the costs and uncertainties mentioned above.

Suppose, for example, that the external market exhibits only one type of imperfection in the form of transportation cost which has to be incurred both by seller and buyer. In this case the seller receives P_s (the market price *less* transportation cost) and the buyer pays P_b (the market price *plus* transportation cost) such that $P_b > P_s$. The question now is: what is the optimal transfer price? The following numerical example illustrates this problem and derives the optimal transfer price.

International Fabrics Plc produces textiles for a variety of household uses. Its intermediate division I transforms raw cotton into yarn, which can be sold externally or alternatively to the final division F. Division F turns the yarn into finished textile which is sold externally. The current market price for yarn is £550 per 1000 lb. If either division transacts in the external market, it has to incur transportation cost of £50 per 1000 lb. The detailed cost and revenue information for a typical week of operations, and the solution, are contained in Table 4.1.

The solution derived in Table 4.1 was first suggested by Gould (1964), who pointed out that the optimal transfer price depends on the precise relationship between P_b, P_s, and $\bar{P}$, where $\bar{P}$ is defined as the point at which MC_I intersects NMR_F (£400 in the example). The curve NMR_F is the net marginal

Table 4.1 International Fabrics PLC. Revenue and cost data: slightly imperfect intermediate market

Quantity (lb)	Intermediate total cost (£)	Division (I) marginal cost (£)	Final division (F)[a] Net total revenue (£)	Net marginal revenue (£)
1,000	100	100	700	700
2,000	300	200	1,300	600
3,000	600	300	1,800	500
4,000	1,000	400	2,200	400
5,000	1,500	500	2,500	300
6,000	2,100	600	2,700	200
7,000	2,800	700	2,800	100

[a] This is total revenue excluding the separable costs of the final division.

Solution:

Given a market price of £550 and transportation cost of £50 per 1,000 lb, P_b = £600 and P_s = £500. The marginal cost of division (I) and the net marginal revenue of division (F) are listed above. International Fabrics should produce internally as long as the marginal cost of the intermediate division is below £600 per 1,000 lb, above this level it will be cheaper to buy externally. Similarly, the company should sell yarn internally as long as the net marginal revenue of the final division is greater than £500 per 1,000 lb, below that level it is more profitable to sell externally.

The optimal solution is determined by the intersection of the effective MC_I curve (that is the curve which takes into account the opportunities of purchasing externally when this is cheaper than producing internally) and the effective NMR_F curve (that is the curve which takes into account the opportunities of selling externally when this is more profitable than selling internally). This occurs at Q = 5,000 lb where MC_I = effective NMR_F = £500. This is the optimal transfer price. The intermediate division (I) should produce 5,000 lb of yarn; sell 3,000 lb to the final division (F) at £500 per 1,000 lb, and sell the remaining 2,000 lb in the external market at the same price.

revenue of the final division (i.e. its marginal revenue less its marginal cost except the price for the intermediate product). The relationship between these terms can be one of: $P_b > P_s > \bar{P}$; $\bar{P} > P_b > P_s$ and $P_b > \bar{P} > P_s$.

The first relationship corresponds to the one represented by the example. The last case, which is discussed later, is similar to the situation where there is no external market for the intermediate product.

When $P_b > P_s > \bar{P}$, setting the transfer price $P^* = P_s$ maximizes company profits, as is shown in Figure 4.1. In that figure the *effective* marginal cost curve for the firm is ABC, since beyond point B it would be cheaper for the firm to buy externally rather than make further quantities of the intermediate product. The *effective* net marginal revenue curve is JKL, since beyond point K it would be more profitable for the firm to sell further units of the intermediate product in the external market rather than to division F. The intersection of

ABC and JKL determines $P^* = P_s$, and the optimal level of activity for division I at OQ_I. At $P^* = P_s$, division F handles the quantity OQ_F. Compared with outside trading, internal trading increases the profit of division F and of the overall company by the amount $P_s P_b SK$. In the case of International Fabrics Plc, this is reflected in an increased level of activity for the final division F from 2000 lb to 3000 lb. The quantity $Q_I - Q_F$ should be sold on the outside market at P_s. It is straightforward to establish that when $\bar{P} > P_b > P_s$, the transfer price should be set equal to the purchasing price ($P^* = P_b$).

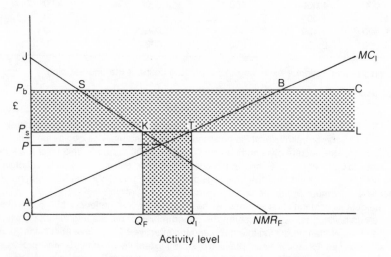

Figure 4.1   The optimal transfer price in a slightly imperfect market

Several important observations emerge from this analysis. First, once some form of intermediate market imperfections are assumed, the benefits to the parent company of internal trading become obvious (an increased profit by the amount $P_s P_b SK$ in Figure 4.1). Second, if the overall goal of the parent company is profit maximization, divisions can no longer have complete autonomy in making their operating decisions. When $P_b > P_s > \bar{P}$, enforcement rules must be designed and applied by top management to ensure that division I sells the quantity OQ_F to division F at $P^* = P_s$. If division I exercises its monopolistic power over division F and charges $P^* > P_s$, the company will operate below its optimal activity level. A similar argument applies to division F when $\bar{P} > P_b > P_s$. Hence, in this analysis, some division discretion is sacrificed in favour of aiming to attain overall company optimality. Third, there are incentives for only one division to trade internally — only one division reaps all the benefits of internal trading. Either the selling price, P_s, or the buying price, P_b, is taken as the optimal price. For example, in the case of International Fabrics Plc it is the final division F which benefits from internal trading, by expanding its activity level by 1000 lb. Fourth, divisional profit cannot be used to assess rationally divisional viability. For example, in Figure 4.1 if the intermediate division I is to be discontinued, the loss to the company as a whole will be more than apparent divisional profit (A P_sT less divisional fixed costs) by the amount P_sP_bSK.

Discriminating monopoly markets

The preceding situation involved only minor imperfections in outside markets. Frequently, the extent of market imperfections is much greater, thereby making internal trading even more advantageous. An example of this is the situation where the intermediate division I has monopolistic power sufficient to allow it to sell the intermediate product internally at a price lower than the one it receives from its external sales. Hirshleifer (1956) has shown that in this case the optimal transfer price, P^*, should be set equal to the marginal cost of the intermediate division (MC_1) at the output level which maximizes company profit ($P^* = MC_1$). This is illustrated in Figure 4.2.

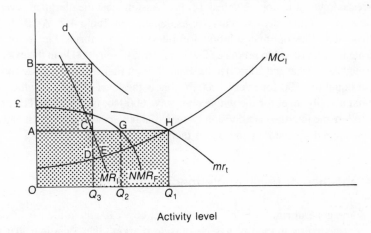

Figure 4.2 The optimal transfer price for a discriminating monopolist

In Figure 4.2 the output OQ_1 of the intermediate division I is established by the intersection of MC_1 and mr_t ($MR_1 + NMR_F$) at point H, giving a price $P^* = OA$. The quantity to be sold to the final division F is OQ_2, where $P^* = NMR_F$. The quantity OQ_3 is to be sold in the outside market at OB > P^*. The above solution may be derived by the head office assuming that it has knowledge of the divisional demand and supply functions. Alternatively, the same solution can be derived by the divisions if either provides the other with its demand or supply function. Thus, if division F were to determine the optimal solution, it would need to obtain details of d (the demand curve facing the intermediate division I), MR_I, and MC_I from division I. If instead division I were to derive the optimal solution, it would need to obtain information about NMR_F. In Figure 4.2 it is assumed that division I plays the dominant role in determining the transfer price after securing the demand function of division F, NMR_F. However, top management would need to impose enforcement rules in order to ensure that division I does not exercise its monopolistic power and charge division F a higher transfer price, which would be against overall company interest.

Once more, most of the limitations associated with imperfect competition are present here. First, apparent divisional profit does not reflect 'real' divisional contribution to company profit. Second, interference by central management greatly restricts divisional autonomy. Third, because of information asymmetry, even with central management interference, there is no guarantee that divisional managers will not manipulate cost and revenue functions to their advantage.

To illustrate this case refer back to International Fabrics Plc. Assume now that the intermediate division I can sell the yarn in an imperfect market where it faces a downward-sloping demand curve. Assume that the marginal revenue associated with that demand curve is as depicted in Table 4.2. As is shown in that table, the optimal solution for International Fabrics Plc is for the intermediate division I to produce 6000 lb of yarn, to sell 4000 lb in the external intermediate market and 2000 lb to the final division F. The transfer price should be set equal to £600 for every 1000 lb (this is the level of MC_I at which the optimal activity level for the whole company, 6000 lb, is reached). The price charged by the intermediate division I to external buyers would be much higher, as determined by the demand curve facing that division.

The absence of outside intermediate markets

The same general rule of pricing at marginal cost extends to the case where the intermediate commodity has no outside market. If we assume that the company faces a competitive market for the final product, the best solution for the firm is to produce that level of output at which the company's overall marginal cost equals the price in the final market. Again, this optimal solution can either be achieved by top management or by individual divisions subject to central supervision. In the earlier case of an imperfect intermediate market, the intermediate division I played the dominant role in arriving at the optimal solution. To demonstrate that either division can play this role, division F is given the task of deriving the solution in the present case which is achieved as follows (Figure 4.3):

Table 4.2 International Fabrics PLC. Revenue and cost data: highly imperfect market

Quantity (lb)	MC_I (£)	MR_I (£)	NMR_F (£)
1,000	100	950	700
2,000	200	850	600
3,000	300	750	500
4,000	400	650	400
5,000	500	550	300
6,000	600	450	200
7,000	700	350	100

Solution:

The general rule is to sell each batch in the most profitable market as long as the marginal revenue is higher than the marginal cost of production. This means that we have to compare the marginal cost of each batch with the marginal revenue in each market. Hence:

$$MR_I \quad NMR_F$$

The first 1,000 lb go externally;	950	> 700
The next 1,000 lb go externally;	850	> 700
The next 1,000 lb go externally;	750	> 700
The next 1,000 lb go internally;	650	< 700
The next 1,000 lb go externally;	650	> 600
The next 1,000 lb go internally;	550	< 600

The intermediate division I should produce 6,000 lb, sell 4,000 lb externally at a price derived from the downward sloping demand curve facing it in the external market, and sell the remaining 2,000 lb to the final division F at £600 per 1,000 lb (this is the level of MC_I at 6,000 lb of yarn). Production should stop at 6,000 lb because the marginal cost of the next 1,000 lb (£700) exceeds the net marginal revenue of the final division at 3,000 lb (£500), and the marginal revenue in the external market at 5,000 lb (£550).

1. Division F obtains from division I its supply schedule showing how much it would produce at any transfer price $P*$ for the intermediate commodity. This should be the same as MC_I, if division I is to behave rationally and set its output level where $MC_I = P*$.
2. Division F derives a curve showing the difference between the final market price and the transfer price for any level of output, $P - P*$. Division F sets its output level where $MC_F = P - P*$ at Q_1, establishes the transfer price $P* = OR$, and then passes it on to division I.
3. Division I, given $P*$, produces Q_1, since this is where $MC_I = P*$. The profit of division I would be equal to the area DSR and that of division F would be equal to the area ABC. Top management, however, should ensure that division F does not sub-optimize to increase its profit at the

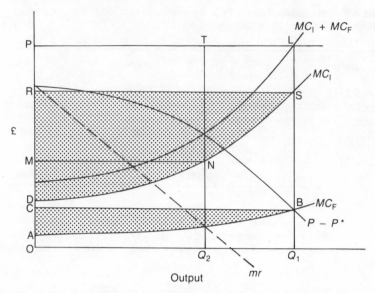

Figure 4.3 The optimal transfer price when there is no outside market

expense of the company. If division F is left free, it can derive a 'quasi-marginal' revenue curve marginal to $P - P^*$, the one denoted mr, and set its output at Q_2 with the lower transfer price OM. At a joint output level of Q_2, the profit of division F will be greater than before, but overall company profit would be less at Q_2 than at Q_1.

Evaluation

Despite its valuable contribution towards a better understanding of some of the issues related to transfer pricing, the traditional economic theory model has several limitations.

First, it overemphasizes the attainment of corporate optimality at the expense of maintaining divisional autonomy, and this is likely to result in adverse behavioural implications. The very idea of divisionalization is frequently interpreted to imply significant delegation of decision-making power, and hence divisional managers are likely to feel alientated if top management imposes great constraints on the manner in which they run their divisions. The model also assumes that central management can induce divisional managers to act in a manner consistent with its interests, but this may not occur for the following reasons:

1. Top management is unlikely to know divisional cost and revenue functions and hence may not know which action is optimal.

2. Divisional managers may engage in sub-optimal strategies, for example changing the resource allocation pattern to their advantage, which are difficult to detect by central management.
3. Perceptions of risk by divisional managers and their attitudes towards risk may induce them to operate at levels different from those deemed optimal by top management. For example, they may extend their product range in order to smooth out divisional periodic profits and hence consolidate their positions as managers, even though the new product lines may be less appropriate from the company's point of view.

Second, marginal cost-based transfer prices reasonably reflect opportunity cost only when the market for the intermediate product is highly competitive, or if there exists one demanding division requiring the product. If there is more than one demanding division, the opportunity cost will be the highest of the marginal cost and the revenue forgone by diverting resources from alternative uses (see Dopuch and Drake 1964). Further, accountants use variable cost (which is assumed constant per unit within the relevant range of output) as a proxy for marginal cost. To set the transfer price equal to variable cost would leave the intermediate division with a loss equal to its total fixed costs, and this implies that it cannot operate as a genuine profit centre. Finally, marginal cost pricing could result in obscuring true divisional profitability by passing on cost efficiencies/inefficiencies across divisions.

Third, the traditional model assumes that company divisions are independent of each other with regard to both production technology and demand. However, the prevalence of technological and demand interdependence in practice restricts the applicability of the model significantly.

Mathematical programming models

It has been suggested that some of the above limitations can be reduced if mathematical programming models are used to determine transfer prices. One such model is linear programming, the optimal solution of which yields a set of prices known as 'shadow prices'. A shadow price is the opportunity cost of a unit of a scarce resource in terms of the amount of contribution that will be added to company profits if one more unit of that resource becomes available. Typically, the transfer price of a resource, P_i^* is set as

$$P_i^* = VC_i + W_i \tag{4.1}$$

where VC_i is the variable cost of resource (i), and W_i is the shadow price of resource (i). In order to investigate the implications of such a technique in the context of transfer pricing let us refer back to International Fabrics Plc.

Let us assume now that International Fabrics Plc consists of three intermediate divisions, I_1, I_2 and I_3, and two final divisions, F_1 and F_2. Suppose also that:

I_1 has a capacity of 2,000 units of product X_1, the variable cost per unit is £5

I_2 has a capacity of 3,000 units of product X_2, the variable cost per unit is £3

I_3 has a capacity of 6,000 units of product X_3, the variable cost per unit is £3

Assume that each of the two final divisions produces one final product, Y_1 and Y_2 respectively, as in Table 4.3. The associated LP model would then be as follows:

$$
\begin{aligned}
\text{maximize } Z = {} & 15Y_1 + 10Y_2 && \text{(total contribution)} \\
\text{subject to} \quad & 4Y_1 + 2Y_2 \leq 2,000 && \text{(capacity of } I_1, X_1) \\
& 3Y_1 + 4Y_2 \leq 3,000 && \text{(capacity of } I_2, X_2) \\
& 4Y_1 + 4Y_2 \leq 6,000 && \text{(capacity of } I_3, X_3) \\
& Y_1 \text{ and } Y_2 \geq 0
\end{aligned}
$$

Table 4.3 Revenue and cost details: International Fabrics PLC

| | Selling price (£) | Variable cost (£) | Input required of intermediates | | | Net contribution margin (£) |
			X_1 (unit)	X_2 (unit)	X_3 (unit)	
Y_1	65	9	4	3	4	15
Y_2	60	16	2	4	4	10

The optimal solution for the firm is; $Z = £9,000$, $Y_1 = 200$ units, and $Y_2 = 600$ units. At this level of activity, all the productive capacities of intermediate divisions I_1, and I_2 are fully utilized, but intermediate division I_3 has a spare capacity equivalent to 2,800 units of product X_3. The shadow prices associated with the capacities of the intermediate divisions are $W_1 = £3$, $W_2 = £1$, and $W_3 = 0$.

Using equation 4.1, the transfer prices for X_1, X_2 and X_3 are:

	X_1 £	X_2 £	X_3 £
VC_i	5	3	3
W_i	3	1	0
P_i^*	8	4	3

The net contributions of divisions F_1 and F_2 are shown in Table 4.4.

Table 4.4 Net contribution of divisions F_1 and F_2

Division F_1					Division F_2
Selling price			£65		£60
Less cost of intermediate input	£			£	
	X_1 4×£8 = 32			2×£8 = 16	
	X_2 3×£4 = 12			4×£4 = 16	
	X_3 4×£3 = 12			4×£3 = 12	
	—			—	
Total cost of transfers		56			44
+variable cost of final divisions		9			16
Total variable cost		—	£65		— £60
			—		—
Net contribution		—			—
		—			—

Linear programming thus permits the determination of the mix of products which is consistent with the optimal allocation of resources, and generates good proxies for opportunity cost in the form of shadow prices. However, in the context of transfer pricing this model has several limitations.

First, it assumes that cost and revenue functions are linear whereas in reality they tend to be non-linear.

Second, shadow prices are accurate measures of opportunity cost only if: (1) the product mix does not change and (2) resources are utilized efficiently. These conditions do not always hold in practice. Changes in either of these conditions can result in changes in shadow prices and can thus render previously derived shadow prices inappropriate for transfer pricing. Moreover, shadow prices can be helpful to divisional managers only in so far as they guide them towards the selection of the optimal product *combination*, but not in deciding on the optimal *level* of activity. Given the assumptions of constant variable cost (marginal cost) and contribution margin (marginal revenue) per unit, the marginal cost curve and the marginal revenue curve will not intersect and hence divisional managers will be indifferent to production levels at the optimal transfer prices. (The reader should check the effect on the net contributions of Y_1 and Y_2 of the transfer prices just calculated.) Hence other mechanisms will have to be employed in order to motivate divisional managers to pursue optimal production policies.

Third, if the resources used in producing the intermediate product are non-binding (non-scarce) constraints in the optimal solution the shadow price will be zero and the transfer price will equal the variable cost per unit. Hence, the division cannot operate as a profit centre. An example of this is the intermediate division I_3 of International Fabrics Plc, which in the optimal solution has a spare capacity of 2,800 units of X_3. Because the resources of this division are not scarce, the shadow price per unit is zero and the transfer price is set at £3, which is the variable cost per unit. Further, shadow prices may lead to sub-optimal decisions in the long term. For example, divisional managers may avoid acquiring excess plant capacity for future expansion since this would reduce their shadow prices and, hence, their transfer prices if plant capacity becomes non-binding in the short term.

Fourth, divisional autonomy is restricted under linear programming since the optimal solution for the company is usually derived by central management. Moreover, given this centralized structure, potential economies in processing and transmitting information usually associated with decentralized structures will be forgone.

To overcome some of these limitations the use of the decomposition model has been suggested (see Baumol and Fabian 1964). This model, it has been argued, offers greater decision-making autonomy to divisional managers without adversely affecting the overall interests of the company. According to the decomposition model, the total programme is divided into the headquarters plan and the divisional plans/programmes. The headquarters and the divisional managers will each solve their own programme independently but with relevant information being communicated in both directions.

To illustrate this idea, refer back to International Fabrics Plc. Assume now that in addition to the capacity constraints with which each of the intermediate divisions operates, division F_1 has available a maximum of 1,000 machine hours, and division F_2 has a maximum of 1,800 man hours. Each unit of Y_1 requires 5 machine hours where each unit of Y_2 requires 3 man hours. The total programme for International Fabrics Plc 'will be:

$$\text{maximize } Z = 15Y_1 + 10Y_2$$

$$
\begin{array}{llll}
\text{subject to} & 4Y_1 + 2Y_2 \leq 2,000 & \text{(capacity of } I_1) & (4.2) \\
& 3Y_1 + 4Y_2 \leq 3,000 & \text{(capacity of } I_2) & (4.3) \\
& 4Y_1 + 4Y_2 \leq 6,000 & \text{(capacity of } I_3) & (4.4) \\
& 5Y_1 \quad\quad\;\; \leq 1,000 & \text{(capacity of } F_1) & (4.5) \\
& \quad\quad 3Y_2 \leq 1,800 & \text{(capacity of } F_2) & (4.6) \\
& \text{all } X_i, Y_i \geq 0
\end{array}
$$

The headquarters plan consists of the objective function plus constraints 4.2, 4.3 and 4.4; it is assumed to be unconcerned with the constraints 4.5 and 4.6 of the final divisions. Expressions 4.2, 4.3 and 4.4 represent the constraint sets of the intermediate divisions which are demanded by both final divisions. As such, they represent common corporate resources. The programme of each of the final divisions consists of its objective function which can be directly derived from the corporate objective function (e.g. maximize $15Y_1$ — the contribution from Y_1 for division F_1), and its own constraints, equation 4.5 for division F_1 and equation 4.6 for division F_2. Neither of the final divisions need concern itself with the corporate constraints represented by the capacities of the intermediate divisions. The mechanism of the decomposition algorithm operates as follows:

1. Given that the optimal transfer prices for the relevant commodities are not initially known, the headquarters announces a set of provisional transfer prices as a starting point.
2. Each division optimizes its contribution subject to the prices announced and its own resource constraints and submits the solution to the headquarters.
3. The headquarters compares divisional demands for each commodity resulting from step 2 with the supply of that commodity. Most likely, demand will not exactly match supply. The headquarters would then announce a revised set of transfer prices in an attempt to match supply with demand, by increasing the prices if demand was greater than supply or decreasing the prices if demand was below supply. These new prices are then communicated to divisions.
4. Steps 2 and 3 are repeated until the headquarters reaches an optimal solution, where supply and demand are exactly matched. Divisions are then informed of the optimal transfer prices, which they subsequently use to determine their activity levels.

To summarize, the decomposition model derives optimal values for scarce resources by treating the organization as an internal market. It determines transfer prices for multi-product, multidivisional firms, and hence it is more realistic than the traditional economic theory model which usually deals with a two-division firm with only one intermediate product. It can also model explicitly divisional interdependencies, for example demand interdependence, in the constraint set of the relevant divisions. Finally, compared with the linear-programming approach it attains significant economies in the cost of information transmission through division of information. Each division solves a problem which contains only its own technological coefficients and imputed prices, while the central management solves a problem which contains only the overall linking information, that is the objective function of corporate profits, corporate as opposed to divisional resource constraints, and the divisional production levels.

Yet the decomposition model has some important limitations. First, divisional autonomy is restricted since final output decisions regarding both quantity and product mix are made by the central management rather than by divisional managers. Thus even though divisional managers deal with their own parts of the plan, it is top management who decides when an optimal solution is reached and instructs divisional managers accordingly to accept the transfer prices determined. As with the traditional economic theory and linear-programming models, attaining corporate optimality is the overriding priority even if that results in significant reductions in the levels of divisional autonomy. Second, as is the case with the previous models, there is no guarantee that the final solution will be optimal at corporate level because divisional managers have a vested interest in manipulating the data which they supply to their own advantage. This criticism is rooted in the fundamental notion that prices alone are not sufficient to ensure making optimal decentralized decisions, since a decision which is optimal for the company as a whole can be sub-optimal, and hence undesirable, at divisional level. Although several incentive schemes have been developed in order to induce truthful supply of information by divisional managers, such as the Groves (1973) scheme, they have had limited success in practice because they are based on many restrictive assumptions.

Organizational-based transfer pricing

Transfer pricing, differentiation and integration

The analysis of transfer pricing presented thus far has two main limitations: it oversimplifies economic reality and it ignores behavioural issues. Thus, in order to facilitate the analysis, most models abstract away from situations of complex interdependencies between divisions and reduce the transfer pricing problem to simply a microeconomic model or a mathematical programming exercise. This emphasis produces models of limited value. Moreover, in seeking to make decisions which are optimal at corporate level, the models allow for only limited measures of autonomy for divisional managers. The models have not explicitly linked transfer pricing to the organizational and behavioural contexts of the firm. Explicit consideration of these contexts is needed for a more informed knowledge of transfer pricing techniques and implications. The transfer pricing problem is as much a behavioural and organizational issue as it is a purely economic issue.

One immediate organizational issue in transfer pricing systems is the extent to which they can contribute to the attainment of the requisite differentiation and integration of company divisions. Differentiation can be defined as the segmentation of the company into specialized sub-units and the differences in the behaviour of organizational members caused by this segmentation. Integration refers to the quality and extent of collaboration between sub-units in response to the extent of co-ordination and unity of effort imposed upon them by their environments.

The transfer pricing mechanism enhances differentiation in so far as it helps separate and illuminate responsibility for different stages of production. Furthermore, if the transfer pricing mechanism is routine, as is the case when it is based on a well-defined formula such as cost-plus, it helps to achieve the required integration in situations of low to moderate complexity. In these situations, standard operating rules and procedures are relied upon frequently. Moreover, when designing a management accounting system, the requisite degree of differentiation should be considered carefully. Thus, if differentiation necessitates the segmentation of the organization in a manner that is different from the one consistent with the accounting system, the segmentation based on differentiation should prevail. For example, it may be convenient from a reporting point of view to separate a number of highly dependent functions into divisions. Such temptation should be avoided because it is opposed to the notion of integration suggested above. In summary, the accounting system should not impose artificial profit centres on the organizational structure.

Transfer pricing can thus be considered as an important mechanism for achieving integration and resolving conflict in organizations. In this respect, negotiated transfer prices offer a promising means for achieving effective integration by helping to resolve inter-divisional conflicts.

It is worth noting, however, that in the absence of a relevant outside market, the transfer price is likely to reflect the divisional manager's ability to negotiate rather than his ability to control economic variables. Moreover, negotiations between divisional managers may degenerate into personal conflicts, although the potential for this can be reduced for the following reasons. First, although organizational members could have different perceptions and working styles they may have many common attributes by virtue of being members of the same organization, and hence agreement among them can be frequently attained. Second, the use of skilful mediators would help in maintaining the rational flow of negotiations. Third, guidelines can be provided for conducting negotiations. Empirical evidence, however, indicates that in several cases agreement between negotiators is not automatically secured without central directives.

Bailey and Boe (1976) combined some of the behavioural analysis discussed above with mathematical modelling and developed a behaviourally orientated transfer pricing model. The model has the following characteristics: (1) it is dependent upon the organizational structure of the firm, (2) it uses multiple goals, and (3) divisional managers are not expected to subscribe to organizational goals. The model assumes that the firm's organizational structure consists of: Corporate Management (CM), Division Management (DM) and Operating Management (OM). While remaining deterministic, the model specifically allows for the possible existence of alternative production characteristics at the operating level. The optimal solution to the problem is guided by derived shadow prices and is organizationally dependent; it is a satisficing rather than a global solution.

The model explicitly accounts for pooled, sequential and reciprocal interdependencies. Pooled interdependence means that two or more tasks can be performed independently of one another. Sequential interdependence refers to situations where tasks have to be performed according to strict ordering, say task 1 before task 2, task 2 before task 3 and so on. Reciprocal interdependence occurs when a constant input–output interrelationship has to be observed among several tasks, so that individuals involved in these tasks co-ordinate their efforts through frequent interactions.

In the Bailey and Boe model, pooled interdependence is represented at any of the three levels, CM, DM and OM. Sequential interdependence is represented along the lines: CM → DM → OM; this establishes the order of the tasks associated with the three organizational levels. This means that each higher organizational level is responsible for integrating the activities of lower sub-units. Direct contact between sub-units not sequentially linked is not permitted. Reciprocal interdependence is reflected in the formulations at the next-higher organizational level. Thus, if OM_1 and OM_2 were reciprocally dependent, this would be reflected in the formulations of the relevant DM (the one to which OM_1 and OM_2 belong). The model also allows for the existence of gaming, given the possibility that multiple and conflicting goals exist at each organizational level. Gaming is also likely to be problematic in the case of reciprocal interdependence, particularly when it is not uniquely known to the higher management level.

The Bailey and Boe model offers a good illustration of how some important organizational concepts can be combined with formal modelling to generate a plausible transfer pricing scheme. However, the model has many of the limitations associated with mathematical programming techniques described earlier.

Organizational interpretations of transfer pricing

The above discussion indicates, to some extent, that underlying any transfer pricing system developed is a theory of the organization. This particular notion has been elaborated by Swieringa and Waterhouse (1982). They argued that, in relation to issues like transfer pricing, different models of the organization emphasize different events, lead to different definitions of the problem, raise different diagnostic questions and provide different answers to the questions. To illustrate their argument, they contrasted five models of the organization: (1) the traditional model (used predominantly in the literature on transfer pricing,) (2) the Cyert and March behavioural model, (3) the Cohen and March garbage-can model, (4) the Weick organizing model and (5) the markets and hierarchies model. They compare these models through the use of four dimensions, or what they call 'paradoxes': goals *versus* action determinants, process *versus* outputs, adaptability *versus* stability, and simplicity *versus* complexity.

Goals *versus* action-determinants

The traditional model of the organization is premised on the notion of well-defined, predetermined organizational goals. Goals are assumed to precede actions. The analysis typically focuses on identifying actions which are consistent with predetermined goals. Thus, from this perspective actions relating to transfer pricing are analysed in terms of their contributions to well-specified organizational goals. Optimal actions are assumed to be consistent with organizational goals. Whenever possible, central management interferes and modifies actions which threaten the supremacy of such goals.

The remaining four models of the organization do not view goals and actions as following a specific order. Their main focus is on understanding factors that determine outcome. The Cyert and March behavioural theory views goals as fluid, being influenced by the nature of bargaining that takes place between organizational members, the composition of the coalition and the definition of organizational problems. Goals are viewed as emerging through experience. In this model, activities related to transfer pricing can be seen as reflecting long-term bargaining between divisional managers with the aim of arriving at an acceptable pricing rule. Such a rule can then be used to negotiate the internal environment in which managers operate and to contribute to the avoidance/reduction of uncertainty.

In the garbage-can model, goals are decoupled from actions; actions result from a context-dependent set of problems, solutions, participants and choice opportunities. Outcomes are not likely to appear closely related to goals. Choices are made when the combination of these elements makes action possible. In this context, the transfer pricing situation is viewed as a choice opportunity which can lead to specific actions. The problems brought to this choice opportunity could include, for example, the inability of divisions to exploit their external markets, and the manoeuvering by divisions to exploit each other by attempting to arrive at favouable transfer prices. The solutions for these problems can include, for example, divisional bids and dual pricing schemes.

According to Weick's organizing model, past histories are used to endow actions with plausibility and legitimacy. Actions are related to the reduction of uncertainty rather than to pre-specified goals. Thus the choice of a specific transfer pricing system can be seen as a means of explaining, or legitimizing, past actions and making them appear consistent with highly valued organizational goals. For example, the use of negotiated transfer prices can be legitimized in terms of freedom of action and liberal managerial style. In contrast, transfer prices imposed by top management can be legitimized in the name of integration and subordination of individual interests to group interests.

Markets and hierarchies rely on the mechanisms of internal organization and the norms of socialization to curb the tendency towards opportunism in situations of small numbers bargaining and asymmetric information. The argument that there exist various economies in mediating transactions does not have to be based on the existence of well-specified goals. This theory focuses on using transfer pricing mechanisms to settle disputes, to act as incentives which foster co-operative internal trading, and to economize and regulate the flow of information. Hence, the transfer pricing system is viewed as a means of minimizing the costs of trading intra-company products.

Process *versus* outputs

The traditional model focuses on the development of transfer pricing systems and procedures which motivate divisional managers to act in a manner consistent with the interest of the company as a whole. Divisional interests are assumed to be subordinated to company interests. The remaining four models focus on the process of determining transfer prices, and related rules and procedures. The Cyert and March behavioural model views this process as an episode of ongoing, long-term bargaining between divisional managers. The garbage-can model treats it as a choice opportunity into which problems and solutions are dumped by divisional managers and the headquarters. Weick's organizing model views this process in terms of enactment and legitimation of past actions. According to the markets and hierarchies theory, the process is viewed in terms of mediating transactions through markets or hierarchies and curbing tendencies towards opportunistic behaviour by divisional managers. These latter models then emphasize the process through which transfer prices are determined, rather than the prices *per se*.

The analysis of Swieringa and Waterhouse (1982) suggests that, by emphasizing transfer pricing processes, shared beliefs and co-operative behaviour are promoted and thus different expectations held by various divisional managers can converge. Shared understandings of situations, and agreements on future actions can be attained by exchanging information and fostering interactions between managers.

Adaptability *versus* stability

Viewing transfer pricing as a process through which structure and control evolve, this process can be subject to pressures for organizational adaptation and learning which may conflict with pressures for organizational stability and predictability. All four non-traditional models (the behavioural, the garbage-can, the organizing and the markets and hierarchies) emphasize organisational learning and adaptation to cope with information asymmetry and uncertainty. They also show awareness of the presence of stabilizing elements in organizations as reflected in programmed activities, rules, standard procedures and incremental changes in behaviour.

Swieringa and Waterhouse suggest that transfer pricing can contribute to both organizational stability and change. Thus the transfer pricing system can act as a stabilizing force if the pricing rules become part of the organization's enacted reality. Such rules can also help to stabilize the organizational coalition by determining the basis for the distribution of rewards and by legitimizing authority. To contribute to organizational learning and adaptation, transfer pricing rules can be coded with expiry dates. This is likely to introduce greater uncertainty and to stimulate search behaviour for new transfer pricing rules, and to encourage experimenting with them.

Simplicity *versus* complexity

Under the traditional model, the transfer pricing problem is greatly simplified because that model is based on the assumptions of economic rationality, existence of well-defined goals, and antecedence of goals to actions. This also permits the abstraction of the transfer pricing process from its organizational context. Swieringa and Waterhouse note that such a situation requires little information. The locus of emphasis is simply on evaluating the degree of consistency of transfer pricing methods and procedures with the predetermined goals of the organization.

The remaining models offer more complex views, in which the dimensions and the process of the transfer pricing choice situation are intertwined with many dynamic organizational features, so that it is not sensible to abstract them from their organizational context. For example, in the garbage-can model transfer prices are the outcome of context-dependent problems, solutions, participants and choice opportunities. Thus the nature of the problems facing internal trading influences transfer prices — and so also do the personalities of divisional and top managers involved in the transfer pricing process.

The insightful analysis of Swieringa and Waterhouse demonstrates the richness and complexity of transfer pricing in an organizational context. Their work also warns of the serious limitations of analysing transfer pricing through the lens of any one model of the organization to the exclusion of others. Considered in combination, these models together offer a more comprehensive view of transfer pricing.

Summary

The main purpose of this chapter has been to provide a review of the literature on transfer pricing schemes which have been developed in order to facilitate the allocation of resources within a company and the evaluation of divisional performance. The success of the pricing system in performing these tasks depends largely on its ability to capture the relevant economic and organizational characteristics of the company. In essence, the divisionalized organization is a dynamic and interactive web of interdependent divisions, which seek the attainment of some goal(s). Transfer pricing schemes employed by the company not only impact on the degrees of co-operation and integration that take place between divisions, but they also influence the extent of decision-making autonomy enjoyed by divisional managers.

The transfer pricing systems developed by economists and management scientists range from the less sophisticated traditional economic model of a two-division firm with no externalities, to the more sophisticated mathematical programming models dealing with multi-product, multidivisional firms with differing externalities. The development of the more sophisticated models has made the transfer pricing problem setting more realistic. However, these models share some underlying assumptions which reduce their validity.

First, these models assume goal consensus. The possibility of goal conflict, which is considered inevitable under modern organization theory, is not explicitly entertained in these models (with the exception of the model developed by Bailey and Boe). Further, participants are assumed to submit complete and honest information either to each other, as under the traditional economic model, or to the central management, as under mathematical programming models. Thus information manipulation by divisional managers is not assumed to occur. To the extent that both goal conflict and gaming occur in reality, control over the allocation of resources within the divisionalized organization may be dictated by forces other than the pricing mechanism, for exmaple personal power or specialized knowledge of divisional managers.

Second, underlying the above transfer pricing models is the common belief that the price mechanism is a theoretically sound tool for regulating economic activities. However, the price system may not always be useful. For example, when the activities of some divisions are highly interdependent, prices do not lead to an optimal solution unless they have been appropriately modified to motivate divisions to take cognisance of such interdependence. Even if these modifications were introduced, they typically lead to increased levels of centralized control.

Third, the problem of uncertainty is hardly, if ever, considered by transfer pricing models. Thus, under the traditional transfer pricing model uncertainty is generally assumed away, while under the decomposition model uncertainty is introduced but only in a very rudimentary way. Uncertainty is likely to affect greatly the detemination of appropriate transfer prices. The divisionalized organization can be viewed as an economic entity facing different sets of transfer prices with each set corresponding to a particular state of the world. Hence each divisional manager will be faced with a probability distribution of transfer prices. Under such conditions it may be appropriate to emphasize the utility of profits in decision-making.

Fourth, existing transfer pricing models do not capture all the relevant organizational and behavioural issues. The pricing mechanism has not as yet completely penetrated all organizational levels, nor has it appropriately taken account of reciprocal or even sequential divisional interactions. Furthermore, the trade-off between corporate optimality and divisional autonomy is an issue of major importance; it is not entirely clear, when in conflict, which of the two should be sacrificed in favour of the other.

The above argument does not imply that the price mechanism should be discarded altogether. All that it implies is that it is necessary for the price mechanism to be buttressed by 'non-market' mechanisms to ensure that resource allocation within the divisionalized organization more fully reflects the relevant economic, organizational and behavioural characteristics.

References

Bailey, A.D., Jr and W.J. Boe (1976) 'Goal and resource transfers in the multigoal organization', *Accounting Review*, July, pp. 559–73.

Baumol, W.J. and T. Fabian (1964) 'Decomposition pricing for decentralization and external economies', *Management Science*, September, pp. 1–32.

Dopuch, N. and D.F. Drake (1964) 'Accounting implications for a mathematical programming approach to the transfer price problem', *Journal of Accounting Research*, Spring, pp. 10–24.

Gould, J.R. (1964) 'Internal pricing in firms where there are costs of using an outside market', *Journal of Business*, July, pp. 61–7.

Groves, T. (1973) 'Incentives in teams', *Econometrica*, July, pp. 617–31.

Hirshleifer, J. (1956) 'On the economics of transfer pricing', *Journal of Business*, July, pp. 172–84.

Swieringa, R.J. and J.H. Waterhouse (1982) 'Organizational views of transfer pricing', *Accounting, Organizations and Society*, vol. 7, no. 2, pp. 149–65.

Chapter 5

Strategic management accounting
RICHARD M.S. WILSON

Strategy and strategic decisions

While strategy has been defined in lots of different ways, there is no standard definition. Some writers have identified different levels of strategy along the following lines:

1. *corporate strategy*, which deals with the allocation of resources among various businesses or divisions of an enterprise;
2. *business strategy*, which exists at the level of a particular business or division, dealing primarily with the question of competitive position;
3. *functional strategy*, which is limited to the actions of specific functions (e.g. distribution) within particular businesses.

Our main concern will be with the role of managerial accounting in relation to business strategy as above. In this context we can define strategy as *an integrated set of actions aimed at securing a sustainable competitive advantage.*

The notion of *competitive advantage* requires that a given business be viewed relative to its competitors, and continuing success requires that a competitive advantage (e.g. in superior product quality, lower costs or more efficient distribution) be sought and maintained. It will be apparent from these comments that a period-by-period statement of a business's profits (whether by segment or overall), its cash flow or any other traditional accounting measure of performance, is blinkered in at least two respects. First, it is an artificial exercise at best to divide time up into arbitrary periods. Second, seeking to gauge a business's performance in isolation of changes in its strategic position relative to competing businesses ignores its capacity for generating future cash flows and achieving other aims.

'Strategy' is not synonymous with 'long-term plan' but rather consists of a business's attempts to reach some preferred future state by adapting its competitive position as circumstances change. While a series of strategic moves may be planned, competitors' actions will mean that the actual moves taken will have to be modified to take account of those actions.

The *characteristics of strategic decision* can be summarized as follows:

1. They are concerned with the scope of an organization's activities, and hence with the definition of the organization's boundaries.
2. They relate to the matching of the organization's activities with the opportunities in its substantive environment. Since the environment is continually changing, it is necessary for this to be accommodated via adaptive decision-making that anticipates outcomes — as in playing a game of chess.
3. They require the matching of an organization's activities with its resources. In order to take advantage of strategic opportunities it will be necessary to have funds, capacity, personnel, and so on, available when required.
4. They have major resource implications for organizations — such as acquiring additional capacity, disposing of capacity or reallocating resources in a fundamental way.
5. They are influenced by the values and expectations of those who determine the organization's strategy. Any repositioning of organizational boundaries will be influenced by managerial preferences and conceptions as much as by environmental possibilities.
6. They will affect the organization's long-term direction.
7. They are complex in nature since they tend to be non-routine and involve a large number of variables. As a result their implications will typically extend throughout the organization.

In broadening our perspective into a strategic setting we need to recognize that most managers have a functional role (whether as a personnel specialist or as a transport manager) and thus tend to see the world in terms associated with their function. Accountants are no exception to this, and they usually view matters in financial terms that are associated with existing activities. Thus there exists a risk of managerial accounting systems being designed as a reflection of past experience, with environmental changes being interpreted in the light of what has gone before. This tendency towards retrospective introspection needs to be changed in a fundamental way if strategic control is to be achieved. For example, traditional managerial accounting methods might give attention to: controlling working capital, decreasing work-in-progress, reducing wastage rates and negotiating modest wage increases — in order to improve an enterprise's performance. But if the enterprise is in a declining industry or is suffering from intense competitive pressures or is lagging behind in the adoption of current technology, no amount of marginal adjustment to insignificant details will improve its fortunes. Of central importance to organizational prosperity is the ability to acquire, allocate and utilize resources to take advantage of environmental opportunities and avoid environmental

	Strategic	Operational
Tangible	• Debt charges • New plants • Product development • Market development	• Labour • Materials • Energy • Supplies • Contract services
Intangible	• Poor product positioning • Technological obsolescence • Poor location of facilities	• Poor quality • Absenteeism • Labour turnover • Low morale • Lost output • Late delivery

Figure 5.1 A total view of cost categories (source: Richardson 1988, p. 30, adapted)

threats. The focus for the management accountant is therefore outward and forward.

The contrast between traditional and strategic approaches to cost categorization is highlighted in Figure 5.1. This suggests that the traditional focus of managerial accounting on operations represented in the top right-hand quadrant is inadequate if a comprehensive view is required. The latter encompasses strategic as well as operational matters and intangible as well as tangible issues.

An accounting systems framework for strategic decision-making

In a rare attempt at detailing the design of an accounting system that would facilitate the process of strategic decision-making, Gordon and his colleagues (1978) proposed the following parameters (Figure 5.2) as being generally applicable: Parameter 1, in Figure 5.2, deals with the question of who should be allowed to enter information into the system, while parameter 2 is concerned with who should be allowed access to its output, and parameter 3 refers to the technology to be used. Our main interest, however, is in parameter 4, relating to the specification of information characteristics.

In Figure 5.3 the general parameters from Figure 5.2 are specified more precisely in relation to a prototypical cost account system.

The content of Figure 5.3 is both familiar and unhelpful in the context of

1. Identification of information preparer(s).

2. Identification of information recipient(s).

3. Identification of the technology employed for information transmission.

4. Specification of the information characteristics:
   (a) which data items are to be communicated;
   (b) what the format of the data items is to be;
   (c) what the form of the data items is to be;
   (d) what the focus of the data items is to be;
   (e) what the orientation of the data items is to be;
   (f) what the time horizon covered by the data items is to be;
   (g) how frequently the data items are to be communicated.

Figure 5.2 Design parameters for an accounting information system (source: Gordon *et al*. 1978, p. 207)

1. Preparers — accounting clerks.

2. Recipients — production superintendents.

3. Transmission technology — written reports.

4. Information characteristics:
   (a) data items — direct labour hours worked per project, percentage completed, wage rates, overtime hours, overtime rates, overhead rates, cost standards, etc;
   (b) format — tableau of numbers, totals and summaries, identifying verbal statements;
   (c) form — quantitative, of both a financial and non-financial nature;
   (d) focus — narrow and specific;
   (e) orientation — internal;
   (f) time horizon — *ex post*;
   (g) frequency — periodically, say every fortnight.

Figure 5.3 Design parameters for prototypical cost accounting system (source: Gordon *et al*. 1978, p. 209)

strategic decision-making, so what might more helpfully fit the bill? Gordon and his colleagues tackle this question by breaking the process of strategic decision-making down into three phases: (1) problem identification, (2) generation of alternative courses of action and (3) choice among alternatives.

They argued that each phase requires different specifications for the accounting system's design parameters. Thus, for the problem identification phase, Figure 5.4 applies; for the generation of alternatives phase, Figure 5.5 applies; and for the choice phase, Figure 5.6 applies.

These design parameters give valuable guidelines for designing strategy-oriented managerial accounting systems. However, prior to reviewing other

1. Preparers — long-range planning taskforce.

2. Recipients — top echelon executives.

3. Transmission technology — primarily oral reports.

4. Information characteristics:
   (a) data items — competitors' actions, demand shifts, technological changes, new governmental regulations;
   (b) format — verbal statements;
   (c) form — primarily non-financial and qualitative;
   (d) focus — broad and diffuse;
   (e) orientation — primarily external;
   (f) time horizon — mostly current, some *ex ante*, little *ex post*;
   (g) frequency — non-periodic, triggered by monitoring key variables.

Figure 5.4 Design parameters for the strategic problem identification phase (source: Gordon *et al*. 1978, p. 209)

1. Preparers — corporate staff.

2. Recipients — one echelon below the top.

3. Transmission technology — written and oral reports.

4. Information characteristics:
   (a) data items — resources, skills, time availability, lines of credit, geographical sites and characteristics, demand forecasts;
   (b) format — tableau of both verbal statements and numbers;
   (c) form — primarily quantitative, of both a financial and non-financial nature;
   (d) focus — narrow and specific;
   (e) orientation — both internal and external;
   (f) time horizon — both current and *ex ante*;
   (g) frequency — non-periodic, triggered by completion of previous phase.

Figure 5.5 Design parameters for the strategic generation of alternatives phase (source: Gordon *et al*. 1978, p. 210)

significant contributions to strategic management accounting, there are three important issues that warrant coverage. Each has relevance to each phase identified by Gordon *et al*. They are the product life cycle, the experience curve and the product portfolio matrix.

Further underlying concepts

Products and services typically pass through a series of distinct phases in what is termed the *product life cycle*. The major characteristics of this concept are:

1. Preparers — corporate staff and line managers one echelon below the top.
2. Recipients — top echelon executives.
3. Transmission technology — primarily written reports.
4. Information characteristics:
   (a) data items — action possibilities, costs, payoffs, probabilities, decision trees;
   (b) format — tableau of mostly numbers, some verbal statements;
   (c) form — primarily quantitative, with emphasis on financial data;
   (d) focus — very narrow and quite specific;
   (e) orientation — internal;
   (f) time horizon — *ex post*;
   (g) frequency — non-periodic, triggered by completion of previous phase.

Figure 5.6 Design parameters for the strategic action selection phase (source: Gordon *et al*. 1978, p. 210)

1. Products have limited lives, and a given product's life can be represented by an S-shaped curve tracing its sales history.
2. The stages of the product's life cycle are identified by the inflection points in the sales history — introduction, growth, competitive turbulence, maturity, extension, decline.
3. Profit per unit varies as products move through their life cycles, falling following the growth phase.
4. Each phase of the product life cycle poses different threats and opportunities that give rise to different strategic actions.

The above points are summarized in Figure 5.7.

The second important concept is the *experience curve*. The essence of experience curve theory is that the real costs of generating products and services decline by between 20 and 30 per cent whenever cumulative experience doubles.

An important distinction needs to be drawn between the experience curve and the learning curve. The latter was initially observed during the 1920s, and it was a significant feature of the labour hours required for building aircraft during the Second World War — but it only relates to labour hours (hence labour cost). As a consequence, the reduction in costs due to the learning-curve effect is much lower than that due to the broader-based experience curve. *All* costs and cost effects are reflected by the experience curve.

Several causes of cost reduction act together within the experience curve, such as the learning experience, the effect of labour specialization and scale effects due to increased volume. The experience curve is not derived from accounting costs but by dividing the cumulative cash inputs by the cumulative output of end products, and the cost decline is shown by the rate of change in this ratio over time. From this rate of change managers can see how and

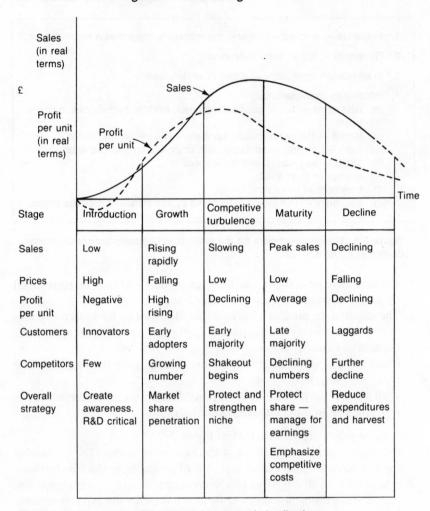

Figure 5.7 The product life cycle and its strategic implications

why their competitive costs are shifting. If estimates can be made of competitors' experience curve effects, this should reveal which are the low-cost competitors and which are not, and hence which are at risk and from whom.

The main strategic message from the experience curve is that if costs per unit in real terms decrease predictably with cumulative output, then the market leader has the potential to achieve the lowest costs and the highest profits. This is illustrated in Figure 5.8.

Firm A has less experience than Firm B, hence the latter has a significant cost advantage. In this rather extreme (but not implausible) example, A's unit cost is higher than the current market price, so it sustains a loss on each unit

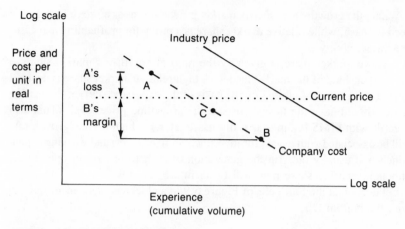

Figure 5.8 Advantages of experience

sold. By contrast, B's unit cost is well below the prevailing price, so it achieves a substantial margin on each unit sold. Firm C is operating profitably, but firm B could take advantage of its leadership position in the following way: since the industry price falls with cumulative volume, firm B can cut prices as its costs also fall due to its greater experience. Firm A has virtually been driven out, and the same fate could befall firm C.

Given the empirical existence of the experience curve, then, the use of cash will be less than directly proportional to a product's rate of growth. Similarly, the generation of cash will be a function of the product's market share. From these relationships the Boston Consulting Group constructed the *growth share matrix* (also known as the *product portfolio matrix*). This is the third important issue and is illustrated in Figure 5.9 below.

		Relative market share	
		High	Low
Market growth	High	Star (may be cash generator or cash absorber)	Wildcat (cash absorber)
	Low	Cash cow (large cash generator)	Dog (modest cash generator or absorber)

Figure 5.9 Product portfolio matrix

Within the growth-share matrix market growth serves as a proxy for a firm's need for cash, while relative market share is a proxy for profitability and cash-generating ability.

Relative market share is given by the ratio of any firm's market share to the market share of the market leader. A high relative market share is deemed to lead to higher profitability on the basis of the experience curve: the market leader should have the lowest costs at the prevailing price level. (This also accords with PIMS findings as is discussed later.) A high market growth rate will be associated with a need for investment in fixed assets and working capital which will usually outstrip the generation of cash from current operations, although securing share now will bring future rewards.

Let us look at the four cells of Figure 5.9 in a clockwise sequence, starting with the bottom left.

High market share, low market growth: This is a position of strength as the high market share should facilitate economies of scale, low unit costs, and so on, and give market dominance. Because market growth is low, the need for new investment will be minimal, with the result that products in this cell will tend to be large generators of cash (i.e. 'cash cows'). A reasonable aim might be to maintain market share to enable the generation of cash to continue rather than seeking to increase market penetration.

High market share, high market growth: This cells contains potential cash cows, at present termed 'stars'. If their competitive position is improved, involving heavy expenditure, they will be cash absorbers until the market growth rate declines and they become cash generators. The important requirement is to obtain and maintain a large market share.

Low market share, high market growth: Any product in this cell will be a cash absorber ('wildcat') because of the need to invest to keep a foothold in a market that is dominated by others. If an aggressive attempt is made to move a wildcat product into a *high* market share position, then it may become — eventually — a cash cow. However, if resources are not available to pursue this strategy, it may be advisable to withdraw.

Low market share, low market growth: Within this cell are the 'dogs' that produce very little cash (if any). It would be prohibitively expensive to seek market dominance from this position, so the best strategy may be to delete dogs from the range. The existence of dogs suggests a failure to obtain a leadership position during the growth phase, so further failures through cash absorption should preferably be avoided.

The choice of a strategy in the light of the growth-share matrix will be influenced by both feasibility (bearing in mind that market share can be influenced more readily than market growth) and desirability (in that a balanced product portfolio will probably be sought in which some products generate cash and acceptable profits in the short-run to support those needing cash for their long-run growth).

A strategic success sequence is likely to emerge via the following steps:

1. The cash generated by cash cows (high market share, low market growth) should be invested in building the market share of wildcats. If this is done well sustainable advantage will be provided by which wildcats will become stars and then cash cows, thereby being able to finance subsequent strategies.
2. To be avoided is the sequence by which wildcats are not supported so that they become dogs when the market matures: low relative share in a low-growth market is not the place to find oneself.
3. Also to be avoided is the sequence by which stars lose position and become wildcats as market growth slows, with the risk of their becoming dogs.

Key contributions to strategic management accounting

In formulating strategies there is a need to search for alternative directions and means of pursuing those directions. Three major contributions to these tasks which give a basis for strategic management accounting come from Porter, the PIMS study and Simmonds.

Porter's approach

Porter's (1985) influential contributions to strategy formulation and implementation are premised on two basic questions. First, how attractive, from the viewpoint of long-term profitability, are different industries? Differences exist from one industry to another, and changes occur over time. Since a given enterprise's profitability will be influenced by the profitability of the industry it is in, this is a key question. It is also significant because the choice of an industry determines an enterprise's competitors.

Whatever the industry, there are five competitive forces central to formulating and implementing strategy:

1. the threat of new entrants;
2. the threat of substitute products or services;
3. the rivalry amongst existing organizations within the industry;
4. the bargaining power of suppliers;
5. the bargaining power of consumers.

Taken together, they significantly influence whether organizations can generate returns in excess of the cost of capital. Thus in the pharmaceutical, soft drinks and data-base publishing industries, the five forces are favourable, and enterprises within these industries can earn attractive returns. However, in other industries — including rubber, steel and video games — pressure from one or more of the forces is so intense that few enterprises can generate high returns.

Why do these forces have such an influence on industry profitability? The answer is in the constituents of profitability — prices, costs and investment. Prices are influenced by the bargaining power of consumers and the threat of substitutes. Costs are influenced by the bargaining power of suppliers and the rivalry among competitors. Investment is influenced by the threat of entrants and other factors including rivalry and consumers' requirements.

The relative strength of each competitive force tends to be a function of *industry structure* (i.e. its underlying economic and technological characteristics). This can change over time, with the result that the relative strength of competitive forces will also change, hence the industry's profitability. At the very least, an enterprise should monitor its environment to identify shifts in its industry structure and the competitive forces. But an enterprise can also induce change — primarily by its innovative endeavours, such as the development of new products or processes. Any change by one competitor is likely to bring a response from others, and so on, with the result that the final outcome (in terms of impact on an industry's profitability) may be extremely difficult to predict.

Porter's second fundamental question is: what is the enterprise's relative position within its industry? This question is significant because it influences whether an enterprise's profitability is greater or less than the industry's average. The basic way an enterprise might seek to achieve above-average returns into the long term is via *sustainable competitive advantage*. This can be achieved by *generic strategies*, of which there are three:

1. cost leadership, whereby the enterprise aims to be the lowest cost producer within its industry;
2. differentiation, through which the enterprise seeks some unique dimension in its product/service that is valued by consumers, and which can command a premium price;
3. focus, which has two variants — cost focus and differentiation focus — as depicted in Figure 5.10. While cost leadership and differentiation strategies strive for competitive advantage in broad market segments, the focus strategies are directed at narrow segments to the exclusion of others. If the structure of the segments chosen is favourable, then above-average returns should result.

Porter's view is that any enterprise seeking a sustainable competitive

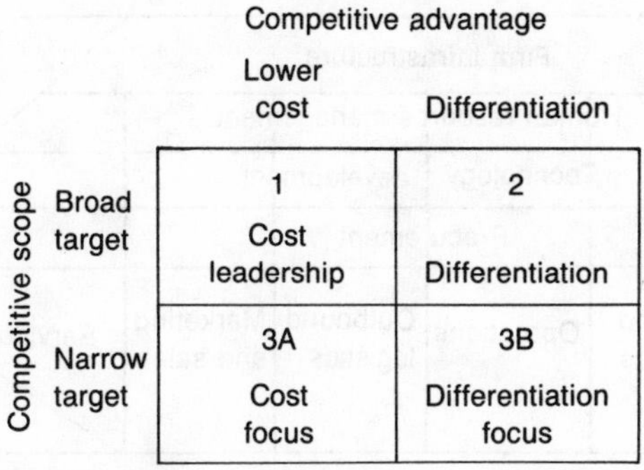

Competitive advantage

		Lower cost	Differentiation
Competitive scope	Broad target	1 Cost leadership	2 Differentiation
	Narrow target	3A Cost focus	3B Differentiation focus

Figure 5.10 Generic strategies

advantage must select one of these generic strategies rather than attempting to be 'all things to all people' or 'stuck in the middle'.

In so far as competitive advantage is cost based, we need to recall that conventional cost analysis:

1. concentrates on manufacturing activities;
2. ignores the impact of other activities;
3. overlooks linkages among activities by analysing each activity in a discrete way;
4. fails to assess the cost positions of competitors in relative terms;
5. relies too heavily on existing accounting systems.

In contrast strategic cost analysis focuses on:

1. the determinants of relative cost position;
2. the ways in which a firm might secure a sustainable cost advantage;
3. the costs of differentiation.

Following Porter's (1985) approach, the initial step is to define the firm's *value chain*, which he introduced as a way of breaking down a firm's strategically relevant activities in order to understand the behaviour of costs. Competitive advantage comes from carrying out these activities more cost-effectively than one's competitors.

The value chain of a firm is composed of nine categories of interrelated activities, as shown in Figure 5.11. These activities are, in part, primary activities and, in part, support activities: the latter exist to facilitate the former. The particular arrangements reflect an enterprise's history, strategy and the underlying economics of its situation.

The value aspect is found in the price that customers are willing to pay. Hence the margin depends upon the cost-effectiveness of the primary and support activities on the one hand, and the market's perception of the firm's offering on the other.

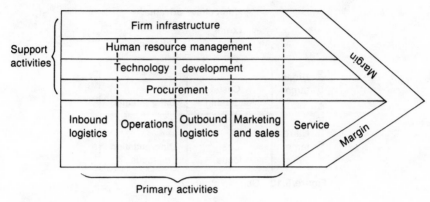

Figure 5.11   The value chain (source: Porter 1985, p. 37)

Each activity in the value chain has operating costs and assets (whether fixed or current) associated with it. The amount of assets assigned to an activity, along with the efficiency of their utilization, both influence that activity's costs. Assigning assets and operating costs to the activities constituting the value chain involves similar problems to those in any allocation exercise. Formulas and procedural rules will need to be established to deal with this problem, bearing in mind the ways in which competitors' cost analyses are to be carried out.

Any enterprise's cost position (relative to its competitors) is derived from the cost behaviour patterns associated with the activities constituting its value chain. These cost behaviour patterns in turn depend upon a number of *cost drivers*, which Porter has defined as the structural determinants of an activity's cost. Some cost drivers are within the firm's control, but some are not, and a given activity's cost may be due to several cost drivers acting together. A particular firm's cost position on any value activity will depend on whichever cost drivers are at play, but the impact of different cost drivers will vary among firms — even within the same industry.

Ten key cost drivers have been identified. If an enterprise can understand which affect its relative cost position, it should be able to improve its cost advantages over its competitors. The key cost drivers identified by Porter (1985, pp. 70–83) are economies (or diseconomies) of scale; learning; pattern of capacity utilization; linkages; interrelationships; integration; timing; discretionary policies; location; and institutional factors.

Figure 5.12 suggests how cost drivers impact upon the cost behaviour of value activities within a consumer durables manufacturing firm. In this type of analysis attempts should be made to quantify the impact of each cost driver influencing the cost of a value or activity. However crude, it should help to indicate the relative significance of each cost driver. Moreover, it will help in showing the extent to which the interactions among cost drivers tend to reinforce or counteract each other.

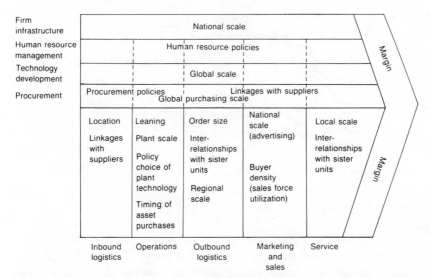

Figure 5.12 Cost drivers in a consumer goods manufacturing firm (source: Porter 1985, p. 86)

The next step is to do the above analysis for one's competitors. A given enterprise will have a cost advantage if its cumulative costs of carrying out all the activities within the value chain are less than those of its competitors. This advantage will only have strategic significance if it can be sustained. This requires that competitors are unable to readily imitate it. The scope for imitation will depend upon the structure of the enterprise's value chain relative to those of competitors, and the enterprise's key cost drivers relative to those of competitors. A cost advantage (which is equivalent to cost leadership) needs to be maintained, and this requires determined effort on a day-to-day basis in improving cost-effectiveness.

In summary, Porter (1985, p. 118) specifies the steps in strategic cost analysis as follows:

1. Identify the appropriate value chain and assign costs and assets to it.
2. Diagnose the cost drivers of each value activity and how they interact.
3. Identify competitor value chains and determine the relative cost of competitors and the sources of cost differences.
4. Develop a strategy to achieve a lower relative cost position through controlling cost drivers or reconfiguring the value chain.
5. Ensure that cost reduction efforts do not erode differentiation.
6. Test the cost reduction strategy for sustainability.

Brock (1984, p. 226) has portrayed this diagrammatically as in Figure 5.13.

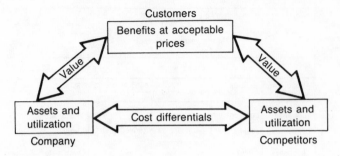

Figure 5.13 The strategic triangle

The PIMS study

Another important and influential approach to guiding strategy formulation is the PIMS (profit impact of market strategy) study. Work has been going on in the United States on this project since 1972, during which time a huge data base has been built up from over 2,800 businesses. The aim of the PIMS programme is to identify the features of businesses that account for performance (in terms of cash flow and profitability). Persistently influential factors are competitive position (including market share and relative product quality); production structure (including investment intensity and the productivity of operations); and attractiveness of the served market (as shown by its growth rate and customers' characteristics).

These factors explain between 65 and 70 per cent of the variability in profitability among the firms in the PIMS data base. By examining the determinants of profitability it is possible to address such strategic questions as:

1. What rate of profit and cash flow is normal for this type of business?
2. What profit and cash flow outcomes can be expected if the business continues with its present strategy?
3. How will future performance be affected by a change in strategy?

A key notion underlying strategic management accounting is the relative position of a firm among its competitors regarding unit costs, profitability, market share, *inter alia*. This is reflected in the PIMS approach, as shown in Figure 5.14.

The contribution of each variable in Figure 5.14 to overall profitability is estimated by a multiple regression model. This allows the impact of weak variables to be offset by strong variables — such as a small market share being offset by high product quality. Once the model has been applied to one's own company — requiring as input more than 100 separate variables — it can then be used to assess the relative strengths and weaknesses of competitors in order to identify the best source of competitive advantage.

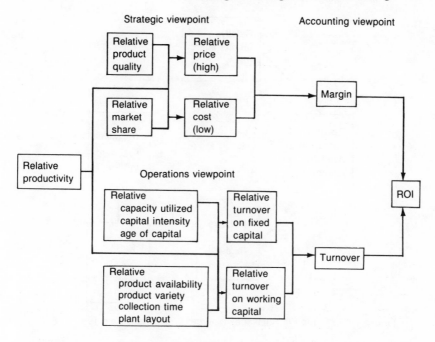

Figure 5.14 The determinants of relative profitability (source: Day 1986, p. 120)

The PIMS approach has been subjected to an increasing amount of critical comment regarding measurement errors, deficiencies in the model and interpretations of the findings. Perhaps the main concern is over the practice of deriving prescriptions about strategy from unsupported causal inferences. Hence it is important when using PIMS data to understand its limitations. When so used the PIMS programme can provide valuable insights.

Some of the broad conclusions from the PIMS programme are:

1. In the long run the most important factor affecting performance is the quality of an enterprise's products/services relative to those of its competitors.
2. Market share and profitability are strongly related: first, the rate of investment (ROI) increases steadily as market share increases; second, enterprises having relatively large market shares tend to have above-average rates of investment turnover; and third, the ratio of marketing expenses to sales revenue tends to be lower for enterprises having high market shares. The PIMS programme has demonstrated the linkages among superior relative quality, higher relative prices, gains in market share, lower relative costs and higher profitability. These linkages are portrayed in Figure 5.15, which indicates the causal role of relative quality upon business performance.
3. High investment intensity acts as a powerful drag on profitability: first,

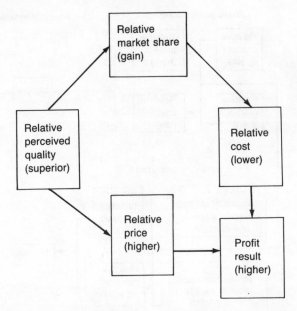

Figure 5.15 Some PIMS linkages (source: Buzzell and Gale 1987, p. 81)

the higher the ratio of investment to sales, the lower the ROI; second, enterprises having high investment intensity tend to be unable to achieve profit margins sufficient to sustain growth.
4. Many dog and wildcat activities generate cash, while many cash cows do not.
5. Vertical integration is a profitable strategy for some kinds of enterprise but not for others.
6. Most of the strategic factors that boost ROI also contribute to long-term value.

Simmonds' approach

The contribution of Simmonds is perhaps the most significant from the viewpoint of showing how strategic management accounting might be undertaken. Simmonds (1981) defined strategic management accounting as 'the provision and analysis of management accounting data about a business and its competitors for use in developing and monitoring the business strategy'. (p. 26)

He emphasizes the particular importance of relative levels and trends in real costs and prices, volume, market share, cash flow, and the proportion demanded of an enterprise's total resources. The key notion here is that of an enterprise's position *relative to* competitors' positions. In so far as strategy is concerned with competitive position, it has been largely ignored by management accountants, but in a number of papers Simmonds (1981, 1982, 1985, 1986) has proposed how this failing might be overcome.

A basic plank in his argument is the preoccupation of accountants with the recording, analysing and presentation of cost data relating to existing activities. This 'data orientation' begs some fundamental questions — such as why the data is being collected in the first place. An alternative, and preferable, approach is one of 'information orientation' which starts with the diagnosis of problems, leading to the structuring of decisions, and thence to the specification of information for making appropriate decisions. The focus shifts from the analysis of costs *per se* to the value of information.

Managers wishing to safeguard their organization's strategic position must know by whom, by how much and why they are gaining or being beaten. In other words, strategic indicators of performance are required. Conventional measures, such as profit, will not suffice.

Let us take comparative costs as a starting-point. Intuitively, organizations having a cost advantage (i.e. lower unit cost for a product of comparable specification) are strong and those having a cost disadvantage are weak. If we relate this to the previous discussion on experience curves, it will be appreciated that if costs can be made to decline predictably with cumulative output, then that enterprise which has produced most should have the lowest unit cost and therefore the highest profits.

Apart from cost, an enterprise may seek to gain strategic advantage via its pricing policy. Here the management accountant can attempt to assess each major competitor's cost structure and relate this to their prices — taking care to eliminate the effects of inflation. Applying cost—volume—profit analysis to one's competitors is likely to be more fruitful than simply applying it internally.

> Clearly, competitor reactions can substantially influence the outcome of a price move. Moreover, likely reactions may not be self-evident when each competitor faces a different cost—volume—profit situation. Competitors may not follow a price lead nor even march in perfect step as they each act to defend or build their own positions. For an adequate assessment of the likelihood of competitor price reactions, then, some calculation is needed of the impact of possible price moves on the performance of individual competitors. Such an assessment in turn requires an accounting approach that can depict both competitor cost—volume—profit situations and their financial resources. (Simmonds 1982, p. 207)

After dealing with costs and prices the next important (and related) variable to consider is volume — especially market share. By monitoring movements in market share, an enterprise can see whether it is gaining or losing position, and an examination of relative market shares will indicate the strength of different competitors. Reporting market-share details in financial reports can help make managerial accounting more strategically relevant.

Competitive position has been highlighted by Simmonds (1986) as the basic determinant of future profits and of the business's value. Since competitive position can change over time, so can profits and value,,but it should not be assumed that an improvement in competitive position will be associated with an improvement in short-run profits. In fact, the opposite is likely to be the case due to the cost of building up a competitive position, which depresses current profits in favour of future profits. This raises the question as to whether competitive position can be measured in accounting terms — not just for a given business but also for its main competitors, and not just at a point in time but also over time. Simmonds has attempted to do this by applying strategic management accounting. He makes it clear, however,that it is not possible to express competitive position as a single figure. But it is possible to offer an array of indicators relating to the competitive situation which will give managers insights into a business's competitive position.

Simmonds recommends that competitive data is built up for the market leader, close competitors and laggards rather than for all competitors. The following data might most usefully be developed (Simmonds 1986).

Sales and market share

Sales revenue of each firm relative to the total market is a cornerstone. Changes in market share should be closely monitored for they indicate changes in competitive position, with implications for future profits. Adding market share details to management accounting reports enables managers to make more sense of what is happening. Table 5.1 gives sales and market share data for firm A and total market for product X. We can see from Table 5.1 that, despite an increase in sales revenue of 20 per cent for firm A, its market share has slipped from 19 to 16 per cent. The total market grew by 44 per cent. It seems probable that the firm's failure to keep pace with the overall market growth will be reflected in a poorer competitive position: not only might competitors

Table 5.1 Sales and market share data: product X

	Firm A	Total market
Sales (£000s)		
Last year	1,000	5,200
This year	1,200	7,500
% change	+ 20	+ 44
Market share (%)		
Last year	19	100
This year	16	100

have gained market share at the firm's expense, but this is likely to be accompanied by cost advantages — hence improved profits. Some details are given in Table 5.2.

Relative market share is calculated by dividing each competitor's market share by that of one's own firm. As Table 5.2 makes clear, firm A has slipped relative to both the market leader and its closest competitor. The leader's market share has increased to three times that of firm A, and this will almost certainly have lowered its unit costs.

Table 5.2 Relative market shares

	Sales (£000s)	Market share (%)	Relative market share
Total market:			
Last year	5,200		
This year	7,500		
Firm A			
Last year	1,000	19	
This year	1,200	16	
Leading competitor			
Last year	2,200	42	2.20
This year	3,600	48	3.00
Close competitor			
Last year	1,200	23	1.20
This year	2,000	27	1.67

Profits and return on sales

If a competitor has a higher return on sales than firm A it may well reduce price, or improve quality, or increase its marketing efforts to improve its competitive position further.

The data in Table 5.3 shows sales, market share, relative market share, and profit (before tax but after interest) over the last three years for all firms supplying product X. Over that period the market leader's profit has grown by 400 per cent, the closest competitor's by over 200 per cent, and firm A's by only 90 per cent. In absolute terms the market leader's profit in year 3 is almost five times that of firm A, giving a huge source of funds for expansion, R & D, etc. In relative terms the leader's return on sales of 22.2 per cent in year 3 is well ahead of any other competitor.

Firm A's task seems to be to reinforce its competitive position relative to laggard firms and to develop a defence against the strong competitors.

Table 5.3 Sales, market shares and profits for all suppliers of product X

	Sales (£000s)	Market share (%)	Relative market share	Profit (£000s)	(%)
Firm A:					
Year 1	700	17.5		90	12.8
Year 2	1,000	19.2		130	13.0
Year 3	1,200	16.0		170	14.2
Leading competitor:					
Year 1	1,400	35.0	2.0	200	14.3
Year 2	2,200	42.3	2.2	400	18.2
Year 3	3,600	48.0	3.0	800	22.2
Close competitor:					
Year 1	1,000	25.0	1.4	120	12.0
Year 2	1,200	23.1	1.2	170	14.2
Year 3	2,000	26.6	1.7	260	13.0
Laggard 1:					
Year 1	500	12.5	0.71	55	11.0
Year 2	500	9.6	0.50	60	12.0
Year 3	500	6.7	0.42	50	10.0
Laggard 2:					
Year 1	400	10.0	0.57	40	10.0
Year 2	300	5.8	0.30	20	6.7
Year 3	200	2.7	0.17	5	2.5
Total market:					
Year 1	4,000	100.0		505	12.6
Year 2	5,200	100.0		780	15.0
Year 3	7,500	100.0		1,285	17.1

Volume and unit cost

Details of volume and costs are given in Table 5.4. Changes in unit costs reveal each firm's relative efficiency: the further a competitor's relative cost falls below unity, the more of a threat this becomes, and *vice versa*. (Costs are calculated by subtracting profit from sales revenue, and unit costs are obtained by dividing the costs by volume, year by year.)

The market leader has a cost advantage in year 3 of £0.69 per unit relative to firm A, whereas laggard firm 2 has a cost disadvantage relative to firm A of £0.73 per unit. Perhaps more significant than these figures are those that compare volume and cost changes. Thus, for example, firm A's two main competitors both increased volume between years 2 and 3 by more than 70 per cent, yet the close competitor's cost per unit only fell by 3 per cent or

Table 5.4 Volume, costs and unit costs

	Volume in units (000s)	Increase (%)	Cost (£000s)	Cost per unit (£)	Relative cost per unit
Firm A:					
Year 1	100		610	6.10	
Year 2	156	56	870	5.58	
Year 3	192	23	1,030	5.36	
Leading competitor:					
Year 1	200		1,200	6.00	0.98
Year 2	350	75	1,800	5.14	0.92
Year 3	600	71	2,800	4.67	0.87
Close competitor:					
Year 1	140		880	6.29	1.03
Year 2	190	36	1,030	5.42	0.97
Year 3	330	74	1,740	5.27	0.98
Laggard 1:					
Year 1	70		445	6.36	1.04
Year 2	75	7	440	5.86	1.05
Year 3	80	7	450	5.62	1.05
Laggard 2:					
Year 1	56		360	6.42	1.05
Year 2	45	(20)	280	6.22	1.16
Year 3	32	(29)	195	6.09	1.14
Total:					
Year 1	566				
Year 2	816	44			
Year 3	1,234	51			

so while the market leader's cost per unit fell by more than 9 per cent. Is the explanation to be found in the close competitor's investment in competitive position — such as Research and Development, marketing programmes or new plant?

Unit prices

Table 5.5 shows the unit prices charged for product X by each competitor over the last three years, along with costs and the profits and market shares that have resulted. (Unit prices are simply calculated by dividing sales revenue by units sold.) The pattern of price changes reflects the use of price as a competitive variable. This can be related to cost and market share data to see

Table 5.5   Unit prices, profits and market shares

	Average price per unit (£)	Average cost per unit (£)	Profit per unit (£)	Market share (%)
Firm A:				
Year 1	7.00	6.10	0.90	17.5
Year 2	6.41	5.58	0.83	19.2
Year 3	6.25	5.36	0.89	16.0
Leading competitor:				
Year 1	7.00	6.00	1.00	35.0
Year 2	6.29	5.14	1.15	42.3
Year 3	6.00	4.67	1.33	48.0
Close competitor:				
Year 1	7.14	6.29	0.85	25.0
Year 2	6.31	5.42	0.89	23.1
Year 3	6.06	5.27	0.79	26.6
Laggard 1:				
Year 1	7.14	6.36	0.78	12.5
Year 2	6.66	5.86	0.80	9.6
Year 3	6.25	5.62	0.63	6.7
Laggard 2:				
Year 1	7.14	6.42	0.72	10.0
Year 2	6.66	6.22	0.44	5.8
Year 3	6.25	6.09	0.16	2.7

how competitive positions are changing. For example, the market leader has
reduced the price by more than any other firm, but its price reductions have
not been as great as its cost reductions, hence profit per unit has increased
each year — as has the number of units. This places that firm in a very strong
competitive position. Patterns of price, cost, profit and volume change for firm
A and its closest competitor are less clear, but for the laggards the picture
of a downward spiral is clear enough.

Cash flow, liquidity and resource availability

Competitive gains and losses will arise over longer periods than the financial
year, and the capacity of a competitor to continue in the fray is a function
of more than simply profit or market share at a particular point in time. A
firm's ability to continue to compete will also depend upon its liquidity and
the availability of other resources over time. For example, a firm with poor
cash flow, a high level of debt, and out-of-date production facilities is not likely
to be able to compete for long.

The future

Having analysed the relative positions of each firm supplying product X over the past three years, the major task is formulating the next move.

The management of firm A can see that the market leader is controlling the competitive situation with the highest volume and profits, plus the lowest unit costs and price. If that firm reduced its price by, say, 10 per cent, it would force the laggards out of the market and limit the close competitor's profit (assuming it followed suit and reduced its own price). Firm A needs to reduce its costs and strengthen its position against its two main competitors while there is scope for growth in the overall market for product X.

Using Tables 5.2 to 5.5 as a basis, various possibilities can be projected for the future, each building on explicit assumptions regarding future market demand, likely competitive actions, likely competitive reactions and competitors' liquidity and solvency. This takes us a long way from conventional single-entity, single-period management accounting, yet the necessary adaptations are not so difficult to comprehend — but the benefits from gaining a clearer picture of one's competitive position and how this is changing should be enormous. Strategic management accounting can help realize these benefits.

References

Brock, J.J. (1984) 'Competitor analysis: some practical approaches', *Industrial Marketing Management*, vol. 13, pp. 225–31.

Buzzell, R.D. and B.T. Gale (1987) *The PIMS Principles: Linking Strategy to Performance*, New York: Free Press.

Day, G.S. (1986) *Analysis for Strategic Marketing Decisions*, St Paul, Minnesota: West.

Gordon, L.A., D.F. Larcker and F.D. Tuggle (1978) 'Strategic decision processes and the design of accounting information systems: conceptual linkages', *Accounting, Organizations and Society*, vol. 3, no. 3/4, pp. 203–13.

Porter, M.E. (1985) *Competitive Advantage: Creating and Sustaining Superior Performance*, New York: Free Press.

Richardson, P.R. (1988) *Cost Containment: The Ultimate Advantage*, New York: Free Press.

Shank, J.K. and V. Govindarajan (1988) *Strategic Cost Analysis*, Homewood, Illinois: Irwin.

Simmonds, K. (1981) 'Strategic management accounting', *Management Accounting*, vol. 59, no. 4, pp. 26–9; reprinted in R. Cowe (ed.) (1988). *Handbook of Management Accounting*, 2nd edn, Aldershot: Gower.

Simmonds, K. (1982) 'Strategic management accounting for pricing: a case example', *Accounting and Business Research*, vol. 12, no. 47, pp. 206–14.

Simmonds, K. (1985) 'How to compete', *Management Today*, August, pp. 39–43, 84.

Simmonds, K. (1986) 'The accounting assessment of competitive position', *European Journal of Marketing*, vol. 20, no. 1, pp. 16–31.

Chapter 6

Agency theory and contracts of employment

DAVID ASHTON

As was outlined in the introductory chapter, the key assumption in principal—agent (PA) analysis is that the employee or agent, while economically rational, acts out of self-interest rather than necessarily in the interests of his employer or principal. What prevents the organization, in such circumstances, from degenerating into anarchy is the series of binding agreements or contracts between the owners and the various employees of the firm. These contracts specify the actions to be undertaken by employees as well as designating the rewards that will accrue to the employees from their actions. Before proceeding to explore the consequences of this view of the firm and examining the mathematical structure of contracts[1] it is useful to identify and discuss those features of a contract of employment which are of particular interest in this approach.

Consider the case of a wealthy person who wishes to invest some capital in a small business. For the sake of simplicity, it is assumed that the wealthy person, who acts as the principal in the contract, is the sole owner of the business and employs a manager to act as his agent. The manager or agent is charged with the responsibility of running the business. One possible form of contract of employment is for the owner or principal to pay the manager a fixed salary. Here the principal carries all the risk associated with the success or otherwise of the business. In contrast, the agent bears none of the risk and is assured of a constant salary irrespective of profits or losses. The major weakness of such a contract from the principal's point of view is obvious. The

---

1. This analysis is more usually referred to in the literature as agency theory. However, agency theory covers a much broader spectrum of contracts, for example contracts in financial markets, insurance and auditing. For the purposes of management accounting, we will largely restrict our discussion to contracts of employment and follow the analysis as originally presented in Holmstrom (1979).

manager, whom we shall assume is honest though motivated by greed, has no incentive to work hard and maximize the profits from the business. This of course assumes that we are dealing with a one-period contract, thus eliminating the possibility that the manager loses his job and salary as a result of bankruptcy of the business. A more attractive contract or sharing rule from the principal's point of view — where, as is quite likely, the principal cannot easily monitor and control the actions of the manager — is to make the manager's salary dependent upon the profitability of the business. With such a sharing rule, the manager has an incentive to ensure the success of the business. Such a contract is termed incentive-compatible. A further feature of such a contract is that it reduces the owner's exposure to risk. When trading is poor and profits are low, so are the expenses in the form of the salary or share to be paid to the manager. This simple example of an *incentive-compatible risk-sharing rule* illustrates some of the specific features of contracts which will form the substance of the subsequent analysis.

More formally, the contract is an *ex-ante* specification of a sharing rule for the division of an uncertain monetary outcome. In the example cited, the gross profits from the business constitute the uncertain monetary outcome, and the profit-related salary shares these profits between the owner and the manager. This sharing rule also ensures that the manager, while selfishly seeking a higher salary, also acts in the interests of the owner. The agreed sharing rule or contract of employment cannot be based upon the manager's effort, because this is unobservable, but is based on the related performance measure of profits. The actual choice of profits as the appropriate measure of performance arises for two reasons. The first is that profits provide a performance measure which is observable by both the owner and the manager. Second, profits are calculated according to a given set of rules. As such, profits can be used as the basis of a legally enforceable contract. The need to write a contract on some observable and well-defined surrogate of management performance rather than on a direct measure of management performance would appear to have profound implications for the design of management accounting systems. It is these implications which (PA) theory purports to analyse.

The concept of an optimal sharing rule

The first problem which we face in attempting to draw up a contract of employment is what reward schedule, or share $S(x)$ of the profits x, should be given to the agent. It should be noted that this sharing rule is a function of the outcome or profits and hence varies with profits. Examples of some possible sharing rules are given below.

Rule 1: $S(x) = \lambda$ (a constant)

Rule 2: $S(x) = \dfrac{x}{2}$

Rule 3: $S(x) = \dfrac{x}{3}$ if $x \geq 0$

$\qquad\quad = 0$ if $x \leq 0$

Rule 4: $S(x) = a_0 + a_1 + a_2 x^2 + a_3 \log x$ (a_0, a_1, a_2, a_3 are constants)

Since a sharing rule represents a division of profits between the principal and the agent, the principal's share is the residual $x - S(x)$. Rule 1 therefore corresponds to the agent receiving a fixed fee while the principal receives $x - \lambda$. In Rule 2 the agent receives half of any profits or losses, while in Rule 3 the agent receives one-third of any profits but nothing if the venture makes a loss. Rule 4 is merely a reminder that, in theory, a sharing rule can be arbitrarily complex with an infinite number of parameters. This is what makes the mathematics of agency theory so difficult. In general, the principal is trying to find the best reward function. Now functions are infinitely many, the optimal choice of just one function from many is dealt with in a branch of mathematics called functional analysis. In constrast, most other optimization problems in management accounting deal with a few (or at least a finite) number of variables. Here, the methods of differential calculus or mathematical programming are usually sufficient.

As we have already discussed, the contract or rule for sharing the profits is drawn up before either the principal or the agent know what the profits, x, will be. So that we can carry out a mathematical analysis of the contract, we need some probability distribution to represent the possible level of profits. Perhaps not surprisingly, the most convenient distribution for our purposes is the normal distribution. The average or expected level of the profits is simply the mean μ of the normal distribution while the riskiness of future profits is given by the variance σ^2.

Analysis of simple sharing rules

Having defined the various ingredients in our model, we can now proceed to analyse it. In practice, of course, any sharing rule or bonus system which is so complex as to be improperly understood by employees is at best likely to prove ineffective and at worst dysfunctional. Mathematically, the only restriction which will be imposed on sharing rules is that they are differentiable functions of x. Clearly, all of the above, with the exception of Rule 3 (which has a corner at $x = 0$) satisfy these conditions.

An important feature of any sharing rule is that it not only apportions the monetary outcome but also apportions the risk attached to that outcome. Thus Rule 1 apportions all the risk to the principal, with the agent enjoying a certain income irrespective of the success of the business. Rule 2 divides the risk equally between the principal and the agent. Which of these sharing rules is preferable depends on the attitudes to the risk and return of the principal and the agent. Thus, in order to investigate sharing rules, we really need to incorporate the attitude to risk of the principal and the agent.

An individual's attitude to monetary risk and return can be modelled using Von Neumann—Morgenstern (VM) utility functions. Thus we shall assume that we know the utility functions $U_p(w)$ and $U_A(w)$ — where w denotes wealth — of the principal and the agent and that both the principal and the agent are expected utility maximizers. The subsequent mathematical analysis is considerably eased if we assume that the principal is risk-neutral and has a VM utility function over wealth given by

$$U_p(w) = w \tag{6.1}$$

We will assume that the agent is risk-averse. While, in theory, any risk-averse (concave) utility function is acceptable, the mathematical analysis is considerably simplified if we assume that the agent's utility function is of the form

$$U_A(w) = 2\sqrt{w}, \quad w \geq 0 \tag{6.2}$$

The first sharing rule $S_1(x)$ we shall consider is one where the principal pays the agent a fixed amount. In order to avoid the subsequent use of a square root, we shall denote this amount by λ^2. Thus for the agent we have

$$w_A = S_1(x) = \lambda^2 \tag{6.3}$$

The expected utility of the agent ϕ_A is given by:

$$\phi_A = E[U_A(S_1(x))] = E[2\sqrt{\lambda^2}] = 2\lambda$$

or equivalently:

$$\lambda = \frac{\phi_A}{2} \tag{6.4}$$

The corresponding value,[2] for the expected utility of the principal is given

---

2. Extensive use in the text is made of the properties of the moments of the normal integral. Then, if x is normally distributed, mean μ and variance σ^2, $E(x) = \mu$ and from the definition of variance $\sigma^2 = E(x^2) - \mu^2$ it follows that $E(x^2) = \mu^2 + \sigma^2$ while $E(c) = c$ is a constant. Elementary properties of the expectation operator also give the following useful forms

$E(Mx + N) = M\mu + N$

$E[(Mx + N)^2] = (M\mu + N)^2 + M^2\sigma^2$

where M, N are constants.

by

$$\phi_P = E[U_P(x - S_1(x))] = E[x - \lambda^2]$$

$$= \mu - \lambda^2$$

$$= \mu - \frac{\phi_A^2}{4} \quad \text{or} \quad \phi_P + \frac{\phi_A^2}{4} = \mu \tag{6.5}$$

Figure 6.1 shows the relationship between the expected utility of the principal and that of the agent. As λ increases, the share paid increases from zero at point A to $2\sqrt{\mu}$ at point B. The arc AB therefore repesents all possible divisions of the profits that can result from using the sharing rule $S_1(x) = \lambda^2$.

Let us now consider a different sharing rule, namely the sharing rule $S_2(x) = (\lambda_1 + \lambda_2 x)^2$. For this sharing rule, the agent's expected utility is given by:

$$\phi_A = E[2\sqrt{S_2(x)}] = E[2(\lambda_1 + \lambda_2 x)]$$

$$= 2(\lambda_1 + \lambda_2 \mu) \tag{6.6}$$

The principal's expected utility is given by:

$$\phi_P = E[x - S_2(x)] = E[x - (\lambda_1 + \lambda_2 x)^2]$$

$$= \mu - (\lambda_1 + \lambda_2 \mu)^2 - \lambda_2^2 \sigma^2 \tag{6.7}$$

In this case, ϕ_A, ϕ_P are now related by the equation:

$$\phi_P = \mu - \frac{\phi_A^2}{4} - \lambda_2^2 \sigma^2 \quad \text{or} \quad \phi_P + \frac{\phi_A^2}{4} = \mu - \lambda_2^2 \sigma^2 \tag{6.8}$$

So far we have concentrated purely on possible forms for the sharing rule. We cannot determine the optimal shares unless we have some further rules for the division of the profits. It is conventional to assume that, while the principal chooses the terms of the contract, the principal must be prepared to pay at least the market rate to the agent. Hence, unless the agent's expected utility is at least H units, it is assumed that the agent will go elsewhere and take no further part in the contract. These H units can be thought of as the market rate for the job.

A comparison of equations 6.5 and 6.8 show that sharing rule S_1 gives a higher utility to the principal for any given value of $\phi_A (=H)$, provided $\lambda_2 \neq 0$. Equally, for any fixed level of utility for the principal, the agent also obtains a higher utility with sharing rule S_1. Hence we can conclude that the sharing rule $S_1(x) = \lambda$ is preferred by both the principal and the agent to the sharing rule $S_2(x) = (\lambda_1 + \lambda_2 x)^2$ for any non-zero λ_2 (Fig. 6.1). We say that

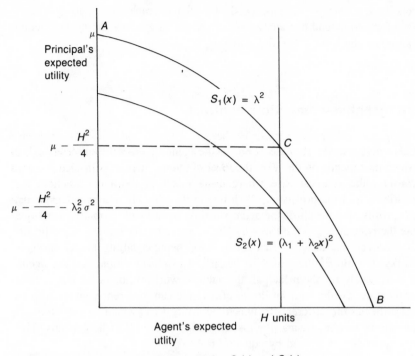

Figure 6.1 Comparison of the sharing rules $S_1(x)$ and $S_2(x)$

S_1 Pareto dominates S_2. In fact, it can be shown, though we will not do so here, that of all the possible sharing rules which one could devise, the one which pays the agent a fixed fee is Pareto superior to any other. Perhaps this is not too surprising; we have assumed that the principal is risk neutral (i.e. indifferent to risk), while the agent is risk-averse. Hence the agent requires compensation in the form of a higher (expected) fee for any risk which he has to carry. It is preferable, therefore, for the principal to (costlessly) accept the risk rather than pay a compensation premium to the agent for carrying risk. Thus the optimal sharing rule chosen by the principal will be such that he satisfies the agent's minimum requirement of H units of utility while maximizing his (the principal's) own utility. This is achieved by setting $\phi_A = 2\sqrt{\lambda} = H$ or $S_1(x) = H^2/4$. This sharing rule corresponds to point C of Figure 6.1.

The analysis just presented is one of pure risk-sharing, neither the action of the principal or the agent influence the outcome and the level of profits. As such, it is one of limited interest to the management accountant who is concerned with the measurement and motivation of employee activity. We need, therefore, to extend our analysis to cover the case where the agent's action can affect the level of profits available for sharing.

An incentive-compatible contract

Let us now consider the case where, as the agent increases the amount of effort which he expends on the task, the level of output increases. In fact, we will consider the simplest case where, as a result of the agent's action, the distribution of the profits is just shifted to the right. In mathematical terms, the profits, as a result of the agent's action, a, are still normally distributed but their mean is given by $\mu = a$. The variance or uncertainty in the profits is, however, unaffected. Hence, other things being equal, the harder the agent works, the bigger the 'cake' to be shared by the principal and the agent. Unfortunately for the principal, the agent is workshy, or in the language of economics, exhibits a disutility of effort. We can thus represent the agent's net utility as the difference between the utility $U(w)$ which he gets from his income or wealth, w, and the disutility $V(a)$ of the effort he expends. This net utility is represented by equation 6.9.

$$\phi_A = E(U_A(w)) - V(a) = \frac{1}{\sqrt{2\pi}\sigma} \int U_A(S(x)) e^{-(x-a)^2/2\sigma^2} dx - V(a) \quad (6.9)$$

As before, it will be assumed that $U_A(w) = 2\sqrt{w}$ and that the agent can gain a utility of H by not entering into a contract. If the principal were to adopt the optimal (pure) risk-sharing contract of $S_1(x)$, the principal would be giving the agent a guaranteed salary regardless of the agent's effort. The doctrine of self-interest proposed in the introduction would result in zero or minimal effort expounded by the agent. Our selfish agent would merely collect his salary of H utility units. What is needed by the principal is some sort of incentive scheme or sharing rule which rewards the agent for his efforts. Hence, some part of the agent's share must be made dependent on his efforts. Since effort is not readily observable without constant monitoring, the incentive scheme is based on profits, since these are (statistically) dependent on the agent's effort. Thus, the harder the agent works, the higher the expected profits and hence the higher the expected payments to the agent.

Again the principal is faced with the problem of what is the best form for the contract. It turns out that of all the possible forms for 'contracts of employment' which could be devised, the one which is mutually preferred by the principal and the agent is the one rejected in the case of pure risk-sharing, namely $S(x) = (\lambda_1 + \lambda_2 x)^2$.

The agent's problem

While the choice of the form and detailed structure of the contract are the prerogative of the principal, the choice of the effort expended on the task is that of the agent. The agent will trade off his dislike of providing effort against his likely reward to decide his optimum level of effort (a). The agent's net expected utility is given by equation 6.10:

$$\phi_A = 2(\lambda_1 + \lambda_2 a) - V(a) \tag{6.10}$$

His optimal action is obtained by equating the marginal utility of reward to the marginal disutility of effort as in equation 6.11:

$$\frac{d\phi_A}{da} = 2\lambda_2 - \frac{dV}{da} = 0 \tag{6.11}$$

Again, in order to make progress with this example, a suitable functional form for $V(a)$ needs to be hypothesized. A solution to the agent's problem is guaranteed provided that the agent exhibits increasing disutility of effort. In other words, the higher the level of effort, the higher the dislike of further effort. The function $V(a) = \frac{1}{2}e^{a/8}$ not only satisfies these conditions but simplifies the subsequent mathematics. With this form, the agent's optimal action can be derived from equation 6.11.

$$2\lambda_2 = \frac{dV}{da} = \frac{1}{16}e^{a*/8}$$

or $a^* = 8 \ln 32\lambda_2$ (6.12)

The agent's problem is illustrated graphically in Figure 6.2. This figure shows the agent's net (i.e. expected utility from salary, less disutility of effort) utility plotted against the effort.

The principal's problem

The principal's problem is to choose the best contract. In this case, the choice is that of values for λ_1 and λ_2, such that the principal maximizes his own expected utility, while still ensuring that the agent receives the market rate. Thus the problem is to maximize with respect to both λ_1 and λ_2, the expression for ϕ_P given by equation 6.13:

$$\phi_P = E[x - (\lambda_1 + \lambda_2 x)^2] = a - (\lambda_1 + \lambda_2 a)^2 - \lambda_2^2 \sigma^2 \tag{6.13}$$

At this stage, the algebra gets a little 'heavy'. What we are trying to do

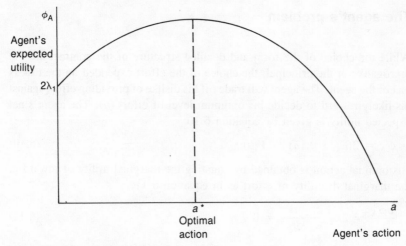

Figure 6.2   The agent's problem

is to find how the expected utilities of the principal (ϕ_P) depend on the choice of λ_2 (and λ_1). Thus equation 6.10 can be used to eliminate λ_1 by replacing the middle term in equation 6.13 to give

$$\phi_P = a - \tfrac{1}{4}(\phi_A + V(a))^2 - \lambda_2^2\sigma^2$$
$$= a - \tfrac{1}{4}(\phi_A + \tfrac{1}{2}e^{a/8})^2 - \lambda_2^2\sigma^2 \tag{6.14}$$

The optimality condition (equation 6.12) can be used to eliminate the agent's action a^* from the above expression to give equation 6.15

$$\phi_P = 8 \log 32\lambda_2 - \tfrac{1}{4}(\phi_A + 16\lambda_2)^2 - \lambda_2^2\sigma^2 \tag{6.15}$$

Hence, equation 6.15 relates the principal's expected utility to the agent's expected utility for different values of λ_2, assuming of course that the agent acts in his own self-interest. Before we formally derive the optimal value of λ_2, it is instructive to consider how the principal's and the agent's expected utility depend on this choice of λ_2. This is shown in Figure 6.3.

As the principal chooses different values of λ_2, he generates the different sharing rules represented by *AD, CF, BE*. The principal's own expected utility is maximized when he just pays the minimum market rate of *H* and, simultaneously, chooses λ_2, such that the ordinate at *H* intersects with the highest possible sharing rule. Hence the principal's welfare is maximized for the sharing rule *CF* when he finishes with expected utility *HG*. Assuming a market rate for the agent of *H* = 4, say, the principal's problem can be solved by setting $\phi_A = H = 4$ in equation 6.15 and differentiating with respect to λ_2.

$$\frac{d\phi_P}{d\lambda_2} = \frac{8}{\lambda_2} - 8(4 + 16\lambda_2) - 2\lambda_2\sigma^2 = 0 \tag{6.16}$$

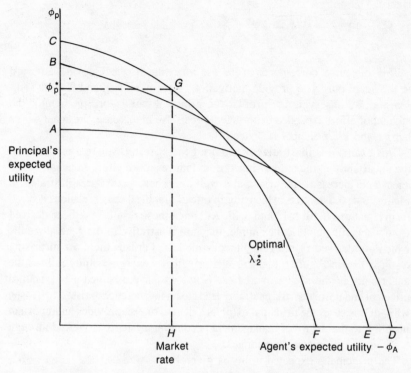

Figure 6.3 The principal's problem: the choice of the parameters of the contract

The solution to this (quadratic) equation has a positive root given by:

$$\lambda_2^* = \frac{2(\sqrt{80 + \sigma^2} - 4)}{(64 + \sigma^2)} \qquad (6.17)$$

Putting $\sigma^2 = 64$ gives a value for $\lambda_2^* = 0.125$, while $a^* = 8\ln(32\lambda_2^*) = 11.09$. The value of λ_1^* needs to be chosen so that the agent receives the minimum 4 units of utility. Hence, if we set $\phi_A = H = 4$ in equation 6.10, we get

$$\phi_A^* = 2(\lambda_1^* + \lambda_2^* a^*) - \tfrac{1}{2}e^{a^*/8} = 4$$

This gives us the only remaining unknown value, that for $\lambda_1^* (= 1.614)$.

If we want to compute the principal's utility, this can be done by substitution of the values into equation 6.13. This gives a value for ϕ_P of 1.09 units.

Let us now consider the case where there is no uncertainty, i.e. $\sigma^2 = 0$, the new values for the parameters become:

$$\lambda_1 = 1.267, \quad \lambda_2^* = 0.154, \quad a^* = 12.78$$

Hence,

$$\phi_P^* = 12.78 - \tfrac{1}{4}(4 + \tfrac{1}{2}e^{\frac{12.78}{8}})$$
$$= 2.31 \tag{6.18}$$

This, of course, corresponds to the case where the principal provides a reward to the agent purely to provide motivation; there is no risk and thus no risk-sharing. By observing the profits, the principal can deduce or monitor the amount of effort expended by the agent precisely. In this case, the agent works harder and the principal is better off.

This example is illustrative of a more general result, where a reduction in the uncertainty in the monitoring system induces more effort on behalf of the agent and increases the principal's welfare. These points are illustrated in Figures 6.4, 6.5 and 6.6, which are, in effect, graphical representations derived from equations 6.10, 6.12 and 6.17. Although these results have been derived from a specific numerical example, they are illustrative of the general results which are derived from agency theory models. Perhaps the most surprising result is that in Figure 6.6. Here, the principal's expected utility falls as the uncertainty in the system increases. Now, we have assumed a risk-neutral principal and normally risk-neutrality leads to an indifference to risk. The reason why, in this case, the principal exhibits a dislike of risk provides an important insight into the nature of management accounting systems as viewed through the lens of information economics.

The principal's expected utility is given by

$$\phi_P = E(x - S(x)) = a - E(S(x)) \tag{6.19}$$

where, in this example, since for the principal $U_P(w) = w$, wealth and utility are synonymous. The principal's expected wealth can be treated as the expected 'profits' from the venture after paying the agent's shares or salary $S(x)$. Now, the agent's expected utility is given by

$$\phi_A = E\{U_A(S(x))\} - V(a) = H = 4$$

where the first term $E\{U_A(S(x))\}$ represents that part of the agent's expected utility derived from his salary. Since $E\{U(S_A(x))\} = 4 + V(a)$, his salary (measured in utilities) can be thought of as a basic market rate of 4 plus additional compensation for his effort.

If we return to a more traditional economic model, where agents carry out in selfless and altruistic fashion the owner's commands, the principal would merely have to instruct the agent to carry out action a^* (say) and pay the appropriate compensation or fee F utilities to the agent for his efforts. This fixed fee F is given by equation 6.20

$$E\{U_A(S(x))\} = 2\sqrt{F} = 4 + V(a^*) \tag{6.20}$$

In this case, the principal's expected labour costs, which is just the share

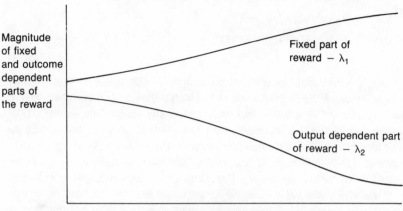

Figure 6.4 The form of the optimal contract

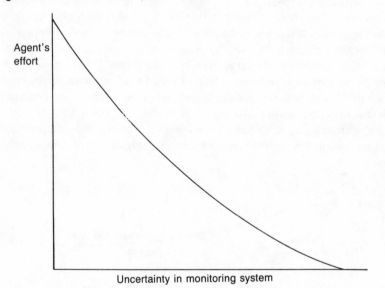

Figure 6.5 Effect of monitoring noise on agent's efforts

paid to the agent, is given by:

$$E(F) = \tfrac{1}{4}(4 + V(a^*))^2 \tag{6.21}$$

However, in the absence of altruism, the principal needs to provide an incentive compatible contract. In this case, the agent's monetary compensation is given by $S(x) = (\lambda_1 + \lambda_2 x)^2$. The principal is thus faced with labour costs of:

$$E(\lambda_1 + \lambda_2 x)^2 = (\lambda_1 + \lambda_2^2 a)^2 + \lambda_2^2 \sigma^2$$
$$= \tfrac{1}{4}(4 + V(a^*))^2 + \lambda_2^2 \sigma^2$$
$$= F + \lambda_2^2 \sigma^2 \tag{6.22}$$

Here, the principal has not only to compensate the agent for his effort by paying the fee F, but also for the risk which the agent is forced to carry. If we trace through the effort of increasing risk on the sharing rule and the action, we see that, as the risk increases, the principal finds it optimal to reduce the dependency of the agent's compensation on the increasingly risky outcome (see Fig. 6.4). The principal reduces λ_2 and correspondingly increases the agent's fixed part of the fee λ_1. Unfortunately for the principal, a reduction in λ_2 reduces the agent's incentive to work and as a result a^* falls (see Fig. 6.5). Nevertheless, it is preferable to accept a lower expected output than to pay the agent a disproportionate amount to carry a larger share of the risk.

The principal's expected utility, where there is no uncertainty in the monitoring system, is called the first best solution and is shown by the curve AB in Figure 6.6. It represents the solution where the principal has a precise knowledge of the agent's actions. The incentive compatible solution, or second-best solution, is shown by the curve AC in the same figure. The principal suffers a loss due to Moral Hazard. Moral Hazard is said to arise where the principal cannot distinguish between genuine uncertainties (in this case, uncertainties in the business environment affecting profits) and favourable or adverse results stemming from the agent's actions (or inactions). In other words, the principal is not sure whether poor profits result from adverse trading conditions or from

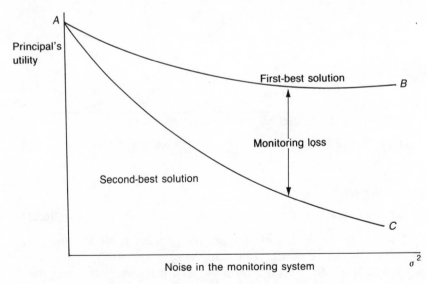

Figure 6.6 A comparison of the first-best and second-best solutions

a lack of effort on the part of the agent. In this example, because the agent's net expected utility is held constant at the market rate, the principal must bear all the loss due to Moral Hazard.

Where the principal is able to monitor and measure the agent's actions precisely, then a loss can be avoided. While precise monitoring may not be possible, the principal might be able to install a system which provides an improvement over the method of merely gauging the agent's effort from the uncertain profit or output. Such a problem would seem to be at the crux of designing an accounting information system. The principal agent analysis would thus appear to offer a framework for at least a partial answer to the question of what do we mean by 'a better accounting system'. Such a discussion forms the basis of the next section.

A more effective accounting system

It was shown in the previous section that, according to our model, where the agent is motivated purely out of self-interest, then it is the principal who carries the burden for an inefficient monitoring system. We have also seen that the difference between the principal's preferred, first-best, contract and the incentive-compatible, second-best, contract can be quite considerable (see Figure 6.6). This accords with casual empiricism, that imprecise performance measures are likely to result in a substantial reduction in effort and a consequent reduction in profits. In this section, therefore, we wish to explore more fully, albeit at an abstract level, what we mean by a more efficient or effective accounting system. Throughout this section, we will concentrate solely on the accuracy of the accounting system and ignore the costs of producing the information.

Let us assume, therefore, that rather than just rely on 'profits' or in the notation of the previous section, x, to monitor the agent's actions, the principal introduces some separate monitoring system signal, y. Again, it will be assumed that the mean value of y is determined by the agent's action and is equal to a, while y itself is normally distributed about a. This time, the variance (σ_y^2) of y is less than the variance of σ_x^2. Intuitively, we would think of y as a better measure of the agent's actions than x. Both produce unbiased estimates of the agent's actions, Figure 6.7, but the distribution of y is more closely centred on a. Indeed, if it were a simple choice between the two signals, x and y, then y would be the principal's preferred choice. However, in general, x and y provide information about the agent's action, and their use in conjunction would be preferred to the use of only one of the signals. The sharing would be of the form $S(x,y)$. The contract would, in accordance with our intuition, attach more weight to the more accurate measure of, performance y.

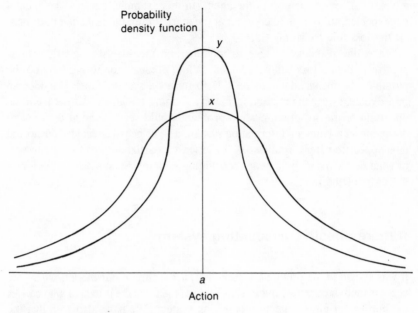

Figure 6.7 More informative signals

The signal y, by itself, would only provide an adequate performance measure if it were related to x by the statistical relationship of equation:

$$\tilde{x} = \tilde{y} + \tilde{z} \tag{6.23}$$

where $\tilde{z}$ is normally distributed with zero mean and variance σ_z^2, with $\tilde{y}$ and $\tilde{z}$ independent. The implication of this is that when $\tilde{y}$ has been observed, an observation of $\tilde{x}$ would tell us nothing more about the agent's actions. This is because the observation x is just really a 'noisier' version of the observation y (i.e. it is formed from y merely by adding a random noise term. $\tilde{y}$ is said to be a sufficient statistic for $\tilde{x}$. In this case, the optimal contract or payment to the agent can be expressed in the form:

$$S(x,y) = (\lambda_1 + \lambda_2 y)^2 \tag{6.24}$$

and depends only on y. Moreover, the principal's expected utility is of the form:

$$\phi_P = a - (\lambda_1 + \lambda_2 a)^2 - \lambda_2^2 \sigma_y^2 \tag{6.25}$$

Here, both the agent's actions and the difference between the first-best and second-best solutions depends on the smaller variation σ_y^2. As can be seen from Figure 6.6, this will result in the principal being unambiguously better off.

The above analysis also captures the essence of what in PA analysis is meant by a better accounting system. An accounting system which produces a signal *y* is better than (or at least as good as) one which produces a signal *x*, if observing *x* tells us nothing more than that which we could have gained by observing *y* only. More formally, an accounting system which produces a signal *y* is preferable to one which produces a signal *x*, if *y* is a sufficient statistic for *x*. The concept of a sufficient statistic is based upon the notion of how precisely an event can be pinned down. As such, it accords with intuition about the quality of an information system.

While the foregoing analysis may capture the essence of the principal−agent relationship, the mathematical model, in spite of its apparent complexity, represents a gross simplification. Nevertheless, the example presented is sufficiently rich to be used as a basis for mapping out possible extensions and consequences, as well as identifying the major weaknesses of PA analysis.

Multi-period contracts

Most contracts of employment, in effect, are repeated contracts over successive time periods. The agent or employee receives a bonus or an incentive reward annually, or monthly, or even on a weekly basis. This also has the impact of reducing the problem of Moral Hazard. If, in the example outlined, all parameters are held constant and outputs or profits in successive periods are statistically independent, then the effective variance of the signal *x* over n periods is just σ_x^2/n. Hence, over an infinitely large number of periods, it would appear that Moral Hazard is eliminated. In other words, a person cannot hide behind incompetence or lack of effort indefinitely and always blame poor performance on bad luck. Of course, in practice, all the parameters of the model are likely to vary. Thus, it cannot be assumed that the distribution of outcomes or even the agent's utilities over wealth and effort are constant. Neither can we assume the statistical independence of outcomes. What is clear though, is that repeated contracting is likely to reduce, at least in part, the problem of Moral Hazard.

Responsibility accounting and relative performance

The essence of responsibility accounting is that the employee should only be evaluated on the basis of those factors under his/her control. This has traditionally been interpreted as those factors which can be directly attributed to the employee. A large part of management accounting systems has been designed with the aim of assigning costs and revenues to individual responsibility centres.

Agency theory does not fundamentally disagree with this idea; it merely recognizes that considerable information problems arise in any attempt to implement it. Indeed, it may be that in many circumstances it is preferable to incorporate into incentive schemes information about factors over which the agent has no control. This enables some of the 'noise' which exists in performance measures to be screened out, resulting in performance measures more closely related to the agent's action. Frequently, reward systems based on relative rather than absolute performance measures are attempts at devising such incentive schemes. Two examples will be used to illustrate the arguments involved and the nature of such schemes.

In the case of a sales manager, it may make more sense to reward performance on the basis of market share (i.e. relative sales) rather than the actual level of sales. The actual sales figure is likely to be influenced by many (random) economic factors outside the control of the sales manager. In using market shares as the performance criterion, an attempt is being made to remove some of the 'noise' in the performance measure and concentrate on a measure more closely related to managerial effort. Although the uncertainty in this example is multiplicative (as opposed to additive), the formal analysis is similar to that carried out in the previous section. The market share ($\bar{y}$), is more closely related to the sales manager's effort than is the total sales ($\bar{x}$), which consists of market share multiplied by the (random) noise term of total sales ($\bar{z}$) in the economy.

An example of a relative performance measure, which eliminates additive noise effects, can be devised for a chief executive who is responsible for maximizing the return to shareholders. According to modern finance theory, the return ($\bar{x}$) to shareholders in the form of dividend yield plus share price appreciation can be decomposed into a return ($\bar{z}$) reflecting general economic conditions and a return ($\bar{y}$) due to firm specific factors. It is only this return ($\bar{y}$) relative to market conditions that can be influenced by the chief executive and hence should form the basis of any contract. In effect, we are using information about all the firms in the economy to gauge and reward performance of a manager in just one of those firms. This requires nothing more than comparing the firm's return with one of the numerous stock market indices such as the FT-All Share Index or the appropriate Industrial Sector Index.

Limitations of agency theory

To the mathematically accomplished, as well as to those who feel uncomfortable with the many and apparently conflicting views of behavioural scientists, agency theory is very appealing. It seems to bring a hitherto missing consistency and rigour to the theory of accounting control systems. Unfortunately, this is only a partial truth, for agency theory itself is only a partial analysis of a limited number of aspects of an accounting control system. The core models of agency theory are relatively simple, even though they require sophisticated mathematical techniques to analyse them. Indeed, the sophistication of the mathematics is a weakness rather than a strength. Mathematical tractability prevents us enriching the models and widening the scope of application. What we would like, ideally, is a fairly complex and contextually 'rich' model requiring only simple mathematics for its exploration. The great virtue of our agency model, as with any mathematical model, lies in the internal consistency between its conclusions and its assumptions. However, as in many mathematical models, the assumptions are frequently so deeply embedded into the structure of the model that they are effectively hidden from the casual reader, or indeed the casual modeller. A fuller discussion of these begins to shed some light on the technical limitations and range of applicability of the PA model.

All the analysis we have carried out, and indeed a great deal of analysis carried out in the literature, assumes a risk-neutral principal. This, for many applications in the theory of employment contracts, is not a particularly restrictive assumption. The principal or shareholder is assumed to hold a well-diversified portfolio of assets, and fluctuations in labour costs due to performance related payments from specific firms are not considered significant. The reason, as opposed to the justification, for this assumption of risk neutrality, is one of mathematical tractability — a reason that dictates many of the other features of PA analysis. It is also mathematical tractability which dictates the simplistic structure of the agent's problem. The agent faces a straightforward choice between effort and reward. The impact of the agent's effort is to increase the expected level of output or profits without increasing the risk. The effort effectively ensures a higher probability of favourable outcomes by 'shifting' the probability distribution of outcomes to the right.

Such a model, where the agent displays disutility of effort, while any effort unambiguously increases output, would seem more appropriate for modelling workers who face relatively uninteresting, repetitive and physically demanding jobs. However, not only do managers frequently appear to display a positive relish for work, but normally a manager's decision would affect both the expected level of profits as well as their risk characteristics. Moreover, managerial activities are many and varied. It is extremely unlikely that the relationship between effort devoted to different managerial tasks and profitability are well defined, even in some probablistic sense.

However, it is perhaps in its model of agent motivation that agency theory, at least in its mathematical form, is most vulnerable to criticism. The agent is assumed to be an economically rational utility maximizer who trades off the utility derived from earnings against the loss in utility from having to work for those earnings. No other factors influence his effort or reason for working. While such a model is an improvement on the altruistic model of an employee who unselfishly maximizes the principal's welfare, it remains a very simplistic model of motivation. The reader need only refer to the chapter on performance measurement and appraisal in this book to realize the simplicity of the economic model of motivation incorporated into agency theory models.

The optimal contract is an equilibrium contract which neither principal nor agent can improve upon. Mathematically, it is brought about by a simultaneous optimization of the action by the agent and the reward specification by the principal. It is not clear, as in many equilibrium models, just how this equilibrium emerges. According to conventional wisdom, the contract comes from the principal's protracted negotiations and experiences with current and past agents. It is presumably during this negotiation phase that the principal learns everything about the agent's attitudes to money, risk and work — no mean feat on the principal's part.

It is further assumed that the final choice of contract is brought about by some competitive (in terms of utility) market for agents, whereby the agent has the alternative of going elsewhere in return for a fixed fee H. The market for agents is, in itself, a complex market. Just two aspects which are of particular relevance to us are in the selection of the agent. First, the existence of a market for agents is in itself sufficient to provide motivation. A manager on a fixed salary may well work very hard to increase the profitability of an enterprise in order to increase his own market value and the salary he may then command elsewhere. Second, the output in the PA model is determined by the equilibrium between the marginal utility of money and the disutility of effort. Among the key determinants of this disutility of effort are the intellectual ability, physical stamina and attitudes of the agent. The contract itself serves in part to screen potential applicants. Thus, a piecework contract requiring a great deal of physical effort is unlikely to be attractive to either a weak or physically lazy individual. Equally, the salesman's contract, based on commission, is unlikely to prove attractive to those who do not have the requisite skills and energy to pursue orders from customers. We shall not pursue this issue further here, since it takes us into a different area of information economics known as 'signalling'. We shall leave the discussion having merely introduced the notion that the form of the contract is more strongly influenced by the market for labour than a cursory inspection of the assumptions would reveal.

Finally, it must be remembered that what has been analysed is just a single contract between a principal and an agent. Organizations consist of many interlinked contracts usually arranged in some hierarchical structure. It is not immediately clear what impact this hierarchy might have on individual contracts. For instance, the sharing rule on profits embeds the sharing rule on all lower-order incentive schemes. The divisional manager's share may ultimately depend on the share awarded to line managers which in turn may depend on the share awarded to production workers. In such circumstances, the assumption of risk neutrality of the various principals in such contracts is no longer tenable.

A further difficulty, of course, arises because such contracts are no longer just between a single principal and a single agent. Even the design of a contract is likely to involve many such agents. For example, consider the role played by the management accountant in such contracts. The management accountant presumably is largely responsible for the design of the management information system which provides the basis of all contracts. Moreover, he or she is also likely to be quite closely involved in the design of individual incentive schemes. Hence, any contract between the manager and production workers is likely to involve at least one other person, the management accountant. What is not clear, at least within the rigid PA scheme of analysis, is the form of any incentive-compatible contract to the management accountant. We leave this unsolved puzzle to the reader, with the warning that rewarding accountants on the basis of reported profitability may well invite, rather than eliminate, Moral Hazard!

References and further reading

Baiman, S. (1982) 'Agency research in managerial accounting: a survey', *Journal of Accounting Literature*, Spring, pp. 154–213.

Holmstrom, B. (1979) 'Moral Hazard and observability', *Bell Journal of Economics*, Spring, pp. 74–91.

Kaplan, R.S. (1982) *Advanced Management Accounting*, Hemel Hempstead: Prentice Hall.

Scapens, R.W. (1985) *Management Accounting: A Review of Recent Developments*, Basingstoke: Macmillan.

Walker, M. and N. Strong (1987) *Information Economics and Capital Markets*, Oxford: Basil Blackwell.

Chapter 7

Performance appraisal and rewards
PETER MOIZER

'O world! world! world! thus is the poor agent despised. O traitors and bawds, how earnestly are you set a-work and how ill requited! Why should our endeavour be so loved and the performance so loathed?'
Pan in *Troilus and Cressida*, Act 5 Scene 10

This chapter is concerned with one of the fundamental problems faced by senior management: how to encourage subordinates to perform to the best of their abilities, in accordance with the behavioural requirements of the organization. The solution that is commonly employed is to introduce a system of performance appraisal and to link organizational rewards to levels of performance. The performance appraisal system contains two main elements: (1) a specification of the job that the subordinate has to do and the criteria that will define what constitutes good performance (e.g. operating budgets or specific production targets) and (2) a mechanism for gathering information about the adequacy of the behaviour that takes place (e.g. monthly management reports comparing budgeted and actual performance, or at the production level, the dials and gauges on machines). Once the performance of an individual has been evaluated, then some form of reward (or more rarely punishment) has to be given which the individual can relate to the effort that he or she expended on their job. The rewards can be either economic (e.g. money or prizes) or psychological (e.g. praise or blame). The essence of all performance appraisal and reward systems is the assumption that if good performance is rewarded, then an individual employee will be motivated to expend more effort in order to improve his or her performance so that he or she can enjoy the rewards that follow from the improvement in performance.

In any form of performance appraisal, one of the most significant aspects is identifying criteria to evaluate performance. For example, in a recent study of the performance evaluation of audit managers by their audit partner three factors seemed most important: (1) the quality of the audit work carried out, that is the degree of confidence felt by the audit partner that all significant errors in the financial statements had been spotted by the audit team; (2) the profitability of the audit, that is the degree to which the audit fee earned by the audit firm exceeded the costs of the audit; and (3) the extent of the goodwill between the client company management and the audit firm, that is, the chance that the client company might appoint another firm of auditors.

One feature of the previous example is that the superior is evaluating the performance of the subordinate on the basis of first-hand experience. There is, therefore, no need for an information system to relay details about the performance of the subordinate. However, in most organizational contexts, the superior will be remote from the subordinate and so the superior's evaluation will have to be made on a second-hand basis. In these instances, performance is usually evaluated using accounting measures. Budgets and plans are often used for this purpose, and even when the performance measures have a wider scope, accounting information is generally seen as being the most important. For example, while the evaluation of the performance of hospital administrators is couched in terms of the quality of the health care provided by their hospital, one of the most important determinants of their performance is their control of cost. In this chapter we shall be using accounting examples of information systems concerned with performance appraisal, not only because this book is concerned with management accounting issues, but also because of the importance that accounting information plays in most organization's performance evaluation systems.

Motivation

The main aim of a system of performance appraisal and rewards is the motivation of subordinates to perform well. The term 'motivation' is of relatively recent origin (1863) and means 'furnishing with a motive' or 'causing (someone) to act in a particular way' (*Shorter Oxford English Dictionary*). In psychological terms, motivation is that which energizes, directs and sustains behaviour. Two principal elements have been identified within motivation: goal congruence and effort. *Goal congruence* is a measure of the extent to which an individual shares the goals and aspirations of the organization's top management (i.e. those individuals who decide on the organization's overall policy). In an ideal state of goal congruence, each subordinate makes the same decisions that would be made by top management if it had been consulted. Subordinates act in this way because they identify their own perceived best interests with furthering the aims of top management. *Effort*, on the other hand, is the amount of physical or mental power that is exerted by the individual in pursuit of a goal. In the sense used in this chapter, effort is not simply undertaking an activity at a faster rate; it encompasses all those actions (such as watching and waiting) that a conscientious employee would perform in order to further the organization's goals.

The motivating role of a performance appraisal system is to define what will be regarded as 'good' performance (i.e. to specify the goals that the employee should aim at) and what rewards will follow for achieving this level of good performance. Note that it is performance that is rewarded and not the effort expended. Performance appraisal systems traditionally involve measuring the results of an individual's labours rather than the effort expended.

Performance model

A common model asserts that an individual's performance at a particular task is determined by three factors: the amount of effort expended, the ability of the individual at the task, and a series of uncontrollable factors (luck) which makes the task harder or easier than is normal (Moizer and Pratt 1988). These three factors will be discussed in turn starting with luck.

In an ideal world the element of luck would be incorporated into the benchmark against which performance is measured. However, in the real world there will always be occasions when subordinates feel that their performance was judged too harshly because their supervisor had failed to allow sufficiently for unexpected problems. The element of luck is felt, for example, by civil engineering contractors, who are judged by how quickly they complete a particular job (e.g. building a stretch of motorway, office block, etc.). The contractors have no control over the weather or the quality of ground upon which they are asked to build. Consequently, whether or not they are 'on time' will be partially the result of luck. Some performance evaluation systems allow for the impact of random events. For example, the performance of portfolio managers of institutional shareholders is usually evaluated every three months in relation to the performance of the average fund rather than in absolute terms. Hence, in the fourth quarter of 1987 when world stock markets 'crashed', the vast majority of funds suffered substantial losses, but few fund managers were replaced. The stakeholders accepted that most of the performance of the funds in that quarter was outside the control of the managers.

The second factor of ability relates to an individual's competence at performing a particular task. It will be the result of that individual's inherent aptitude at the task and by his or her training, and work experience. In order to find and allocate individuals who have the right characteristics for a particular job, it is necessary to have a good employee selection system. Such a system involves a thorough analysis of the specific requirements of a job, a comprehensive assessment of whether potential candidates possess the characteristics that are important for successful performance, and a monitoring system for validating whether the selection procedure does in fact produce performance on the job. While this is an important management issue, it is outside the scope of this chapter. Accordingly, from now on it will be assumed that the abilities of subordinates have been satisfactorily matched to the requirements of the job.

The third factor of effort is the main subject of this chapter. It relates to the amount of energy that an individual devotes to a particular task. Most performance appraisal and rewards systems assume that the performance of an individual will be improved if he or she expends more effort and hence rewarding good performance will encourage employees to work harder. Obviously, the above performance cycle will only work if more effort produces better performance. There will be occasions when the performance of individuals is constrained by factors beyond their control and in these circumstances performance will be limited to the maximum allowed by the constraint. At the production level, examples are common and usually relate to the capacity of technology to perform a particular task; for example, a piece of machinery may be able to perform only a certain number of operations in an hour. Returning to the example of the audit manager, it will be apparent that the quality of the work performed by the audit team is not necessarily improved by the audit manager spending more time supervising. More supervision might impair the overall performance by wasting time answering unnecessary queries.

Theories of motivation

There are many models of motivation, but most rely on notions that motivation is the degree to which an individual *wants* and *tries hard* to do well at a particular task. There are thus two aspects to motivation: *arousal* (those mechanisms which get the individual energized, i.e. in a state of readiness to do something) and *choice* (those pressures which cause an individual to engage in a particular form of behaviour). Individuals are aroused, because they believe that they are not receiving as much of something as they want. They wish to reduce this discrepancy and so they are ready to undertake some activity. The type of activity chosen and the amount of effort that the individual chooses to exert will depend on the value that he or she places on the results of the activity. A system of performance appraisal and rewards needs to take account of both the arousal and choice aspects of motivation. Rewards and incentives will influence motivation only if they are related to what employees need (arousal) and to what employees can do (choice).

Theories of arousal

The most often quoted cause of arousal is *need deprivation*. Human beings are stimulated or aroused by a set of needs — some internal state in a person that causes objects of outcomes to become attractive to that person. Empirical results suggest that needs can be arranged in a two-tier hierarchy. On the lower level are existence and security needs (such as the need for oxygen, water, food, temperature regulation, sleep, sex and protection from physical harm), while on the higher level are social, esteem, autonomy and self-realization needs (the self-realization need is the need to make full use of one's talents, capabilities and potential). The higher-level needs begin to become significant when the lower-level needs are satisfied. If the satisfaction of the lower-level needs is threatened, then the importance of the higher-level needs will be substantially reduced. Evidence shows that, in modern society, most needs can be satisfied and that once enough outcomes are obtained to satisfy a given need, then people stop seeking outcomes relevant to that need. The exception to this rule is the need for self-realization, which seems to be insatiable. The more individuals obtain the outcomes that satisfy this need, the more important the need becomes and the greater is the satisfaction required. Hence, once the self-realization need appears, it usually remains as a strong motivator. One difficulty that presents itself to the designers of reward systems is that some rewards can satisfy more than one need, for example, salary, which can satisfy not only existence and security needs (as the money received can be used to provide a reasonable standard of living) but also esteem needs (since the size of a person's salary often confers a particular level of social status).

It is also worth noting that individuals may have different needs and therefore dissimilar reactions to particular job outcomes. These differences will cause individuals to view the same job in different ways and so could result in different on-the-job behaviour. Hence a job that one person finds satisfying and motivating could be dull and uninteresting to another. Such differences in need strength can be predicted if the personal characteristics of the individuals are known. Personality profiles can be constructed for individual employees and hence reward and control systems can be tailored to the individuals who will be covered by them.

More recently, there has been a move away from need-based theories of arousal to theories which concentrate on external factors. The most significant external factor is the presence of other people and the processes involved are termed *social facilitation* and *evaluation apprehension*. These theories suggest that people are aroused by the presence of others and the feeling that they are being evaluated. Individuals wish to impress and hence they will undertake actions that they think will make them look good and avoid actions which might make them look bad. Employees will therefore be motivated to do well in the presence of their co-workers and their superiors. The important point for a performance appraisal system is that employees need regular feedback on the key aspects of their work, so that they will be under constant encouragement to perform to the best of their abilities. Evaluation apprehension must operate at the appropriate level, and so the level of appraisal should rest with people who most frequently observe the work of the individual. This technique is often used in large firms of chartered accountants where individuals tend to be evaluated by their immediate superior on an audit job, for example an assistant by the in-charge senior, the in-charge senior by the audit manager and the audit manager by the audit partner.

Theories of choice

There are three principal theories of the internal causes of behavioural choice: expectancy theory, equity theory and goal-setting theory. The three theories emphasize different aspects of human nature. They have an internal focus in that they attempt to explore the thought processes that determine choice. Theories with an external focus have also been developed and they concentrate on the external factors that affect intended behaviour: the nature of the job and its social setting. Jobs that are *enlarged* (i.e. where there is an expansion in the tasks that an employee is asked to perform) and *enriched* (i.e. where the employee's autonomy and responsibility is increased) have greater motivational content. The attitudes of an employee's co-workers are also important to the motivational appeal of a job. Individuals who have co-workers who like their job are likely to obtain greater satisfaction from their work than when the co-workers dislike the task.

The three internal theories of choice will now be discussed and their implications examined.

Expectancy theory

In this theory, originated by Victor Vroom in 1964, individuals are assumed to be rational decision-makers who evaluate alternative courses of action in terms of the probability that each alternative will lead to valued rewards. The course of action chosen is the one that will maximize satisfaction. The theory has two principal concepts: expectancies and valences.

A summary of the theory is as follows. Having been aroused into a state of feeling that something must be done, an individual then examines the various courses of action open to him or her. For each course of action, the individual makes an estimate of the probability that directing a given amount of effort into a particular activity will result in a given reward or positively valued job outcome. This *effort—reward* probability is itself the product of two subsidiary subjective probabilities: *expectancy* — the probability that a certain amount of effort will result in a particular level of performance and *instrumentality* — the probability that this level of performance will result in a particular reward or outcome. The significance of the reward or outcome to the individual will depend upon its *valence* — the individual's perception of its value to him or her. The valence of rewards or outcomes will derive from their perceived ability to satisfy the individual's needs. The rewards or outcomes can be either extrinsic or intrinsic to the individual. Extrinsic rewards are part of the job environment and are given by others (e.g. pay, promotion, praise etc.). They are determined by external events and tend to satisfy lower order needs. In contrast, intrinsic rewards stem from the level of performance achieved. These rewards are internally determined, because the individual rewards him or herself. They satisfy higher-order needs such as self-esteem and self-actualization and involve feelings of accomplishment and achievement derived from using and developing one's skills and abilities.

Research on the expectancy model is considerable and over eighty studies have been carried out (e.g. Moizer and Pratt 1988). In general, the results show that expectancy models are partially successful at predicting job effort. This less than complete result has many causes including the difficulty of experimentally measuring the variables and the inherent complex nature of the model's formulation.

There are five important implications of the theory for a performance appraisal and reward system. First, the subjective probability estimate of expectancy, needs to be as high as possible. Expectancy captures the belief that a given amount of effort will produce a particular level of performance. Accordingly, this probability will reflect the individual's own estimate of what performance is possible given the effort he or she can expend and the performance of the machinery used on the job. If a job is ill-defined with no clear measure of what constitutes good performance, an individual's expectancy will inevitably be lower than for a well-defined job. This is a particular problem when evaluating the performance of managers using accounting measures. Accounting reports by their nature cannot include all the relevant dimensions of managerial performance, since they are primarily concerned with representing objective outcomes, whereas managerial activity is concerned with the detailed processes that give rise to these outcomes. Hence a manager might have expended a considerable amount of effort during a period, but that period's accounting reports may show only a poor level of performance as a result of factors beyond his or her control. For a fair evaluation, the reports should be structured so that the activities over which the manager has direct control are isolated from those controlled by other factors. Unfortunately, this problem is insoluble, because the determination of whether a budget variance was caused by the efforts of the manager or by uncontrollable effects in the environment requires a level of knowledge which senior management are unlikely to possess. Indeed, if senior management did possess such knowledge, then there would be no need for the accounting report. One undesirable consequence of managers being continually asked about budget variances over which they have no control, is that there is a tendency to try to pass their apparent failure on to colleagues. As a result, rivalries ensue, and the resulting conflicts often impede the co-operation which is necessary for controlling interdependent activities.

A second implication of expectancy theory is that the subordinate's probability estimate of the instrumentality of a particular level of performance needs to be as high as possible. Instrumentality reflects the employee's confidence that his or her supervisors will recognize good performance when it is achieved and reward it accordingly. Hence employees need to be able to associate rewards with their perceptions of the performance that they have achieved. Hopwood (1976) describes some of the problems of using budgetary information as a comprehensive measure of managerial performance. Managers are primarily evaluated on their ability continually to meet the budget on a short-term basis. This criterion of importance is stressed at the expense of other important criteria, and the manager will receive unfavourable feedback from his or her superior if actual costs exceed the budgeted costs, regardless of other considerations. Hopwood quotes one manager as follows:

'I don't think [the name of the supervisor] properly evaluates my performance. He looks at the figures, but he doesn't know what they are doing. He's real good at seeing that you are over your budget. He is as straight and narrow as the book is written.'

The result of superiors relying primarily on deviations from budget to measure performance is that managers are tempted to manipulate their accounting reports in order to improve the probability that their supervisor judges them as having performed well.

A third implication of expectancy theory is that because individuals wish to achieve high performance evaluation ratings, they will use the performance criteria against which they are assessed to clarify the role that they see themselves as playing in the organization. Therefore, if the subordinate perceives that his or her superior is obsessed by the cost of particular activities, then he or she will also be concerned about those costs. Hopwood (1976) reports that a simple-minded concern with the budget led managers to make decisions which were less innovative and which sometimes increased the total processing costs for the company as a whole. Costs were charged to incorrect accounts and repairs delayed until the money was available in the budget, in spite of this resulting in higher costs. One revealing quotation is given by Hopwood:

'Simply no-one will take the decision to spend. Most people in this position try to make themselves look good. They don't want to see negative signs on their reports. They're aiming for promotion without worrying about the future. It's let's look good today, tomorrow I'll get promoted. It's someone else's problem then.'

A fourth implication of expectancy theory is that rewards need to be associated with those activities that are desired by the organization's top management. External rewards, such as pay and promotion, are relatively easy to link to activities. However, internal rewards will be determined by the individual's reaction to the job, and this will be affected by a number of factors, including: (1) the nature of the task (e.g. if there are certain activities which an individual finds inherently satisfying, he or she will pursue them even if they are not particularly desirable to top management), (2) the form of the performance appraisal system related to the job (e.g. the criteria used to evaluate performance, the freqeuncy of feedback, etc.) and (3) the extent to which the targets representing good performance are both challenging and attainable. The aim, therefore, is to design jobs and performance appraisal systems which satisfy top managements' goals as well as being internally satisfying to the higher-order needs of employees.

The fifth implication is that different employees will have different valences or reactions to particular rewards or job outcomes. Hence individual employees need to be matched to jobs, not only in terms of their abilities but also in terms of their appreciation of the rewards or outcomes that are associated with the particular job.

Equity theory

This theory first outlined by J.S. Adams in 1963 starts with the assumption that people tend to compare themselves with other similar individuals. The theory is one of a number called *exchange theories*, in which social relationships are viewed as exchange processes where individuals make contributions (inputs) for which they expect certain outcomes. In a situation where a person exchanges his or her services for pay, inputs could include previous work experience, education, effort on the job, and training. The most important outcome is pay, but other outcomes can exist, such as supervisory treatment, job assignments, fringe benefits and status. The theory suggests that an individual will weight his or her inputs and outcomes in accordance with their importance to him or her. The individual will then total these weighted inputs and outcomes and compare the ratio of outcomes to inputs with those of another individual or group doing a similar job (called the 'other'). Equity is said to exist whenever the ratio of a person's outcomes to inputs is equal to the ratio of the other's outcomes to inputs. Inequity exists whenever the two ratios are unequal.

The motivational aspects of Adams's theory result from the effects of perceived inequity. Perceived inequity creates a tension which the individual is motivated to reduce in proportion to the size of the perceived inequity. The methods of reducing tension include changing inputs, seeking to alter outcomes, changing one's perceptions of the inputs or outcomes (i.e. cognitively distorting them), taking steps to alter the reference individual or group's inputs or outcomes, changing the reference group or simply changing one's employment.

The choice of the method of reducing inequity will depend on the particular situation's circumstances. Two conditions of inequity (underpayment and overpayment) are usually identified as well as two types of compensation system (salaried and piece rate). Four specific predictions can be made from the theory:

1. Underpaid, salaried employees will reduce their inputs by producing less or poorer-quality output than equitably paid subjects.
2. Overpaid, salaried employees will increase their inputs by producing more or higher-quality output than equitably paid subjects.
3. Underpaid, piecework employees will produce a larger number of low-quality units in comparison with equitably paid subjects.
4. Overpaid, piecework employees will produce fewer units which are of higher quality than produced by equitably paid subjects.

Empirical evidence provides some support for the above predictions. The strongest support appears to be for the predictions about underpayment inequity. The studies of overpaid inequity can be explained by other factors than inequity. For example, it has been argued that overpaid employees will simply adjust their idea of what constitutes an equitable payment in order to justify the pay they are receiving. Another point is that *perceived* overpayment is more likely to occur between close friends, and hence individuals only react to overpayment inequity when they believe that their actions have led to someone else being treated unfairly.

The main implication of this theory for a system of performance appraisal and rewards is that attention must be given to the attitudes of employees to the rewards that result from their effort. Relatively under-rewarded employees will be dissatisfied and reduce their effort accordingly. Relatively over-rewarded employees might initially experience tension but may well resolve it by altering their expectations. Hence it will be difficult to change a system which creates relative overpayments. The major contribution of the theory is to highlight the importance of the relative nature of an employee's reward—effort assessments. It is not the absolute size of the reward that matters, but how it compares with the rewards of other people doing the same job. Hence, when targets are set based upon accounting data, it is important that they are reinforced by appropriate rewards, because individuals are responding to rewards rather than the targets themselves (the exception being when individuals 'reward themselves' for achieving or bettering a target — a phenomenon termed 'intrinsic activity valence').

Goal-setting theory

This theory, originated by Edwin Lock in 1978, suggests that an important determinant of an individual's choice of how much effort to expend is the individual's own chosen goal and the extent of his or her commitment to that goal. People aspire to accomplish both short- and long-term objectives, and these then influence specific behaviour. Empirical evidence indicates that situations in which goals are present lead to higher performance than situations without goals. Furthermore, the research suggests that specific, difficult goals which are accepted by employees as attainable if challenging, lead to better performance than easy or non-specific goals. Hence a non-specific goal such as 'as soon as possible' is not likely to be effective. The evidence is less clear on whether goals are made more or less effective if employees have participated in their determination. If anything, the results show that goals which are solely determined by an employee's supervisor have a greater motivational impact than those goals which the employee has influenced. However, when budgetary data are used in managerial performance evaluation, it has been noted that participation in setting the budget can have a significant effect (see Hopwood 1976). With only minimal participation, the imperfections in the budgetary system tend to heighten the tensions created by the rigid evaluative use of budget reports; but when subordinate managers are allowed to participate in the setting of their budgets, many of the problems inherent in the process are discussed with supervisors who, having become aware of the problems, alter their evaluative behaviour. Hence the role of participation in budgetary evaluative systems is not simply associated with determining the level of the target, but rather with providing a mechanism for exchanging information between supervised and supervisor. The degree of participation that is required will vary depending on the circumstances. For example, a greater degree of participation is likely to be required in situations of change and uncertainty (where new information is continually needed) than in more stable situations (where supervisors can rely to a much greater extent on the insights gained from their own previous experiences).

The two implications for a performance appraisal system are: (1) that it needs to include specific, well-defined goals and (2) that these goals have to be sufficiently difficult so that an employee can just achieve them given maximum effort. The difficulty of using accounting information to define the goals is that the accounting performance measures themselves influence how the manager sees his or her role. Even when performance measures are instituted solely for the purpose of information, they are often interpreted as definitions of important dimensions of the job and have important implications for motivation behaviour. Many researchers have noted the tendency of managers to pad their budgets either in anticipation of cuts by superiors or to make the subsequent variances more favourable. There are also more disturbing examples of managers making decisions in response to performance indices, even though the decisions are contrary to the wider purposes of the organization. For example, there is a well-documented tendency on the part of managers to avoid replacing old or outdated items of equipment because there would be an unfavourable effect on their return on capital employed statistics.

The second implication for any budgetary information system is that the targets contained within the manager's budget should just be achievable, given an ideal set of circumstances. However, if the budgets are also to be used as planning devices, there will be a conflict of objectives. Planning budgets which are likely to be achieved are unlikely to provide the maximum motivation, since motivation results from the provision of a challenging target to which a manager can aspire, but which he or she will not usually be able to reach. Hence, motivating budgets will not be achieved on average and so adverse budget variances will be generated if a motivating budget is set. This is only a problem if motivating budgets are interpreted as if they are planning budgets. Small, adverse variances in a motivating budget could be indications that the budget set a challenging target, rather than indications that the manager has failed to control costs adequately. Financial planners within an organization will, however, have to allow for potential adverse variances in their planning (the so-called 'aspirations gap'). This is an example of a wider problem where an information system has more than one purpose (performance measurement and planning) when the information from the system has to be interpreted carefully by decision-makers.

Summary of the three theories

The three theories presented above provide differing insights into people's behaviour and hence are complementary rather than opposing. The most obvious difference between them lies in their assumptions about the causes of behaviour. In expectancy theory, individuals are assumed to want to achieve the greatest possible satisfaction from work; in equity theory, individuals are assumed to desire that their outcome to effort ratio is fairly rewarded in comparison with their co-workers; and in goal-setting theory, individuals are assumed to be motivated by challenging, specific goals. In order to use the results of these theories in a performance appraisal and reward system, top management needs to be able to link rewards to the behaviour of subordinates, set specific and challenging goals and be seen to reward all employees in accordance with their performance. These then represent the problems that have to be solved. How this might be done is described in the next section.

Performance appraisal systems

There are five general steps which have to be taken when creating a performance appraisal system: selection of the measures to be used; definition of these measures; selection of measurement principles; selection of appropriate standards; and timing of feedback. These five steps will now be examined.

Selection of measures

The performance measures should be chosen to represent the goals of the organization's top management. The measures can be of two types: objective and subjective. *Objective* measures provide a quantifiable measure upon which to assess performance — for example, output quantity measures, such as volume produced; output quality measures, such as the number of spoiled items; diligence measures, such as the amount of time lost because of absenteeism or tardiness; and progress measures, such as the time taken to acquire a particular skill or to be promoted to a particular position. Of particular relevance to this book are the measures based on accounting information such as budgeted revenues, cost and net profit. For example, managers of divisions within a company are frequently·evaluated on their *return on investment* (ROI — the net profit of the division divided by its total capital employed). Advocates of ROI would argue that it encourages divisional management to maximize revenues, minimize costs and minimize the amount of money tied up in capital employed. It would thus appear to harmonize with the overall goals of top management. An alternative, less popular divisional performance measure is *residual income* (RI — the division's net profit less an imputed interest charge on invested capital). This measure should also encourage divisional managers to increase revenues and decrease costs, including the interest cost imputed to the division's capital employed. The use of these measures will be discussed later as examples of the more general issues associated with 'objective' performance measures.

As well as objective measures, there are two types of subjective measures that can be used: other people and absolute standards. In the first approach an employee's performance is assessed by comparing it with that of others performing similar tasks, such as by ranking the performance of all similar employees. In the second approach, the jobs performed by employees are analysed to determine the skills and behaviours necessary to produce effective performance. The usual result of this type of analysis is to produce a behavioural checklist such as that used by accounting firms to assess staff performance, for example oral skills, written skills, organizational skills, technical ability and so on.

Any particular measure usually suffers from two related problems: *deficiency* (when the measure does not assess all the relevant aspects of the person's performance) and *contamination* (when the measure assesses things that are irrelevant to the person's performance). Accordingly, it is preferable to use more than one performance measure, because multiple measures reduce deficiency and because their contamination effects should relate to different areas and hence are more evident.

Definition of the measures

Having chosen the measures to be used, there then follows the need to produce a definition of what should be included in the measures. For example, when using either ROI or RI, a choice has to be made whether fixed costs should be included and, if so, whether they should include allocated head-office costs. The capital-employed base also requires defining. For example, should it comprise all the assets available, all the assets in active use, working capital or shareholders' equity?

Selection of measurement principles

Once the items to be included in a measure have been defined, there is then the problem of determining how they should be measured. For example, capital employed (however defined) can be measured in terms of historic cost, replacement value, realizable value or economic value (i.e. the present value of an asset's future net cash inflows). Each measure has its advantages and disadvantages — for example, replacement cost will usually approximate closely to the value in use of an asset, but it is a subjective figure and hence open to manipulation by divisional management. In contrast, historic cost may be largely meaningless for old assets and its use will encourage divisional managers to avoid replacing old assets for as long as possible; but it is a figure which is difficult to manipulate.

Selection of appropriate standards

Having decided how actual performance will be determined, a suitable yardstick has to be produced to assess how good the actual performance is. For example, should all divisions be expected to achieve the same ROI and RI? If tailored standards are to be used, how are they to be determined? When accounting information is used to provide the standard against which results can be monitored, it is usual to use budget information to create the standard. The problem is that if the budget is so used, then rewards become directly connected with achieving the budget. Given a manager's natural desire to appear to be performing well, the consequences of budget-based standards are that (1) the budget standard itself is likely to be challenged and hence become less of a target, (2) the reported accounting information will be manipulated to make the manager's performance look as good as possible, and (3) the manager's behaviour will be altered in adverse ways, because he or she will be attempting to maximize particular accounting numbers rather than acting in the organization's overall best interests.

Timing of feedback

As discussed in the section on motivation, timely, regular feedback is essential. Ideally, each employee should be informed about his or her level of performance as soon as a particular task has been completed. In the case of one continuing job, such as divisional management, the reporting interval will be a balance between evaluating the manager too frequently when he or she may feel threatened and too infrequently when he or she will find no timely feedback or recognition of improvement.

Reward systems

The central issue in implementing a reward system is distributing rewards so that they have a positive impact on an individual's motivation to take part and put effort into the activities that are desired by the organization's top management. In order to create an effective reward system it is essential that the organization has an effective system for assessing the performance of employees. If the performance appraisal system is unreliable or lacks validity, then the rewards that are distributed on the basis of its results will be ill directed and so have little motivational impact. In this section, it will be assumed that a satisfactory performance appraisal system exists and the issue is then how to design a suitable reward system.

Creating a reward system

The first issue to be addressed is which parts of performance should be rewarded. Rewarding a particular aspect of performance may concentrate employees' attention on it, to the detriment of other desirable aspects which are not similarly rewarded. In addition, there is the possibility that rewarding certain individuals for good performance will have a negative influence on other individuals who are not able to produce good performance in that area, however hard they try. Another important consideration from expectancy theory is that employees must be able to associate rewards with performance. It is not sufficient for top management alone to recognize the link. Equity theory also suggests that employees should feel fairly treated when they evaluate their rewards for particular levels of performance against other employees' reward—performance ratios.

A second implementation issue concerns the level of aggregation to be used when deciding to reward performance; for example, should it be at the level of the individual, a work group or a manufacturing plant? The advantage of choosing higher levels of aggregation is that the resulting performance measures are more reliable and objective than the ones available at lower levels. The disadvantage of higher levels is that it is more difficult for individual employees to see the connection between the effort they have expended and the rewards they receive. Annual bonuses based on a company's net profit are a good example of the problem. The amounts received are calculated on a basis which is so far removed from most employees, that there is hardly any discernible link between their effort and the bonus.

Another issue in reward systems concerns the extent to which rewards are kept secret or are made public. The importance of this issue will depend on the extent of the variations in pay for individuals at the same level within an organization. Survey results show that there is a wide range of organizational practices. Public-sector bodies tend to be fairly open about how their rates of pay are determined and about what amounts are paid out, whereas private-sector companies tend to be rather secretive. Some private-sector companies will provide information on pay rates, but little on the amounts paid, while others will provide virtually no information about either. It is usual for managers in the private sector to be told only about their own bonuses or salary increments. This is in contrast to what managers would actually like to know, which is where they stand relative to others using their bonus as a guide. A more open system also has the benefit that managers will be able to judge to what extent their pay is tied to their performance by judging the relative size of their pay against their performance relative to that of their colleagues. This should increase a manager's motivation to perform well in the future.

Finally, a more complex issue in implementing a reward system concerns the degree to which the reward system matches the management style that is characteristic of the organization. Management styles can be categorized on a scale whose extremes are open/participative and traditional/authoritarian. Reward systems can be similarly classified on scales based on the degree of employee participation, ranging from a high degree of participation to zero participation (rigid reward systems). Rigid reward systems are likely to suit a traditional/authoritarian management style and participative reward systems are likely to suit an open/participative management style.

Types of reward available

The final decision relating to a reward system concerns the types of reward to be distributed. Two principal types of reward have been identified theoretically: intrinsic rewards and extrinsic rewards. *Intrinsic rewards* are often categorized as rewards that are produced from having undertaken an activity 'for its own sake'. *Extrinsic rewards* in contrast are provided to individuals by their supervisors for having done a good job. As in all such distinctions, the split is much less clear-cut in practice, where it is frequently difficult to disentangle intrinsic from extrinsic rewards. However, the dictonomy does provide a useful taxonomy and so will be used here.

Intrinsic rewards

These rewards take the form of feelings of competence, accomplishment, self-fulfilment and pride in a job well done. Strictly, intrinsic rewards cannot be part of an external rewards system, but there are a number of ways of improving the intrinsic reward aspects of a job, and these largely revolve around providing employees with greater job satisfaction. A brief summary of the ways of improving intrinsic rewards is as follows:

1. Employ considerate supervisors, who take note of problems and achievements.
2. Provide job challenge, such as variety on the job, the need for creativity, difficult goals and the need to use one's own skills.
3. Provide job clarity, because people prefer a clear, unambiguous work environment.
4. Provide a moderate amount of both standardization and specialization, since without either an employee has difficulty knowing what to do or how to do it.
5. Improve social cues, because job satisfaction is influenced by the satisfaction of co-workers and others in the work environment who might act as role models.

Extrinsic rewards

Extrinsic rewards can be considered using the theory of *operant conditioning* as well as the three theories of internal choice discussed earlier (expectancy, equity and goal-setting). In an operant-conditioning world, extrinsic rewards are tangible, external 'reinforcers' which are controlled by the organization. The theory of operant conditioning suggests that an individual's behaviour will be modified by the rewards or punishments that occur as a result of some action or failure to act on the part of the individual. A *reinforcer* is thus some event that increases the probability that a target behaviour is repeated. *Positive* reinforcement occurs when an employee receives a bonus for good performance. *Negative* reinforcement occurs when an employee is rewarded by the removal of some unpleasant or undesirable environmental detail (e.g. by replacing a piece of equipment which has not been working properly). Note that negative reinforcement is not the same as *punishment*, which is used to decrease the probability that an undesirable behaviour will be repeated. Punishment is not usually part of a reward system because of its negative nature. It indicates only what is undesirable, it does not indicate what employees should do. For this reason (as well as for humanitarian and legal reasons) punishment is rarely used as a way of motivating employees.

The various forms of extrinsic reinforcers that are in use at present include the following:

1. *Promotion*: This is a fairly weak motivator because promotion is a relatively infrequent experience for most employees.
2. *Piece-rate pay systems*: Employees are paid for the number of items completed regardless of the amount of time and effort expended. The motivational problem is that the employee's performance will not simply be a function of the effort expended but also of the employee's skill, and the quality of machinery and raw material available etc.
3. *Salary increments and bonuses*: An individual bonus system is usually a more effective way of rewarding performance than a salary increment system, because bonuses can disappear in the event of future poor performance whereas salary increments are hardly ever lost. Bonus pay systems, therefore, have a much more powerful effect on motivation than salary increments.
4. *Group bonus plans*: Rather similar to salary increments except that the bonus is dependent upon the organization's performance rather than an individual's. Company profit-sharing schemes are a good example of the type.
5. *Skill evaluation pay plans*: People are paid for the skills they have rather than the jobs they do. Its greatest strength is that it communicates to employees a concern for the development of their skills. There are, however, problems of people reaching the top of the pay range, the cost of training and the difficulties of controlling people who want to do new jobs.
6. *Lump-sum salary increases*: The impact of an annual salary rise is usually lost when it is buried in a weekly or monthly pay slip. Lump-sum increase programmes aim to make salary increase more flexible and visible. Under a lump-sum increase programme, employees are given the opportunity to decide when they will receive their annual increase.
7. *Cafeteria benefit programmes*: Employees have a total pay figure, but they can decide how much of it they wish to take as money and how much as fringe benefits (e.g. car, pension plan, insurance policy, etc.).

Summary

This chapter has considered three aspects of the management process: motivation, performance appraisal and rewards. Motivation was described as that which energizes, directs and sustains behaviour. Two aspects were considered: arousal (how individuals get energized, i.e. in a state of readiness to do something) and choice (how individuals choose to engage in a particular form of behaviour). Two different types of theories of arousal were considered: the need-deprivation theories deriving from the work of Maslow and the external social theories based on the concepts of social facilitation and evaluation apprehension. Three principal theories of the internal causes of behavioural choice were considered: expectancy theory, equity theory and goal-setting theory.

The process of creating a performance system was then examined, and five stages were identified: (1) selection of the measures to be used, (2) definition of those measures, (3) selection of measurement principles, (4) selection of appropriate standards and (5) timing of feedback. These stages were considered using two accounting performance measures as examples: return on capital employed and residual income.

Finally, reward systems were discussed from two aspects: how to create one, and the types of reward that exist. The implementation decisions that were discussed were: (1) which parts of performance to reward, (2) what level of performance aggregation to use (i.e. individual or group), (3) whether rewards should be public or secret and (4) how the reward system could match the management type of the organization. A number of different rewards were considered using the basic distinction of intrinsic (self-reward) and extrinsic (external reward). The theory of operant conditioning was discussed when considering extrinsic rewards.

References and Further Reading

Emmanuel, C., A. Merchant and D. Otley (1990) *Accounting for Management Control*, 2nd edn, London: Chapman and Hall.

Hopwood, A.G. (1976) *Accounting and Human Behaviour*, Hemel Hempstead: Prentice Hall, London.

Lawler, E.E. and J.G. Rhode (1976) *Information and Control in Organizations*, Pacific Palisades, Calif.: Goodyear.

Mitchell, T.R. and J.R. Larson (1987) *People in Organizations: An Introduction to Organizational Behaviour*, 3rd edn, New York: McGraw-Hill.

Moizer, P. and J. Pratt (1988) 'The evaluation of performance in firms of chartered accountants', *Accounting and Business Research*, Summer, pp. 227–37.

Otley, D. (1987) *Accounting Control and Organizational Behaviour*, London: Heinemann.

Steers, R.M. and L.W. Porter (1987) *Motivation and Work Behaviour*, 4th edn, New York: McGraw-Hill.

Chapter 8

Budgeting, creativity and culture

ALISTAIR M. PRESTON

The purpose of this chapter is to explore the way in which budgeting may contribute towards, or impede, the creative process within organizations. The first section examines the model of the creative process implicit in the conventional textbook treatment of budgeting. This model is referred to as the rationalist model of creativity. The chapter then explores the characteristics of organizations and budgeting prescribed under this model for dealing with high environmental uncertainty. It is suggested that the rationalist model is an inadequate representation of how creative or innovative behaviour manifests itself in organizations, which casts doubt upon the efficacy of using traditional budgeting techniques in conditions of high environmental uncertainty. The second section proposes an alternative model of creativity, referred to as the humanist model. Drawing on contemporary research on budgeting, the humanist perspective is seen to shed a different light upon the process of budgeting in organizations. Budgets are seen to be part of, and give shape to, the shared meanings, beliefs, value and distribution of power within the organization. It is argued that these elements must be considered in making prescriptions about the appropriate nature of budgeting under conditions of high environmental uncertainty. The final section tentatively considers what form budgeting systems, intended to foster creative behaviour in organizations, might take.

The rationalist model

The rationalist model is part of a general theory which professes to explain the natural order. The natural order is seen to be an interlocking system of objective elements, arranged in a logical and rule-governed manner. This natural order is ultimately knowable and may be fully explained, providing all the relevant variables in the system are identified and the rules governing their relationship understood. Events within the natural order, which include physical, social, economic and organizational events, are the inevitable outcome of a determinate principle, and therefore, with the correct knowledge, may be predicted. The reason why creativity is still regarded as being mysterious, is simply because all the relevant factors have not been identified, and the interplay between the elements are still ill understood. Research into creativity, as with research in general within the rationalist perspective, involves uncovering those variables and rules, of which we are still ignorant.

The following section explores how rationalist assumptions are used in the management and accounting literature to explain the workings of organizations environments, uncertainty and various organizational processes, including budgeting. The way in which organizational characteristics may impede or enhance creativity will also be explored.

Organizations, environments and uncertainty

Environmental uncertainty

Within the management accounting literature, environments are defined as a complex system of interrelated economic, market, technological and, to a lesser extent, social and political variables. These variables may be placed on a continuum ranging from low to high uncertainty. Low environmental uncertainty is characterized by situations in which future events may be extrapolated from the past with some degree of accuracy. In this case the variables and rules which make up the environment are well understood. Therefore the outcome of a course of action, say a proposed investment in plant and equipment, may be predicted with a high degree of confidence. In contrast, high environmental uncertainty is characterized by dynamic, variety-rich environments which manifest themselves in highly unpredictable changes. In this case the relevant variables and rules of the environment are misunderstood or only partially understood. The outcome of a proposed investment may therefore be highly uncertain.

In accounting, considerable effort has been directed towards improving quantitative techniques for dealing with uncertainty. These techniques, which include probability theory, conform to the rationalist perspective in that they are directed towards determining all the relevant environmental variables and the rules governing their relationship, based upon the belief that environments operate according to a predetermined order. The reduction of uncertainty may be achieved by gathering information, and therefore knowledge, about the environment. Perfect information would permit a reliable predictive model to be constructed, and the outcomes of particular courses of action would then be determinable.

However, even within the rationalist perspective, it is generally accepted that perfect information, and therefore adequate predictive models of highly uncertain environments are unobtainable. It is recognized that an organization's strategy for dealing with high uncertainty may not be restricted to the application of quantitative or statistical techniques. Rather, an organization's survival is reliant upon its ability to respond creatively to the threats and opportunities that a highly uncertain environment poses. Creativity, or as it is usually expressed in the management literature, adaptability and flexibility, is seen to occur when the correct combination of variables or organizational characteristics are brought into play. These characteristics include the organizational structure, leadership style, the information system and the planning and control process. Each of these elements may be seen to be part of, or interact with, the budgeting process. Implicit within this perspective is the assumption that particular combinations of these elements are appropriate to different environmental conditions. Some combinations foster bureaucratic and highly rigid behaviour, while other combinations result in creative, adaptable and flexible behaviour.

In essence, organizational structures and processes may be designed to promote creativity. The following examines three organizational characteristics typically associated with budgeting under conditions of high environmental uncertainty. These are the organization structure, the information system and the management control system. Although the three elements are highly interrelated, each will be explored separately.

Organizations as a combination of elements

Organizations are traditionally portrayed as a series of interlocking subsystems, representing patterns of authority and control, communication and information flow. Organizations are seen to differ in the way that their subsystems are arranged, the way in which information is communicated and the way in which control is exercised. Under conditions of high environmental uncertainty, where creativity is at a premium, the ideal combination of structure, information and control systems conforms to the *organic* type of organization rather than to the *mechanistic* type.

Organic structures are typically decentralized, with relatively low degrees of hierarchical authority and with few formal rules and regulations. Ideally, subsystems within the organization will have a high degree of autonomy in decision-making, planning and control. Within an organic structure, contact with the environment, and therefore information gathering, is dispersed throughout the organization. In conditions of high environmental uncertainty, organizations are required to produce greater volumes and varieties of information in order to plan for, and respond to, changes in the environment. For example, organizations will require information about the future as well as about the past, about events within the organization and about external events in the environment. Much of the information will be generated through informal sources and may be qualitative and non-financial in nature. The planning and control of the organization's activities is likewise dispersed throughout the organization to facilitate adjustments in current operations and future plans, in response to environmental conditions. Ideally there will be few formal rules and regulations to allow for flexible and adaptable behaviour. Organic structures are loosely coupled, flexible and adaptable and permit creative and innovative behaviour. Without going into details, mechanistic organizations are essentially the opposite of the organic type and are characterized by rigid hierarchical structures, formalized information and control systems, and numerous formal rules and regulations.

Two questions are posed by the depiction of organic organizations. First, does budgeting as typically presented in management accounting textbooks conform with the organic type of organization? Second, does the rationalist depiction of organizations represent the way in which organizations actually operate? These questions are explored below.

Budgeting, organizations, information and control

The extreme case

There is a close relationship between budgeting and organizational structure. Budgeting is based upon the concept of responsibility accounting which emphasizes formalized, hierarchical structures. Organizational subsystems are defined as responsibility centres with individual managers held responsible and accountable for the performance of their division or department. Typically, performance is measured against some clearly defined target or standard, often determined by senior managers in the organizational hierarchy and communicated downwards through the budgeting process. Budgeting is involved in co-ordinating the activities of the individual subsystems so that the goals of the organization as a whole are achieved. As such, budgeting, through its formalized system of responsibility and accountability, may have the twin effect of establishing and reinforcing structures which emphasize hierarchical and rigid patterns of relationships within the organization. The typical organizational charts found in management accounting textbooks appear to be more in keeping with mechanistic rather than organic organizations. Such monolithic structures may promote inflexible responses with little room for creativity, thus impairing an organization's ability to adequately respond to rapidly changing and dynamic environments.

As noted above, organic organizations require a considerable variety of information, often informal. Yet the information which budgeting systems typically provide is highly quantitative and economic in nature and forms part of the formal and often computer-based information system. Indeed, budgets are typically defined as a quantitative or financial expression of a company's plans. However, formal information systems have been criticized for their failure to provide the correct type of information in conditions of high environmental uncertainty (Mintzberg 1975). The criticisms are as follows, and are applicable to budgeting systems as well.

Budgeting concentrates on the easy-to-measure routine events, while under conditions of high environmental uncertainty, managers require information about unfamiliar and hard-to-measure events. Where events are rapidly changing and unpredictable, information from budgets is often outdated, is historical rather than future oriented, and arrives too late for managers to base their decisions upon. Formal information is not sufficiently rich to adequately describe complex and unfamiliar environmental events. Finally, formal systems tend to concentrate upon events internal to the organization rather than upon events in the external environment. These criticisms have led to the suggestion that formal information systems produce an overload of irrelevant information about routine events and very little relevant information about important unfamiliar events.

To illustrate these inadequacies, a group of managers at a large plastics container factory were found to systematically ignore formal production information which reported labour and material variances as part of the budgetary control system. One production manager claimed that the information was too late. He said, 'Information is bound to be so far behind and managers must react much quicker. They've got to react on an hour-by-hour basis.' The production planner claimed that 'the overall picture might be good enough, it's just that the detail is not good enough in some cases'. Another production manager commented on the type of information provided: 'I don't know what I can do about it, they are just showing me some bloody figures aren't they? What can I do about figures? They just mean 60, 70, 80 or whatever the bloody figure is. It doesn't tell me how to get better figures.' Finally, even the factory accountant admitted that 'there are too many inaccuracies. If you get it wrong at one stage then it's invariably wrong throughout.'

Mintzberg argued that these insufficiencies are not the result of a poorly designed system but are inherent to all management information systems, including budgeting systems. Given the type of information provided by the typical budgeting system, it is questionable whether it contributes towards creativity, flexibility and adaptability in organizations.

The model of control which has dominated management accounting and budgeting thought is that of 'control over'. Managers set and communicate targets or standards, measure and evaluate performance and prescribe corrective action if actual performance deviates from planned. Within the conventional textbook wisdom, control is typically portrayed as being located at the top of the organization and the allocation of tasks, setting standards, the evaluation of performance and the budgetary process are top-down. Control is exercised through managerial dictate and the establishment of numerous rules and regulations to guide behaviour. Motivation is based upon a system of incentives designed to provide economic reward for good performance. The underlying assumption of this style of control has been characterized by 'Theory X', which suggests that individuals are rational economic beings, are inherently lazy and require constant supervision and motivation through economic gain. However, such autocratic control is typically associated with mechanistic organizations. The concentration of authority and control at the top of the hierarchy creates a monolithic organization which will have difficulty responding to changing environmental conditions. Such methods of control within a budgeting system are said to impede organizational learning by positively reinforcing existing practices rather than developing new, innovative and creative strategies.

Softening the case

The above portrayal of budgeting may seem extreme and to some extent dated, nevertheless it is still common in textbooks. Others, while still operating within the rationalist perspective, suggest that budgets need not reinforce mechanistic structures, nor incorporate all of the problems associated with formal information systems and need not rely on autocratic control. In particular, contingency theorists (see Otley 1980) suggest that budgetary control systems may be designed to respond to, rather than ignore, changes in the environment. Decentralized structures may be complemented with decentralized systems of budgeting. Greater autonomy in formulating plans, setting standards, evaluating performance and determining corrective action may be devolved throughout the organization rather than being concentrated at the top. The type of budgeting system operated within an organization will be contingent upon environmental conditions which confront it. Flexible budgeting and control systems are ideal for uncertain environments, and more bureaucratic methods are applicable for organizations operating in stable conditions. In addition, informal, non-quantitative and non-financial information may complement the more formal and quantitative calculations found in the typical budget.

In terms of control, these authors would suggest that autocratic control need not be the only form practised in rational organizations. Consensual control, which emphasizes participation in budgeting, when setting standards and the evaluation of performance, may be practised. This style of control is based upon 'Theory Y', which emphasizes the 'human' side of management. Individuals are defined as responding to a wide range of incentives such as greater autonomy and control over their own tasks, job enrichment, and group participation. By encouraging participation in the budgetary process, a greater variety of information and perspectives will be introduced which will promote more innovative strategies. By dispersing information throughout the organization, and allowing all members to participate in the budgeting and control process, organizations will be better able to identify, learn about and respond to changing environmental conditions. Under consensual control the budgeting process will be bottom-up, with top management's role confined to approving standards proposed lower down in the hierarchy. It is assumed that if individuals are involved in the setting of standards and in the evaluation of their own performance, they will internalize and strive to achieve the standards set.

Another alternative to Theory X which proposes even fewer formal controls, is 'Theory Z' (Ouchi 1979). A Theory Z organization is likened to a clan, where each individual becomes a member of the organization in a much more intimate sense. The clan functions by socializing the individual completely, so that the goals of the individual merge with the goals of the organization. The clan is culturally homogeneous and members share a common set of values and beliefs. Unlike hierarchical organizations, in which each member is dependent on the structure to provide guidance for action and levels of performance to aspire to, clan organizations are said to have relatively few rules, regulations and control systems. This enables the members to individually adjust and adapt their behaviour to suit changing conditions. Chaos is avoided because a system of mutual interdependence is established between the individual and the organization. This relationship is characterized by the motto 'what is good for the organization is good for the individual'. Thus, formalized control systems for ensuring consistency between individual and organizational goals are unnecessary, because the goals of the organization are already the goals of the individual. In clan organizations, control takes the form of socially integrating the individual into the organization. Theory Z was apparently developed by observing the practices of Japanese firms and has been prescribed as an appropriate model of control in rapidly changing environments.

In summary, certain authors advocate organic structures, a budgeting system which provides relevant and timely information and a style of control that minimizes the number of rules and regulations, either through participation or through a process of social integration. It is argued that suitably designed budgeting systems are possible and may facilitate the necessary flexibility and adaptability to promote creative and innovative responses to environmental uncertainty. However, these prescriptions are based upon the same rationalist perspective which underpins mechanistic structures, formal systems and autocratic control. Implicit in all of the above models is the assumption that creative and adaptable behaviour will automatically result from the correct combination of organization structure and information and control systems.

Dismissing the case

What is missing from this perspective is that organizations *create* as well as *respond* to their environment. Take for example the deregulation of the financial services in the United Kingdom. The environment, namely the financial services market within which brokerage firms and investment banks operated, underwent a radical transformation. The environment became highly uncertain; Japanese and American investment firms moved into London. London companies began to restructure through a rash of takeovers and mergers, and by introducing new operating procedures in order to better position themselves for the new conditions they anticipated. So far this is consistent with contingency theory. However, after deregulation, the nature of the financial services market was created by the actions of the people and companies in that market. The mergers themselves, reducing commissions, offering different services and the introduction of American and Japanese styles of management, all helped shape the environment within which the firms operated. In this respect the organizations created their own environment.

There is a degree of reciprocity between organizations and environments. Environments may be contingent upon the actions of the organizations, and in turn an organization's structure and process may be contingent upon events in the environment. Where an environment begins and an organization ends is a lot less clear, and the relationship between organizations and their environment is more complex and mutually interrelated than contingency theory would lead us to believe. Even budgeting, and the plans of action it contains, may impact upon and change the environment. In short, environments do not operate according to immutable laws but rather are created and reproduced by the actions of individuals and organizations. The idea of mapping out environmental variables and matching them with organizational variables and appropriate budgeting systems is a fallacy, simply because environmental and organizational variables do not exist as discrete entities which can be identified, measured, modelled and predicted. Rather, environments are constructed by the actions and interactions of competing organizations, governments and customers. As we shall see in the next section each of these entities are themselves constructed by the actions and interactions of individuals and need not operate according to a single determinate principle of order.

Another criticism of the traditional perspective of budgeting rests upon the fact that consensual and clan control have an important characteristic in common with autocratic control. All three are premised upon the principle of 'control over' or of coercing individuals into behaving in accordance with the goals of the organization, normally reflected in the top management's ideology. The purpose of consensual control which allows, and indeed encourages, individuals to participate in the budgeting process is as much to do with ensuring commitment to the budget by the participant, than it is to do with promoting creativity. In a similar way, clan control appears to subordinate the expression of individuality to the organization. Clan control may be likened to a dictatorship of the majority. It is based upon a docile and mute membership, including management, which will comply with unspoken norms and values as if they were their own. There is also the suggestion that the unspoken norms and values are those of the senior management which are internalized by the clan. Conformity rather than creativity may be the likely result.

Finally, what is notable from the rationalist perspective, whether it relates to creativity, budgeting, organizational structure or the natural order in general, is the absence in the analysis of human beings as self-directing individuals. Within the rationalist perspective the behaviour of individuals is seen to be determined by the situation — that is, by the combination of structure and process, including the budgeting process, of the organization. There is no provision within the rationalist perspective for the conscious self-determining actions of individuals. For this reason the rationalist model is referred to as being determinist in nature. Behaviour is explained by the stimulus—response model. An individual's response will be determined by the stimulus or situation which is brought into play and is therefore predictable. The image of the human individual is that of a passive object being tossed around by the force of circumstance.

The absence of the creative human individual in traditional perspectives on budgeting is its most severe limitation. In response, a number of studies have sought to introduce the human being into their analyses of the budgeting process. We shall refer to these as the humanist perspectives. There are a number of overlapping schools of thought within the humanist perspective, each emphasizing different aspects of social reality or individual behaviour. However, they have sufficient in common for them to be treated as a single perspective for the purposes of this chapter. .

The humanist model

In the humanist perspective, behaviour, including creativity, is not the result of the correct combination of elements or a predeterminate order, but is a product of the creative individual. One school of thought called symbolic interactionism (see Blumber 1962) suggests that human behaviour may be understood in the following manner. First, individuals act towards 'things' — that is, towards objects, situations, events and possibly each other — on the basis of the *meaning* that things have for them. There is a critical process between encountering an object, situation or event and an individual's response to it. This is referred to as the process of interpretation, in which the individual constructs a meaning or definition of the situation, event or object and acts in accordance with that meaning. Meaning is therefore not inherent in the object or situation, but is brought to it by the individual. Second, meanings do not simply pop out of the air, rather they are said to be derived through social interaction, that is through the ways in which people meet, talk, work and play together and in turn construct and share meanings. Meanings are therefore socially constructed, internalized and shared between individuals. Third, meanings may be expressed symbolically through language. (Hence the title symbolic interactionism). In this respect, words, formulas, information, financial accounts and budgets are all symbolic representations of reality and carry meaning which may be communicated to others. Finally, meanings are not immutable but rather may be changed by individuals themselves and/or through further social interaction.

For example, during a lorry drivers' strike, when pickets refused to permit products to leave the plastic container factory mentioned earlier, the managers met to discuss the problem. Throughout the interaction various managers suggested that the factory should be closed, that stock should be built up until the strike was over or that part of the factory should be closed and certain select items of stock should be built up. The managing director finally asked the following question. 'If we cut back or close down, how do our customers stand?' One of the production managers commented. 'It doesn't matter. If we are picketed they're going to be picketed as well! If they can't get anything out they won't need any containers.' The production planner however, interjected 'Ah is that right? They're not picketing food manufacturers. ... Birds Eye, Express Dairies, Rowntree, Van den Berghs won't be picketed' (these companies were the factory's largest customers). The managing director then said, 'If you look at it that way, we're part of the food industry ourselves.' After discussions with the regional offices of the union, plastic containers used in the food processing industry were allowed to leave the factory. The factory was able to continue operations at a slightly reduced capacity throughout the strike.

This example demonstrates how meanings and definitions may be altered through social interaction. In effect, the managers had redefined the very nature of their business. From being in the plastic container industry the company was now defined to be part of the food-processing industry. The interaction is also an example of the creative process at work. The redefinition of the business brought a significantly different meaning to the situation, and it resulted in a creative solution to the problem. The source of creative and adaptable behaviour lies in the potential to construct and redefine meanings.

The creative process is often defined as being intuitive or inspirational. However, these are only metaphors for a mystery that eludes rational enquiry, because the creative process is itself non-rational. Within the creative process, something that has no apparent precedent, or has only a loose connection to previous experience, emerges and this phenomena is difficult to reconcile with the rationalist perspective. Nevertheless, creativity, the process of introducing new and novel interpretations and actions, is an observable phenomenon. Ultimately it rests upon the potential in individuals to look at the world anew and to interpret what they see differently. The question this perspective poses is what organizational context and budgeting process will promote or impede creative behaviour. To answer this question it is first necessary to redefine the nature of organizations under the humanist perspective.

Organizations as culture

Within the non-rationalist perspective, organizations are seen as gatherings of people. However, football crowds may also be described as gatherings of people, and yet in many obvious respects 'they differ from the typical organization. What makes an organization different from a football crowd, and indeed one organization different from another, is the manner in which people gather — that is, the manner in which individuals interact with one another and thereby align their individual courses of action. As noted above, human behaviour is not determined by a rational order, but neither is it completely irrational or anarchic. Rather, an individual's behaviour is guided by the meanings, values and beliefs that are constructed by, and shared between, the members of an organization. An organization may therefore be defined as a socially constructed order. It must however be noted that the actions of organizations may ultimately be traced to the actions of individuals.

These shared values, beliefs and meanings have come to be collectively defined as organizational culture. Within the organization and accounting literature two conceptions of culture have emerged and it is important to distinguish between them. On the one hand, culture is defined as merely another variable to be combined with the organization structure and processes in order to bring about desired results. Organizations are portrayed as *having* a culture which may be crafted and manipulated by management intervention to instil particular company values and attitudes and to create particular forms of behaviour. The work on clan organizations belongs to this tradition as it interprets culture as a 'thing' which may be manipulated. On the other hand, organizations may be thought of *as* culture (Dent, forthcoming). From this perspective, culture is not a separate element but rather it constitutes or *is* the organization. Organizations *are* the shared meanings, values and beliefs — that is, the culture, which over time, has been formed by the organizational members.

This humanist perspective does not preclude the existence of organizational structures and processes, but rather it suggests that they are symbolic representations of a particular view of organizational reality. They are subject to interpretation by individuals who will act towards them on the basis of the meaning they have for them. In this respect the structure, and in particular, processes including budgeting, may form part of the culture of the organization, and indeed may be active in shaping the pattern of shared meanings, values and beliefs.

A particular organizational culture may impede or enhance creativity. Culture may be seen to define the limits of currently acceptable behaviour or of current practices and beliefs. In other words, it prescribes a line between that which is 'done' and that which is 'not done'. Such prescriptions may be seen as rules, but these differ from the predetermined rules of the rationalist model. They are 'rules in process' and are often unstated. They are continually produced and reproduced, or else modified and changed, through the actions and interactions of the participating individuals. Creativity, by definition, lies beyond acceptable or current practice: it operates on or beyond the border of 'that which is done'. For creativity to thrive, individual behaviour which transcends the current order must be accepted by other members and, if judged worthy, incorporated into, or change, current practices. For creativity to thrive, a culture of acceptance of new and innovative behaviour will have to evolve. The above perspectives on individual behaviour, organizational culture and creativity provide some interesting ways of reinterpreting budgeting in general and also budgeting under conditions of high environmental uncertainty.

The meaning *of* budgets

Budgets or budgeting, like any other object or activity, are subject to the interpretation of individuals whereby meanings are assigned to them. While many of the meanings of budgeting may be shared by the organizational participants, there need not be complete consensus. Budgets may mean radically different things to different people.

For example, during a study of the introduction of management budgets into a district in the British National Health Service (NHS) a number of conflicting meanings of the budgeting process were evident. The Department of Health and Social Security defined management budgeting in the following manner: 'The overriding objective of introducing management budgeting in the NHS is to give better services to its patients, by helping the clinicians and other managers to make better informed judgments about how the resources they control can be used to maximum effect' (DHSS Health Notice, Jan. 1985). The above definition conforms fairly closely to traditional definitions of budgeting, which emphasizes efficiency, and improved services. However, an administrator, within the district, revealed his scepticism of this definition and offered his own. 'The general view is that this is yet another tool for cuts within the District. So no matter how cleverly one might attempt to disguise this in a language that talks about improvements in services, what we are actually talking about in this District is achieving less for less money. . . . In this district we want to be doing less by 1993 at less unit cost than we are doing now.' For this administrator, budgeting meant cost-cutting or the constraining of financial resources. For the doctors within the NHS budgets meant a device which would impinge upon their clinical freedom. Doctors defined budgets as an 'Orwellian nightmare' and argued that if they participated in the process, it would be a 'Trojan horse' to their autonomy.

Each of these and other definitions were laden with deep-felt meaning and guided the various individuals' responses to the management budgeting initiative. Ultimately the entire national initiative to introduce management budgets was suspended because of the conflict it caused between national and district managers and the entire medical profession. The outcome of the budgeting process is in part determined by the meaning that people hold for it and the culture within which it is placed. In the case of the National Health Service, the proposed new budgeting system was placed in a complex culture in which there were multiple shared meanings, values and beliefs. Indeed, the NHS at the time of the study could be defined as a culture of conflict. The new budgeting system not only reflected this conflict but helped to fan the flames. In this sense the new system enhanced and even created conflict within the organization.

Another example of the meaning of budgets found in the literature is that the presence of budgets within an organization give the impression of a rational, efficiently-run operation. In this sense budgets are synonymous with good management and confer legitimacy upon the organization. They create the appearance of a rational approach to the uncertainties of the future. This may be very important to organizations trying to raise funds from financial institutions or government departments. Financial institutions usually require operations and capital budgets before considering a loan. For example, one author noted that the power of the administrators in the Polaris missile programme came from their ability to convince others both in and outside the US defense department that they were effective and rational managers. They did this through the use of sophisticated management techniques including forms of budgeting. Even though these techniques were not employed in making the critical decisions (Sapolsky 1972).

In this sense budgets are a form of advertisement for rational economic behaviour. Budgets may also be used as advertisements in another sense. Managers may inflate their expected level of performance in the budget, against which they will subsequently be evaluated. This advertises determination and motivation, which may be valued and rewarded qualities within the organization. This strategy may seem risky. However, the same budgets may be used as a means of defence if the budgeted performance is not achieved. Budgets contain numerous assumptions about anticipated future events.

Managers who fail to achieve their budgeted performance, may appeal to these assumptions claiming that events outside of their control did not work out as expected. In essence, they may claim retrospectively that the budget was rendered meaningless by unpredictable and uncontrollable events.

Given that budgets may be interpreted differently in different situations by different people, the budget as an artifact and budgeting as a process in itself can neither impede or promote creative behaviour. However, the meaning that budgets and budgeting have for people certainly may. If budgets are seen as a divisive means of cutting cost and constraining growth, or as a pernicious form of control as in the case of the administrator in the NHS, this may influence values and beliefs in an organization and create a culture in which creativity is stifled.

To avoid the possibility that budgeting might impede creativity, the directors of an independent record company simply refused to budget in the early days of the company. One director commented as follows: 'I think budgets are totally irrelevant, you are never going to know [whether a record is going to be profitable] in this kind of business. It's either going to be a good idea or a bad idea.' When asked what constituted good or bad the director replied, 'It's good if you like it.' He then asked rhetorically, 'Do you make a record because you think the man on the street is going to like it? Na, you're going to make it because *you* like it.' The principal philosophy of the company was to subordinate economic analysis to aesthetic appreciation in order to allow creative music and ideas to surface and develop. Their principal concern was that a good idea should not be rejected on its perceived unprofitability, when revenue and costs were highly uncertain. Budgets were therefore seen as meaningless or might mean giving up a good idea.

Budgets are not only meaningful to people — they may be involved in the shaping of meaning. The following section explores this point.

The meaning *in* budgets

Budgeting is typically presented as a neutral process, or as a passive technique which mirrors but does not create a purely objective reality. However, this claim to neutrality and objectivity has been criticized because it neglects to consider that budgets are symbolic representations of the reality they express. Budgeting brings a selective visibility to particular events or particular characteristics of events and thus sets the agenda for the future. In this respect, budgets or budgeting may define what is important and in need of consideration. Budgets emphasize the economic aspects, the revenues, expenses and cash flows, of future anticipated events or current operations. Budgets, by what they measure and how they measure it, may shape the interpretative process of individuals and the meaning that things have for them. Because of budgeting's focus upon the measurable, quantitative elements of a situation, those hard to measure non-quantitative elements may be ignored. What is measured gets attention, what is not measured gets ignored. Budgets may have the effect of narrowing the focus of managers' interpretations to consider only the economic and in turn stifle the possibility of new and innovative interpretations. It must be noted that the capacity of budgets and budgeting to shape meaning is not inherent in the budget or the process of budgeting. It is because budgets have come to mean something that they in turn shape meaning. Budgets may be seen as part of the overall management trend towards quantitative and economic analysis, that is towards an increasingly rational organizational culture. It is because quantification and economic measure have come to mean so much in commercial organizations that budgeting and other quantitative techniques may in turn shape people's interpretative process and create meaning.

An example of how meanings may be affected by accounting, concerns the independent record company mentioned above. One of the bands who recorded with the company was investigated by the Inland Revenue. The record company was required to provide information on earnings for each album and single, tape and CD that the band had recorded with them. This required calculating the sales revenue and costs of each item, something the company had not done until this point. This constituted an enormous elaboration of the accounting system of the company. What is relevant is that after the investigation, the new accounting system continued in operation. It began to be used to evaluate the success of particular projects. For example, one director commented to the manager of a band, 'You know your last single made a loss.' The band manager replied, 'I dispute that.' The director interjected saying, 'You can't dispute the figures [referring to the new accounts]. Costs: recording and mixing 60, video 40, printer's bill 110 . . . that's where we really got caught. Pressing was 65, with royalties, the total costs are 315 grand. Total money in was about 260 . . . . We made a loss of about 55 grand.' The new accounts finally evolved into a crude form of budgeting which would not have been acceptable a few years previously.

This example suggests that budgets and accounting in general may not only shape the meaning given to events but might impact upon the culture of an organization more generally. With the increased use of accounting, the directors of the record company admitted that they had moved into an era of financial realism. In turn, other practices within the organization changed. More aggressive 'hyping' (meaning advertising and promotion) of the music and a greater concern for profits began to emerge. In consequence, the culture of the organization slowly evolved from one which emphasized aesthetics to a more economic orientation.

Another example of how budgets may shape culture is found in a study of a company referred to as European Rail. Dent (forthcoming) noted that when financial considerations were given a greater profile in the organization, economic interpretations began to eclipse the engineering interpretations which up until this point had been an integral part of the organization culture. Dent noted that this reorientation had a significant impact upon the culture of the organizations. This example of European Rail and the new financial realism at the record company, suggest that accounting in general and budgets in particular may be mechanisms of change and power within organizations.

The power of budgets

Within an organization, groups of individuals or indeed a single individual may have the ability to influence the budgeting process and therefore the allocation of resources. Resource allocation is subject to a considerable amount of power play in organizations, in that it may set the level of resources assigned to departments and determine which capital projects will be funded. Budgets have been defined as a political bargaining process which reflects systems of power and influence in organizations. The manner in which resources are allocated and the capital investment projects chosen are not necessarily the outcome of a rational decision-making process but, rather, reflect the ability of certain groups or individuals to influence the allocation process.

For example, a media director of a leading advertising company in London commented that he wished to have the largest media budget in the advertising industry. He admitted that it was important for him to have a large budget because this would reflect the relative importance and status of the media department within the company and the industry as a whole. Higher status would enable him to have a greater say in the running of the company. Given this interpretation, the media director was deliberate in his attempts to influence the budgeting process in his favour. Thus the size of the media budget, relative to other departments in the organization and the industry, reflected the director's power and his ability to affect subsequent resource allocation.

Thus budgets may mirror the extant patterns of power and influence in the organization and may reflect changes in these patterns. Apart from the political bargaining of powerful individuals, the allocation of resources and the acceptance of projects under capital budgeting may be influenced by those individuals involved in the budgeting process. Certain individuals may have the influence to determine the selection of information to be included in the budget; this may help shape the outcome of the budgeting process and affect the future direction of the company, and possibly the distribution of power and influence. In this respect, budgets are an instrument of power as well as being a reflection of power. Determining the input of data may have other consequences. Certain managers may underestimate performance and build slack into their budgets. Subsequently, when their performance is evaluated they appear efficient and effective. This in turn may enhance their position in the organization.

Lastly, budgeting, especially capital budgeting, through the manipulation of data may be used to justify decisions already made rather than playing a role in the decision-making process *per se*. In this respect a capital budget may be a *post hoc* rationalization of a decision that has already been taken. For example, a company which ran a chain of catalogue showrooms in the United Kingdom determined that any new showrooms must show a positive net present value using the company's regular cost of capital figure. The estate manager, who was responsible for searching out and evaluating new showroom sites was set the objective of opening twenty new stores per year. As the prime sites were slowly used up, it became increasingly difficult for prospective showrooms to satisfy the company's investment criteria. In order to fulfil his quota the estate manager used more and more generous estimations of those factors which would affect his anticipated revenue calculations, such as the spending power in the area, and flow of pedestrian traffic past the store. In effect, the capital budget was manipulated to justify the opening of new stores and satisfy the quota requirements set by the company.

Budgets and the process of budgeting are complex, and tightly interwoven with organizational life. In particular, budgets form part of, and help shape, the shared meanings, values, beliefs and distributions of power which make up the culture of the organization. The question remains as to how this conceptualization of organizations and budgeting, impacts upon the creative process.

Budgeting and creativity

Budgets and budgeting in themselves neither impede nor enhance creativity. Rather, it is what budgets mean to organizational members, what meaning budgets bring to situations, and how budgets are used to reinforce or shape the patterns of power in an organization that will impact upon the creative process. This impact may enhance or impede creativity. For example, in the case of the media director mentioned above, his striving to increase his budget had a more pragmatic intention than simply to increase his status and power. By increasing the size of the media budget the director could buy in talent, meaning the best media planners and buyers in the industry. This would enable the director to operate the media department more effectively. In fact, the department won a number of national awards for the best media campaign. This success in turn enhanced the media department's standing in the company and in the advertising industry.

Here, influencing resource allocation increased creativity in the media department by permitting the buying in of talent. The buying in of talent is a common way for organizations to attempt to enhance creativity. However, if the power to influence resource allocation lay in the hands of those committed to preserving the status quo, new and innovative projects might not receive funding, or departments which might enhance the company's ability to operate in conditions of high uncertainty might be starved of funds. For example, organizations which experience a downturn in earnings after a period of high profitability tend to develop rigid budgetary control systems and cut research and development, even though it was product innovation which created their success in the first place. Such organizations become inward-looking rather than exploring possible new products and markets and fail to meet the challenges of the environment.

Even if powerful individuals in an organization are committed to creativity, change and development, the dominant culture or cultures of the organization might suffocate the best intended attempts to change. Rigidity may be integral to the socially constructed order. Particular approaches to problems or situations may become ossified into culturally accepted 'ways of doing things'. Innovation and novelty may be socially unacceptable and mechanisms may exist to resist change and restrict creative endeavour. The notion of rigid cultures suggests that there are particular characteristics of organizational culture which might impede creativity. March (1976) identifies a number of agents of rigidity commonly found in organizations. He notes that in organizations decision-making and subsequent action are typically viewed as being purposive. That is directed towards achieving a predetermined goal or objective. March notes, however, that in highly ambiguous situations, managers often have to act in order to find out what they are doing. Even if managers operate on a trial and error basis, they are obliged to rationalize their actions to appear as if they were purposive and goal-directed. Managers are required to give the impression that they know what they were doing, and most organizations place a premium on rationality. Indeed, rational behaviour is rewarded and non-rational behaviour is frowned upon. Decisions clouded by emotions are actively discouraged in most organizations and justifying a choice because it 'feels right' is rarely acceptable.

In addition, in most organizations, courses of action are evaluated in terms of whether they are consistent with the actions of other managers and subunits and with the goals of the organization. Actions are also evaluated in terms of whether they are consistent with past actions, which coerces managers into familiar and routine patterns of behaviour. Purposiveness, rationality and consistency have a strong appeal in organizations and are often highly valued and rewarded. However, organizations confronted with rapidly changing and highly uncertain environments require a very different type of culture. Purposiveness, rationality and consistency may promote a cautious and risk-averse approach to unfamiliar situations. Procedures may become standardized and formalized and create a culture of preserving established customs and practice. Such a culture may promote repetitive and imitative rather than original behaviour.

If we examine the principles and practice of budgeting one can see how they may be involved in reinforcing a culture of rationality, consistency and purposiveness. Budgets, by reducing events to financial measures according to basic accounting formulas, represent a paragon of rationality. Moreover, because managerial performance is often evaluated against these measures, budgets may not only reflect rationality but may actively promote and reinforce rational behaviour. The role of budgeting in co-ordinating the activities of the various subunits in an organization is valued because it promotes consistency and goal congruence. But insistence upon goal congruence and consistency may limit creative ideas and experimentation and instead it may promote imitative behaviour which displays very little originality. Finally, budgets, conceived as a means of compelling planning in organizations, promote the ideal of purposive behaviour and the need to justify decisions and actions in terms of intent and purpose. Having expressed one's intention through the budget, performance may be evaluated against achieving the goals set. Failure will be defined in terms of the inability to meet the budget. This may promote rigid, unidirectional behaviour as well as slavish adherence to budgets even if they are made obsolete by changes in the environment. Budgets represent a highly formalized approach to planning in organizations and, as we have seen, represent a narrow picture of reality. These characteristics may have the effect of guiding behaviour down one path in accordance with one strategy. Therefore budgeting may constrain and limit an individual's ability to creatively explore and experiment with alternative approaches to decision-making and planning and thus different ways of representing or interpreting environmental conditions.

Below we explore how organizations might design or develop organizational processes which either complement or replace traditional budgeting procedures and which may in turn enhance creative and adaptable behaviour. The final section is necessarily tentative in that there are few examples of creative forms of budgeting in the management accounting literature.

Budgeting for creativity and creativity in budgeting

What is notable in research which advocates alternative conceptualizations of budgeting in conditions of high environmental uncertainty (see Cooper, Hayes and Wolf 1981) is the absence of concrete prescriptions for appropriate budgets or budgeting systems. This is understandable given the perspective these papers normally adopt. When one considers that within a single organization budgets mean different things to different people and different organizations evolve different cultures, and given that cultures are dynamic and changing, or at least have the potential for change, then a simple formula for budgeting is inappropriate. A budgeting system which in one organization might compel planning and encourage innovative ideas might be the source of conflict and retrenchment in another organization. It might therefore be undesirable to prescribe or construct a general model of budgeting for all people in all organizations.

A normative, model-based conception of budgeting belongs to the rationalist perspective which believes that an organization's structure and processes, including the budgeting process, may be modelled to match environmental conditions. Therefore a particular model of budgeting will have a general application for all organizations existing in similar environments. Within the humanist perspective this is simply not the case. The interpretations and interactions of people within a shared culture of meanings, values and beliefs, shape how organizations operate, rather than predetermined, immutable laws. Thus, budgets and the budgeting process must reflect the role of the human individual in interpreting and constructing reality and the meanings, values and beliefs of the organization. Boland (1979) suggests that the design of information and control systems should be 'action based' rather than 'model based'. He notes that an action-based approach is not a question of the way in which a system fits a particular model of the environment but, rather, how it fits into the culture of the organization and how it is used in the symbolic process of constructing meanings and definitions. This fit may only be achieved by the active participation of the organizational members in the design process. An appropriate metaphor of this principle of design is that of the jazz 'arranger'. Mike Westbrook (1981) describes the role of an arranger of jazz music as follows: 'My job is to provide a structure and then work on it within the band. The music is a collective concern with ample room for improvisation and individual ideas. Working together we create a chain reaction and that's what provides the thrills.' Compare this to an orchestra playing a classical arrangement where the music is precisely defined and minutely specified, with little or no room for individual interpretation. The design process of a budgeting system should likewise provide ample room for improvisation and individual ideas rather than being based on the imposition of a precisely defined model. In this respect the outcome of the design process, that is the way in which a budget may look and operate, is unpredictable. The outcome is a product of the process rather than a product of a predefined model.

The outcome of such a design process could be that the members of an organization might choose to ignore budgeting as did the independent record company in its early days. However, in our increasingly rationalist and measurement prone society there is considerable pressure for managers to seek the reassurance that budgets give in guiding and justifying action. In addition, financial institutions, government agencies and investors provide additional pressure for rational accounts and business plans. There are strong imperatives towards rational, purposive and consistent behaviour. It is therefore difficult for organizations to give up budgeting and rely instead on creative and intuitive behaviour for which there is no clear means of evaluation and no rational or quantitative way of accounting.

The action design approach might relax mechanisms within an organization which foster purposive, rational and consistent behaviour. Certain authors, notably Cohen *et al.* (1972), advocate quite different modes of management for organizations operating under conditions of high environmental uncertainty. These may be referred to as organized anarchies. Cohen and his colleagues describe the 'garbage can model', where amongst other things, there is a partial decoupling of problems and solutions. Organizations are characterized as a series of solutions looking for problems and problems looking for solutions. Decisions and the choice of a course of action are the fortuitous confluence of streams of problems, solutions, participants and choice opportunities. These meet together like streams of garbage in a garbage can (or rubbish in a dustbin). The outcome is an unpredictable but creative matching of solutions and problems. The garbage can provides an interesting, if a little unfortunate, metaphor of organizations which represent less rigid imperatives, less formalized systems and less standardized procedures. March (1976) provides further suggestions, in the form of aphorisms, about how organizations might generate less rigid, formal and standardized responses. He refers to these, again in a somewhat unfortunate metaphor, as the 'technology of foolishness', which is designed to encourage playful, experimental and creative behaviour. The aphorisms are as follows.

1. *Treating goals as hypotheses*: This prescription implies that minimum faith should be placed in goals under conditions of high environmental uncertainty. Rather, they should be treated as ideas or possibilities with the recognition that these are possibilities that may never actualize. The plans which budgets represent must be taken for what they are; a series of assumptions or hypotheses about the future. In this sense they should not be slavishly followed as if they were objective facts. Goals, plans and budgets should be continually reconsidered and challenged by other and possibly more appropriate interpretations of the future.

2. *Treating intuition as real*: Although the origins of creative ideas are not clearly understood, the potential for new and surprising ideas should be recognized. Such ideas may not be easily rationalized within a conventional framework, but should nevertheless be accepted as legitimate. Accepting ideas and behaviour for which 'no good' reason exists opens up new arenas for analysis and comparison. Budgets, which require a rationalized, and quantitative justification for proposed courses of action cannot accept intuition as real in their present form. It may be necessary to have budgets that 'don't add up' or budgets that are part quantification and part narrative. Storytelling, analogies, anecdotes and parable may be included in budgets to allow the expression of intuitive ideas.

3. *Treating hypocrisy as transitory*: Hypocrisy may be defined as a discrepancy between actions and stated goals or plans. Inconsistencies between action and goals are typically referred to as deviant or goal-incongruent behaviour and not normally sanctioned in organizations. Budgeting is a process where actual outcomes are compared with plans and performance is judged on discrepancies between the two. Yet behaviour which contradicts goals may be providing new opportunities to enrich the organization's stock of experience and provide new and innovative strategies. It has been suggested that semi-confusing information and control systems which recognize and report contradictory data should be used to promote the inconsistencies necessary for generating new forms of behaviour. Another strategy may be to decouple planning and control. If people are not held responsible and accountable for plans, then possibly more interesting ones will develop.

4. *Treating memory as an enemy*: This prescription is intended to break the link between the past and the future. Treating the past and current practices as something to be avoided places a greater reliance upon the generation of novelty. It has been suggested that organizations should disbelieve the familiar, taken-for-granted ways of doing things and encourage minimal commitment to the status quo. Instead they should be encouraged to have faith in the new, the unfamiliar and doubtful. Although textbooks on budgeting caution the use of the past as a model of the future, they nevertheless proclaim the need for consistency with the past and claim that historical information may be the best gauge of the future. As an alternative, budgets which most deviate from previous plans and those that might seem most outlandish or have no supportable, rational explanation, might be valued and rewarded. Such budgets might not be fully implemented, but they might provide a wider variety of alternatives.

5. *Treating experience as a theory*: This aphorism suggests that previous experience may be seen as a process of learning rather than as a given, indisputable fact. Previous experience may be re-examined, possibly by different groups, in order to reveal what lessons it may teach. The past may be reinterpreted and expressed in new and unique ways thereby promoting new ways of thinking and allowing the organization to learn about itself. Within budgeting, the evaluation process should not simply be based upon analysis of variance, but rather should be seen as a learning experience. The underlying assumptions built into the budget about anticipated future events and the theoretical underpinning of budgeting itself, should be open to question, analysis and reinterpretation within deliberately set up group processes.

As a final point, most of management theory, including budgeting theory is normative. This means that they prescribe how organizations ought to be and how budgeting ought to be done, according to their rational economic model. Few management theories are based upon how organizatioins actually operate. The dearth of descriptive studies on alternative ways of budgeting is due in part to the reluctance of researchers to study budgeting in action or within its organizational context. There are, however, companies which creatively respond to environmental conditions. In this sense the creative potential is there and this needs to be explored before any more prescriptions are made.

For example, in the plastics container factory mentioned above, the managers who systematically ignored the formal production information system, constructed their own processes of informing whereby they gathered and shared information within the organization. These processes of informing included interaction whereby managers met and swapped information. As one departmental manager commented, 'One of the biggest effective ways of keeping things ticking over, is obviously fairly regular word-of-mouth contact.' The sales manager likewise commented, 'It's back to word-of-mouth. We'd like to think that people can come over, which happens a lot, and say they've got a problem.' Another source was direct observation, where, when it was possible, managers directly observed the problematic event taking shape. The material control manager commented, 'I've got to get on my feet and walk down there to see what's going on. I come in . . . in the morning and see a machine still running (when the order quantity should already have been produced) and have to go to the machine setter and ask what is going on.'

Another mode of informing was the keeping of personal records, in which important and often hard-to-measure events were recorded, for future reference. The sales manager kept customer record cards on which he recorded the number of containers produced and the quantity dispatched in order to calculate the level of stock on hand. This enabled him to answer customer enquiries promptly and compensate for inaccuracies in the official stock reports. The managers actually created arrangements to inform, whereby individuals could be relied upon to provide richly descriptive, accurate and timely information. Moreover, these arrangements to inform were forums in which unfamiliar or intractable problems were analysed, interpreted and made meaningful. Based upon the meanings that the managers constructed, new and innovative courses of action were decided upon. As the sales manager commented, 'You hear something and then you go and check on it. You probe and you try and find out what is happening and you then find out what you feel to be the true picture. There are a lot of cases still, where you think you ended up with the true picture. Then you talk to somebody else about it or you put forward your theory, just to find you've got the whole thing wrong anyway, or there have been developments.'

Although this example relates to production managers and information systems, there is evidence to suggest that informal planning and control systems in addition to information systems exist at all levels in organizations. Within the rationalist perspective informal processes are referred to as 'grapevines' or as 'butcher or black books' or as 'gossip' and 'hearsay'. They are criticized for their inconsistency, for duplicating effort and for not being factual. Conventional textbook wisdom suggests that they should be eradicated and replaced with more formal, efficient and rational planning, information and control systems. Yet these informal processes are an integral part of creativity in organizations. They provide a rich source of alternative interpretation and are a means by which novel and innovative behaviour may emerge. They are also an integral part of the process of modifying the organizational culture and thus current custom and practices. In this sense the potential for creativity may already exist in organizations. The informal processes, which are systematically ignored or criticized in conventional textbooks on management accounting, may already generate the kinds of creative and innovative behaviour necessary in a rapidly changing environment. The irony is, that by imposing formalized systems, the very behaviour necessary for an organization's survival may be systematically eradicated or at best severely constrained.

References

Blumer, H. (1962) 'Society as symbolic interaction', in A. Rose (ed.) *Human Behaviour and Social Process*, Boston: Houghton Mifflin.

Boland Jr, R.J. (1979) 'Control, causality and information system requirements', *Accounting, Organizations and Society*, vol. 4, no. 4, pp. 259–72.

Cohen, M.D., J.G. March and J.P. Olsen (1972) 'A garbage can model of organizational choice', *Administrative Science Quarterly*, vol. 17, no. 1, pp. 1–25.

Cooper, J.D., D. Hayes and F. Wolf (1981) 'Accounting in organized anarchies: understanding and designing accounting systems in ambiguous situations', *Accounting, Organizations and Society*, vol. 6, no. 3, pp. 175–91.

Dent, J.F. (forthcoming) 'Accounting and organizational cultures: a field study of the emergence of a new organizational reality', *Accounting, Organizations and Society*.

March, J.G. (1976) 'The technology of foolishness', in J.G. March and J.P. Olsen (eds.) *Ambiguity and Choice in Organizations*, Bergen: Universitetsforlaget.

Mintzberg, H. (1975) *Impediments to the Use of Management Information*, New York, National Association of Accountants.

Otley, D.T. (1980) 'The contingency theory of management accounting: achievement and prognosis', *Accounting, Organizations and Society*, vol. 5, no. 4, pp. 413–28.

Ouchi, W. (1979) 'A conceptual framework for the design of organizational control mechanisms', *Management Science*, vol. 25, no. 9, pp. 833–48.

Sapolsky, H.M. (1972) *The Polaris System Development*, Cambridge, Mass.: Harvard University Press.

Westbrook, M. (1981) 'Jazz and the art of living dangerously', *The Sunday Times*, 10 May, p. 35.

Chapter 9

Accountable management in the public sector

CHRISTOPHER HUMPHREY

The performance of the public sector is an issue these days which seldom fails to make headline news and to generate a wide range of analysis and comment. Some topics which have received considerable publicity include the efficiency of the National Health Service in treating patients and reducing waiting lists; the effectiveness of social workers in preventing/detecting child abuse; the improvement in the performance of schools that could be generated through greater local autonomy; the cost-effectiveness of electronic security tags *vis-à-vis* supervision by probation officers; the extension in the contracting out of local authority services; and the benefits of separating the policy advising and administrative functions of the civil service. In considering such developments it is important to realize that a concern with the performance of the public sector has not been the sole preserve of Conservative governments. While the political impetus provided by recent Conservative administrations has dramatically forced the pace of change, their attempts to influence the management of public-sector resources need to be placed in an evolutionary context and not be simply regarded as the product of the post-1979 revolution of Thatcherism.

The reforms of the 1960s and 1970s

The report of the Fulton committee (Cmnd. 3638, 1968) is generally regarded as giving the first real impetus to the development of accountable management in central government. It urged the civil service to modernize itself and move away from its 'amateurish' way of managing resources. This report was seen as the expression of a body of criticism that had first developed in the 1950s. At this time the complexity of administering a greatly expanded public sector became apparent. As economic growth deteriorated in the 1960s, the view that the civil service was not very competent at managing the economy started to spread and its generalistic culture (with an emphasis on the detached provision of balanced advice) no longer looked capable of 'producing officials with the kind of technical and managerial skills now thought by many to be necessary for effective performance of the functions of government' (Johnson 1985, p. 418). The case for reforming what politicians increasingly saw as a 'hostile' bureaucracy was strengthened by the growing interest in more rational and scientific means of planning and organizing work such as management by objectives, cost—benefit analysis and planning, programming and budgeting systems.

The pursuit of better managerial skills and the promotion of scientific management techniques also permeated other public-sector organizations. Major reorganizations of the managerial structures of the National Health Service and local authorities took place in 1974. Developments in American federal government such as planning, programming and budgetary systems and zero-based budgeting also began to influence local authority control systems in the 1970s, although they were not formally implemented on a nation-wide scale.

Formulating a 'grand strategy'

What has distinguished the Thatcherite reforms from its predecessors has been the maintenance of a strong political commitment to reform. This can best be illustrated by further analysis of the reforms in the civil service. The government's experiences with the civil service also played a key role in crafting out the major mechanisms by which change could be effected throughout the public sector.

Many of the recommendations of the Fulton Report were either never implemented or failed to impact on the Whitehall culture. Despite widespread critical views on the civil service there was no great rush to change. However, by the time of the 1979 election there had been significant shifts in public expectations. The relative economic decline in the 1970s eventually stimulated the desire not just to control but also to reduce public expenditure, and with the election of the Conservative government this became a fundamental element of government policy.

Once elected, one of Mrs Thatcher's first appointments was that of Lord Rayner (chairman of Marks and Spencers PLC) as 'Special Adviser on Efficiency', and this was quickly followed by the setting up of the 'Efficiency Unit', to assist in designing and implementing a programme to improve efficiency and eliminate waste in government. The savings identified by the Rayner scrutinies compared favourably with the initiatives of previous administrations, but the pressure for change continued to increase as a series of administrative reforms were introduced in 1981. These included the abolition of the civil service's pay mechanism (the Priestley Pay System) and, overall, sought to give the Treasury much greater control over civil service expenditure. These reforms were unexpected as it was widely believed that the government would be frightened by the prospective electoral consequences of 'sound money' and effect a U-turn (similar to the 'Barber boom' of 1972). However, things turned out differently. The government defeated the civil service strike arising from the abolition of the Priestley Pay System and

> the predicted U-turn did not take place; the Thatcher Government's blows continued to rain down on the civil service; and far from petering out the quest for 'efficiency' eventually came to be translated into something akin to a grand strategy in the form of the Financial Management Initiative (FMI). (Fry 1984, p. 323).

The Financial Management Initiative

The efficiency scrutiny programme's officially stated intention was to encourage and develop better management of resources by working with, rather than against, departments. While the official intention may well have been for the scrutinies to be more than low-level cost-cutting devices, publicity given to them in the early 1980s tended only to discuss cost savings (with no reference to effects on service quality). Furthermore, close links were often drawn between the scrutinies and cuts in the numbers employed in the public sector. A similar concern with costs and savings was evident in the economy drives undertaken in the NHS. For instance, in 1981–2 regional health authorities were required by the DHSS to make savings of 0.4 per cent of their total revenue allocations. Likewise, a major aim of the Local Government Planning and Land Act 1980 was to limit the extent of perceived overspending amongst local authorities.

Doubts about the merits of the government's policy towards the public sector were raised by the Treasury and Civil Service Select Committee, which reported in March 1982. The committee categorized resource management into three components, namely 'economy' (a concern with inputs and the acquisition of resources at the lowest cost), 'efficiency' (translating inputs into outputs and defined as obtaining the maximum output from a given level of resources) and effectiveness (the extent to which an organization's output has met its goals and objectives). The report stressed that proper resource management necessitated much greater attention being given to outputs and the effectiveness of performance. There was little point in doing the wrong things quickly or cheaply.

Part of the government's response was to launch the Financial Management Initiative (FMI) in May 1982. Its main aim was to:

promote in each department an organisation and system in which managers at all levels have:

(a) a clear view of their objectives and means to assess and, wherever possible, measure outputs or performance in relation to those objectives.

(b) well defined responsibility for making the best use of their resources, including a critical scrutiny of output and value for money and

(c) the information (particularly about costs), training and access to expert advice which they need to exercise their responsibilities effectively. (Cmnd 8616, 1982, para. 13).

That success was now to be judged in terms of outputs rather than reduced costs and inputs, and for managers to be conscious of results and not just costs suggested the start of a more comprehensive approach to resource management. However, the FMI is propounding a very traditional management by objectives view to organizational control. Management is portrayed as a scientific activity involving the specification of objectives, the measurement and monitoring of performance in relation to the chosen objectives and the taking of corrective action where appropriate.

It was noted above that the FMI has been held to be the government's 'grand strategy'. Indeed, all main central government departments were required to respond to the plans laid down in the White Paper. The FMI, though, is not the only initiative to be applied to the public sector since 1982. Its importance for the purposes of this chapter, however, is that its underlying philosophy is evident in a number of other initiatives. It could even be argued that this view of accountable management is becoming the dominant theme behind the reforms of the managerial and administrative functions in the public sector. For instance, cost improvement programmes in the NHS; value-for-money auditing in local authorities and central government departments; local financial management initiatives in schools and the increasing delegation of authority and power to school boards; and the wide-scale generation of performance indicators in nationalized industries, local authorities and the NHS, all embody an approach to management and control which is similar to that propounded by the FMI.

The remainder of this chapter examines the appropriateness of this approach in the public sector, particularly in areas where the majority of objectives are non-financial and performance is difficult to quantify. The question which has really stimulated the following analysis is: can it be this easy? Is the development of such systems all that it takes to improve public sector performance?

In search of effectiveness

A reading of the 'official' government literature on the FMI, or other initiatives such as value-for-money auditing, will reveal frequent reference to words such as the efficiency and effectiveness of performance. In a sense these concepts are portrayed in such a way that they appear to be synonymous with the common good.

However, what is notable by its absence is any adequate explanation of what such terms mean. The positive manner in which they are used tends to disguise their complex and controversial nature. Bluedorn (1980), for example, regards the topic of organizational effectiveness as a 'can of worms'. The White Papers on the FMI do acknowledge that the measurement of effectiveness in non-financial areas is complex, but the statements which explore effectiveness only get as far as saying it is concerned with achieving goals, which hardly seems sufficient given its fundamental importance to the FMI.

Defining organizational effectiveness

The most common, and the oldest, definition of effectiveness is the goal model which developed from theories viewing organizations as machines. Organizations are assumed to be goal seeking entities and their effectiveness is judged by their degree of goal attainment (a goal being defined as a desired state of affairs). A secondary but related assumption is that an organization's chances of attaining its goals are maximized by maximizing the number of 'goal-related' activities.

The government has clearly adopted this model, but despite its apparent simplicity it does have several operational problems. One such problem is the identification of an organization's goals. The easiest goals to identify are official goals — those stated in charters, annual reports or public statements by key executives and so on. However, they are often vague, and it has been argued that they serve a legitimating function to protect the organization from external pressure and do not have much impact on actual behaviour. A good example of the limitations of such goals is provided by research in local authorities (see Neilson 1986) which found that staff were hesitant to provide any clear unambiguous statements of future intentions because they would only be 'hostages to fortune', which could do them untold harm when the time came to account for their performance.

An alternative approach is to focus on operational goals. These goals include the unofficial goals pursued by various groups within the organization. However, it is difficult to identify such goals — particularly in large, complex organizations with a variety of sub-groups. Even if goals can be identified, the model of organizational effectiveness still has to assign relative weightings to each goal before effectiveness can be assessed. Ambiguity is therefore immediately introduced as the weights may vary depending on the views of the evaluator.

The weaknesses of the 'goal model' led to some effectiveness researchers utilizing a different approach — the 'open systems' model. This attempted to dismiss the concept of organizational goals and argued that effectiveness should be measured in terms of the organization's ability to exploit its environment in the acquisition of scarce and valued resources. It claimed that the most effective position was where an organization *optimizes* its resource procurement. An organization which maximized, rather than optimized, its resource procurement would not be effective as it would deplete its environment and destroy its capacity for self-renewal. This type of model, however, is rather weak theoretically. In particular, it fails to show how the optimal position should be determined. Also, in situations where several resources are required, there is a circular problem. The aim of the organization has been taken to be the optimization of the procurement of valued resources, yet the values of such resources depend on the aims of the organizations — that is, its goals!

Despite its limitations, the open-systems approach does provide a different insight into the effectiveness issue by promoting the idea that organizations are not machines but rather organic, social systems. The emphasis is shifted from goal maximization to the ability to cope with problems and uncertainty. The environment is seen as more fluid and the operational process less technical. Effectiveness is dependent not just on 'output criteria' (such as profitability) but also on 'process criteria' such as the capability to deal with conflict and the co-ordination of sub-units.

Operationalizing effectiveness

Given such differences in defining effectiveness, it is not surprising that when researchers have attempted to measure organizational effectiveness, there have been significant differences in the evaluation criteria used. The criteria used have included adaptability, productivity, satisfaction, profitability, resource acquisition, absence of strain, efficiency, environmental control, growth, employee retention and organizational survival. Some authors have called for better models, with more care to be taken over the selection of variables. However, others have argued that the problem is insurmountable. According to Hopwood (1979), 'there is no such thing as effectiveness *per se*':

Concepts of corporate effectiveness are socially constructed, their meanings and roles stemming from the articulation of particular social concerns, interests and demands and the specific contexts in which the concepts operate. And, as such interests and contexts vary and change over time, so do the prevailing notions of effectiveness (p. 82)

An appreciation of the subjectivity of the issue of organizational effectiveness is a critical first step in understanding the inherent limitations of the scientific management approach. Its practical significance for the FMI is more observable when it is linked with a second strand in the organizational effectiveness literature which focuses on the use of 'imperfect' performance measures in practice (as distinct from the search for 'real and true' measures). In this regard, the conclusions of Hopwood (1979) make for potent reading. He argues that performance is not affected by the selection of performance/effectiveness criteria in themselves, but by the way they are used and communicated within the organization. He stresses the importance of having an awareness of the potential power of accounting information — which rests in the selective visibility it can give to certain organizational actions and customs, in its ability to create facts out of uncertainty and to disguise underlying conflicts of opinion.

What is striking from the literature examining accounting in action is the ease with which it can be misused and generate dysfunctional decision making. For instance, a budgetary constrained style of management has been found to encourage decisions which ensure that the budget target is met, even if such actions could have a negative impact on longer-term profitability, for example where budgets are met by cuts in the quality of service an organization's reputation as a supplier of a high-quality product can be damaged, resulting in a reduced ability to earn future high rates of return. Hopwood summarizes such cases as ones where accounting information is used as an end in itself rather than a means to an end.

Another example of the misuse of performance measures can be provided by allegations of the manipulation of crime clear-up rates in a regional police force (see Davies 1986). It was claimed that detectives 'under pressure for results' were getting criminals in prison falsely to confess to unsolved crimes, or to crimes 'invented' by detectives. This was being done on the understanding that any confession would not lead to a prosecution. Another allegation concerned the bailing of one of the region's most active juvenile criminals ('a one-man crime wave') after he had been arrested for burglary. This was apparently acceptable as detectives knew

> that if they didn't oppose bail, he would go out and commit more offences, but they didn't mind as long as he agreed to ask for a lot of offences to be taken into consideration. It didn't matter that the people of Kent were burgled, as long as the books looked good. (Davies 1986, p. 11)

The effect of such practices on the crime clear-up rates was dramatic, with some divisions reporting nearly threefold increases. One senior detective was noted as stating that 'he now had so many crimes written off, that he could clear up every offence in his patch for the rest of the year' — although he would have to feed them through slowly so that 'the figures didn't go over the top' (Davies 1986, p. 11). Disciplinary action was eventually taken against certain officers, whose attempts to improve clear up rates bore little relation to an overall policy of reducing crime.

The separation between targets (means) and ultimate objectives (ends) is most pronounced where non-financial objectives predominate. As a consequence the information content of performance measures is lower and the risk of dysfunctional decision-making is increased. When it is also recognized that most organizations pursue multiple objectives, and that there are usually numerous measures of performance that can serve as surrogates for an overall objective (e.g. an objective of local labour relations can be measured by staff turnover rates, staff sickness days, number of days lost through strikes, number of complaints, etc.), the inherent subjectivity of any performance evaluation becomes more evident.

Changing the emphasis

Mayston (1985) provided evidence of improvements in the reliability and usefulness of performance indicators in the public sector. However, he concluded that in many parts of the public sector (education and social services in particular) the problems of using performance measures are so great that the emphasis placed on performance indicators should change. The major difficulties are that many costs and benefits accrue over a long period of time; that uncontrollable, environmental factors are likely to distort results and that small sets of summary statistics are being used to represent the whole distribution of performance variables in the absence of any explicit evaluation function. Given these problems, Mayston argued that general performance indicators would always suffer from natural imperfections and should not be used to evaluate performance directly. Rather, they should operate as pre-screening devices, serving as 'triggers for further investigation and possible remedial action'.

The strength of Mayston's conclusion is well illustrated by reference to the work of Sheldon (1986). Sheldon examined social-work effectiveness experiments between the periods of 1940 to 1970 and 1971 to 1986. The general conclusion from studies in the first period was that social work had little impact on clients. Sheldon, though, criticized these studies for failing to control adequately for the independent variables and for using a methodology which tended to cancel out individual effects. He likened the position of someone trying to use these findings to that of a football manager trying to determine a new game plan on hearing that his/her team had lost, but without knowing how the individual team members had played! The post-1971 studies were better organized and the results showed social workers as having much more positive impacts. Clearly, if it takes tightly controlled experiments to provide a reliable assessment of social-work effectiveness, it would appear that the type of broad, summary performance indicators, which are continually being produced in the public sector, should be used with great care. One way that has been suggested to overcome the difficulties facing those responsible for performance assessment is the adoption of a multifaceted approach to performance measurement. This would combine overall performance measures with more detailed and controlled studies of individual performance. The effectiveness literature also points to a clear role for training so that decision-makers become more aware of the limitations of accounting information.

The concept of management

The messages coming from the organizational effectiveness/performance measurement literature do much to bear out the statement by the government that the FMI cannot be expected to provide instant remedies for the ills in public-sector management. However, a number of writers have gone further and argued that the FMI is fundamentally flawed by its adoption of an impoverished concept of management.

It is unusual in the management control literature to find unqualified support for the accountable management systems continually advocated for the public sector. For instance, Hopper (1986) found it ironic that conventional management accounting techniques were being advocated in the public sector at a time when academic accountants have become increasingly sceptical about their use in the private sector. Much of the criticism is directed at the rigidity of the management function implicit in the reforms and the over-emphasis being placed on the design of information systems. According to Metcalfe and Richards (1984), the government is confusing management with control. Management really starts where control is problematic, where situations are encountered which defy the corpus of available knowledge. It is an interactive process requiring an ability to manage people, and not just information systems. As Earl and Hopwood (1980) note, 'it is the managers ... who put the management into Management Information Systems'.

The importance of being aware of the potential impact that individuals can have on control systems was apparent in the previous section. However, the management control literature points out that this is not just because of the subjectivity of accounting information, but also because accounting has the power to impact on organizational values. As Boland and Pondy (1983) note, 'Because accounting is symbolic, not literal, vague not precise, value loaded not value free, dealing with meanings not just things, it tries humans as moral agents' (p. 229). Thus changes in accounting and control procedures can present a threat to the existing organizational order and what is deemed to be appropriate behaviour. If such reforms are rejected by participants, the inherent subjectivity of accounting data lends itself conveniently to manipulation by the dissatisfied.

The management of cultural change

Harvey-Jones (1984), the ex-chairman of ICI PLC, commented that the art of management is to preserve the essential core of an organization's tradition in a period of change. This need to consider people is also a strong theme running through an analysis by Peters and Waterman (1982) of some of the most successful companies in the United States. Such findings are particularly worrying because it suggests that the FMI, with its mechanistic view of organizations is proposing a rather outdated view of even private-sector management.

This questioning of the technical conception of accounting information, and the importance of cultural considerations is well illustrated by studies of the government's reforms in the civil service since 1979. Plowden (1985) is concerned that the FMI, with its narrow view of management, could destroy the existing culture of the civil service without putting anything in its place. He sees the 'widespread and completely unprecedented industrial action of recent years' and the 'prevalence of leaks' as symptoms of a failure to properly manage reforms.

Similar conclusions are reached by Metcalfe and Richards (1984), who argue that a blind reliance on political clout, while important in initiating reforms, underestimates the extent to which the obstacles to reform are cultural. They believe that long-term change can best be achieved by policies which seek to establish change from within rather than by imposing change from above. In relation to the FMI and the civil service, they point out that to achieve long-term change, the FMI must overcome the civil service's 'disbelief system'. The main elements of this psychological defence mechanism include a belief that reforms fail, that efforts to establish change are always shortlived and a refusal to take management concepts and ideas seriously. 'In summary, the civil service has seen it all before' and it is not impressed by 'managerial jargon'. If the FMI fails to address this barrier to change, it is unlikely that it will succeed in getting its philosophy accepted by civil servants. For example, people who have seen it all before may view references to effectiveness in the FMI official papers rather sceptically and react in expectance of cost cuts rather than in a way which reflects the official spirit of the initiative.

The need for a thinking and insightful approach to reform is also emphasized by Johnson (1985). He notes that the logical extension of the accountability principles inherent in the FMI should mean that ministers cannot be held responsible for actions taken by civil servants. Johnson, though, doubts whether the government's pursuit of management will extend this far. He believes ministers will continue to prefer civil servants who can provide policy advice rather than managerial, administrative support. Furthermore, he argues that ministers will not want to see their scope for intervention narrowed as a result of a more autonomous and accountable civil service. Such a move would go against the belief to which politicians are naturally prone, 'that efficiency will be served only when they give an external impulse to the administrative machine'. The danger of ministers maintaining this stance is that civil servants would quite quickly realize that actions which may be efficient would not be followed if ministers perceived them to be 'politically inopportune. Consequently, civil servants would remain in the position of agents rather than of managers accepting responsibility for their actions, and would be unlikely to view the FMI in any positive light. The likelihood of such situations occurring would appear quite high when one observes the comment of Clucas, a former Permanent Secretary, that 'the more possible it is in any area of work to set an attainable objective, and realistically allocate a budget to it, the further away this is likely to be from current political interest and sensitivity' (Clucas 1982, p. 35). The consequence for the FMI if such attitudes continue to prevail, is that its intended reforms could be frustrated by the very people who introduced it.

A role for formal management control systems?

The merits of scientific management control systems have been analysed in the management/organizational behaviour literature. Hofstede (1981) developed a typology for management control, based on four main aspects of organizational activities: the ambiguity of objectives; the measurability of outputs; the understanding of the effects of managerial intervention; and the repetitiveness of activities. By considering alternative combinations of the four aspects, Hofstede derived six different types of management control. These ranged from the easiest form of control (routine control), where objectives are unambiguous, outputs measureable, effects of interventions known and activities repetitive, to the most difficult (political control) where objectives are ambiguous, the effects of management intervention unclear and where control depends on power structures and negotiation processes.

Hofstede concluded that traditional management control systems are really only applicable in situations of 'routine control', which are likely to be rare in the pubilc sector. From the previous discussions, many public-sector organizations appear better suited to the more complex forms of control which derive from social psychology disciplines and assume non-rational decision processes. Indeed, in ambiguous and uncertain environments research has shown that the prospects for organizational survival can be enhanced by less emphasis on rationality and consistency. For example, Hedberg and Jonsson (1978) argued that accounting systems which transmit experimental and semi-confusing information can help sensitize managers to the need for innovation and change and avoid creating a false atmosphere of certainty which can result in managers missing the vital signals for change. The creativity and inspiration necessary to survive in such environments is more likely to spring out of the more socially interactive forms of information processing which allow for choice and flexibility (see Earl and Hopwood 1980; Cooper, Hayes and Wolf 1981). This point has been used by Gray and Jenkins (1986) to cast doubt on the FMI's prospects for success. They highlight the interrelated nature of governmental activities and fear that the FMI will inhibit the effectiveness of government by subdividing departments into 'self-contained' cost-centres.

This analysis of the concept of management appears to deny any appropriate role for conventional control systems in the civil service (and the public sector in general). However, research suggests that they do have a role to play, because without them organizations can be vulnerable to claims that they are negligent, irrational and even unnecessary. According to Meyer and Rowan (1977), formal accounting systems can help to legitimize the actions of an organization and keep its participants satisfied. For example, a manager whose plans have failed, can fall back on conventional systems to demonstrate that procedures were prudent and decisions were made by rational means. This leads to the type of compromise position adopted by Cooper, Hayes and Wolf (1981), where formal control systems are deemed necessary, but that systems must also accommodate the flexibility and creativity necessary for operating in uncertain environments.

The implications for managers

The implication of the discussion so far for organizational management is that there is little to be gained from the implementation of ill-thought-out and inappropriate control systems. Conventional management control systems should not be used *en masse*. Control systems must adapt to the organization in which they are going to operate with sufficient attention being given to the existing organizational culture and the way information is currently used and processed. For long-term change to be achieved, reforms have to be seen as legitimate and accepted by managers and employees alike. Thus, just as performance effectiveness has been shown to be a difficult and subjective issue, so too has the whole process of organizing and managing the provision of public services. The continued promotion of terms such as 'efficiency', 'effectiveness', 'value for money' and the need for objectives and performance indicators should not be allowed to disguise the messages of the last two sections: there are no simple solutions to the complex problems of improving the performance and accountability of the public sector.

A political perspective

All of this analysis points to an uncertain future for the FMI if it continues to propound a mechanistic view of organizations. However, before examining the FMI in action, it is worth referring to the public policy and politics literature, particularly given the multi-disciplinary nature of the FMI. This provides another dimension to the analysis, but interestingly confirms many of the doubts expressed above.

Parsons (1988) focuses on the desire of initiatives like the FMI to encourage 'entreprenurial activity' in the public sector. In an intriguing article, he draws on the very literature that is supposed to be the bed-rock of the Thatcherite approach to government (the Austrian school of economics) to question its approach to reform in the public sector. The basic tenet of Parson's argument is that the ideological justification of entrepreneurial activity in the private sector (namely, the ability of the entrepreneur to create profit opportunities out of disequilibrium and uncertainty) is directly contradicted by the type of management systems being advocated for the public sector (which assume inappropriate levels of certainty and objectivity). He contrasts the government's approach in the public sector with its encouragement of entrepreneurship in the private sector — where the subjectivity of data and uncertainty of the environment precludes it from running the economy through a 'grand computer'.

Parsons concludes his assessment of recent public-sector initiatives with two examples of the government's apparent misunderstanding of the concept of entrepreneurship. First, he shows how an *ex-ante* perspective is critical to the entrepreneur — 'it is the acting according to the anticipated exploitation of profit opportunities which defines entrepreneurial activity'. This forward looking approach is not, however, promoted in the public sector where the *ex-post* perspective dominates in the pursuit of value for money and accountability. Second, Parsons stresses that the assumption that individuals can be singled out and decreed to be entrepreneurs is the complete antithesis of the Austrian school which states that entrepreneurs cannot be identified in advance of success.

Concern about the ideological basis of the government's reforms in the public sector has been expressed in another strand of the political literature. This is not concerned with analysing the limitations of the scientific management philosophy, but more with exposing the government's 'real' objectives of cutting the size of the public sector and expanding the role of the market in the provision of public services. Rhodes (1987) argues that central government policy towards local government since 1979 has been dominated by these objectives — which have resulted in capital and cash limits, the introduction of the block-grant system, the abolition of supplementary rates, the introduction of rate-capping and the privatization of local government services. To illustrate the concern of central government with narrow expenditure controls, he notes that between 1979 and 1983 there were seven major changes in the grant system.

Rhodes discusses the main consequences of these policies, which include a reduction in central–local negotiations; increasing litigation over the validity of expenditure controls or local authority policies; creative accounting whereby current expenditure is reclassified as capital expenditure to avoid 'overspending', the refusal of many local authorities, both Conservative and Labour controlled, to comply with central government's demands and a whole series of other unintended consequences (one of which revealed that the cuts in local authority expenditure had not been draconian and in many cases had been matched by increases in central government expenditure on complementary services).

Evidence of the desire to cut the size of the public sector without much regard for the quality of service can also be found in the literature on privatization. In this area, the government has frequently been accused of adopting a narrow cost function which does not take into account the full public costs of privatization, for example the cost of redundancy payments, loss of income tax and National Insurance, increased unemployment benefits (for those made redundant and not attaining other employment), increased housing benefits, cost of employment schemes and increased health-care costs caused by higher unemployment.

What is striking from this analysis is the lack of significance given to improving the effectiveness of local government services. Whether it can be used to describe the FMI's aims is open to question. After all, it should be remembered that the FMI was born out of a lack of concern with outputs and effectiveness, and a better assessment can be made of its real aims following the next section, which examines the FMI in action. However, even if the government does have a genuine intention to improve the all-round performance of the public sector, it should give due consideration to the 'political' literature. Research suggests that the views of Rhodes and others are more likely to be representative of public-sector employees' perceptions of government policy than the official rhetoric contained in White Papers.

Progress in financial management

This section looks beyond the officially stated intentions of the FMI, and the theoretical debate, to see what has happened as it has been applied in practice. Studies of the FMI are rather sparse, so this section will also draw on the results of similar initiatives in the NHS and in local authorities to provide a sufficiently comprehensive view of the effect of Thatcherite reforms on the management of public services.

The FMI in action

A White Paper (Cmnd 9297, 1984) reported on early experiences with the FMI. This concentrated on three main areas — meeting the needs of ministers and senior managers; managing programmes of expenditure; and budgeting control subjects. Progress had been slow in the first two areas. Difficulties had been experienced in using information systems. This was confirmed by the work of the Financial Management Unit (FMU 1985a) in the Department of the Environment, which found that a concern with functional details had hindered any significant use of the systems in policy analysis and performance assessment. Developments in the specification of objectives were only briefly reported on and reports of individual departments contained some rather surprising references. For instance, the Department of Education and Science reported that output measures were being developed from more refined *cost per graduate* data, which would be used to make across subject comparisons and to assist in the development of the future strategy for higher education. Similarly, in the Department of Transport, outputs for road building were to be measured in terms of annual mileage of roads constructed and the number of local by-pass schemes started. In both these situations, and numerous others reported in the White Paper, the measures are not saying anything abut the effectiveness of programmes (which was supposed to be one of the main purposes of the FMI). Just because more miles of road have been built does not mean that the construction programme has been effective, as anyone who has experienced the rush hour on the M25 will no doubt appreciate. A second report by the FMU (1985b) confirmed the difficulties that departments had experienced in formulating output measures but stressed the need for such efforts to continue.

Most progress has been made in the area of budgetary control systems, but these had not got much further than an analysis of departmental running costs. This led Gray and Jenkins (1986) to conclude that, despite the constant references by the government to the concepts of efficiency and effectiveness, the emphasis was still very much on costs and inputs. A report by the National Audit Office on the FMI (NAO 1986) contained basically the same message, stressing the need for the FMI to focus on programme expenditure and not just departmental running costs. The significance of this point is apparent when it is recognized that for 1986−7, gross running costs of the civil service amounted to £13,000 million compared to £100,000 million for direct central government expenditure.

The FMI also appears to have struggled to change attitudes, with departments not making any significant progress regarding the measurement of service quality and effectiveness. Several writers have attributed the lack of progress to the influence of the Treasury. However, a study by Flegmann (1985) of the new departmental select committees (set up to improve Parliament's ability to monitor and control the activities of government) suggests that the problem is more deep rooted than this. The Flegmann found very little interest in the FMI among the members of the committees, with few having read anything contained in the White Papers on the FMI and most expressing little interest in finance and value for money. With such a lack of top-level commitment to the FMI philosophy it is not surprising to find Fry (1988) concluding that the 'old civil service' recognizably survives.

A recent, detailed study by the author (Humphrey 1988) of the FMI in the Probation Service has also highlighted the difficulties of the task being set for the FMI. The period from 1982 to 1985 saw the setting of national and local statements of objectives, an attempt to devise a set of performance indicators and the undertaking of 'pilot-FMI studies' by the Probation Inspectorate. The lack of meaningful progress in applying the principles inherent in the FMI led eventually to the appointment, by the Home Office, in 1986, of private-sector consultants with the remit of devising a Financial Management Information System (FMIS) for the Service. The consultancy project is continuing at present, and is unlikely to be completed until 1990. While assessment of the relative merits of it are best left until then, the process by which work was undertaken in the first two stages of the assignment has important implications for the future of the FMI. By the end of the fact-finding, first stage of the assignment, the consultants had generated a strong sense of optimism within the civil service regarding its potential achievements. This atmosphere changed rapidly, however, once the detailed systems work got underway. Apart from a number of technical, measurement difficulties relating to probation work, many of the factors which hindered progress seemed to be a product of the nature of the consultancy assignment. The consultants struggled to remove fears of hidden agendas, especially amongst operational staff who were providing much of the source FMIS data. Rather than observing the collaboration of consultants and practitioners, what was more in evidence was the use of strategies to protect interests. Mistakes were made, but it is questionable whether they are not an inevitable consequence of a centrally funded assignment which created an intensely pressurized environment within which to work. The significance of the lack of progress is amplified when it is recognized that the consultants were a highly regarded, international firm and that much of the detailed prototype work was performed in a division of the Service relatively well versed in the use of information systems.

The National Health Service

Since 1979 the NHS has experienced cost-cutting drives, cost-improvement programmes, national performance indicators and reorganizations of its managerial structure. According to the National Audit Office (NAO 1986) the cost-cutting drives generated as much creative accounting (transfers from capital, etc.) as they did in savings. This led to the development of 'cost-improvement' programmes which tried to shift concern towards productivity improvements and away from pure cash savings, in line with the official philosophy of the FMI and the Griffiths Report's (DHSS 1983) recommendations concerning the management of the NHS. The NAO also reviewed the achivements of the cost-improvement programmes, and while it noted that they were the main thrust in the pursuit of value for money, it suspected that some savings were being made by reducing the standard of health care provided. The probability of districts passing off cuts in service quality as 'efficiency savings' is increased by the difficulties in measuring standards of health care. This places a strong emphasis on performance review procedures, but the NAO found that in several districts such procedures were not being operated properly. There was evidence that regional health authorities were passing on data to the DHSS without submitting them to any form of check.

Developments with performance indicators have had a similarly troubled path. The first set of national indicators, published in 1983, was heavily criticized for being too cost orientated. A revised package of indicators, issued in 1985, was supposed to give more attention to service quality matters but came in for much of the same criticisms. One significant difference between the two sets of indicators was the numbers produced, which rose from 123 to 418. While this has not reached the amazing numbers of 3,500, indicators produced by the US Federal Government Programme, it has still been criticized for accepting without question that information is a good thing (Smith 1987) and for not properly assessing the relative costs and benefits of performance indicator packages. Pollitt (1985) questioned the impact of the indicators on the operational activities of the NHS when noting that junior staff had frequently been allocated the task of analysing the indicators at the district level.

A major failing of the managerial reforms in the NHS has been the inability to get clinicians involved. This is particularly important given that clinicians largely dictate the use of NHS resources. The majority of cost-improvement programmes have focused on areas such as catering, domestic and gardening services and energy conservation. These are not normally regarded as the mainstream operations of the NHS. Similarly, none of the performance indicators refer to the effectiveness of treatment and measures using the concepts of 'avoidable deaths' have only just started to be produced in 1988. Bourn and Ezzamel's (1986) analysis suggests that the push for financial accountability has had little impact on the overriding doctrine of clinical freedom and efforts for improved value for money have been pushed to the periphery.

Much of the NHS's experiences with the pursuit of accountable management serves to emphasize the points made earlier in this chapter regarding the need for reforms to give sufficient attention to the organizational contexts in which they are going to operate. Creative accounting, cuts in service quality, lack of reviews, little used performance indicators and so on are indicative of the failure of government initiatives, to date, to be seen as legitimate and to impact on the existing culture of the NHS.

Local authorities

The scale of change required to produce the managerial, entrepreneurial culture sought by initiatives like the FMI is made clear in a study by Hamblin and Adams (1983) which focused on supervisors of manual workers employed by local authorities. Many supervisors found it impossible to develop realistic effectiveness criteria. They did not expect to be rewarded for better performance and saw little incentive to improve performance. Hamblin and Adams concluded that any managerial reforms would struggle to improve performance unless the wider character of local government was altered. Further, supervisors' experiences were that cuts had been, and always would be, based on arbitrary decisions of government (central or local) and not on the relative effectiveness of their performance.

Concern about cost cutting has also hindered the development and impact of value-for-money auditing, a legally required element of the external audit of local authorities since 1982. Neilson (1986) found that value-for-money auditing was seen by councillors and finance/executive officers as synonymous with cost reduction (even given that the legislation requires auditors to examine the efficiency and effectiveness of service provision) and that auditors' recommendations were not being integrated into the managerial and operational processes.

These suspicions had been strengthened by some of the early actions of the Audit Commission when it published 'spending' league tables and singled out those local authorities spending above average, even though a low league position could also indicate poor value for money. The lack of attention to effectiveness issues was confirmed by the work of Grimwood and Tomkins (1986). Other studies, though, have noted that the Audit Commission has not been helped by existing local authority systems (which themselves gave scant attention to effectiveness measures) and by the action of the government in requiring local authority annual reports to include cost comparisons with similar authorities (but with no such requirement for service quality comparisons).

Earlier in this chapter, a case was made out for detailed studies of performance, capable of controlling for the wide variety of independent variables which influence service effectiveness. Value-for-money audits are ideally placed to assume this role, but instead, it would appear that they are doing more to confirm beliefs regarding cost cutting. However, the Audit Commission is showing increasing awareness of the need to rectify this position and has stated several times that it wanted more emphasis placed on service effectiveness. It has also made public its dissatisfaction with some of the private-sector accounting firms undertaking VFM audits, which even led to the drawing up of a secret list of firms to be replaced. Although this was eventually shelved in 1986, it is indicative of the increasing pressure being placed on value-for-money auditors to broaden the scope of their work. Some of the Audit Commission's special studies have also illustrated a desire to provide the detailed investigations of performance so recommended by the literature. A report on care for the elderly (Audit Commission 1985) made repeated reference to the need for detailed research and for practitioners to get more involved in assessing the effectiveness of the services they are providing.

Despite such developments, scepticism remains as to their likely impact on the dominance of cost-concerns. Whynes (1987) argues that in an atmosphere of financial stringency detailed research will not prove attractive because it is not immediately productive. The desire for quick results and easy solutions is likely to encourage inadequate and inappropriate reforms. He sees reports by the Audit Commission (which even they accept are rapidly produced and often, by necessity, are quite narrow in perspective) being used as hard-and-fast rules rather than as guidelines to assist future practice. Similarly, Pollitt (1986) believes that the push for a greater emphasis on service effectiveness will not be taken up because it reduces the political attractiveness of VFM auditing and like minded initiatives:

> For it would then become clear that the whole process was irredeemably political. It would be seen that the assessment of the performance of a complex public service can be neither neutral (value free), nor simple, nor complete if left to the 'experts' and a few interested politicians. (p.28)

One possible explanation for the government maintaining a cost-cutting atmosphere is that it is a way of putting pressure on local managers to take the initiative and improve service performance through their own locally developed schemes. Costs may be the only feasible way for the government to direct policies and set targets because, at present, it is the major component of information passing from local to central administration. In other words, the government is setting the boundaries within which local management operates. It is doubtful, though, whether the FMI can be viewed as a catalyst to reform, given the emphasis placed on it by the government as a long-term process. The FMI is too prescriptive of what management should be doing to serve such a role.

Even if the catalyst argument is accepted, this chapter has hopefully indicated how such an approach can generate adverse consequences. The work of Burgess (1986) is relevant in this regard. He examined attempts by Cambridgeshire Education Authority to apply FMI principles through the introduction of decentralized, school-based, budgeting systems. Burgess (acting as an independent, external assessor) saw much merit in Cambridgeshire's policy of not seeking cuts in expenditure. Joint consultation between officers and teachers helped remove any lingering cost-cutting fears and created confidence in the project's ability to improve educational effectiveness. Savings made by schools enabled them to employ more teachers, and in-service training was also expanded. Burgess notes that much innovation was generated by participant teachers, but he provides little detail of how improvements in effectiveness were monitored. Even so, the apparent success of the scheme can be monitored by the willingness of other schools in the region to participate. The spirit generated by this project stands in contrast to that reported by Rhodes (1987) when commenting on the prevalence of the practice in local authorities of off-loading cuts to the periphery (just as in the NHS). According to Rhodes, such behaviour had been encouraged by the inadequate approach of the government, which had made it more expedient for local authorities to protect services by off-loading, than to spend time making them more efficient and effective. Burgess supported the call for a more considerate, less deterministic and centralistic approach to reform and saw danger in the government acting in a more traditional vein.

> In order to act at all, central government has to eliminate differences — and in doing so, it eliminates the experience which should inform its actions. One is left with an increasingly ignorant central government, which becomes remote, filled with fear and distrust for the service it finds so intractable. . . . The paradox is that central government responds to the disintegration it causes by being more dictorial. Pursued much longer, this will lead through chaos to collapse. (p. 23)

Recent indications that the government is planning to introduce league tables of performance indicators by which to assess school performance would suggest that the more enlightened approach to reform is still some way off.

Concluding comments

It would appear that to date the FMI, and similar initiatives such as value-for-money auditing, have failed to shift the balance away from inputs to a consideration of service effectiveness. While apparently being set up to promote the latter concern, they have struggled to make any real progress and have frequently been seen in much the same light as earlier, more cost-orientated approaches. As a consequence, the barriers facing future progress with these reforms are twofold: not only have they to tackle the difficult issue of service effectiveness, but the reforms have got to be introduced in such a way that overcomes the prevalent fears of hidden agendas.

The literature abounds with suggestions as to what needs to be done — including the undertaking of detailed research studies, exercising positive discrimination in favour of outputs and service quality, the use of more adaptive and responsive information systems, better training programmes, the establishment of a less-pressurized atmosphere in central—local relations and a greater involvement of the consumer to promote better accountability within government. While many of these recommendations have been derived from detailed investigations of the failings of various public-sector initiatives, it could be argued that as yet they remain somewhat untested and will also struggle to reform 'stubborn and hostile bureaucracies'. However, what they have in their favour is a proper appreciation of the complexity of the task of improving public-sector performance. A recognition that there are few simple solutions is a crucial first step in building a firm base for a reforming programme. Further, as this literature becomes more widely known, it will become increasingly difficult for the government to refute claims that its main concern is cost cutting, the longer its approach fails to incorporate the findings of detailed research.

The basic messages of this chapter are equally relevant to those providing and managing services at the operational level. People should not allow themselves to be deceived by the apparent objectivity of performance data. They need to learn how to exercise discretion in the management of staff — in the same way that practitioners do with their clients. With regard to determining a strategy for responding to government initiatives, the implications depend on practitioners' perceptions of the governments 'cost-cutting' intentions. For those who see cost reduction as the prime aim, regardless of officially stated intentions, the mystifying properties of performance measurement can be seen as a useful asset in a policy of non-cooperation. This avenue of thought can also find comfort in Fry's (1988) observation that the 'old' civil service remains largely intact after eight years of apparently resisting all that can be thrown at it by the Thatcher administration.

Alternatively, if the concern with effectiveness is seen as genuine, the lack of progress to date points clearly to the need for practitioners to get involved in investigating, identifying and promoting the more effective ways of working. Indeed, reforms such as the FMI could be seen as ideally set up for practitioners to promote their own, professional criteria, and they do not have to take a passive role in the reforming process. There is evidence to suggest that the government would prefer practitioners to develop their own effectiveness measures and a lack of progress on this front could lead to the criteria of others being imposed. It is through an extension of this argument that some writers, such as Sheldon (1986) and McWilliams and Pease (1990), have argued that practitioners should take an active role in monitoring their effectiveness, regardless of the intentions of the government. This approach sees the pursuit of better service provision as the natural and legitimate responsibility of all staff, and management in particular. It also doubts whether future governments, of any doctrine, are likely to reduce the pressure on the public sector and sees the issue as one of 'measure yourself or be measured'.

For those remaining wary of the need to get involved in performance measurement, it is worth noting Sheldon's observation on the effectiveness of social work. The research studies he reviewed showed that social work was most effective when a 'thick wedge of influence' was brought to bear on a problem. Sheldon fears that the 'spinning plate' philosophy encouraged in today's cost-orientated world (where social workers give limited attention to many clients and try to keep problems (plates) from 'wobbling too dangerously') is likely to make social workers increasingly ineffective. In his view, it was up to social workers, and public-service professionals in general, to take the initiative. A fear that more effective organizations are likely to experience cuts as they subsidize more ineffective ones has been countered on the grounds that they will be better able to defend themselves by being aware of how their resources are utilized. This provides the organization with a defence mechanism additional to the protection provided by a subjective performance reporting process.

The main purpose of this chapter has been to open up the debate on the performance and accountability of the public sector, and to highlight its complex nature. It would therefore be inappropriate to close by putting forward a purported, definitive solution regarding future strategy. Given the nature of the subject, it is doubtful that one exists. Instead, it is hoped that the material covered will stimulate readers to adopt questioning and searching approaches to this issue in the future, and thereby help to generate an enlightened reforming mood in the public sector.

References

Audit Commission (1985) *Managing Social Services for the Elderly More Effectively*, A report by the Audit Commission, February, London: HMSO.

Bluedorn, A.C. (1980) 'Cutting the Gordian Knot: a critique of the effectiveness tradition in organisational research', *Sociology and Social Research*, vol. 64, no. 3, pp. 477–96.

Boland, R.J. and LR. Pondy (1983) 'Accounting in organisations: a union of natural and rational perspectives', *Accounting, Organizations and Society*, pp. 223–35.

Bourn, M. and M. Ezzamel (1986) 'Organisational culture in hospitals in the NHS', *Financial Accountability and Management*, vol. 2, no. 3, pp. 203–25.

Burgess, T. (1986) 'Cambridgeshire's financial management initiative for schools', *Public Money* June, pp. 21–4.

Clucas, Sir K. (1982) 'Parliament and the civil service', in RIPA (ed.) 'Parliament and the Executive', London: RIPA.

Cmnd 3638 (1968) *The Civil Service*, London: HMSO.

Cmnd 8616 (1982) *Efficiency and Effectiveness in the Civil Service*, London: HMSO.

Cmnd 9297 (1984) *Progress in Financial Management in Government Departments*, London: HMSO.

Cooper, D.J., D. Hayes and F. Wolf (1981) 'Accounting in organized anarchies: understanding and designing accounting systems in ambiguous situations', *Accounting, Organizations and Society*, vol. 6, no. 3, pp. 175–91.

Davies, N. (1986) 'Crime: the great cop-out', *The Observer*, 13 July.

DHSS (1983) *Report of the Inquiry into Management Arrangements in the National Health Service*, London: DHSS.

Earl, M.J., and A.G. Hopwood (1980) 'From management information to information management', in H.C. Lucas Jr, F.F. Land, T.J. Land and K. Supper (eds.) *The Information Systems Environment*, Amsterdam: North Holland.

Flegmann, V. (1985) 'Public spending: too selective', *Public Money*, June.

FMU (1985a) *Top Management Systems*, Financial Management Unit, June.

FMU (1985b) *Policy Work and the FMI*, Financial Management Unit, June.

Fry, G.K. (1984) 'The development of the Thatcher Government's "Grand Strategy" for the civil service: a public policy perspective', *Public Administration*, vol. 62, Autumn, pp. 322–35.

Fry, G.K. (1988) 'The Thatcher Government, the financial management initiative and the 'new' Civil Service', *Public Administration*, vol. 66, Spring, pp. 1–20.

Gray, A.G. and W.I. Jenkins (1986) 'Accountable management in British central government: some reflections on the financial management initiative', *Financial Accountability and Management*, vol. 2, no. 3, pp. 171–86.

Grimwood, M. and C. Tompkins (1986) 'Value for money auditing: towards incorporating a naturalistic approach', *Financial Accountability and Management*, vol. 2, no. 4, pp. 251–72.

Hamblin, A.C. and P. Adams (1983) 'Criteria of effectiveness in local authorities: the position of supervisors in public and private organisations', *Local Government Studies*, vol. 9, no. 2, pp. 21–34.

Harvey-Jones, J.H. (1984) 'The development of management as an art in the private sector', *Royal Society of Arts Journal*, May.

Hedberg, B. and S. Jonsson (1978) 'Designing semi-confusing information systems for organizations in changing environments', *Accounting, Organizations and Society*, vol. 3, no. 1, pp. 47–64.

Hofstede, G. (1981) 'Management control of public and not-for-profit activities', *Accounting, Organizations and Society*, vol. 6, no. 3, pp. 193–211.

Hopper, T. (1986) 'Private sector problems posing as public sector solutions', *Public Finance and Accountancy*, October.

Hopwood, A.G. (1979) 'Criteria of corporate effectiveness', in M. Brodie and R. Bennet (eds.) *Managerial Effectiveness*, London: Thames Valley Regional Management Centre.

Humphrey, C.G. (1988) 'The financial management initiative (FMI) and the Probation Service, 1982–87', paper presented at the EIASM Public Sector Workshop, Maastricht, The Netherlands, December.

Johnson, N. (1985) 'Change in the Civil Service: retrospect and prospects', *Public Administration*, vol. 63, Winter, pp. 415–33.

McWilliams, W. and K. Pease (1990) 'Probation practice and an end to punishment', *The Howard Journal*, vol. 29, no. 1, pp. 14–24.

Mayston, D.J. (1985) 'Non-profit performance indicators in the public sector', *Financial Accountability and Management*, vol. 1, no. 1, pp. 51–74.

Metcalfe, L. and S. Richards (1984) 'The impact of the efficiency strategy', *Public Administration*, vol. 62, no. 4, pp. 439–54.

Meyer, J.W. and B. Rowan (1977) 'Institutionalized organization: formal structure as myth and ceremony', *American Journal of Sociology*, vol. 83, no. 2, pp. 340–63.

National Audit Office (1986) *The Financial Management Initiative*, HC 588 (1985−86), London: HMSO.

Neilson, A. (1986) 'Value for money auditing in local government', *Public Money*, June, pp. 52−4.

Parsons, S. (1988) 'Economic principles in the public and private sectors', *Policy and Politics*, vol. 16, no. 1, pp. 29−39.

Peters, T.J. and R.H. Waterman (1982) *In Search of Excellence: Lessons from America's Best-run Companies*, New York: Harper and Row.

Plowden, W. (1985) 'What prospects for the civil service?', *Public Administration*, vol. 63, Winter, pp. 393−414.

Pollitt, C. (1985) 'Measuring performance: a new system for the National Health Service', *Policy and Politics*, vol. 13, no. 1, pp. 1−15.

Pollitt, C. (1986) 'Beyond the managerial mode: the case for broadening performance assessment in government and the public services'. *Financial Accountability and Management*, vol. 2, no. 3, pp. 155−70.

Rhodes, R.A.W. (1987) 'Mrs Thatcher and local government: intentions and achievements' in L. Robins (ed.) *Political Institutions in Britain*, London: Longmans.

Sheldon, B. (1986) 'Social work effectiveness experiments: review and implications, *British Journal of Social Work*, vol. 16, pp. 223−42.

Smith, P. (1987) 'Performance indicators in the National Health Service', *Public Money*, March, pp. 35−9.

Whynes, D.K. (1987) 'On assessing efficiency in the provision of local authority services', *Local Government Studies*, vol. 13, no. 1, pp. 53−68.

Chapter 10

MRP, JIT and automated manufacturing and the role of accounting in production management

JIM MACKEY

Over the last decade, traditional manufacturing practices have been challenged and are being replaced. This chapter traces how the evolution of manufacturing processes has impacted upon accounting systems. Four significant manufacturing environments are considered: traditional, materials requirement (resources) planning (MRP), just-in-time manufacturing (JIT) and automated manufacturing. Each is examined with respect to three vital aspects of accounting systems: usefulness, measurability and the cost of information.

The traditional model

Traditional manufacturing processes evolved from the breaking up of craft production systems into a series of small individual tasks. Consider, for example, the making of a musket. The craft approach lay in one highly skilled artisan directly making or supervising several apprentices making a complete weapon from stock to barrel. The factory approach mechanized and divided this process into a series of relatively simple activities, each of which could be easily taught and controlled with less-skilled labourers. Similar machines were grouped together; for example, gunstock making, barrel making, and assembly. These functions evolved into individual departments and usually formed the basis for cost centres.

In manufacturing, the flow of materials through the plant defines the production technology. Two production extremes exist — a job shop and a flow shop. Job shops utilize job costing, and flow shops employ process costing. Most traditional manufacturing falls somewhere between these extremes. Understanding these two extremes is important because recent innovations shift complex, costly job shops to more of a flow process.

Figure 10.1 compares the materials flow of these two extremes. Arrows

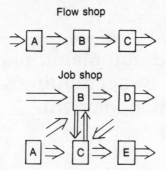

Figure 10.1   Comparison of materials flows of job and flow shop

represent flows of work-in-process, while each box is a cost centre. For example, in a job shop, we would start in the wood shop for stock making, A, then progress to B for sanding, then to C to add the stock and fixtures, then back to B to sand and finish, and finally, to D for testing. Other products might follow a different path through the process.

Consider a more modern illustration comparing a typical job shop with a flow shop. The job shop, for example, may make custom store fixtures while the flow shop processes corn. Each square represents a machine group. The arrows illustrate the flow of work-in-process. In the job shop each job or store fixture may follow a unique path through the production process, spending different times in each department. On the other hand, all jobs follow the same sequential route for the corn processor — department A to B to C. Some jobs may spend more or less time randomly at each stage because of varying quality of inputs or outputs, but the flow of products is identical. To get a better idea of how this flow approach allows us to classify products, examine Figure 10.2.

Figure 10.2 represents a product-process matrix. The vertical axis identifies the extremes of product flow; while the horizontal axis qualifies products from custom, like store fixtures, rocket shuttles *versus* commodities, such as corn, oil or forest products. Electronics may employ elements of both types of process since the more varied the product, the greater the management complexity. In general, job shops stand as the more difficult management challenge.

Table 10.1 illustrates some of the environmental differences between job and flow manufacturing. This represents how new management changes are moving from job to less costly flow shop environments. The impact on the usefulness, accuracy and cost of accounting systems because of this trend must be understood. Consequently, this chapter begins with the traditional environment and moves successively to more recent management systems.

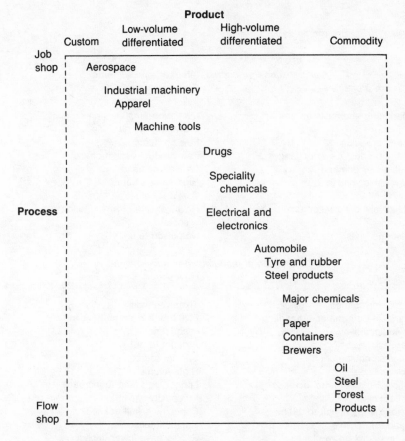

Figure 10.2 Traditional product–process matrix (source: Taylor *et al*. 1981)

Management of the process in the traditional environment

Five key management issues are the management of raw materials, buffer work-in-process, cost/responsibility centres, the overall production system, and finished goods and marketing (see Figure 10.3). The analysis here concentrates on the job shop environment as it evolves with technological innovations.

The management of raw materials

Three management issues — quality, delivery, and cost — should be considered for purchases. Conventionally, purchasing buys large inventory stocks to

Table 10.1 Environments

Comparison of product and market environments

Custom products	*Commodity products*
Marketing emphasis on product features	Marketing emphasis on product availability and price
Many products	Few products
Many product design changes	Few product design changes
Consumer demand	Derived demand
Low sales volume	High sales volume
High unit value	Low unit value
Relatively low transportation costs	Relatively high transportation costs
Discrete units	Non-discrete units

Comparison of manufacturing environments

Job shop	*Flow shop*
Variable routings	Fixed routings
Variable path material handling equipment	Fixed path material handling equipment
Process layout	Product layout
Flexible equipment	Specialized equipment
Low volume	High volume
Shorter lead time to increase capacity	Longer lead time to increase capacity
Capacity is difficult to define	Capacity is well defined
Labour intensive	Capital intensive
Strikes shut down plant	Strikes have lower impact
Skilled craftsmen who build the product	Highly specialized, trained operators who monitor and control process equipment
Significant work-in-process inventories	Low work-in-process inventories
Often warehouse work in process	No warehousing of work in process
Jobs not overlapped between work centres	Jop overlapping
Equipment failure shuts down a machine	Equipment failure shuts down the plant
Late receipt of a purchased part delays a customer order	Raw material shortage for a basic raw material shuts down the plant

---

Source: Taylor *et al.* 1981

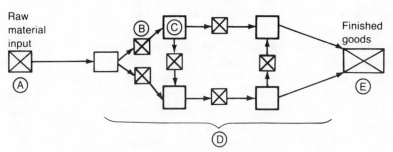

Figure 10.3 Management of the traditional manufacturing process

smooth production and create purchasing economies. The traditional manufacturing environment operated under considerable uncertainty with respect to delivery dates and quality of materials. Excessive inventories allowed management a cushion or buffer, so that manufacturing operations could be carried on despite these uncertainties. Large inventory stocks separated the purchasing function from manufacturing, thus allowing purchasers considerable freedom in negotiating delivery, quality and price. High inventory levels are an underlying assumption of traditional manufacturing. They permit the day-to-day operations of manufacturing and purchasing to be, for the most part, separately controlled activities. Consequently, accounting measures concentrate on the remaining controllable issues of purchasing budgets and price variances. Traditionally, accounting tends to ignore delivery and minor quality problems because these are coped with by excess inventories. Inventories are global investments in the management of the overall factory and are measured by return-on-investment (ROI) ratios.

The management of work-in-process (WIP)

Quality, delivery or output quantity failures of one cost centre can influence the performance of other cost centres. However, high levels of buffer work-in-process inventories between work centres allows for relatively independent activities which reduces problems for shop-floor (cost centre) management. A large number of jobs queued-up waiting to be worked upon allows department managers to pick and choose among jobs; to match men to machines; to batch together compatible job set-ups, while deferring less suitable jobs. This strategy, however, creates problems with scheduling production because jobs tend to get lost or delayed, often forcing costly expediting. Traditional accounting provides few incentives to actively reduce these inventories, but rather anticipates excessive inventories so that independent cost-centre performance is measurable.

The management of cost centres

Within cost centres, additional factors regarding labour and machinery must be considered by shop-floor managers. Early manufacturing systems assume that direct labour often suffers from low skills, low motivation levels and high absenteeism; while machinery often proves unreliable and produces inconsistent quality. On the other hand, these same machines could often handle a variety of products and activity rates. However, set-ups can be costly and require skilled labour; consequently batching jobs (grouping jobs with similar set-ups) provides opportunities for cost savings. And these potential savings motivate management to keep high levels of WIP.

Accounting systems measuring responsibility cost centres frequently evaluate shop-floor managers in terms of efficiency, based upon the relationship between inputs and outputs. Long production runs offset expensive set-ups and contribute to higher input—output efficiencies. Consequently, budgets and variances can create situations where meeting production schedules are of secondary importance to shop-floor managers. Further, budget setting motivates managers to pad their budgets. Finally, managers often ignore the efficient use of WIP on the shop floor because this is rarely evaluated. In fact, larger WIP levels, as illustrated previously, makes cost centre management easier. Again, WIP levels stand as an underlying non-quantified assumption of the traditional operating environment and its accounting systems.

Management of the overall factory

Overall factory management involves the co-ordination of purchasing, manufacturing and sales, as well as the efficient scheduling of production through the shop. A master production schedule, similar to the accountant's master budget, drives capacity planning of the scheduling and co-ordinating of jobs. The nature, however, of the production flow leads to significantly different management difficulties.

Flow shops possess less varied production and sequentially linked machine centres (see Fig. 10.1). A fully loaded 'bottleneck' department determines short-term capacity. For most flow shops, the bottleneck usually lies in the same easily identified 'bottleneck' department. Job shops, on the other hand, present a more difficult problem, since they produce a variety of products. In this situation bottlenecks float (i.e. move among departments) as the demand for products change. Maximum utilization of machinery, however, usually requires a uniform flow of production to all departments. This flow can be comfortably managed in a flow shop by balancing work centres, but it is more difficult in a job shop. The traditional job shop solution 'pushes' more jobs (WIP) into the workplace to ensure that all work centres have the materials necessary to keep busy. This strategy, while eliminating one problem, leads to many others, including long due dates and expediting jobs. Expedited jobs are given first preference and are forced through the shop, often ignoring batching economies.

In this environment, management accounting begins with a master budget to test the feasibility of the *pro forma* income and to communicate to each manager the performance required through a series of sub-schedules. Two critical purposes, therefore, are met by accounting budgets — planning and the control of activities. Annual budgets impose a longer-term perspective that influences the nature of factory management. Accrual accounting becomes a relevant issue because performance is gauged against annual *pro forma* financial statements. Since full costs constitute a part of their performance evaluation, management must consider these in its decisions. This consideration does not contradict the usefulness of relevant or marginal cost analysis, but rather emphasizes the influence that accrual accounting may have on the behaviour of factory management.

Once budgets are determined, short-term decision-making becomes an issue for consideration. The accountant faces two concerns: the potential for the distortion of decision-making, because accrual accounting is employed in incentive systems; and reconciling an accrual data base with relevant costs.

The management of finished goods and marketing

The management of finished goods and marketing also reflects the manufacturing environment. Marketing management deals with uncertain demand and manufacturing, long manufacturing lead times, quality and warranty problems. These conditions can all be lessened by large amounts of finished goods thereby allowing marketing to decide retailing issues relatively independent of manufacturing. However, pricing and product profitability using the accountant's costs present a problem. Since accountants usually define and apply overhead costs using only one allocation base (e.g. direct labour hours, direct labour costs or machine hours), many costs that vary with production levels are classified as fixed. Set-up costs provide a good example. Set-up costs vary with the number and similarity of jobs, but not with the number of units in the job. For accounting purposes, set-up costs can be treated as fixed or variable per unit. Both treatments can be incorrect for pricing but they do not normally lead to material errors for financial statement purposes. To provide accurate pricing data, more than one cost-basis must be employed, and the criteria for costing precision should be related to pricing requirements.

Other problems created by full costing result from the allocation of fixed costs. For many companies, inventory valuations represent only an approximate cost of production and may not be suitable for the decisions at hand. With these management uses in mind, how do traditional accounting systems influence management?

The influence of accounting on traditional manufacturing

If accounting profits serve as a basis for factory manager evaluation, then managers feel compelled to increase production in spite of weak sales demand. The more units produced, the lower the fixed cost allocated to each unit, and hence the lower the production cost per unit. Suppose the set-up cost is £100. A job lot of 100 units would bear a charge of £1 per unit while a job lot of 200 units would cut this cost per unit in half. Full costing which uses accruals motivates factory managers to fully utilize fixed capacity and use long production runs. Both conditions' lead to high inventory levels.

Other problems can arise. Cost control systems can create a fascination with the efficient use of the direct materials and labour. Since costing systems have become dominated by the materiality standards of financial statements, overhead costs remain less precise than for direct costs. Traditional accounting defines fixed and variable costs by their response to changes in a specific activity base such as units of output for homogeneous products, or direct labour hours for heterogeneous products. Virtually any costs not varying directly with the activity base will normally be pushed into the overhead burden. Few companies demand detailed standards for overhead costs. This encourages managers to shift costs into overhead categories less easily measured and controlled by the costing systems. Accounting systems, however, are not the sole reason for the increase in overhead costs; accounting cost control for overheads simply is not as precise as for direct costs.

When the underlying traditional manufacturing assumptions change, responsibility accounting can cause a number of motivational problems. First, the separation of management functions can create hostility and internal competition, since each manager is responsible for a theoretically distinct set of controllable costs. The accounts, representing each manager's defined activities, measure performance. New production economies generated more by teamwork than individual effort violate these conditions of unambiguously defined activities. Second, when shop-floor managers understand the process better than higher-level management, evaluation based upon budgets motivates game-playing between shop-floor and upper management and so creates slack or the existence of excess resources. Since negotiated cost budgets serve as the basis for evaluating shop-floor management, managers have an interest in making the cost budgets easily attainable. A third motivational problem relates to innovation and improvement. The original conditions under which standard costing evolved assumed that the industrial engineer (or management) understood the process as the 'one best way' to do the job. This thought process can be regarded as innovation from above. Implicit historical assumptions about quality (erratic), reliability (uncertain) and industrial reations (hostile) also existed. Consequently, while direct labour and shop-floor management may be able to innovate for improved efficiency (innovation from below), they may be discouraged to do so by the budgetary consequences of their innovations, namely the subsequent tightening of cost standards.

Most of these problems stemmed not from the need for accounting systems to provide cost data for financial statements, but rather from the assumptions of traditional manufacturing management.

Materials requirements planning

MRP, first introduced by IBM in 1970, essentially substitutes excessive inventories for better information systems. MRP schedules the production of jobs through the factory so that managers no longer require excessive WIP to compensate for job-scheduling problems between cost centres. MRP does not deviate from most of the previous underlying assumptions about co-ordinating machine centres. Instead, MRP co-ordinates the flow of materials by releasing work orders for parts to the factory based upon a master production schedule *and* the current number and location of parts in the factory. Figure 10.4 presents an overview of the information base used by MRP.

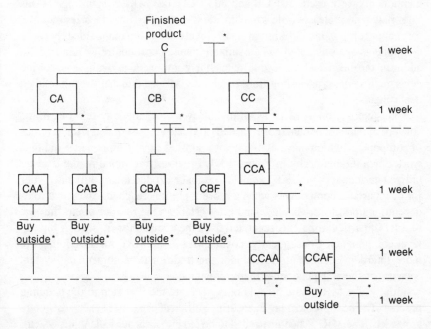

* Inventory stocks

Figure 10.4 The information base of MRP

A sales forecast or a specific order specifies that sales of product C will average 100 units per week. A version of the economic order quantity (EOQ) model, an economic lot size (ELS) model, determines that 500 units should be produced in one job lot. Bills of material for each product, in our case product C, are programmed into the computer. The hierarchy in the exhibit represents the information included in a typical bill of materials.

The computer records the number of inventory components in each form along with time standards for moving, waiting, setting-up and running each component. This information allows production to be time phased or co-ordinated so that at the final assembly of C sufficient CA, CB and CC components (i.e. 505 of each) will be ordered. The 505 parts allow for approximately a 1 per cent spoilage rate on assembly. In this sample, each level of production is assumed to take the same amount of time; for example, one week. This assumption need not always be considered true and, indeed, is highly unlikely to be the case in practice. The computer, however, can easily handle the variety that our illustration cannot.

Scattered throughout the factory may be isolated sets of subcomponents left over from previous orders or from the need to produce certain specified lot sizes. (Say, for example, in order to complete the assembly of C, 500 CA components were used, 501 CB and 505 CC.) The MRP system ingests this information and releases orders to coincide with the necessary lot sizes required for each component. Minimum WIP levels may be maintained because components are scheduled to be available to each cost centre as required. In addition the need to hit the due dates for component arrivals in specified departments encourages shop-floor discipline. Missed due dates result in idled departments.

A key innovation of MRP as an inventory management system lies in the concept of dependent demand. Finished products are assembled from families of components which may subdivide into families of subcomponents and thus work down the hierarchy in Figure 10.4. Previous traditional manufacturing utilized various types of EOQ models to signal a production or purchase order for new parts or components when a reorder point is reached. Statistical rules depending upon forecasted demand rates establish the reorder point; thus the reorder of particular parts is separated from the demand for finished or higher-level components. Consequently, cost centres using MRP for scheduling are more interdependent than those under the traditional manufacturing system because of these dependent demand phenomena.

Initially, the MRP system could only generate the first step in the planning process. The next problem lay in ensuring sufficient capacity in each cost centre as needed. The MRP schedule needed to be fed into a capacity planning system. MRP II adds the MRP schedule into a capacity planning system and then builds the information into the production schedule. Later versions of the system, MRP III, continually expand by integrating the MRP system with accounting, purchasing, and capacity planning.

MRP's impact on accounting systems

The impact of MRP systems upon cost accounting, however, remains quite subtle and perhaps not fully understood as yet. But some observations should be recognized. First, significant decreases in inventories render previously separate functions more interdependent. Second, MRP creates additional nonaccounting performance criteria related to meeting due dates. Third, as due dates take priority over budgets, shop-floor managers lose some discretion. This redistribution of authority does not indicate a decline in the importance of costs but rather that due dates must now also be considered. Finally, better data discipline also encourages better shop-floor discipline. Management now recognizes WIP levels and product flows because each computer run generates this data. (Computer runs can be in real time.)

Depending upon the type of MRP used — I, II, or III — accounting budgets may be more or less closely integrated with the MRP system. Planning tends to be more accurate and detailed; thus the building of slack into the process is difficult because activities are more easily observed. Therefore, tighter budgets will more likely be implemented. As control shifts from a cost orientation to include due dates, management becomes less decentralized. The performance of each manager can directly interfere with purchasing, manufacturing or sales functions. Shop-floor management exercises much less discretion over the selection of jobs because of scheduling priorities and reduced WIP levels. In addition, managers are now responsible for timely, accurate data reporting. Unless incentives are changed to enforce schedules while providing accurate data to control costs, behavioural problems can occur. Failures to do so have contributed to the high failure rate of MRP systems.

The role of accounting in decision-making has also changed. Make *versus* buy, capacity change, and even overtime decisions, carry implications not limited to any one department. Because MRP requires more precise standards to function, accounting standards for pricing and inventory valuation should also be upgraded.

MRP systems introduce new information and more efficient management co-ordination but they do not represent a radical change in manufacturing philosophy. Just-in-time or zero inventory systems, however, do so.

Just-in-time manufacturing (JIT)

Dr Ohno, the inventor of JIT manufacturing at Toyota, found that his system would only work after the accountants had been banished from the plant. Further, he insisted that his management team receive no training in accounting. Nor could he justify JIT using any existing accounting analysis. JIT manufacturing represents a different philosophy and is changing the way we regard the role of inventory. In traditional manufacturing, WIP buffers occur between cost centres, allowing independent responsibility centre management. Traditional scientific management solutions would typically consider some optimal WIP levels or trade-offs between spoilage and outputs. System-wide effects would be ignored.

On the other hand, the economics the Japanese faced did not coincide with those of traditional manufacturing. Japan lacked raw materials, capital, space and energy, and needed to raise foreign credits to pay for scarce natural resources. Her inexpensive resources represented the opposite economies assumed by the traditional manufacturing system. Japan possessed a plentiful supply of motivated, skilled labour that shared the Eastern philosophy of the group over the individual; teamwork over individual success. This group-orientated philosophy led to a use of low cost, flexible labour and teamwork wherever possible.

Since transportation costs were excessive, consumer goods with a high value to weight content were most suitable for foreign export. Good warranties were required. Quality became both a marketing strategy and a method to reduce the need for foreign repair locations and inventory caches. However, the Japanese knew little of foreign markets, their products faced long costly sea voyages; and because of their inability accurately to forecast demand, they required flexibility of production to quickly adapt to changes in consumer tastes. These viciously competitive conditions motivated JIT manufacturing. JIT consists of a set of ideas and approaches that systematically introduces constant improvement. JIT philosophy strives to remove costly non-value adding co-ordinating assets (e.g. the substitution of WIP and expensive control systems through greater manufacturing flexibility and quality improvements). These ideas simultaneously decrease the response time required to adapt to market changes and they help reduce costs.

In general, the Japanese employed labour if savings could be achieved in materials either through the reduction of waste (scrap) or buffer stocks. Quality became important in two contexts. First, quality expectations for inputs to manufacturing processes were that material specifications must be met exactly, thus removing a need for the excess WIP. Second, quality for the consumer also influenced product marketing and the required level of finished goods and helped minimize warranty costs.

Japan's motivated workforce — trained to be flexible in skills, working hours and salaries — could handle both production and cost flexibility. In Japan, bonuses based upon company profits can account for up to 50 per cent of a worker's annual income. Reduced company profits result in a reduced bonus. Besides the obvious motivational effects, this system directly improves the company's competitiveness. Labour costs can be reduced directly, thus allowing companies to cut prices without labour negotiations to maintain market share. These conditions provide direction for improvements. But none of these approaches are expressed in the accountant's cost–benefit terms. Current accounting data is not being collected to evaluate accurately these decisions because of the difficulty of determining the exact benefits.

Factory management under JIT

The major changes initiated by JIT are the management of factory environments and the restructuring of production departments into work cells. The JIT philosophy aims to find practical ways to eliminate the need for inventories; it regards inventories as a means of hiding problems rather than resolving them as in traditional manufacturing. JIT attempts to minimize inventories through small incremental reductions rather than prescribe particular techniques or methodologies. The focus rests not on the decomposition of tasks but upon the interaction of activities and the production process as a whole. Whereas traditional production methods group similar machines together to simplify the tasks within each cost centre to create the simple and 'hopefully' efficient production of 'like' parts, under JIT such cost centres become cells manufacturing 'families of components' not 'parts'.

Figure 10.4 illustrates an MRP system in the traditional manufacturing environment where like machines are grouped together into work centres. Jobs may return to the same production department again and again as they are combined into larger components. For example, parts CAA, CAB and CA may be returned to grinding after each is combined. The JIT approach strives to create different work cells which may include a variety of different machines. A JIT cell aims to produce a particular product or a family of components, *not* perform specific functions. For example, JIT cells may produce component CA including the production and assembly of parts CAA and CAB; or component CB from another cell and CC from a third cell and so on — all with no (or minimal) idled WIP. Ideally, any WIP will be in the process of conversion and never sit idle. A JIT cell, then, may be comprised of a mix of machinery and require the line workers to be flexible with respect to overtime and the performance of a variety of tasks. Each cell manufactures families of similar component parts. JIT cells, unlike traditional cost centres, are grouped by family of components not function (like, grinding, assembly, etc.). The philosophy is the reverse of traditional. Traditional reduces the complexity of tasks within the work centre but produces a large variety of subcomponents. JIT increases the variety and complexity within the work cell but produces fewer components. Both produce the same number of final products.

Normally, management sets a monthly/weekly production schedule so that a balanced mix of components can be produced each day (ten of A, two of B, twelve of C, etc.) in each cell. This organization of the cell balances the flow of work through the cell and the shop (i.e. to the next cell, etc.). Once set, the production schedule requires absolute discipline in order to meet the planned production so that work is not unintentionally idled by the lack of components.

Factory management changes from the traditional push to a pull system. Because forecasts form the basis for the traditional system, orders are released to the shop in the order determined by the master schedule. Long lead times from starting to completing a product necessitate this approach. For pull systems, on the other hand, individual components are not built until specifically requested by the succeeding (downstream) department. The Toyota Kanban system operates as a pull system. Workers stand-by idle until an order (*kanban*) is placed for the parts they produce. Often the Kanban works as little more than a carrying box with cards indicating the units required. The orders to initiate production originate from upstream production cells and sales.

This approach is a distinct contrast to the traditional accounting notion of efficiency, namely keeping workers and machines working constantly and eliminating idle time. In the JIT process direct idle labour time supplants the traditional overhead functions such as maintenance. Workers use idle time for maintenance thus reducing overhead costs. The use of work cells and minimizing set-up times enhances the desired flexibility. The time spent setting up a machine reduces the time available to run it and consequently reduces its production capacity. As the number of components requiring different set-ups increases, more run-time is lost and the opportunity cost of machine time per component increases. Therefore reducing incremental set-up costs allows for smaller lot sizes while not significantly increasing per unit costs (as discussed previously) and increases plant capacity despite the variety of products and demands. The production system now possesses a greater degree of flexibility, WIP levels are reduced and capacity is increased. Greater production flexibility also reduces lead times; as a result, fewer finished goods are required for warranty work and to protect against stockouts.

Simplication is another key concept. Since the design of new products centres around existing families of components, the variety of components required remains at a minimum. The objective lies in simplifying the production process even in the face of product redesign. By concentrating more machining variety in each cell, the production flow between cells is less complex and co-ordination is made easier. However, significantly more demands are made of labour, both in skills and task discipline. Emphasis falls on team work and behavioural or cultural controls rather than traditional bureaucracies because separate work cell activities are much more difficult to evaluate. Workers must be motivated to make sacrifices for the whole. Slack exists in the form of machine and labour flexibility, not inventories.

Quality control is extremely important in the reduction of WIP. In the Toyota system each line worker exercises constant quality control. If the worker locates a defect, or runs short of time, he or she can shut down the entire line. Lights and whistles literally go off indicating where the shutdown occurred. Engineers and fellow workers descend upon the station to solve the problem. Since the failure represents an opportunity to improve the system it receives reverential attention. In this philosophy, no guilt-laden finger-pointing occurs. Exceptions are considered an opportunity to improve the system. Therefore part of the JIT philosophy is to *cause* failures to improve the process.

Other reasons for excessive inventories are unreliable vendor deliveries and vendor quality. JIT solves purchasing problems by forgoing the short-term benefits of competitive bidding in order to develop special long-term relationships. In exchange, the vendor coincides his production schedule and quality standards to the plant's needs, thus reducing uncertainty and hence the need for excess inventories. As an example, for the California Nummi plant, a joint venture between Toyota and General Motors, deliveries from local suppliers must be within a three-hour window. In addition, the production schedule at the California plant co-ordinates with the component manufacturer in Japan. Unloading containers from the boat and parts from each container occur in the appropriate order for the production line. This is attention to detail!

In conclusion, JIT manufacturing becomes more like a service industry. One author compares a JIT system to a McDonald's restaurant, able to instantaneously meet the luncheon needs of three unannounced bus loads of boy scouts.

Innovation and improvement

Ultimately the manufacturing process would utilize zero inventories and respond exactly to demand. This ideal, however, is virtually impossible to achieve. An important advantage of JIT lies in its superiority in identifying just where improvements should be made. Traditional push systems with excessive inventories are engineered to fully utilize the capacity of each cost centre. It is assumed that variation in the mix of products demanded will in the long run even out the demands on each department. Production activity in each department will vary randomly day to day, week to week and, in a job shop at least, product routings may not be co-ordinated but are, rather, random. Each department therefore operates relatively separately. If accounting is employed to evaluate performance, and engineering does not know the one best way to accomplish all the required tasks; labour and shop-floor management will be motivated to create slack to give them protection against tight budgets. Consequently, the incentive to communicate innovation from the shop floor is reduced through *negotiated* budgets with upper management, which are likely when the production process is not well understood or not observable by higher management.

Worker incentives also tend to reflect the accounting notion of efficiency.

Piecework emphasizes maximum output levels for individual sub-tasks, not the manufacturing process as a whole. Because each department strives to operate at full capacity (thus maximizing efficiency) bottlenecks appear less obvious. Engineers and middle to upper management tend to spur improvements which may be capital intensive. The 'kneejerk' engineer's and management's reaction may include replacing costly, unpredictable labour with more expensive, predictable machinery.

JIT systems allow controllable incremental improvements where the benefit is greatest. To repeat, the steps involve systematic removal of buffer inventories until errors occur. The detected problem could be due to a machine failure, a set-up or quality problem, and so on. Upon tracing the problem to its cause, the removed inventories are replaced into the system until a solution can be found. Then the inventories are again removed until another failure signals an opportunity to improve the system somewhere else. This approach of continual trouble-shooting and replacement leads to a series of minute, usually low-cost, improvements as well as, more importantly, a culture of constant analysis and improvement. Under this system, no final plateau of success is ever reached. Since the objective is to create temporary failures in order to improve the system, an 'optimal' standard of manufacturing performance is never achieved.

When engineers/workers locate a severe problem, automation may be considered to remedy the situation; but the key lies in the idea that the investment in automation occurs where it will exact the greatest benefit; an observation not always possible in a traditional system where underutilized automated equipment commonly exist. Many practitioners consider JIT to be a necessary prerequisite for the efficient introduction of automation. JIT facilitates three aspects of capital investment usually considered difficult under traditional systems: first, accurate identification of potential candidates for improvements; second, estimates of system-wide benefits to the organization as a whole; and third, follow-up monitoring of the performance of the improvements.

Another approach to improvement and cost reduction introduced by JIT separates operations into value-adding and non-value-adding functions or the co-ordinating and production functions of traditional systems. Examples of non-value-adding functions are moving, maintenance and various types of overhead that do not directly improve the product. Further analysis extends this idea to the physical space and assets within the plant.

In summary, consider the changes to the five management functions initially identified with traditional manufacturing — the management of raw materials, buffer WIP, production departments, the overall process, and sales. Purchasing no longer manages raw material inventories nor continually shops for better prices, but monitors due-dates and quality by direct, close relationships with a few suppliers. Longer-term guaranteed contracts and closer connections at the shop-floor level motivate suppliers to be more conscientious about the purchasers' needs. WIP management is very simple due to the reduced need for buffer stocks. Production departments change from a simple set of similar activities to the complex production of families of parts. Management of the overall process has been simplified through fewer work cells. Process control becomes a shop-floor responsibility where failures may be easily and immediately observed; and sales management directly determines short-term, often monthly, production schedules.

Implications of JIT for accounting systems

JIT remains a relatively new concept whose impact on accounting has not yet been clearly determined. But, returning to the purposes of accounting introduced earlier, we can look at what has happened so far, and at what we suspect will happen in the future.

Planning

The long-term scheduling process becomes less crucial to production due to the flexibility built into the production system. However, since companies are now more vulnerable to short-term demand fluctuations, capacity measurement is very important. Manufacturing cells are usually balanced monthly to the planned production. Accounting numbers are employed since profit goals are still important to management and shareholders. However, in Japan where these systems evolved, the long-term perspective is more important than short-term profits. Interestingly, their financial statement disclosure and reporting are significantly more conservative than Western reporting practices.

Budgeting

In the traditional manufacturing environment the budgeting process determines the feasibility of production and profit figures, and it establishes standards for performance. This often takes the form of negotiated budgets between top and bottom management. JIT philosophy aims at attaining fewer levels of management, continuous improvements and relatively visible processes. Thus, the need for, and the complexity of, budgeting processes will be reduced. Cost centres have become work cells which have largely fixed costs, as labour is no longer considered variable. Only materials, some overhead items, and power costs vary. Flexible budgeting, using activity or transaction based cost drivers may be more accurate in this situation. Behavioural controls, stressing team approaches, appear to be more important because of the emphasis on constant improvement, whereas annual budgeting becomes less meaningful. Control in the JIT environment shifts to the production floor and operational control, and away from annual budgets.

Control

The control emphasis has shifted from debating standards to the automatic consideration of each new cost improvement as the new standard. The traditional role of variances needs to be changed as well. Aggregated (by time period, e.g. monthly, weekly) efficiency variances hold little significance because utilization hinges upon sales demand in a pull system. If insufficient demand arises, workers perform other functions. To utilize efficiency variances, therefore, these variances must be calculated job by job and should be thought of as indicating trends of expected improvement. The form of control under JIT is changed. Long before variances are reported or calculated for accounting reports, workers will have observed and pinpointed problems. Variances, therefore, should only be employed for planning, standards should be used with JIT only to 'balance the books'. Variances may be beneficial in the initial stages of JIT, to signal opportunities for improvement or as a running balance tracking new performance standards. Primary control, however, will be at the shop-floor level and in the culture of the plant.

While JIT stresses behavioural motivation in order to create a culture of continuing improvement, some measures may still be useful for internal control. First, while waste and scrap standards may identify areas for improvement, management must, however, allow for frequent revisions. Also while only quantities are necessary for production, these quantities must be converted to monetary equivalents for accounting purposes. Next, measurements of earned hours based upon output and the most recent standards can be useful to monitor and control capacity requirements. However, care must be taken because the emphasis under JIT should lie in maximization of throughput, not earned hours. Inventory turnover or the levels of WIP serve as useful measures of improvement for JIT systems and represent a possible internal control measure. However, old industry-wide standards of performance are obsolete and should be ignored, inventory levels being used only to reflect the progress of JIT implementation in each plant. Due dates or meeting the schedule are absolutely essential to JIT's success as the level of inventories is reduced. Therefore deviations from schedule should be recorded and examined.

Quality performance stands as a cornerstone of JIT, since total quality control eliminates one reason to have WIP, and makes the implementation of automation easier. Quality, therefore, needs to be monitored. Overtime measures, another tool for internal control, aid management purposes. If overtime occurs because manning levels are too low, few problems exist. However, if the manning level is correct and overtime occurs, then many problems demanding attention are present. Transition or cycle time must also be addressed, since shortened cycle times mean increased velocity through the system, and hence increased capacity. Lastly, increased machine flexibility and the training of the labour force are of critical importance to JIT. Measures to evaluate the ability of the system to handle variety are required and need to be developed. The cost of maintaining and increasing this new machine and labour flexibility should be of importance to management, although many of the benefits cannot be measured with existing accounts. While many of these control measures are already monetarized and, consequently, easily fit into accounting-driven budget formats, others are not. The challenge for the accountant lies in creating measures relating to financial statements. While a long-term, non-financial, statement-driven strategy suits the Japanese, Western companies must consider the bottom line due to the nature of their financial institutions. However, given the scepticism about the accuracy and usefulness of such measures accounting control may shift from its current level of detail into more aggregated figures.

Decision-making

Accounting data impacts on decision-making through the provision of relevant data and its motivational influence on decisions. The accountant's role as the master of the data system often demands the identification for others of information useful for the particular decision at hand. This recognition, of course, involves an understanding of the decision models in use as well as the accounting system. The concept of constant improvement creates difficulties for companies adapting to JIT. Japanese applications of cost—benefit analysis look at much longer paybacks, while JIT serves as more of a strategic decision with ROI playing a lesser role. Most Western companies, on the other hand, maintain complex capital budgeting systems. However, once JIT has been accepted as a strategic decision, the capital budgeting system may become less significant. JIT operates as an incrementalist system, and generally it progresses in a series of small inexpensive improvements. Consequently, a set capital budget, probably within the current spending limits of most plants, could provide sufficient funding for several improvements. When the plant-wide spending limits are met, several projects may be added. Justification would be based upon system (plant-wide) performance. This type of validation is not justification 'before the fact' as is usually the case for traditional capital projects; but under the JIT environment, acceptance will be much more a function of personal judgement legitimized by a track record of improving performance. In a similar vein, the method of analysis itself needs to be better understood; in particular, the notion of value-added and non-value-added processes, assets and space. Also, more timely and constant re-evaluation of breakeven points, contribution margins, product-line accounting, and 'make *versus* buy' decisions will be required, while new cost data and analysis techniques will be necessary for the evaluation of market share.

A final decision-making tool lies in engineers' use of value analysis, which breaks down a product into its constituent parts. Each part undergoes analysis for alternative materials and design. This is crucial within a JIT system because simplification and commonality must be recognized as important. However, changes in input prices, provided by the accountants, should initiate value analysis. At the same time, accounting will still be responsible for providing accurate overhead costs required for this analysis. The creation of work cells makes this easier however. Many of the complex functions of co-ordination and maintenance have been shifted to the production unit thereby reducing the amount of arbitrary overhead allocations required.

Traditional definitions of relevant costs will be changed.' Because accountants currently cannot accurately calculate the cost/benefits of quality, machine and labour flexibility, or reduced set-ups, relevant information will not, at least initially, be expressed in monetary terms. The role of accountants as part of a team will lie in developing these costs while simultaneously relating them to financial statements.

Accounting for accrual financial statements

Accounting for the traditional accrual financial statement presentation will also undergo changes, ranging from product *versus* period cost classification, to the phasing out of cost accumulation systems. Direct labour in JIT systems stands as a largely fixed period cost and rarely relates to short-term capacity fluctuations; therefore, the classification of product *versus* period costs may first be questioned.

Smaller lot sizes could increase overhead costs because of more frequent transactions. In response to this, new automated billing and tracking systems have emerged, as well as several purchasing systems utilizing production schedules rather than invoices to initiate payments to vendors. Automatic paperless invoicing sends payments to suppliers based upon scheduled production; only an exception report from the factory floor indicating a problem with purchased components stops payments. Since short-term capacity stands as the only relevant management issue, long-term capacity may no longer be useful as a basis for allocating costs. Consequently new allocation methods may be required. With the greater proportion of costs now fixed (direct labour and overheads), the argument for direct costing using cost driver makes more sense. One more modification may be seen in the decreased employment of direct labour as a basis for the allocation of overhead costs. With large increases in overhead, burden rates could be 800 per cent and inordinately influence decision-making under full costing. Machine time will provide a more relevant basis for overhead application. The disappearance of complex cost accumulation systems and implementation of 'backflush' costing systems makes a final change. Backflush costing breaks the factory into logical input—output points (such as cells, for example), which measure the materials put in and the materials coming out. Because JIT uses level production loads, constant WIP levels exist; consequently, management can ignore goods-in-process. This simplified system is both relatively accurate and timely. It requires an accurate bill of materials, good measures of yield as well as consistent yield, and accurate engineering change notices when yields do change. Simplification of accounting procedures will free the accountant for other roles.

Simplification of pricing issues

Under JIT the proportion of incremental costs should be reduced, and only direct materials and overhead costs (influenced by transactions) will be relevant. Since JIT employs short-term manufacturing capacity in lieu of large inventories to cope with fluctuations in sales demand, the measurement of opportunity costs will become more important for management evaluation and decisions. However, the old axiom that all costs are variable in the long term still holds true. Consequently, for pricing purposes the debate between suitability of full or variable costing supplemented with additional cost drivers may increase. Even with a one-month response time, the potential for rush orders not covered by extra finished goods still exists. The costs of rush orders and the allocation of these costs may require analysis.

Because the JIT philosophy controls the direct shop-floor costs so effectively, accounting control will increasingly stress overhead costs. Some authors suggest that production plants, like service organizations, should keep detailed overhead records to control costs and to identify where the greatest costs, and hence potential savings, exist. While JIT identifies non-value-added assets and activities as overhead, it does not provide a systematic way of identifying where cost savings will be greatest. As a result, new cost analysis techniques stress multiple overhead application bases using different sets of activities or cost drivers.

Automated manufacturing

One of the strengths of a JIT system is that opportunities for automation are readily identified and can be more efficiently analysed. The job—flow shop continuum, illustrated in Figure 10.5, identifies automation as a corollary of JIT. Increased investment in costly support systems represents one significant feature of factory automation; while computer-aided design and computer-aided manufacturing (CAD/CAM) as well as automatic storage/retrieval systems (AS/RS) represent significant, expensive new developments in support systems.

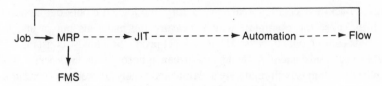

Figure 10.5   Adaptations form the traditional job–flow continuum

Automated machinery comes in many forms with many different attributes, but to maintain consistency we will attempt to keep the job–flow shop differentiation. This split raises comparisons of numerically controlled machines (NC) to flexible manufacturing systems (FMS). NC machines usually require manual set-up, loading and unloading, which can be time consuming and can require highly skilled employees. FMS, on the other hand, consists of a wholly automated group of self-setting-up machines with automated material carriers that load and unload jobs, the entire process operating from a centralized computer. Ideally, support labour is only required for maintenance and to occasionally replace tools.

NC machines, often because of costly set-ups, are most economic with larger jobs; while FMS, concentrating upon families of parts with similar characteristics, stresses rapid set-ups and will often produce lot sizes of only one unit. Once a set of products has been put into the computer system, a complex set of mathematical models schedule and route the work flow to maximize the utilization of each machine in the FMS cell.

However, the economical production of small jobs of customized parts in an FMS system would not be possible without CAD/CAM systems. CAD is a computerized support system replacing the engineering graphics functions. Once CAD combines with other software, production feasibility and routing can also be established. Standards and detailed specifications are, however, essential to fully utilize the potential of an FMS.

Significant material handling advantages can be achieved through the use of AS/RS. The group of automated systems include AS/RS equipment bringing an inventory storage basket to the worker (called a picker). Each worker selects the number of components required from each basket and the basket returns by conveyers to its storage position. Thus components for small jobs or mixed-sales deliveries can be handled quickly despite their complexity. These systems both reduce delivery lead times and increase the variety of parts per order at a lower overall incremental cost. The combination of this group of automated systems (FMS, CAD/CAM and AS/RS) utilize significant investments in technology to allow the efficient production of small jobs. Production typifies that of a job shop. Consequently, automation can be applied to the manufacture of products traditionally produced in either job or flow environments, by NC or FMS respectively.

Predominant characteristics

Quality, in the sense of meeting specifications, is crucial, since automated processes to date tolerate little deviations from specification. Predictability befriends automated systems; uncertainty does not. Simplification and standardization dramatically reduce the software complexity required to run the system. Data discipline may also be recognized as being very important. Because both higher utilization rates and low inventory levels are observed in practice, less slack is available to allow for rejects, planning errors or machine breakdowns. Preventive maintenance of key machinery is also very important.

Finally, a shift in the relationship among labour, overhead and material costs exists. The relative percentages of variable *versus* fixed, and controllable *versus* non-controllable costs have changed. While indirect highly skilled labour has increased, direct labour has shrunk. Overheads have increased and can vary significantly among cost centres, as different activities are automated at different rates with more or less costly equipment. Lower spoilage rates and the need for better quality influence material costs that become the largest variable cost.

Fixed costs grow to become an increasingly significant part of overall costs and hence their control becomes an important management issue. The classification of controllable and non-controllable costs has changed, as many of the controllable costs that remain were formerly lumped into fixed overhead costs. But now because of their increased importance, specific overhead costs should be tracked in order to control costs in general. Again the use of multiple overhead application rates (or cost drivers) becomes more important.

The nature of planning will change since FMS allows shorter master production schedules. But the old job shop problem of balancing machine loading to product mix still haunts these systems. However, mathematical models and simulation can be used as effective means to balance machine utilization. Increased machine reliability, tight quality specifications and the precise timing of work flows have substantially reduced most of the uncertainties viewed as traits of traditional job shops. With the reduced uncertainty, discrete mathematical models combined with computers cope with the variety of job shops. Planning for capacity and flexibility then become more important, and operational control is regarded as a given. Operations rely less on annual plans, instead emphasizing monthly plans; and annual budgeting bears less importance as a control device or as an information source. Automated systems are very sensitive to data and specification errors. Thus necessary day-to-day feedback and mathematical control displaces much of accounting's control and data-gathering roles. However, at least until superior models are developed, management still employs budgeting as a useful means of motivating employees.

Capital budgeting decisions must include the level of uncertainty — both short and long term, and quantitative *versus* qualitative factors. Uncertainty embraces the lack of understanding of the current activities and future activities. Lack of understanding of the current activities often ignites more problems when automation evolves from an MRP or traditional manufacturing environment, as such enterprises tend to evaluate the automation with respect to individual departments or cost centres, and ignore system-wide influences. Automating from a JIT system often ensures a better understanding of the factors influencing the automation process. Future uncertainties are more difficult because much of the machinery is new and subject to modifications. Moreover, management is often not fully aware of its potential uses and they will discover additional productivity improvements only with use.

Automation requires improved quality and better shop-floor discipline in order to generate savings; factors which are not easily quantified. Typically, inventory and lead times drop, less space is required, and delivery reliability improves. The acquisition decision is generally not well serviced by traditional accounting measures such as discounting, ROI or payback measures. Instead customers or the market-place often force the decision upon management. In other words, management perceives that they must increase automation or go out of business. The emphasis becomes to identify the optimal form of that investment rather than its economic feasibility. The issue then becomes a debate as to how we finance it, and not whether or not the net present value is positive.

Short-term decisions, such as make or buy, to drop or add a product, often become easier because more costs become fixed; and costs previously classified as fixed because measurement was difficult are now variable. For example, some systems have been observed which measure the cost of material handling based upon cause and effect. Previously, these costs were simply lumped into fixed overhead because they did not represent a significant proportion of the variable costs.

Pricing becomes a very tricky issue. The popular response of accountants to the pricing issue lies in supporting the use of full or absorption costing since the bulk of automated equipment costs are fixed and long term. Other authors have suggested that full costing be supported by identifying layers of fixed costs separated by their unique time–budget horizons. Separation by time horizons would allow incremental pricing decisions to be linked to suitable strategic decisions.

Regardless, accurate full costing of automated processes will require separate cost pools rather than factory-wide cost pools. Different sets of equipment can vary significantly in cost. Therefore, separate cost pools linked to specific types of equipment are necessary for accurate costing. The classification of the direct labour of machine operators can also create difficulty when one operator operates several machines. Set-up specialists also create new costing problems; and rational cause and effect methods of allocating these costs must be designed.

However, an alternative argument can be created for variable costing as well, since the bulk of the costs are fixed and provide long-term service. Strategic pricing decisions may be more important; strategic pricing matched to the longer life expectations of automated systems promotes the need for variable costing, so that the short-term costs of strategic pricing may be evaluated, especially when machines are underutilized. When machining centres become bottlenecks the measurement of opportunity costs may also be useful.

Conclusions

The accountant must be aware of the influence of new technologies and changes in production management on the usefulness of various accounting techniques. Most of the issues are not new, but their relative significance changes under different sets of conditions. Until very recently only one relatively well understood philosophy of manufacturing existed. A relatively narrow set of techniques were sufficient to meet management's needs. Many of the underlying assumptions about inventories, quality and labour management were simply taken for granted and *not* considered issues important enough to be discussed in accounting textbooks since the underlying philosophy of traditional manufacturing was relatively consistent from plant to plant. But now these assumptions are changing — some for the first time in almost one hundred years. Consequently, cost accountants must carefully analyse their environments, be aware of changes influencing the current costing system; and work with other professionals, like the production engineers, to ensure the implementation of appropriate changes to the accounting systems. The role of the managerial accountant is also changing and becoming more management-orientated. In the future, management accounting systems are needed that produce a variety of costing measures and performance indicators (not always financial) with the emphasis on relevance, even if this entails some sacrifice of precision.

It would be remiss not to offer an opinion on where we are going in the future. Is traditional manufacturing dead? Probably not. At least not in the short term but aspects of it will be radically changed. A key point must be clear to the student by now. Since very few manufacturing systems can be uniquely classified as job, process, JIT or FMS systems, the great majority of situations will consist of a mix of these environments. Even more difficult to cope with, most manufacturing plants will be continually undergoing transitions. Thus, the factory accountants of the future will be unable to apply the relatively clear textbook prescriptions of the past to each new situation. They must be proactive and directly involved in management decisions in order for changes in accounting data to be made compatible with new technologies. Environmental changes within and without the plant can influence the measurability, usefulness and the cost/benefits of accounting systems. As accountants, we need to understand the conditions in each unique environment influencing the accountant's system. Cost accountants will eventually resemble, if not become, more artisans than technicians, more Picassos than Taylors, and more generalists than specialists.

Further Reading

Bennett, R.E., J.A. Hendricks, D.E. Keys and E.J. Rudnicki (1987) *Cost Accounting for Factory Automation*, Montvale, NJ: National Association of Accountants.

Bonsack, R.A. (1986) 'Cost accounting in the factory of the future', *CIM Review*, vol. 2, no. 3, Spring, pp. 28–32.

Capettini, R. and D.K. Clancy (1987), *Cost Accounting, Robotics, and the New Manufacturing Environment*, Sarasota, Flor.: American Accounting Association.

Edwards, J.B. and J.A. Heard (1984) 'Is cost accounting the no. 1 enemy of productivity?' *Management Accounting*, June, pp. 44–9.

Foster, G. and C.T. Horngren (1987) 'JIT: cost accounting and cost management issues', *Management Accounting*, June, pp. 19–25.

Howell, R.A. and S. Soucy (1988) *Factory 2000+ Management Accounting's Changes Role*, Montvale, NJ: National Association of Accountants.

Howell, R.A., J.D. Brown, S. Soucy and A.H. Seed III (1987) *Management Accounting in the New Manufacturing Environment: Current Cost Management Practice in Automated (Advanced) Manufacturing Environments*, Montvale, NJ: National Association of Accountants.

Johnson, H.T. and R.S. Kaplan (1987) 'The rise and fall of management accounting', *Management Accounting*, January, pp. 22–31.

Kaplan, R.S. (1984) 'Yesterday's accounting undermines production', *Harvard Business Review*, July–August, pp. 95–101.

Lee, Y.L. (1987) *Management Accounting Changing for the 1990s*, Artesia, Calif.: McKay Business Systems.

National Association of Accountants (1986) *Cost Accounting for the '90s*, Montvale, NJ: National Association of Accountants.

Taylor, S.G., S.M. Seward and S.F. Bolander (1981) 'Why the process industries are different', *Production and Inventory Managment*, no. 4.

Chapter 11

Financial planning and the micro-computer

MIKE O'HARA

A cursory examination of management accounting texts published prior to 1980 reveals that computers are only seldom mentioned and micro-computers not at all. This must seem very strange to undergraduates in the 1990s who have been used to seeing and using micro-computers at school and university. It is therefore instructive to recall the major changes that have taken place in computing in the 1980s and, in particular, how these developments have changed the financial planning process.

In the mid-1970s two employees of IBM, Steve Jobs and Steve Wozniak, were convinced that micro-computers would form a major element of the future of computing. A lack of support from their employers, IBM, caused them to resign and form their own company, which they called Apple Inc. They started to produce Apple micro-computers from their homes in early 1978 and did not move to a factory and formal production lines until 1980. Despite these modest beginnings, Apple's turnover reached $1 billion by 1983. This spectacular growth was largely attributable to a piece of software called VisiCalc. This was the first electronic spreadsheet package available for a micro-computer and was written in 1979 to run on the Apple II micro-computer.

Financial modelling packages had been available for most mainframe computers for many years, but they were frequently inaccessible to the non-specialist user, including accountants. Their use was largely limited to the data-processing professional. By buying an Apple II with VisiCalc an accountant could have relatively friendly and useful software available at his/her own desk. This lifted Apple out of the, then, normal market for micro-computers as games machines, and into the business world.

In response IBM, realizing their mistake, introduced their own personal computer (IBM PC) in 1981. Many hardware manufacturers soon started to produce their own copies or clones of the IBM PC, and many software houses began to write packages to run on the IBM PC and its clones. Several of these packages were spreadsheets (e.g. Supercalc and Multiplan), but the clear winner in this market was Lotus 1-2-3. Lotus 1-2-3 will be used as a model when discussing spreadsheets in detail later in this chapter.

The micro-computer market has continued to develop since the early 1980s — with the introduction of hard disks, more memory, faster processors and new software — but the rapid acceptance of micro-computers by the business community owes much to the success of spreadsheet software. In this context it is worth noting the rapid growth that Lotus underwent in the early 1980s. The company was only formed in early 1982, and yet had a turnover of $53 million in 1983 and $157 million in 1984. Such are the rewards for a successful software product! Accountants now routinely use spreadsheets for budget preparation and control, cash flow forecasts and analysis, project and investment appraisal, tax computations, cost and variance analyses, consolidations, financial statement analysis and foreign currency conversions.

Spreadsheets: what are they?

As already noted, I will use Lotus 1-2-3 as a model when discussing the design and use of spreadsheets. However, as many other spreadsheet packages are similar to 1-2-3, the principles explained below will be largely applicable whatever package is used. Indeed, rather as hardware manufacturers produce clones of IBM's products, so Lotus's success has caused many software companies to develop 1-2-3 'look-a-like' spreadsheet packages.

A spreadsheet package contains the electronic equivalent of a calculator, a pencil, and a large piece of paper which we refer to as a worksheet. The worksheet is really a large matrix of columns and rows. Each position in the worksheet, which is known as a 'cell', is uniquely defined by its 'address': that is, the 'letter' of the column and 'number' of the row. Thus possible addresses are A16, C511, AB27 and so on.

The first version of 1-2-3 had 256 columns and 2,048 rows available for any particular worksheet. Subsequent versions have even larger numbers of rows and columns available. This may mean that you cannot see an entire worksheet at once. Hence the micro-computer's monitor acts as a 'window' to the worksheet showing a rectangular area of columns and rows, and enabling the user to move around the worksheet as required. The cell that is actually being worked on (in effect, where the pencil is currently being pointed) is highlighted on the screen.

Each cell can have one of three types of information entered into it: a label, a value or a formula. A label is some fixed expression, such as 'Cost of Sales' or 'January 1989'. A value is a number on which it is possible to perform arithmetic operations. Entering a formula into a cell enables a calculation to be undertaken, the answer to which usually depends on the content of one or more other cells in the worksheet. When the content of any particular cell is changed, a powerful recalculation facility built into the software immediately changes the contents of all the other cells which depend directly or indirectly on that particular cell.

It may be helpful for the reader to consider the worksheet as a two-layered block. The lower layer contains the label, value or formula for each cell, and the upper layer shows the actual output arising in the active cells as a result of the current input data. The 'window' to the spreadsheet provided by the micro-computer's monitor generally displays the top layer of outputs, but it is possible to view the lower layer for any particular cell by moving the 'pointer' to that cell. The formula, label or value underpinning the cell is displayed in the working area at the top of the screen, while the output is displayed in the worksheet (see Fig. 11.1).

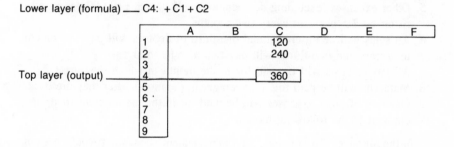

Figure 11.1 Micro-computer spreadsheet

It is also possible to copy the label, value or formula underlying a particular cell, or range of cells (i.e. any rectangular group of cells, including single cells, and parts of a row or a column), to another cell or range of cells. Formulas can be entered into one group of cells and then copied to other parts of the worksheet. Thus a task in which calculations are carried out systematically on a number of rows and columns is a prime candidate for a spreadsheet. Many accounting and related tasks neatly fit this description, and hence the use of spreadsheets is now commonplace in much accounting work. I will illustrate some of the facilities provided by spreadsheet packages by concentrating on an example of producing budgets for a new product.

Spreadsheets: an example

Consider a company which is contemplating the introduction of a new product. The managing director asks the management accountant to prepare a budgeted profit and loss statement, together with a cash flow forecast for the first year of the new product's life, and to present them to the next meeting of the committee considering the new product. Following discussions with several colleagues, the management accountant draws up the following list of assumptions:

1. Initial capital equipment will cost £600,000 and will be paid for in month 1. Depreciation will be provided at 25 per cent per annum using the straight-line method.
2. Sales will be 1,000 units in month 1, rising by 5 per cent per month.
3. The unit sales price will be £100 in month 1, rising by 2 per cent at the end of each quarter.
4. The cost of sales will be 60 per cent of the sales revenue and will be split in the ratio 2:1 materials to labour.
5. Other expenses (excluding depreciation) will start at £10,000 per month, rising by 2.5 per cent every two months.
6. All sales will be on credit, and one-third of debtors will pay one month in arrears and two-thirds will pay two months in arrears.
7. All labour costs will be paid for in the month in which they arise.
8. Materials will be paid for, on average, in the month after they are used.
9. One-half of other expenses will be paid for in the month concerned, and one-half in the following month.

In the absence of a computer, the management accountant would get out a calculator, pencil and a piece of paper, and prepare the necessary calculations. The results would be typed and presented to the next meeting of the committee considering this new product (see Table 11.1).

Problems would arise, however, if the management accountant's colleagues started to ask questions about the figures and to query certain of the assumptions. For example, the management accountant's calculation would need to be completely reworked if:

1. The sales director now thinks that the initial sales will only be 900 units but will rise by 7.5 per cent per month.
2. The production director anticipates that the cost of sales can be reduced to 55 per cent of sales revenue from month 3 onwards.
3. The finance director believes that the suppliers of materials can be induced to allow an extra month's credit.
4. The managing director enquires as to the effect of leasing the capital equipment rather than buying it.

Clearly, the management accountant could not compute the effects of these changes immediately. To recalculate the figures for each different scenario or combination of scenarios will involve a significant amount of work. The inability to respond quickly to revised assumptions and to 'what if?' questions severely limits the extent to which problems can be properly and fully analysed.

A second problem with the traditional calculator, pencil-and-paper method of budgeting is that assumptions are not always stated clearly and unambiguously, and applied consistently and accurately. It is very rare indeed for any other member of the management team to carry out a complete and independent check on the accountant's assumptions and computations. Yet an error could have serious consequences for the entire organization.

In summary then, the management accountant faces two major problems with the traditional method of calculating and presenting figures. First, it is very difficult to explore different scenarios, and second, the assumptions are not always clear or consistently applied. As we shall now see, the use of spreadsheet software can be of major assistance in solving both of these problems. Let us consider how this can arise by working through our example.

After loading 1-2-3 onto an IBM-compatible micro-computer, the management accountant will see the screen illustrated in Figure 11.2. Normally, the first things entered into the worksheet describe such items as the company name, the product under consideration and the type of statement being prepared — for example a profit and loss account. These are all entered as labels. Labels are then entered for the various column headings. As column A is to be reserved for narrative, columns B to M are allocated for the first twelve months under consideration. Thus 'Month 1' is entered as a label in cell B9, 'Month 2' in cell C9 and so on until 'Month 12' is entered in cell M9.

The narrative 'Unit Sales' is entered as a label in cell A10, and now the time has arrived to start entering the figures. The first number is 1000, which is entered as a value in cell B10. This is the unit sales in the first month. To reflect the 5 per cent monthly rise in unit sales, it would be possible to enter 1000*1.05 in cell C10, $1000*(1.05)^2$ in cell D10, and so on. However, the usefulness of 1-2-3 is demonstrated by entering the formula +B10*1.05 in cell C10 (the + sign in front of any expression tells 1-2-3 that a formula rather than a label is being entered). This formula is then copied into each of the cells D10 to M10 using the copy command. This operation is possible because cell D10 bears the same relationship to cell C10 as cell C10 bears to cell B10, and so on all the way across to cell M10. Copying the formula +B10*1.05 in cell C10 into cell D10 converts the formula into +C10*1.05. Similarly, the formula in cell M10 will now be +L10*1.05. This is known as relative copying. When the return key is pressed to signify the end of the copying operation the results of computations based on the formulas will be displayed in the cells D10 to M10.

Having entered the sales in units, the next step is to enter the sales prices, beginning with the label 'Sales Price' in cell A11. The initial selling price of 100 is then entered in cell B11. As there are no increases in months 2 and 3, it would be possible to enter 100 in cells C11 and D11. But it is a general principle of using spreadsheets that it is better to enter formulas rather than values, wherever possible. This is especially so when copying is to take place,

Table 11.1 The ABC Company Ltd. Introduction of product X: budget figures for committee meeting of 21 July 1989

Profit and loss account							
	Month 1	Month 2	Month 3	Month 4	Month 5	Month 6	Month 7
Unit sales	1,000	1,050	1,103	1,158	1,216	1,276	1,340
Sales price	100.00	100.00	100.00	102.00	102.00	102.00	104.04
Sales	100,000	105,000	110,250	118,078	123,982	130,181	139,424
Cost of sales	60,000	63,000	66,150	70,847	74,389	78,109	83,654
Gross profit	40,000	42,000	44,100	47,231	49,593	52,072	55,770
Depreciation	12,500	12,500	12,500	12,500	12,500	12,500	12,500
Other expenses	10,000	10,000	10,250	10,250	10,506	10,506	10,769
Net profit	£17,500	£19,500	£21,350	£24,481	£26,587	£29,066	£32,501

Cash flow forecast							
	Month 1	Month 2	Month 3	Month 4	Month 5	Month 6	Month 7
Equipment	(600,000)						
Sales	0	33,333	101,667	106,750	112,859	120,046	126,048
Labour	(20,000)	(21,000)	(22,050)	(23,616)	(24,796)	(26,036)	(27,885)
Materials	0	(40,000)	(42,000)	(44,100)	(47,231)	(49,593)	(52,073)
Other expenses	(5,000)	(10,000)	(10,125)	(10,250)	(10,378)	(10,506)	(10,637)
Net flow	(625,000)	(37,667)	27,492	28,784	30,453	33,911	35,453
Opening balance	0	(625,000)	(662,667)	(635,175)	(606,390)	(575,937)	(542,026)
Closing balance	(£625,000)	(£662,667)	(£635,175)	(£606,390)	(£575,937)	(£542,026)	(£506,573)

as we shall see shortly. So +B11 is entered into cells C11 and D11. To reflect the 2 per cent price rise at the end of the first quarter the formula for cell E11 needs to be +D11*1.02. The usefulness of the copying facility can now be demonstrated again by copying the formulas in the range C11 to E11 (i.e. cell C11, D11 and E11) into each of the ranges F11 to H11 and I11 to K11, and finally copying cell I11 into each of L11 and M11. The sales price will now be shown for each of the twelve months.

To show the sales revenue it is simply necessary to enter 'Sales' in cell A12, +B10*B11 in cell B12 and to copy this formula into each of the cells C12 to M12. When this operation is complete the sales revenue will be available for each of the twelve months under consideration. To improve the presentation of the figures in the worksheet, it will be helpful at this point to use the formatting facility within the software. This allows the user to insert commas, £ signs and decimal points as appropriate in numerical values and to decide on the number, if any, of decimal places to be displayed. It is probable that when this formatting procedure is complete, some of the numbers in the

Table 11.1 continued

Month 8	Month 9	Month 10	Month 11	Month 12	Total
1,407	1,477	1,551	1,629	1,710	
104.04	104.04	106.12	106.12	106.12	
146,395	153,714	164,628	172,860	181,503	1,646,015
87,837	92,228	98,777	103,716	108,902	987,609
58,558	61,486	65,851	69,144	72,601	658,406
12,500	12,500	12,500	12,500	12,500	150,000
10,769	11,038	11,038	11,314	11,314	127,754
£35,289	£37,948	£42,313	£45,330	£48,787	£380,652

Month 8	Month 9	Month 10	Month 11	Month 12	Month 13	14 Month	Total
							(600,000)
133,262	141,748	148,835	157,352	167,372	175,741	121,002	1,646,015
(29,279)	(30,743)	(32,926)	(34,572)	(36,301)			(329,203)
(55,769)	(58,558)	(61,485)	(65,851)	(69,144)	(72,601)		(658,406)
(10,769)	(10,903)	(11,038)	(11,176)	(11,314)	(5,657)		(127,754)
37,445	41,544	43,386	45,753	50,613	97,483	121,002	(69,348)
(506,573)	(469,128)	(427,584)	(384,198)	(338,446)	(287,832)	(190,350)	0
(£469,128)	(£427,584)	(£384,198)	(£338,446)	(£287,832)	(£190,350)	(£69,348)	(£69,348)

worksheet will mysteriously disappear and be replaced by a series of asterisks. This is no reason to panic! All that has happened is that the value in a particular cell, under the chosen format, is too wide to be displayed in the column. By simply increasing the column width the underlying values will reappear. In fact, to improve the presentation of the worksheet it is probably a good idea to carry out this exercise anyway. Having completed the entering and formatting of the sales information, the worksheet will now appear as in Table 11.2

As the reader now has a flavour of the procedures necessary to create a worksheet, I will not go into the detail of how the management accountant will create the remainder of the worksheet. Working carefully through the rest of the assumptions, and creating the correct relationships between the various cells, it will be possible to produce the budgeted profit and loss statement and cash flow forecast shown in Table 11.1. (At this point the author has a confession to make! Table 11.1 was initially created using 1-2-3 rather than the calculator, pencil and paper implied earlier. As a regular user of 1-2-3 this is the natural route to adopt and it is likely that readers will also soon

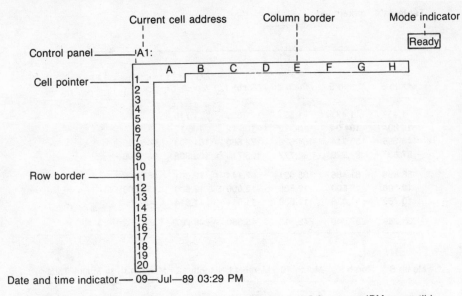

Figure 11.2 Illustration of screen after loading Lotus 1-2-3 onto an IBM-compatible micro-computer

be following this route.)

Initially, a new or inexperienced user of spreadsheets will probably find the electronic solution takes longer than the traditional pencil-and-paper route. This will soon change with practice. However, the benefits of using a spreadsheet are brought sharply into focus when we consider the queries raised by the committee.

To meet the sales director's point (that the initial sales will only be 900 units, but rising by 7.5 per cent per month) it is necessary simply to change the contents of cell B10 from 1000 to 900, to change the formula in cell C10 from +B10*1.05 to +B10*1.075, and then to copy this new formula into each of the cells D10 to M10. *If* all the other formulas underlying the spreadsheet have

Table 11.2 The ABC Company Ltd. Introduction of product X: budget figures for committee meeting of 21 July 1989

| | Profit and loss account | | | | | |
	Month 1	Month 2	Month 3	Month 4	Month 5	Month 6
Unit sales	1,000	1,050	1,102	1,158	1,216	1,276
Sales price	100.00	100.00	100.00	102.00	102.00	102.00
Sales	£100,000	£105,000	£110,250	£118,078	£123,982	£130,181

been correctly expressed, then the effect of the sales director's revised assumptions will now be available.

Similarly, to respond to the points made by the production and finance directors is also a simple matter. For example, to change the costs of sales from 60 to 55 per cent after month 2 it is only necessary to change the multiplier in the cost of sales formulas underlying row 13 (see Table 11.1) from 0.6 to 0.55 for month 3 onwards. Once again, all the other figures will be automatically recalculated.

Dealing with the managing director's query is only slightly more difficult. Leasing rather than buying the equipment has several effects on the figures: the depreciation charge is replaced by the monthly leasing costs; there is no initial cash outlay for the equipment; the time lag in paying the leasing costs needs to be allowed for in the cash flow forecast. Even putting all these changes into the spreadsheet should be accomplished in a matter of minutes.

Furthermore, many other possible variations in the assumptions for our example could be addressed very quickly if the spreadsheet were available. Obviously, as this is only an illustration, the list of assumptions is not exhaustive; a real-life example would be many times more complicated. The ability to revise assumptions and answer 'what if?' questions quickly has been one of the main selling points of spreadsheet software. It overcomes the inability of traditional pencil-and-paper methods to explore more than just a few scenarios.

The way formulas were entered into our example worksheet is typical of the approach most people adopt when first using spreadsheets. Unfortunately, it is also typical of the way many experienced users continue to create their spreadsheets. Earlier I mentioned another problem with the traditional calculator, pencil and paper approach to budgeting. This concerned the assumptions underlying the calculations; in particular, whether they are clearly and unambiguously stated and whether they are consistently and accurately applied. If we are not careful, similar problems can apply to spreadsheets. In our example we are certainly subject to the first of these problems. Our assumptions are hidden within the formulas, rather than being clearly stated.

Table 11.2 continued

Month 7	Month 8	Month 9	Month 10	Month 11	Month 12
1,340	1,407	1,477	1,551	1,629	1,710
104.04	104.04	104.04	106.12	106.12	106.12
£139,424	£146,395	£153,714	£164,628	£172,860	£181,503

At best, our answer to the second problem can only be a qualified yes. If we change the rate of growth in sales, or any of the other assumptions, can we be *sure* that all the consequent changes to the formulas and, thus to the figures, have been made correctly? In our simple example we could probably answer yes, after a careful review. However, in a more realistic and, consequently, more complicated example it will be difficult to ensure consistency between the assumptions and the formulas contained in the spreadsheet. We will return to this issue in the next section when we consider how spreadsheets should be designed to minimize such problems. In the meantime, let us consider some of the other facilities available in spreadsheet software.

So far we have considered only the most basic features of spreadsheet software. Before moving on, I should mention some of the more advanced features which can be of assistance to management accountants. Again, it is beyond the scope of this chapter to go into the detail of how to utilize these functions. There are many books and manuals which do this in great detail — some of which are mentioned in the Further Reading section at the end of this chapter. I will limit myself to listing these facilities and giving a brief indication of how they could be utilized in management accounting.

1. *Graphs*: 1-2-3 and most other spreadsheet packages allow graphs to be produced from data contained in the worksheet. Facilities exist for the user to annotate these graphs as appropriate. The use of graphical output improves the presentation of the data and is a major aid to understanding.
2. *Database management*: 1-2-3 contains a rather rudimentary database function. (Note that 1-2-3 is alleged to have acquired its name as a result of its combining the three main features: spreadsheet; graphs; and database management.) This permits data contained in a worksheet to be sorted or queried on the basis of selected criteria. For example, if we have payroll and personnel data on employees held in a 1-2-3 worksheet, the database commands enable us to answer such questions as which employees work in department X and which employees have an hourly rate of pay greater than £*Y*. Linked with the database function is a data table option. This provides for a more rigorous consideration of the outcome of a series of 'what if?' questions. For example, if the management accountant of our illustrative company wants to explore the effect on profit in the first year of different monthly increases in sales of the new product, a data table could be constructed to show the first year's profit for monthly sales increases of, say, 2.5, 5, 7.5, 10 and 12.5 per cent. In addition, the total cash generated during the year could be computed for each of these monthly sales increases. By viewing such a data table the management accountant could systematically explore a whole range of assumed values. The use of a data table is illustrated in the chapter on 'Short Run Optimization Models' (Ch. 12).

Other functions typically available within spreadsheet software worthy of mention are:

1. *Financial functions*: For example, 1-2-3 supports many financial functions, such as the computation of net present values; internal rate of return; and depreciation under a variety of writing-down procedures.
2. *Statistical functions*: These allow the user to calculate standard statistical measures of mean and dispersion and to perform simple regression.
3. *Mathematical functions*: Functions such as logarithms and square roots are also usually supported.

A final feature that should also be mentioned about 1-2-3 in particular, is macros. These are an attempt to introduce a form of 'programming language' into the software and to enable the user to automate a frequently used set of commands. They are particularly useful in a complex worksheet or when a customized worksheet is being developed for use by someone unfamiliar with 1-2-3. There are many other functions and facilities available within good spreadsheet packages. The reader is recommended to try using one or more of the packages and to experiment with the functions that are of particular interest.

Using spreadsheets: problems, limitations and advantages

Let us now return to our simple example and see what steps can be taken to improve the design of the worksheet to enable us to be more positive in answering the questions we raised about the clarity and consistency of our assumptions. Despite the reservations mentioned above it is worth pointing out that our current worksheet is still a substantial improvement on the calculator, pencil and paper approach. If we had used that approach, a great deal of effort, tantamount to a complete and independent recomputation of the worksheet, would be necessary to make absolutely sure that the assumptions were correctly and consistently applied.

The key step to a further improvement in the worksheet is to remove all assumptions, variables and input data from the formulas, and to locate them in a separate, distinct input area. Then, in general, it will only be necessary to change one or more items in this input area (rather than changing possibly many formulas in the main body of the worksheet) to answer 'what if?' questions. Furthermore, separating the assumptions and input data from the computations facilitates the checking of the assumptions and basic data.

To illustrate this point let us consider some elements of our current worksheet and see how an input area might be used to improve it. Rather than disturbing what we already have in place, we will use column V as our input area and a very wide column U for the related narrative description of the inputs. As before, the discussion will be restricted to the two areas of sales units and prices.

The variables specified in the original problem were:

1. sales in month 1:1,000;
2. monthly rate of increase in unit sales: 5 per cent;
3. initial unit sales price: £100;
4. quarterly growth rate in unit sales price: 2 per cent.

This narrative can be entered into cells U1 to U4 and the values into cells V1 to V4, with the cells suitably formatted. The formula in cell B10 now becomes +V1, and the formula in cell C10 becomes +B10*(1+$V$2). The $ signs in this formula tell 1-2-3 that we want to use the absolute value of cell V2. This use of absolute values is important when copying takes place, as we will want the value in cell V2 to be used in the formula in *each* of the cells D10 to M10. (We do not want to add one column to V for each column we traverse across the worksheet as we did when relative copying took place earlier.) We can now copy the formula in C10 into each of the cells D10 to M10, and on completion of this operation the unit sales figures will appear.

To enter the unit sales prices, we enter +V3 in cell B11 (remember +B11 is already contained in cells C11 and D11). Next, we enter +D11*(1+$V$4) in cell E11, copy the formulas in the range C11 to E11 into each of the ranges F11 to H11 and I11 to K11, and finally copy the formula in cell I11 into each of L11 and M11. As the formulas to calculate the sales values in row 12 are already correctly set up as 'units sales' × 'sales price' (e.g. the formula in cell B12 is +B10*B11) the sales values will be unchanged from when we originally set up the worksheet. Thus, the contents of our new worksheet will be identical to Table 11.2 shown earlier.

This exercise should be continued for the rest of the worksheet so that as many as possible of the assumptions are separately identified in the input area. Questions will inevitably arise as to what is an assumption. The depreciation rate of 25 per cent per annum is clearly an assumption, but what about the twelve periods in a year? There is a school of thought that argues that *no* numbers should be included in formulas, but the author does not subscribe entirely to this view. In this example, changing from twelve monthly periods to say, thirteen 4-weekly periods, would have such a fundamental effect on the figures that a complete redesign of the worksheet would probably be required.

Setting a worksheet up with an input area will take an inexperienced user longer than the method outlined earlier in the chapter. But the benefits of using this method soon become apparent. Let us consider just one of the queries raised earlier. To respond to the sales director it is simply necessary to change cell V1 from 1,000 to 900 and cell V2 from 5 per cent to 7.5 per cent. All the sales and related figures will then be changed automatically. Similarly, many other possible scenarios can be investigated almost instantaneously; thus 'what if?' questions can now be answered quickly and reliably.

In more complex examples this has two particular advantages. First, an accountant or a manager is able to explore the extent of the possible outcomes to a particular problem. Second, it is also possible to identify the critical variables in a particular problem by examining the sensitivity of the outcome to changes in individual variables. More effort can then be put in to improving the estimates of these critical variables.

With the proper use of an input area we should be able to satisfy ourselves that our assumptions are clearly and unambiguously stated. However, we are no nearer answering questions about the consistent and accurate application of these assumptions. Naturally, such questions are far more complex when real-life spreadsheet applications are involved. This can be an important issue when potentially expensive decisions are being taken on the basis of spreadsheet output. There are several strategies which can reduce the chances of incorporating errors into the worksheet. These are listed below:

1. *Design*: Some design issues have already been discussed, but repetition does no harm. The most important advice is that separate areas should be used for headings, inputs, calculations and output. Many organizations have developed comprehensive standards for the design and implementation of spreadsheets, and it is recommended that any organization which intends to become a major user of such software goes at least partly down this route. Another important design issue is perhaps better described as planning. Before starting on a complex worksheet the user should draft out on paper an outline of the worksheet; what is to appear and where it is to appear. Many users cannot wait to actually start using the software, but errors made at the planning stage can have serious consequences later, so 'more haste less speed' is a good motto when constructing complex spreadsheets.

2. *Documentation*: There is a need to produce documentation covering various aspects of a complex spreadsheet application, detailing such matters as how to use it, meaning of inputs, explanation of key formulas, significance of output, and explanation of any macros. Many people dislike producing documentation, but without it the spreadsheet is likely to be unusable by anyone other than its preparer.

3. *Size*: There are two problems here. One problem is the physical limitation of the computer's memory, and the second is the sheer complexity of a large spreadsheet. If either of these issues is likely to arise consideration should be given at the design stage to using two or more separate worksheets, perhaps sharing a common database.

4. *Testing and validation*: It is very difficult, as it is with all programming of computers, to ensure that the spreadsheet does what it is intended to do. While good design helps, a comprehensive testing strategy would involve a return to the calculator, pencil and paper approach from which we are trying to escape. An independent review by another person can help, but it is almost impossible to spot an error in someone else's complex spreadsheet. There is no simple answer. The best advice is to decide on the level of testing by reference to the importance of the spreadsheet output and the likely cost of errors; the more important the output and the more costly the errors, then the greater the level of testing that is needed. There are examples of organizations which have decided that the best testing occurs when two experienced users design and implement a spreadsheet in tandem — an expensive solution, but sometimes necessary.

5. *Macros*: As noted earlier macros are an attempt to add a 'programming' facility into spreadsheet software. If the design of a complex application involves the use of a significant number of complicated macros, this could be an indication that a spreadsheet package is perhaps not the right software for the task in hand. Maybe a financial modelling package on a mainframe computer is required or possibly some other type of micro-computer software package.

Further reading

Jackson, M. (1985) *Creative Modelling with Lotus 1-2-3*, Chichester: John Wiley.
Ross, S.C. (1986) *Understanding and Using Lotus 1-2-3*, St Paul, MN: West Publishing.
Smith, G.N. (1985) *Electronic Spreadsheet Applications for Cost Accounting*, Cincinnati: South-Western Publishing.

Chapter 12

Short-run optimization models
MILES GIETZMANN

Optimization and satisficing sensitivity analysis

After studying undergraduate management accounting courses, the student
would expect to see organizations optimizing production planning and many
other decisions. However, except for in a limited number of industries — such
as oil refining, where linear programming is utilized — the pervasiveness of
optimization is not generally observable. There may be a whole host of reasons
for this; a selected few are as follows:

1. Information on an important variable such as a product demand schedule,
   may be sketchy and unstructured, inhibiting the identification of actual
   relationships.
2. Uncertainty over the specific value of variables may discourage those
   responsible for estimation from quantifying expectational judgements.
3. The historically utilized mode of analysis has been to conduct simple
   simulation analysis to model interactions, without requiring explicit
   optimization.

There may be many other reasons that could be added to this list. For
instance, mathematical considerations arising from inherent non-linearities in
the problem; or behavioural considerations such as the unease with which some
people view mathematical algorithms such as linear programming.

Here attention is restricted to the three reasons highlighted above. The
rationale for this is twofold. First, these three reasons are commonly enunciated
as reasons why linear programming optimization is not implemented and hence
they are sufficiently important to warrant consideration in their own right.
Second, it is the intention to outline how the three issues can simultaneously
be explored by adopting a detailed (parametric) approach to linear-programming
sensitivity analysis.

If the decision problem under consideration is formulated using any sort of simulation methodology such as 'what if?' spreadsheet, then this analysis is called sensitivity analysis. Such an approach is referred to as 'satisficing' sensitivity analysis because with this methodology there is no requirement to either actually formulate the problem as an optimization problem or locate the optimal solution. Parametric analysis will here refer to the analysis of changes in the optimal solution of a linear programming problem, as parameters are varied. (Many authors refer to parametric analysis as sensitivity analysis; this terminology will not be used in this chapter.)

Let us commence by considering the contention that sensitivity analysis adequately deals with many decision problems, freeing us from the need for any explicit formulation and solution of an optimization problem.

A common method of carrying out simulation/sensitivity analysis in organizations is the electronic spreadsheet (see Ch. 11). For instance, with a Lotus 1-2-3 spreadsheet, problems can be modelled by a 'what if?' spreadsheet using the data table option.

To illustrate this approach, a production mix problem is presented below. Results achieved via a data table sensitivity analysis is contrasted with the results generated by a Lotus 1-2-3 linear-programming add-in software package. The reason for the choice of the Lotus 1-2-3 add-in software, rather than a stand-alone package, is so as to allow for a direct comparison between the two approaches, and to show that linear programming can be directly incorporated into financial planning.

The CIC production mix problem

CIC Company produces two types of chemical fertilizers: $5-10-5$ and $6-8-8$. The fertilizers are made from mixes of nitrate, phosphate, potash and with the remaining bulk being made up of an inert filler respectively. The mix of these ingredients in a fertilizer is determined by the type of fertilizer, that is the $5-10-5$ contains 5 per cent nitrate, 10 per cent phosphate and 5 per cent potash by weight. The company forecasts that the two fertilizers will generate a contribution margin of £16.00 for $5-10-5$ and £22.80 for $6-8-8$ per ton. CIC has agreed contracts with suppliers for the provision of 1,200 tons of nitrate and 2,000 tons of phosphate. It is assumed that the suppliers could not provide more nitrate or phosphate during the planning period. CIC has also provisionally agreed a contract with an alternative supplier, to provide 1,500 tons of potash. However, it is envisaged that this additional contract tonnage could feasibly be revised up or down during the planning stage considered in this problem. The company, for the purposes of this problem, is assumed to have an unlimited supply of inert filler on hand. In addition, the company has accepted an order for 8,000 tons of $6-8-8$. During this simulation planning phase, the company would like to determine an appropriate production mix decision that will generate a satisfactory high contribution margin.

A Lotus 1-2-3 data table presentation for the problem is shown in Table 12.1. The formulas for cells D15 and D16 which are referenced in the data table appear below the data table output.

The following heuristic approach was used to determine the table structure. The initial amount of $6-8-8$ proposed is the minimum of amount $6-8-8$ that will meet the order constraint. One thousand unit increase intervals are then chosen until the maximum feasible level of $6-8-8$ is determined. The manual calculation for this is as follows:

$$\text{maximum } 6-8-8 \text{ level} = \min \left\{ \frac{1,200}{0.06}, \frac{2,000}{0.08}, \frac{1,500}{0.08} \right\} = 18,750$$

The interval range is arbitrary, and a much smaller interval could have been chosen without increasing data entry requirements significantly.

The above data table analysis suggests in line 27 the choice of the following production plans.

units	*units*	*contribution*
$5-10-5$	$6-8-8$	margin
6,000	15,000	£438,000

Now consider the explicit formulation of the problem as an LP optimization problem:

Maximize $16Q_1 + 22.8Q_2$
Subject to $0.05Q_1 + 0.06Q_2 \leq 1,200$ nitrate
$\quad\quad\quad\quad 0.1Q_1 + 0.08Q_2 \leq 2,000$ phosphate
$\quad\quad\quad\quad 0.05Q_1 + 0.08Q_2 \leq 1,500$ potash
$\quad\quad\quad\quad\quad\quad\quad\quad Q_2 \geq 8,000$ committed order
$\quad\quad\quad Q_1 \geq 0 \; Q_2 \geq 0$
$\quad\quad Q_1 = \text{level of } 5-10-5$
$\quad\quad Q_2 = \text{level of } 6-8-8$

For a discussion of how to formulate linear programming problems, see for instance, Eppen and Gould (1985). The Lotus 1-2-3 add-in software program OPTIMAL SOLUTIONS was used to solve the above production-mix problem. The results are presented in Table 12.2. This form of output is typical of most commercial packages. The row-3 quantity variables are the decision variables for the problem, the optimal values of which are to be determined, which in turn determines the optimal objective function value at row 9. That is, the maximum contribution margin achievable is £438,000 when 6,000 tons of $5-10-5$ fertilizer and 15,000 tons of $6-8-8$ fertilizer is produced. Other

Table 12.1   Lotus 1-2-3 data table analysis

	A	B	C	D	E	F	G
1		5–10–5	6–8–8		right-hand-		
2		constraint	coefficient		side value		
3							
4	Nitrate	0.05	0.06		1,200		
5	Phosphate	0.1	0.08		2,000		
6	Potash	0.05	0.08		1,500		
7	Order	0	1		8,000		
8							
9		contribution margin					
10		£16.00	£22.80				
11							
12							
13	Initial assumptions						
14	production of 6–8–8			8,000			
15	production of 5–10–5			13,600			
16	total contribution			£400,000			
17					Prod.	Prod.	Total
18					6–8–8	5–10–5	contribution
19						+D16	+D17
20					8,000	13,600	£400,000
21					9,000	12,800	£410,000
22					10,000	12,000	£420,000
23					11,000	10,800	£423,600
24					12,000	9,600	£427,200
25					13,000	8,400	£430,800
26					14,000	7,200	£434,400
27					15,000	6,000	£438,000
28					16,000	4,400	£435,200
29					17,000	2,800	£432,400
30					18,000	1,200	£429,600
31					18,750	0	£427,500
32							
33	Maximum defined contribution margin						£438,000
34							
35							

D15: @ROUND (@MIN (((E4—D14*C4)/B4), ((E5—D14*C5)/B5), ((E6—D14*C6)/B6))
D16: +B10*D15+C10*D14

Linear programming problem in standard inequality form

Max.		16X	+	22.8Y				
subject to								
		0.05X	+	0.06Y	< =	1,200	X = non-negative AMO
		0.10X	+	0.08Y	< =	2,000	of 5–10–5
		0.05X	+	0.08Y	< =	1,500	
				1.00Y	> =	8,000	Y = non-negative AMO
							of 6–8–8

important variables presented on the printout are the slack and shadow price variables presented in rows 30 to 33. A non-zero slack variable indicates that the inequality constraint concerned is non-binding at the optimal solution; that is, for the above problem there is either unused amounts of an input, or production of 6−8−8 is above the committed order requirements. Shadow prices indicate the incremental effect of a unit change in the input resource level or committed-order level on the objective function. This idea will be discussed in more detail later.

The principle of complementary slackness provides comparative results for the relationship between shadow prices and slack values (see Eppen and Gould 1985). If a constraint is binding, the principle implies that the associated slack variable will be zero and shadow price will be positive. In contrast, when a constraint is non-binding the associated slack variable will be positive and the shadow price will be zero. As will be shown in Figures 12.1 and 12.2, the optimal basis (set of variables that can take on non-zero values), binding constraint set for the problem changes if parameters such as the level of potash available vary outside a certain range. The constraint-limit sensitivity analysis presented on row 46 indicates the ranges for which a change in one parameter can occur before any of the zero-valued variables (referred to as non-basic variables) assume positive values (i.e. enter the basis).

To allow for more concise presentation of the results, a summary version of the output will be presented below. Since many values will remain constant for the analysis below, such as contribution margins and constraint coefficients, these values are not included. The summary of Table 12.2 is presented in Table 12.3.

The graphical representation of the constraint set for the problem and graphical solution to the problem are presented in Figures 12.1 and 12.2 respectively.

Graphical analysis can also be used to demonstrate the constraint-limit sensitivity results. Figure 12.1 shows that optimal basis for the above problem is defined by the intersection of the nitrate (NC) and potash constraints (PC), (NC = PC). (Table 12.3 reiterates this result since the basis equations must have zero slack when the solution occurs at the 'limit' of the constraints.) Table 12.3 identifies the constraint-limit sensitivity bands for the potash constraint as 1,600 and 1,400. Figures 12.3 and 12.4 show how the graphical solution changes when the amount of available potash is outside these bands. Figure 12.3 illustrates, if the potash level is reduced to 1,350 then the optimal basis is no longer defined by the intersection of NC and PC but now by the intersection of PhC and PC. There is no basic feasible solution defining an extreme point where NC = PC with the revised potash level, because the reduction in potash has moved the revised potash constraint PC below the nitrate constraint NC (for feasible phosphate levels). At the bound value for potash of 1,400 the basis could be defined by either PC = NC or PC = PhC or

Table 12.2 'Optimal solutions' presentation: Lotus 1-2-3 linear-programming add-in software

	A	B	C	D	E	F
1	Product	5−10−5	6−8−8			
2						
3	Quantity	6,000	15,000			
4						
5	Contrib.					
6	Margin	£16.00	£22.80			
7						
8	Object.					
9	Function		£438,000			
10						
11	Constraints					
12					Used available	
13	Nitrate	0.05	0.06	1,200	1,200	
14	Phosphate	0.1	0.08	1,800	2,000	
15	Potash	0.05	0.08	1,500	1,500	
16	Order	0 .	1	15,000	8,000	
17						
18						
19	Objective	Operation	Achieved		Priority	
20						
21	C9	Maximize	438,000.00		1.0	
22						
23	Variables	Type			Reduced cost	
24						
25	B3	Regular	6,000.00		0.00	
26	C3	Regular	15,000.00		0.00	
27						
28	Constraints	OP value	Slack		Shadow price	
29						
30	D13	< = E13	0.00		140.00	
31	D14	< = E14	200.00		0.00	
32	D15	< = E15	0.00		180.00	
33	D16	> = E16	7,000.00		0.00	
34						
35	Parameters					
36						
37	Display precision		2			
38	Cost coef. sensitivity output		A41			
39	Cons. limit sensitivity output		A46			
40						
41	Cost coefficient sensitivity					
42	Var. cell	Upper bound	Lower bound			
43	B3	19	14.25			
44	C3	25.6	19.2			
45						

Table 12.2 continued

46	Constraint limit sensitivity		
47	RHS cell	Upper bound	Lower bound
48	D13	1,250	1,125
49	D14	Infinity	1,800
50	D15	1,600	1,400
51	D16	15,000	Min. infinity

Table 12.3 Summary solution for potash availability of 1,500

Product	5–10–5	6–8–8	Potash	1,500
Optimal quantity	6,000	15,000	Available	
Obj. function	£438,000			
Constraints	Slack		Shadow price	
Nitrate	0.00		140.00	
Phosphate	200.00		0.00	
Potash	0.00		180.00	
Com. order	7,000.00		0.00	
Potash constraint limit sensitivity				
	Upper bound		Lower bound	
	1,600		1,400	

NC = PhC since all three constraint sets form an optimal basis with $Q_1 = 12,000$ and $Q_2 = 10,000$.

Figure 12.4 illustrates that once the potash level provision is greater than 1,600, the constraint is non-binding and the optimal basis is defined by the basis equations NC and $Q_1 = 0$, labelled by point x. That is, increases in potash provision have 'pushed the constraint out' until there is unused potash.

As can be seen from Table 12.2, the prior sensitivity analysis located the optimal solution exactly. One would not necessarily expect this result to occur always. For instance, the arbitrary interval used may pass over the optimal solution. Therefore in more complicated problems, defining an initial feasible solution and subsequent feasible solutions to iterate to, may not be possible, using a simple heuristic rule as above. Thus in some situations programming methods need to be utilized to deal with the sheer complexity of the problem. However, even where sensitivity analysis can identify solutions that are close to the optimal solution, linear programming optimization offers additional desirable features. The rationale for using linear programming is far more than just to locate the optimal product mix. The features discussed below are especially useful in situations where variable values are uncertain. This requires a discussion on the parametric analysis for linear programming solutions.

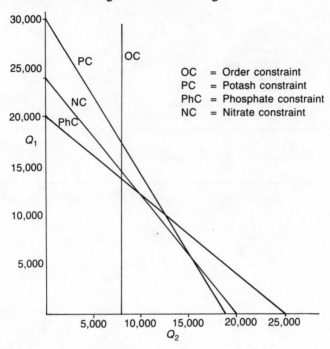

Figure 12.1   Constraint set

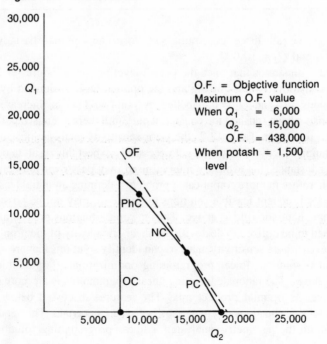

Figure 12.2   Graphical solution over feasible production set

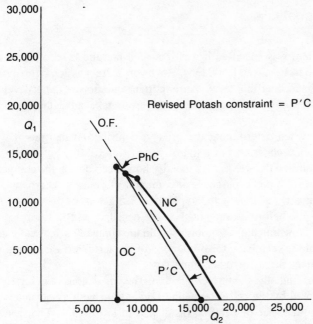

Figure 12.3 Graphical solution over revised feasible production set: potash level of 1,350

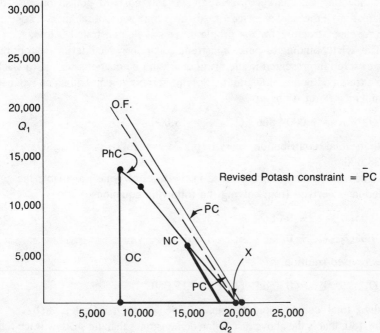

Figure 12.4 Graphical solution over revised feasible production set: potash level of 1,650

Parametric analysis

When the problem was specified it was indicated that the level of potash it was planned to purchase was 1,500 tons. However, there was some flexibility (uncertainty) concerning this level. An important question is: what level of potash should the company purchase in order to take advantage of this flexibility?

Suppose that when determining the product contribution margins it was assumed that the purchase cost of a ton of potash was £200. Does the linear programming solution derived earlier identify how much potash the company should purchase, if it could purchase any amount of potash? Alternatively, suppose the company had contracted to purchase 1,500 tons of potash at £200 sometime ago, just before a dramatic 100 per cent increase in the price of potash to £400. How much of the potash should the company sell at £400 and how much should it keep back for production of the fertilizers, assuming no change in fertilizer prices or other input costs.

Let us consider, initially, the former question. The potash constraint for Table 12.2 is represented by the cell referencing D15 ≤ E15 with associated zero slack and a shadow price of £180.00 (as displayed in row 32). The shadow price indicates the incremental effect on the total contribution margin if an additional unit of potash becomes available. This increase in profitability is after meeting the market price (unit variable cost) of potash because the calculation of the shadow price already takes into account the market cost and the revenue structure for the problem. This is demonstrated below.

The strictly binding resource constraint equations which define the (optimal basic) solution presented in the printout are those equations with zero slack, the nitrate and potash constraints. Solving these two constraints as a pair of simultaneous equations gives

$$Q_{5-10-5} = 6,000 \quad \text{and} \quad Q_{6-8-8} = 15,000$$

with a total contribution margin of $Z^* = 16Q_{5-10-5} + 22.8Q_{6-8-8} = £438,000$.

Hence if there is a unit increase in the level of potash available the new solution is derived from solving the following equations:

$$0.05Q_{5-10-5} + 0.06Q_{6-8-8} = 1,200$$
$$0.05Q_{5-10-5} + 0.08Q_{6-8-8} = 1,501$$

The revised solution is

$$Q_{5-10-5} = 5,940 \quad \text{and} \quad Q_{6-8-8} = 15,050$$

with a total contribution margin of $Z^{**} = 16Q_{5-10-5} + 22.8Q_{6-8-8} = £438,180$, that is the above discussion demonstrates that the shadow price fully reflects required information for assessing a unit change in available potash.

Table 12.4 Cost/revenue structure of 5–10–5, 6–8–8 for potash availability of 1,501 tons compared to 1,500 tons

	Unit price/cost	Quantity		Totals	
Sales revenue					
5–10–5	45	5,940	(6,000)	267,300	(270,000)
6–8–8	57	15,050	(1,500)	857,850	(855,000)
				1,125,150	(1,125,000)
Production costs					
5–10–5 Nitrate	150	297	(300)	45,550	(45,000)
Phosphate	115	594	(600)	68,310	(69,000)
Potash	200	297	(300)	59,400	(60,000)
				172,260	(174,000)
6–8–8 Nitrate	150	903	(900)	135,450	(135,000)
Phosphate	115	1,204	(1,200)	138,460	(138,000)
Potash	200	1,204	(1,200)	240,800	(240,000)
				514,710	(513,000)
				438,180	(438,000)
Contribution margin					
5–10–5	16	5,940	(6,000)	95,040	(96,000)
6–8–8	22.8	15,050	(15,000)	343,140	(342,000)
				438,180	(438,000)

The incremental effect on total contribution margin of one additional unit of potash is $Z^{**} - Z^* = £180 =$ shadow price. However, the value obtained is valid only over a restricted range, often referred to as the right-hand-side range. Outside the restricted right-hand-side range the shadow price may change.

Within the restricted range the set of non-zero basic variables will remain the same, although specific non-zero values may change. Outside the restricted range the set of non-zero basic variables changes. For instance the basic variable values for two levels of potash, one within the restricted range and one outside the range are shown in Table 12.5. When potash availability is increased to 1,650, Q_1 becomes zero and leaves the basis while S_p becomes non-zero and enters the basis.

Table 12.5 Effect of changes in potash availability

Variable	Notation	Potash availability	
		1,500	*1,650*
5−10−5 Production	$Q_1 =$	6,000	0
6−8−8 Production	$Q_2 =$	15,000	20,000
Slacks			
Phosphate	$S_{pH} =$	200	0
Potash	$S_p =$	0	50

The reason for the change in basic variables can be explained by reference to Figures 12.1 and 12.2 for potash $= 1,500$ the optimal solution occurs at the extreme point defined by the intersection of the potash and nitrate constraints, hence $S_p = S_n = 0$ and the remaining variables are positive. For potash $= 1,650$ the solution occurs at the extreme point defined by the intersection of the nitrate constraint with the $Q_1 = 0$ axis, hence $S_n = Q_1 = 0$.

From Table 12.2 it can be seen (line 50) that the shadow prices are valid provided that the availability of potash is between 1,400 and 1,600. The effect of the optimal solution immediately outside this range is illustrated in Tables 12.6.1 and 12.6.2.

When the problem is solved with a potash level of 1,601 tons the shadow price becomes zero (Table 12.6.1). The associated slack variable S_p becomes positive and enters the basis. Any additional potash provision will not increase the total contribution margin. This explains the infinity value placed upon the upper bound on the constraint-limit sensitivity: the zero shadow price holds no matter how much more potash is provided!

When the problem is solved with a potash level of 1,399 tons the shadow price increases to 250 and this shadow price is valid provided potash availability

Table 12.6.1 Potash availability 1,601

Product	5–10–5	6–8–8	Potash available	1,601
Optimal quantity	0	20,000		
Obj. function	£456,000			
Constraints	Slack		Shadow price	
Nitrate	0		380	
Phosphate	400		0	
Potash	1		0	
Com. order	1,200		0	
Potash constraint sensitivity				
	Upper bound		Lower bound	
	Infinity		1,600	

Table 12.6.2 Potash availability 1,399

Product	5–10–5	6–8–8	Potash available	1,399
Optimal quantity	12,020	9,975		
Obj. function	£419,750			
Constraints	Slack	Shadow price		
Nitrate	0.5	0		
Phosphate	0	35		
Potash	0	250		
Com. order	1,975	0		
Potash constraint unit sensitivity				
	Upper bound		Lower bound	
	1,400		1,320	

is greater than or equal to 1,320. Table 12.6.3 presents the summary printout for solution to the problem below this bound.

For the new solution the shadow price for potash is now revised. Tables 12.6.1, 12.6.2 and 12.6.3 demonstrate the intuitive result that as the amount of available potash is reduced, the incremental contribution of additional potash is non-decreasing. The lower bound of 640 tons is the ultimate lower bound because at least 640 tons of potash is required to satisfy the order constraint.

It is now possible to conduct a systematic parametric analysis to calculate the 'optimal value function' for the available potash for the CIC production-mix problem. The level of available potash will now be a variable represent by θ (i.e. the potash constraint in the original problem is replaced by the constraint $0.05Q_1 + 0.08Q_2 \leq \theta$) The objective function now varies as the

Table 12.6.3 Potash availability 1,319

Product	5–10–5	6–8–8	Potash available	1,319
Optimal quantity	13,580	8,000		
Obj. function	£399,680			
Constraints	Slack	Shadow price		
Nitrate	41	0		
Phosphate	2	0		
Potash	0	320		
Com. order	0	2.8		
Potash constraint sensitivity				
	Upper bound	Lower bound		
	1,320	640		

level of potash is varied and we will denote its value by $v(\theta)$. In formal terms the objective function is said to be parameterized by θ. The derivation of the co-ordinates for Figure 12.5 is presented in the appendix to this chapter.

A useful point to note is that the slope of the optimal value function over the respective linear segments will indicate the change in the objective function induced by incremental changes in the level of potash. That is, the slope of the optimal value function is the shadow price on the potash constraint.

It is now possible to resolve the two questions posed at the beginning of the section.

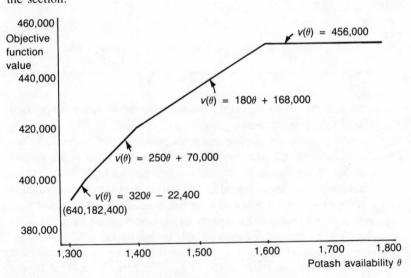

Figure 12.5 Potash optimal value function

First, if the CIC company has complete flexibility to purchase as much potash as it desires at £200 a ton, the company should purchase 1,600 units of potash and will attain a total contribution margin of £456,000 ((180 × 1,600) + 168,000). The solution was obtained by recognizing that the company will always find it worthwhile incorporating more potash into the production process, as long as the shadow price is greater than zero.

Once a zero shadow price is obtained, additional units of potash will not increase the total contribution margin and will, in fact, not be used in the production of the two fertilizers.

Second, if the 1,500 tons of potash that cost the company £200 a ton can now be sold for £400 a ton, the company should sell off 100 tons of potash and, in so doing, achieve a total contribution margin (including potash sales) of £460,000 ((250 × 1,400) + 70,000) + (100 × 400). Again the solution was obtained by referring to the shadow price and the resultant effect by value substitution into the optimal value function. That is, for $1,400 \le \theta \le 1600$ the shadow price of £180 is less than the additional unit proceeds from sale of the potash for £200 (£400 − £200). However, for $\theta < 1,400$, the shadow price exceeds the incremental potash sales proceeds.

The above analysis has illustrated how parametric analysis can be used to answer some simple managerial questions concisely and accurately.

Further sensitivity analysis

Let us now critically evaluate the performance of linear programming *versus* sensitivity analysis. The previous section demonstrated how parametric linear programming analysis could be used as an effective decision support aid for making product-mix decisions when resource provision was variable. Consider now whether sensitivity analysis allows resolution of the two specific problems posed earlier. For those problems where it is possible to identify initial and intermediate feasible solutions readily, sensitivity analysis may be able to identify solutions quite close to the optimal solution. In fact as demonstrated, the heuristic sensitivity analysis presented earlier identified the optimal solution for the CIC production-mix problem. Consider now the two problems.

Given CIC is free to purchase as much potash as it desires, how can sensitivity analysis help to establish what is the correct purchase level?

A new heuristic sensitivity strategy will need to be developed for this purpose. One possible strategy is as follows:

1. Starting with a potash level of 1,500 tons define other possible potash purchase plans using an (arbitrary) purchase amount of say 75 tons.
2. Decide whether to use the additional potash to:

(a) increase production of 5−10−5 while maintaining 6−8−8 constant;
(b) increase production of 6−8−8 while maintaining 5−10−5 constant;
(c) increase production of 5−10−5 and reduce production of 6−8−8;
(d) increase production of 6−8−8 and reduce production of 5−10−5.
3. Decide on the specific increase/decrease levels.

Thus the problem involves searching for an optimal solution over several decision variables. First a choice has to be made about whether the amount of potash should increase or decrease. The production mix needs then to be reinvestigated for each potash level chosen. Effectively a search is being carried out over a three-dimensional decision space by exploring just one dimension at a time. A spreadsheet approach offers no real guidance to the step size of the search or an indication over which search dimension is likely to prove most profitable at each stage. The optimizing or search strategy must be provided by the user.

In short the sensitivity analysis is soon likely to become unwieldy and possibly increasingly inaccurate as one non-optimal decision is used as the data set for another non-optimal decision.

Given the ease and speed with which the software package operates to provide optimal solutions, the shortcomings of sensitivity analysis become clearly apparent. The above analysis demonstrates that important questions about resource allocation are sometimes 'once removed' from locating the static optimal solution. Although sensitivity analysis may be effective for locating 'good' static solutions (for tractable problems), it is not generally effective for analysing the 'once removed' problems that are best addressed from within an optimization framework.

The analysis above presented the arguments favouring the implementation of linear programming rather than relying on spreadsheet sensitivity analysis.

Other arguments introduced earlier against the adoption of linear programming were concerned with uncertainty over the value of variables. One approach to such issues would be to use stochastic programming which explicitly incorporates formalized probability estimates into the procedures. This approach is not considered here as it is outside the scope of this chapter. In addition, there are situations where managers can make decisions without needing to assign (or cannot assign) probabilities to events, as the following example demonstrates.

Reconsider the potash problem. Suppose CIC management have agreed a contract for 1,600 tons of potash at £200 a ton. Management expects the price of potash to increase considerably between the order and delivery date. Should all the potash be incorporated into production of fertilizers, or should it be resold (assuming one can ignore further transaction costs)? Provided managers do not expect the price of potash to rise above £380 the resale decision can be ignored as demonstrated by the optimal value function (shadow price plus original cost = £380). This argument is analogous in the above example to a price rise to £400 a ton for potash. Clearly the required knowledge may not always exist, however, the optimal value function provides an amenable method of dealing with those that do meet the requirement and providing a *benchmark* for decisions.

Parametric analysis (objective function parametries) for the contribution margin value is similar in spirit to the (potash) right-hand-side value parametric analysis. Here, instead of considering the effect on the objective function of changing on input resource provision level, one considers the effect on the objective function induced by changes in the contribution margin arising from say changes in variable costs or revenue. Parametric analysis could be used to answer the following types of questions:

1. If the contribution margin of one product increases, should production be increased?
2. By how much will the contribution margin of a product have to fall in order for it to be optimal to discontinue production?
3. Over what range can the contribution margin of a product vary without necessitating any change in the optimal production plan?

As discussed at the beginning of the chapter, when managers face uncertainty over contribution margins, the answers to questions such as (3) give a useful indication that, if the uncertainty is restricted to a certain range, this will have no impact on the optimal production plan.

Another important extension is to recognize that most real world problems will be of a dynamic (multi-period) nature. The previous section considered how CIC should response to possible changes in potash costs. The model was for a single period and can be formulated quite generally to show this as follows:

$$
\begin{aligned}
\text{maximize} \quad & C_1^1 \, Q_1^1 + C_2^1 \, Q_2^1 \\
\text{subject to} \quad & a_{11}^1 \, Q_1^1 + a_{12}^1 \, Q_2^1 \leq b_1^1 \quad \text{nitrate} \\
& a_{21}^1 \, Q_1^1 + a_{22}^1 \, Q_2^1 \leq b_2^1 \quad \text{phosphate} \\
& a_{31}^1 \, Q_1^1 + a_{32}^1 \, Q_2^1 \leq b_3^1 \quad \text{potash} \\
& a_{42}^1 \, Q_2^1 \geq b_4^1 \qquad\qquad \text{order} \\
& Q_1^1 \geq 0, \; Q_2^1 \geq 0
\end{aligned}
$$

where the superscript indicates the model is for period $t = 1$. In the next period the model would be reformulated, allowing for any revision of coefficients, as follows:

$$\text{maximize} \quad C_1^2 \, Q_1^2 + C_2^2 \, Q_2^2$$
$$\text{subject to} \quad a_{11} Q_1^2 + a_{12} Q_2^2 \leq b_1^2 \text{ nitrate}$$
$$a_{21} Q_1^2 + a_{22} Q_2^2 \leq b_2^2 \text{ phosphate}$$
$$a_{31} Q_1^2 + a_{32} Q_2^2 \leq b_3^2 \text{ potash}$$
$$a_{42} Q_2^2 \geq b_4^2 \qquad\qquad \text{order}$$
$$Q_1^2 \geq 0, \; Q_2^2 \geq 0$$

where the previous discussion on potash provision suggests that $C_1^1 \neq C_1^2$ and $C_2^1 \neq C_2^2$ because of an expected price change for potash, and related to this it is possible that CIC may choose $b_3^1 \neq b_3^2$.

The above methodology treats each planning period as separate, as it is assumed there is no functional dependence between the two planning problems. However, once it is recognized that it may be desirable to build up stocks of raw materials (such as potash) in one period; in advance of an expected price increase in a future period, a functional dependence/linkage is introduced. In general, costs in period t are then determined by both production in the period and purchasing decisions in periods 1 through t. The rest of this section considers how such interdependencies can be formulated and what implications this has for the efficacy of linear programming as compared to 'what if?' sensitivity analysis. The intention of this section is to highlight the need for consideration of multi-period dependencies for realistic problems. For solution techniques and indepth discussion of multi-period linear programming, see Williams (1985).

For a multi-period model it is necessary to establish the material flows equations. For each relevant right-hand-side variable j (such as potash) in each period, the following flow relationship is required to be satisfied:

amount in stock in period $(t-1)$ (i_j^{t-1})
+ amount purchased in period (t) (p_j^{t})
= amount purchased in period (t) (y^{it})
+ amount in stock at end of period (t) (i_j^{t})

In addition the cost of holding stock in period t (h_t), which includes a working capital costs, will need to be included as an argument of the objective function. In general, the n-period planning problem for CIC, where for simplicity, the unrealistic assumption is made that only potash (i_3) may be stockpiled between periods, is formulated as follows:

$$\text{maximize} \quad \sum_{t=1}^{n} c_1^t x_1^t + \sum_{t=1}^{n} c_2^t x_2^t - \sum_{t=1}^{n} h^t i_3^t$$
$$\text{subject to} \quad i_3^t = i_3^{t-1} + p_3^t - y_3^t \text{ (stock flow balance)}$$
$$i_3^{t-1} + p_3^t = b_3^t \qquad \text{(period maximum resource availability)}$$

$$a_{11}^t x_1^t + a_{12}^t x_2^t \leq b_1^t \ \ \text{(nitrate)}$$
$$a_{21}^t x_1^t + a_{22}^t x_2^t \leq b_2^t \ \ \text{(phosphate)}$$
$$a_{31}^t x_1^t + a_{32}^t x_2^t \leq b_3^t \ \ \text{(potash)}$$
$$a_{42}^t x_2^t \geq b_4^t \ \ \text{(order)}$$
$$x_1^t \geq 0, \ x_2^t \geq 0, \ i_3^t \geq 0, \ p_1^t \geq 0, \ y_1^t \geq 0$$
$$\text{for all } t = 1 \ldots n$$

An essential point to note is that for say only three future planning periods there would be eighteen resource constraints, not counting non-negativity conditions. If, in addition, other resources besides potash could be stockpiled, the constraint set would expand further. It should be noted that at the beginning of the planning period, production and resource purchase targets are set for the full planning horizon. However, if revised information becomes available (say the end of the first planning period) the remaining targets should be redetermined by solving the revised problem.

The above discussion demonstrates that resource allocation decisions in an organization can be and usually are of a multi-period nature. Attempting to solve such multi-period problems using 'what if?' sensitivity analysis would require many iterative sample solutions even assuming the problem is tractable.

The above analysis describes the use of 'best guesses' when there is uncertainty associated with a variable. Using parametric analysis then allows identification of a range over which the variable value, predicted, could change without changing the opportunity cost of using scarce resources.

With the parametric analysis results, the decision-maker can formally incorporate the sensitivity of the problem to specification (of an uncertain variable) when constructing flexible financial budgets.

The above analysis has considered parametric analysis with only one parametric variable. However, the analysis can be extended to cover simultaneous changes in parameters. The 100 per cent rule (see Cunningham 1987) can be used to assess simultaneous changes of more than one variable. The rule states that if the sum of percentages of slack used, sums to less than 100 per cent, then the simultaneous change under consideration will not change the basic equations and hence opportunity costs for the scarce resources will not change. Thus the implications of simultaneous changes can be assessed directly.

For instance, consider the following two problems. Suppose the amount of nitrate available is reduced to 1,170 tons and the amount of potash is set at 1,450 tons. What production plan should CIC now adopt? In addition, what would be the minimum decline in total contribution from the £438,000 achieved originally (Table 12.2)?

The 100 per cent rule allows for determination of whether the solutions can be determined directly or whether the problem needs to be reformulated and resolved in full. From Table 12.2 the lower bounds (constraint limit sensitivities) are 1,125 and 1,400 for nitrate and potash respectively, directly implying allowable decreases of 75 tons and 100 tons. Thus the sum change for the simultaneous variations is:

$$\frac{30}{75} + \frac{50}{100} = 0.9 < 1.0$$

This satisfaction of the condition means that the same pair of basis equations (with revised right-hand-side values) will define the new solution as follows:

$$0.05Q_{5-10-5} + 0.06Q_{6-8-8} = 1,170$$
$$0.05Q_{5-10-5} + 0.08Q_{6-8-8} = 1,450$$
$$Q_{5-10-5} = 6,600, \quad Q_{6-8-8} = 14,000$$

The minimum decline in contribution margin can then be directly determined by calculating the respective effects on total contribution of an increase in 5−10−5 by 600 tons and a reduction in 6−8−8 by 1,000 tons as follows:

$$(600 \times 16) - (1,000 \times 22.8) = -13,200$$

revised total contribution margin achievable = 438,000 − 13,200 = £424,800. The 100 per cent rule allows for the determination of benchmark summary measures which are useful for communication to management, who want an overview of parametric analysis results.

Without the guidance of the 100 per cent rule, this type of result cannot necessarily be derived from direct application of the shadow prices, as without the rule one cannot be sure the shadow price values have not changed. It should also be remembered though that most commercial packages will cope with simultaneous changes in more than one resource constraint.

Conclusion

The use of parametric analysis was demonstrated. An understanding of how to conduct parametric analysis is required by management accountants operating in an uncertain world. Once the nature of parametrization of a problem is fully understood, interpretation of optimal value functions becomes a straightforward and helpful tool to aid decision-making.

An assessment of the desirability of formulating and solving problems as optimization models should not be restricted to consideration only of identification of a static solution. The ability and usefulness of being able to conduct parametric analysis within an optimization framework should also be considered.

Table 12.7 Parametric equations

θ range	Equations defining optimal basic solution	Q_{5-10-5}	Q_{6-8-8}	$16Q_{5-10-5} + 22.8Q_{6-8-8} = v(\theta)$
$640 \leq \theta \leq 1,320$	$0.05Q_{5-10-5} + 0.08Q_{6-8-8} = \theta_3$ $Q_{6-8-8} = 8,000$	$20\theta - 12,800$	$8,000$	$320\theta - 22,400$
$1,320 \leq \theta \leq 1,400$	$0.1Q_{5-10-5} + 0.08Q_{6-8-8} = 2,000$ $0.05Q_{5-10-5} + 0.08Q_{6-8-8} = \theta_3$	$-20\theta - 40,000$	$25\theta - 25,000$	$250\theta + 70,000$
$1,400 \leq \theta \leq 1,600$	$0.05Q_{5-10-5} + 0.06Q_{6-8-8} = 1,200$ $0.05Q_{5-10-5} + 0.08Q_{6-8-8} = \theta_3$	$-60\theta + 96,000$	$50\theta - 60,000$	$180\theta + 168,000$
$\theta \geq 1,600$	$0.05Q_{5-10-5} + 0.06Q_{6-8-8} = 1,200$ $Q_{5-10-5} = 0$	0	$20,000$	$456,000$

Appendix

The derivation of the optimal value function below is via the following strategy:

1. Identify basis equations and parameter value (θ = potash level) range for which basis holds.
2. Set the basis equations equal and solve for the decision variables.
3. Substitute decision variable values into objective function to define optimal value function.

The results are as follows:

(A) *Table 12.3*

(1) parameter = θ for $1,400 \leq \theta \leq 1,600$
   basis equations: nitrate
                    potash
   Let $Q_1 = Q_{5-10-5}$, $Q_2 = Q_{6-8-8}$

(2) $0.05Q_1 + 0.06Q_2 = 1,200$ ⟹ $Q_1 = 60\theta + 96,000$
   $0.05Q_1 + 0.08Q_2 = \theta$ $Q_2 = 50\theta - 600,000$
   $Z^* = 16Q_1 + 22.80Q_2$
   $v(\theta) = 1,80\theta + 168,000$ for $1,400 \leq \theta \leq 1,600$

At this stage two simple checks can be made on the validity of the optimal value function:

1. Given the linear nature of the $v(\theta)$ function a unit increase in θ availability (within the allowable range) will increase the $v(\theta)$ value by 180. This unit increase is in fact the shadow pirce for the scarce potash resource. That is, the increase in the attainable objective function value resulting from a unit change in the potash level. Table 12.3 shadow price for potash is 180, confirming the value for the coefficient of the optimal value function.

2. Table 12.3 with $\theta = 1,500$, gives the objective function $Z = £438,000$ and note:

$v(1,500) = (180 \times 1,500) + 168,000 = 438,000$

The above procedure is repeated for values of θ outside the range $1,400 < \theta < 1,600$ so that the complete optimal value function can be determined. The results are presented systematically in Table 12.7.

References

Cunningham, K. and L. Schrage (1986) *Optimizing Lotus 1-2-3 with Vino*, Palo Alto: Scientific Press.

Eppen, G.D. and F.J. Gould (1985) *Quantitative Concepts for Management*, 2nd edn, Englewood Cliffs, NJ: Prentice Hall.

Williams, H.P. (1985) *Model Building in Mathematical Programming*, 2nd edn, New York: John Wiley.

Acknowledgement

The author wishes to gratefully acknowledge the assistance by Enfin Corporation in providing the latest Beta version of the software.

Chapter 13

Forecasting

SYDNEY HOWELL

Forecasts are made in two main ways: by formal mathematical models and subjective human judgement. Mathematical methods take numerical input and process it by fixed rules to produce outputs. The outputs often include the forecasts themselves, plus estimates of the degree of risk or uncertainty attached to the forecasts. Subjective methods are the informal 'feelings' that human judges have. Different judges may make different forecasts on the same data set (and the same judge may do so at different times). In an organization it may be impossible for judges to be aware of all the information sources they are using, and most judges believe they use a vast range of information in a complex way.

However, it is possible to make a mathematical (regression) model that imitates the average pattern of decisions of a human judge, and such models in fact often contain very few items of data, used in simple ways. Such a model of the judge, if applied as a set of fixed rules, may outperform the judge from whom it was originally taken, a concept which is called 'bootstrapping'. Subjective and mathematical methods are not as opposed as they seem. Mathematical methods are not, except under very narrow assumptions, 'objective'. Different mathematical models can produce different forecasts, and different mathematical forecasters make different subjective choices of what system to model, what models to try, what data set to use as input and how to balance any conflicting results — so 'mathematical' forecasting uses 'subjective' skill and judgement.

Forecasts are of no use unless they affect intended actions. Here there is always interaction between 'subjective' and 'mathematical' forecasting methods. Even if a mathematician makes an excellent mathematical forecast, it will not affect the business unless some manager, usually a non-mathematician, decides to act on it, and the non-mathematical manager's decision is a subjective one.

Compared to a specialist forecaster, a line manager usually has more of his or her personal career at risk in the decision, and this may lead to a bias for optimism or pessimism. Unlike the specialist, a manager may not have years of experience in, say, linear regression, which would give them the expert's degree of confidence (or, if appropriate, doubt) in the forecast. For this and other reasons, an expert who has done an intellectually complex, difficult and interesting analysis of some data set may not have helped the organization.

'Subjective' and 'mathematical' forecasting need not differ in accuracy. Human beings can be inefficient in processing statistical data (indeed, if we could all solve statistical decision problems in our heads there would be little need for a science of statistics). However, if the forecasting problem recurs often in a similar form, and the human judge has a chance to learn from experience, subjective forecasts may compare well with mathematical ones. We can in fact use mathematical methods to improve subjective forecasts. If different judges make forecasting errors which are partly uncorrelated (whatever the sizes of these errors), the judges may be absorbing different parts of the available information, and we sometimes get better accuracy by merging their forecasts in some weighted combination. (It is also possible to make statistical combinations of subjective forecasts with mathematical forecasts — or combinations of different mathematical forecasts: Fildes 1987.) The problem of subjectivity remains, however, for the manager: 'I feel in my bones that demand will be 120, but the weighted combination of my belief with other forecasts tells me demand will be 200; do I stake my career by acting on the 120 I believe, or the 200 I'm told?'

Statistical combination of forecasts can only be done if we have a track record of past forecasting performance, and are confident that past differences in performance will continue into the future, so mathematical combination can be unreliable for 'one off' decisions of a major strategic nature, which are probably the most important decisions of all. Mathematical forecasting itself may then be impossible, except for a slightly controversial form known as subjective Bayesianism. For strategic decisions subjective forecasts *are* often combined, for example by working in committees, but in this case no methematical combination is used; there is instead a social process that combines individual subjective judgements. This is partly a 'battle' of beliefs, prestige, power, values, persuasion and so on between shifting coalitions, and partly a negotiated sharing of the risks and benefits of the decision (this may not save some individual from being selected as a scapegoat, at forecasting time or later, if things go 'wrong'). There are some methods for combining subjective forecasts which do not have a directly statistical foundation, such as the Delphi method, consensus forecasting and so on. These methods are readily ignored when political pressures grow intense.

Although subjective and social factors are interesting, pervasive and sometimes dominant in forecasting, the main purpose of this chapter is to alert you to the major mathematical methods, and to warn you of some ways in which they can mislead the forecaster and others in practical decision-making.

Mathematical methods of forecasting

There are many ways to group mathematical forecasts. We will use three groupings:

1. extrapolation;
2. leading indicator (or transfer function or ARMAX);
3. causal.

Extrapolation models

Extrapolation models predict the future values of a variable using only the past behaviour of the variable itself. They are 'naïve' in the eyes of some economists (because they ignore other variables, which must have some influence). Extrapolation models can be mathematically complex, and some require a PhD level of understanding to implement properly, but luckily simple extrapolation models often forecast better than complex ones, and either sort often forecasts as well as elaborate causal models that contain many variables.

The assumption of all extrapolation forecasting is that the variable behaves in some underlying 'true' way, plus or minus random variation which can be removed by averaging or 'smoothing' the past data in a suitable fashion. A limiting case of this is a 'random walk', where there is *no* underlying true level, and any history before the last observation contains no useful information. In this case the best forecast for all future time is simply the latest observed value of the variable. This is a very simple (naïve?) forecast, but it can be shown to be mathematically optimal in efficient markets for traded commodities (e.g. stocks and shares, gold, hides, futures and options, etc.). *Any more elaborate model will eventually make worse forecasts*.

Overfitting

This is an example of an important principle: many industrial variables show surprisingly little structure and are close to a random walk. Fitting an over-complex model to such variables will produce inferior forecasts. But even if a variable has complex behaviour, and so needs a complex forecasting model, a model that is *over*-complex will usually produce inferior forecasts, when used outside the period on which it was estimated.

Why should forecasters ever create over-complex models? Unfortunately most economic data sets are small, and many forecasters do not realize that fitting an explanatory model to a short run of past data has little to do with forecasting the future. It is almost always possible to get a good 'fit' to a short run of past data by building a very elaborate model — even if all the explanatory variables are random numbers! In fact, a model is guaranteed to be a perfect fit to the data if the number of independent coefficients is one fewer than the number of data points. Such a model, which has barely one data point per coefficient, will be useless at forecasting. Opinions vary, but the writer believes that models with fewer than five data points per coefficient are of doubtful value in forecasting (one would not like to estimate a mean and variance in normal statistics with less), and far more data points can be desirable: below I quote an example where a sample of 100 data points was available to estimate a single coefficient, but led to an economically important estimation error of 10 per cent.

The risk of having too many coefficients for the available data is ignored by some quite well respected workers, but even those who understand the risk cannot avoid it. To estimate a model with, say, three independent variables having lagged effects, plus seasonality, may require us to estimate sixteen or more coefficients, which on the 'five data points per coefficient' rule would need a minimum of ninety data points. Few markets, relationships or technologies stay stable for periods of ninety data points, unless the data are measurable (and meaningful) on a weekly basis. If we have fewer than ninety data points it may be impossible *in principle* to estimate this model accurately, or to decide whether it should be replaced by an even more complex one. This problem is called 'overfitting' and is probably the biggest source of confusion in mathematical forecasting. Professional specialists are often tempted to fit over elaborate models because they enjoy using advanced and complex techniques (these show that they are 'earning their money'), and they want to believe that more powerful analysis methods will yield better forecasts. This often simply is not true if the data set is small.

Ex post and *ex ante*

When we fit any model to a past data set we are using hindsight — we adjust the forecasting rules or coefficients to give the best fit to an answer we already know. This is called *ex post* (or 'after the event') fitting, and it is quite wrong to call the fitted values 'forecasts' or 'predictions'. Only when we test the model on completely new data are we truly 'forecasting'. This is called *ex ante* ('before the event') testing. A model that gives a good fit to a small data set (*ex post*) may be useless for forecasting, and also useless in *ex ante* tests, since small data sets give inaccurate estimates of any one model and cannot discriminate reliably between models. Overfitting many coefficients to a few data points can lead to models that look very successful in *ex post* fit, but prove disastrous in *ex ante* tests.

Moving averages

A simple way to smooth past data is to take the average of a fixed number of past time periods (e.g. the latest three months) (for equations see the appendix to this chapter). We ignore seasonality for the moment. How many past periods should we average? If we average very few periods (say the last two) we may have little reduction of the random variation. However, if we average many periods we may get a very 'true' picture of what the variable *was* doing net of the random variation, but for rather a long time ago (halfway through the averaging period).

The 'right' number of periods to average depends on how much trend or movement there is in the data, compared to how much 'noise' or trendless random variation. In fast-changing situations we should average a short period of history, while in situations with little trend but much random 'noise' we should average over a long period (in fact, if we knew there was no trend whatever, we should average all the observations we have, right back to the dawn of history).

Perhaps we might get an even better forecast by 'weighting' the observations in the moving average in some unequal way, or maybe there is some other method of smoothing that is even better than moving average, or should be used in combination with the moving average. This problem is discussed below. The main thing to notice here is that if we have only a short run of past data, we are sure to run the risk of 'overfitting' if we try any of these more complex models.

Advantages of moving averages

It is easy to understand how a moving average handles exceptional data (so called 'outliers'). Say we are using a three-month moving average, and sales in May were three times as high as normal, because of an exceptional event such as a fire at a competitor's warehouse. The moving average calculated in June will contain one-third of the May 'peak' ((March + April + May)/3), and so will be roughly double normal sales, and this excessively high level will remain for three months until the August moving average ((May + June + July)/3). The peak will then be 'forgotten' for ever, as later moving averages do not include May. A manager who knows that the peak will not happen again can easily adjust the June, July and August moving averages for this.

Moving averages can also be a simple way to remove seasonality. For monthly data, a twelve-month moving average always contains both high and low seasons, and likewise a 52-week moving average of weekly data.

Notice that a three-month moving average is more stable than data on complete quarters plus 'current quarter so far': the two agree at the end of each quarter, but in the first two months of the quarter the 'quarter so far' data contain only one and two observations respectively. The same is true for a twelve-month moving average against 'year to date': the 'year to date' figures begin the year as one month's data, but end the year as a highly damped 'twelve-month average' (multiplied by twelve). If seasonality is present, 'year to date' may be meaningless till the very end of the year, except for comparison with the same period last year.

Exponential smoothing

Another way to smooth past data (often the easiest and the best) is to average (in effect) all past data throughout history, but giving more emphasis to recent events. Theoretically we need an infinite supply of past data, but in practice only a short run of realistic observations is needed to supply the most emphasized 'recent' part of the history. Once it has been initialized with any forecast whatever (it matters how we initialise) the process is as follows:

1. A weighting percentage, alpha, is chosen between 0 per cent and 100 per cent (zero and one), for example 20 per cent (or 0.2).
2. The latest actual is compared with the latest forecast.
3. The two are combined in the weighting: 20 per cent of the actual plus 80 per cent of the forecast, to form the new latest forecast.
4. When the next actual becomes available, the process is repeated from step 2.

An equivalent calculation to step 3 above is to make the new forecast the old forecast plus alpha times the forecast error (the forecast error is the latest actual minus the latest forecast). If you need these equations in symbols they are equations (13.2) and (13.3) in the Appendix.

The value of alpha affects the sensitivity of the forecast to recent events. When alpha is tiny, the forecast puts little weight on recent events, and is an almost uniform weighting of a very large number of past actuals. This would be appropriate if the data contain much random fluctuation around the level, but almost no real change of the level itself.

When alpha is large, the forecast is dominated by a few (very different) weightings of recent events. This is appropriate if the data contain relatively little random fluctuation around the level but very real changes of the level itself. In the extreme case alpha becomes 100 per cent (one), and the latest forecast simply becomes the latest actual, which is the correct way to 'forecast' a random walk.

It is interesting to see what happens if we set alpha to zero: we are then placing no weight whatever on the most recent observation. This would be correct if we did already have an infinite number of observations of a completely static process: the latest random observation would tell us nothing new.

How to choose alpha? If we have a short run of past data, we can find by trial and error the exact value of alpha that produces minimum *ex post* fitting errors *for that data set* (and for the initial forecast value chosen), but there is a clear danger of 'overfitting' if the sample size is small. For example, a short run of four observations may by sheer chance show a rising trend (best fitted *ex post* by an alpha of one) while a few more observations may be better fitted by a more usual alpha close to 20 per cent (i.e. 0.2).

What is a big enough sample size to estimate alpha? For non-seasonal data with no erratic behaviour a run of only five to ten observations might give a good idea, but if 'erratic behaviour' is occurring a sample of thirty observations or more might be needed to detect and correctly allow for it, and there is no guarantee that the same pattern will endure into the future.

Work by Brown (1967) and others showed that exponential smoothing is in fact the optimal method of forecasting if we assume that the variable is undergoing two sorts of random fluctuation, first an 'innovation variance' in which the true level of the process undergoes a random walk (i.e. each fresh observation changes the old level by an amount drawn randomly from a normal distribution, with mean zero and statistical variance a^2) and second an 'observation' or 'noise' variance, in which each observation of the true level of the process is corrupted by random noise (which does not change the underlying level of the process), drawn from a normal distribution with mean zero and statistical variance b^2.

The 'best' forecast for the next observation would be the present true level, since both the next change in the true level, and the next noise element, are both random and can only be forecast at their mean level, which is zero. But unfortunately the present true level is *always* unobservable amid random noise, and so recent observations must be 'averaged out' in order to estimate the true level (this is possible because the mean value of the random noise, which does not change the level, is zero).

Under these mathematical assumptions the optimal method of averaging is exponential smoothing, and the correct 'error minimizing' value for alpha depends on how large the innovation variance is compared to the noise variances (a^2 compared to b^2). Much innovation and little noise approaches a random walk, for which an alpha of 100 per cent is optimal, while little innovation but substantial noise is a more static process, which requires a small alpha. An alpha value of 20 per cent seems adequate for some industrial variables, if these change level only slowly and show short-term random measurement errors or other fluctuations. However, different alpha values perform better in many circumstances.

It could happen that the underlying structure of the innovation and noise variances is more complex; for example, either or both of the innovation and noise variances may have a non-zero mean (causing respectively a linear trend in the data and bias in the forecasts). The size of the innovation and noise variances a^2 and b^2 might also change with time. If true, all these would require more complex smoothing models, with several 'alpha' values which could change with time. The risk as before is of *overfitting*: how do we tell from a short run of data that any of these more complex events is truly happening, knowing that we can *always* get a better 'fit' to a past run of data by fitting a more complex model? There is an amusing example of this risk. Brown's classic book on forecasting (1967) contains an attempt to forecast the IBM share price, using a complex exponential smoothing model with three different smoothing coefficients. Box and Jenkins (1976) showed that a simple exponential smoothing model with an alpha coefficient of 90 per cent — almost a random walk — performed better. In fact, even this model was 'overfitted': there is now overwhelming evidence to show that the true behaviour of share prices in the long run is a random walk (alpha 100 per cent), but in a sample of as many as 100 observations the 90 per cent value of alpha 'fitted' better *ex post*. Box and Jenkins did not do an *ex ante* test of their model, which might have shown up the problem. The avoidable error in the Box and Jenkins forecasts would be small, but its economic impact could be great. If either Brown or Box and Jenkins had used their forecasts to decide when to purchase IBM share options they would eventually have lost all their money.

Advantages and disadvantages of exponential smoothing

Exponential smoothing is very economical in computer time and storage, since we only ever need to store one number, the latest forecast (our estimate of the present true level), which encapsulates all we need to know about the whole of past history. This compares with, say, twelve numbers for a twelve-month moving average, plus a requirement for the moving average program to read all twelve numbers and to shift each of the twelve (losing the oldest) each time a new actual is received.

Exponential smoothing seems to be fairly easy for non-mathematicians to understand, but the way it treats outliers or exceptional observations is not so easy to adjust for. To take the same example as for moving average: a high peak in May sales will be immediately fed through by a factor of alpha (say 20 per cent) into the June forecast, which will thus be 40 per cent above normal. On average 80 per cent of this excess will be present in the July forecast, 64 per cent in August, 51 per cent in September and so on, taking until infinity to die away completely. It can be hard for decision-makers to 'aim off' correctly, even if they know the sales peak itself is spurious.

This problem is assumed away in the mathematical theory — there are no outliers or deviants from an assumed perfect normal distribution. Of course, over long periods the normal distribution itself will generate some extreme highs and lows, but over time the 'highs' will counteract the 'lows', and exponential smoothing would still be the best overall rule if the data were indeed normally distributed, and if you had to leave the forecasting system unattended for very long periods, such as a million years. Neither assumption may be true in industry.

Exponential smoothing with a trend

We have so far discussed 'simple' exponential smoothing, which estimates the new level of the process by taking the old (estimated) level plus alpha per cent of the forecast error. Some data show steady trends (consistent changes of level) over long periods of time. These changes of level can themselves be measured and exponentially smoothed.

In exponential smoothing with a trend the forecast (for one step ahead) is the present estimated level plus the present estimated trend (i.e. the forecast predicts next period's level) (see equation 13.4 in the Appendix). The *new estimated level* is updated as before when the actual comes in. It is a weighted combination of the forecast and the new actual (or, equivalently, it is the forecast plus alpha per cent of the forecast error). The *latest trend* is the change between the new forecast and the previous forecast. This is smoothed using a different coefficient, gamma, so that the *new estimate of trend* is a weighted combination containing gamma per cent of the latest change between forecasts, the remainder being the old smoothed change between forecasts.

Symbolic equations are numbers 13.4, 13.5 and 13.6 in the Appendix. For a 'halfway house' between words and equations (which may help to convince you that symbolic equations are actually quite space saving and precise) those equations in words are approximately:

Present forecast = present level + present trend

Present level = alpha × latest actual + (1 − alpha) × last forecast

Present trend = gamma × change in level + (1 − gamma) × old trend

The classic form of exponential smoothing with trend (together with seasonality) is called Holt−Winters after its inventors, and is still among the most successful extrapolation techniques.

Time series analysis

When is it right to use exponential smoothing, and when moving average, and what more complex versions, or combinations, of these should we consider? How do we handle seasonality, and how do we do all of these things without running the risk of 'overfitting'?

To set these questions on a logical, testable base of statistical assumptions, various forms of time series analysis have been developed. Although they sound complex, these methods simply try to pick the best combination of exponential smoothing and moving average methods, and they try to avoid 'overfitting' a complex model when a simple one would do better.

ARIMA (Autoregressive integrated moving average) models

Box and Jenkins (1976) achieved a major synthesis of new and previous methods. They wanted to avoid overfitting by building what they called 'parsimonious' models, that is to say models that use the minimum number of assumed underlying relationships. They took the simplest assumption possible, namely normally distributed random noise, and tried to find ways in which this could be made to relate to itself over time, to produce forecastable structures, using the minimum number of underlying relationships.

Autoregressive models

One possibility is that the present observation is some combination of a fixed number of previous observations together with a new unforecastable random noise element. This is called an 'autoregressive' process, because we can predict the next observation by statistical regression on a few past observations of the variable itself (see equation 13.7 in the Appendix; regression is explained in Wood and Fildes 1976 and many basic statistical texts). But because every observation is generated in an overlapping chain from previous observations (and hence previous random disturbances), there will in fact be an infinitely long chain of relationships between all observations. This is what makes the model 'parsimonious': we can generate an infinite string of relationships with just one, two or three coefficients, and the variable has 'autocorrelations' (i.e. correlations between one value and previous values) which extend, dying gradually away, to infinity.

If we estimate a so-called 'partial correlation' however, we uncover the underlying simple relationship. In partial correlation we ask not simply 'Is there a relationship between May and August?' (in an autoregressive process there is a relationship between almost any two time periods), but 'Is there any relation between May and August that we could *not* have predicted from the intervening relationships between July and August and June and August?' If the answer is, no, then we have at most an autoregressive process 'of order two' (i.e. each month, or whatever other time period we are considering, is explainable by reference to two previous ones, e.g. August can be explained from June and July).

The correct way to forecast an autoregressive process is by a moving average of some sort over the previous observations. The 'order' of the autoregressive process is the number of past observations we need to include in the moving average. The exact weightings in the moving average need not be equal. There can even be negative weights in processes that contain oscillations e.g. jerky movements in a supply chain, or, more interesting to accountants, compensating errors, when inventory is measured in successive time periods and successive processes. To sum up, autoregressive processes allow us to imitate a long and complex pattern of autocorrelations with a very few relationships. Autoregressive processes have few *partial* autocorrelations.

Moving average processes

Unfortunately, many processes do *not* show a simple pattern of partial autocorrelations, so we also need a 'parsimonious' way of imitating a complex pattern of partial autocorrelations with a very few basic relationships. Luckily we have already seen an example of such processes.

The new model is called a moving average model, because each observation is assumed to be based on a moving average, but this time a moving average of random disturbances, rather than of actual observations. Unfortunately, random disturbances, unlike actual observations, cannot be seen directly. This is a variant of the problem we saw in exponential smoothing. Then we needed to estimate something we cannot see (the true underlying level of the process). Since any observation consists of a true underlying level plus random noise, if we have already estimated the true underlying level we have also done the work needed to estimate the noise part.

(The name 'Moving Average' given by Box and Jenkins to this sort of process can be just a little confusing. Unlike an ordinary moving average, which is a relationship between values we can actually observe, the Box Jenkins Moving Average is a process we assume to be going on, between variables we cannot actually observe, namely the random disturbances which form an unknown part of our actual observations. Furthermore it isn't a moving average in the simplest sense, since the weights given to past random disturbances may be unequal, may not sum to one, etc. Finally the correct way to forecast a Box Jenkins moving-average process is NOT any kind of moving average of the data as observed. See equation 13.8 in the Appendix.)

In a typical Box Jenkins moving-average process, the latest actual observation is assumed to consist of a weighted combination of one or more random distrubances. If say two random disturbances are involved (the present and one previous), all random disturbances before those tell us nothing, because any single random disturbance is uncorrelated with all others. Such a process is called a Moving-Average process of order 2 (for 2 we can substitute however many previous random disturbances are responded to by the process). The result of this is that each observation (which is a mixture of recent random disturbances) has no relationship with other observations further away than the order of the moving-average noise process (autocorrelations fall to zero after this gap). However the partial autocorrelations of the observations may die away only very slowly, since the effect of the process is such that if we want to predict the next observation from previous *observations* (as opposed to previous random noise, which we cannot observe directly) we need in theory to use all previous observations throughout history to predict the actual observation today.

The optimal way to do this is some variant of exponential smoothing, which is precisely a way of taking into account an infinite number of previous observations. In this way Box Jenkins moving-average processes pose a generalized class of forecasting problems. The correct way to forecast a moving average process is some variant of exponential smoothing. The number of alpha coefficients, and their exact values, should fit the particular relationships in the moving-average process.

Mixed ARMA processes

Some real world processes have complex autocorrelation *and* complex partial autocorrelation. To imitate them, Box and Jenkins combined their two classes of model. The mixed 'Autoregressive Moving Average' (ARMA) model assumes that the true level of the process is a function of previous observations, as in an Autoregressive model, but that the current observation of that true level contains a noise element which is not pure random, as in the Autoregressive model, but a Moving Average including one or more previous random disturbances (equation 13.9 in the Appendix). The correct forecasting method for a mixed autoregressive and moving-average process is a mixture of autoregression and exponential smoothing i.e. a weighted mixture of the past actual observations, both in their 'as observed' and in 'exponentially smoothed' forms. This achieves the target of integrating and generalizing both the exponential smoothing method and the moving average method.

Integrated AR and MA processes

The processes described so far produce actual observations by combining successive random noise disturbances. The Autoregressive process (best forecast by a weighted moving average of past observations) uses a small number of recent *observations* to summarize the effect of an infinite sequence of past random *disturbances*, while the relevant form of Moving-Average process (best forecast by exponential smoothing) uses an infinite number of past *observations* to reflect the effect of a small number of recent noise *disturbances*. (This is not as inefficient as it sounds, since the entire relevant information in all past observations can usually be summarized in one, two or three smoothed estimates of unobservable 'true levels'.)

It is not always convenient that both an Autoregressive and a Moving-Average process generate the actual observation as a weighted total of previous random noise disturbances (an infinite number of disturbances and a small number of them, respectively). Since the average random disturbance is zero, neither an Autoregressive nor a Moving Average ever moves very far from its fixed mean level (zero or some other level). However, many real-world variables show marked changes of level. In order to imitate these, Autoregressive and Moving-

Average processes are 'Integrated' (added up for ever). This leads to marked and longer lasting changes of level, and to temporary linear trends, as excursions in either direction from the base level.

If the processes are integrated a scond time (the cumulative total of cumulative totals), the result is longer lasting and curved (quadratic) trends, which however occasionally recross the starting level. It is seldom necessary to integrate more than twice to imitate the behaviour of most economic or engineering data (see equation 13.10 in the Appendix). The 'integrated' versions of Autoregressive or Moving-Average processes have an extra 'order' number to indicate the number of times one adds up all previous values of the *process* to get the end product *observation*. For example, a second-order AR process *without* integration can be called an ARI (Autoregressive Integrated) process of order (2, 0), which means that the present observation depends only on two previous observations and there is no adding up. If all values of such a process are cumulatively added, the result is an ARI of order (2, 1). If the result of *that* process is cumulatively added for ever, the result is an ARI of order (2, 2) and so on. (See equation 13.11 in the Appendix.)

Similarly for Moving-Average processes: a simple first-order Moving Average of order 1 without integration is an IMA (Integrated Moving Average) or order (0, 1). If the result is added cumulatively for ever, we obtain an IMA of order (1, 1) and if that result is added for ever we obtain an IMA of order (2, 1) and so on. In fact, simple exponential smoothing as described earlier is the optimal forecasting method for an IMA (1, 1) process (see equation 13.12).

Integrated ARMA or ARIMA processes
An Autoregressive Integrated Moving-Average (ARIMA) process is simply an ARMA process that has been integrated a certain number of times. We write the order of integration between the orders of the autoregressive and moving average parts of the process (see equation 13.10 in the Appendix). For example, an ARIMA (2, 0, 1) process is one in which the present true value of the process depends on two previous observations of the process, but this true value is corrupted by the present, and one previous, value of random noise, and there is no adding up (it is in fact an ARMA (2, 1) process). By adding up for ever the results of the previous process we obtain an ARIMA (2, 1, 1) process, and by adding up for ever the results of *that* process we obtain an ARIMA (2, 2, 1) and so forth. An ARIMA (0, 0, 0) proess is unstructured random noise. The ARIMA processes are an extremely general class of 'parsimonious' models, and the correct methods of forecasting them include many other types of forecasting model as special cases (e.g. simple exponential smoothing, and an ordinary moving average of past observations). Their construction was a great intellectual achievement, and at first great hopes were entertained for their accuracy.

Box Jenkins forecasting methods

So far we have explained how Box and Jenkins started from random noise and brought together ways in which a small number of very simple relationships could process this noise into many kinds of complex time-dependent sequences, similar to data seen in economics and engineering. Even more importantly, Box and Jenkins reminded us that real data sometimes show little structure, and if so should be forecast in very simple ways.

In forecasting we first need to move in the reverse direction, back from the observations to find an ARIMA model which best imitates them. Then when forecasting we exploit the precise amount of statistical information that this particular ARIMA model carries from the past into the future. We have to assume that our set of real observations will behave like one of the ARIMA models, and that the parameters of that ARIMA process will remain constant, and that the 'random noise' process is normally distributed. Even if these assumptions are true, we need a lot of past data to be sure we pick the 'best' ARIMA model. In short runs of data all models may look much alike, or still worse, one model may quite wrongly appear better than others. (The 'best' long-term average model may be 'second best' or worse in a short period.)

Starting with the observations (which we may transform by taking logarithms, etc.), we first 'undo' any possible integration, by differencing the data (subtracting the previous value from each observation) enough times to remove all trends. This leaves us, we hope, with a stationary ARMA process.

Next we must decide the 'orders' of the autoregressive and moving-average parts (respectively these are the number of 'large' partial autocorrelations and 'large' autocorrelations). These orders tell us how many past actual observations (Autoregressive) and what form of exponential smoothing (Moving-Average process) to try to estimate from the data. This stage is called 'identifying' the ARMA process. Identification can be complex but automatic programs are available to do it, and there is some evidence that the ARMA models which these programs identify can forecast as well as those identified by human experts.

The ARMA model is then 'fitted' statistically to estimate the actual Autoregressive and Moving-Average coefficients that best fit (*ex post*) the past run of data. This is easy for pure Autoregressive, but involves a form of trial and error for Moving-Average and mixed ARMA models. Once more there are automatic programs to do this. Again there is a risk of 'overfitting' if the sample is small, as we saw in the case of the IBM share price, where there was only one coefficient and 100 data points with which to estimate it.

If the identification process has been successful, we will have moved from the original observations to fitted values plus errors, which we hope are white noise (random normally distributed disturbances), and this is used as a test that we have omitted no relationships. We check that there is no autocorrelation in the errors made when we fitted the chosen ARIMA process to the data.

We should *not* call the fitted values 'forecasts' since they contain *ex post* 'hindsight'.

In forecasting an ARIMA process we first forecast the ARMA process (each ARMA process carries a different amount of information from the past into the future), then we integrate the results (if necessary) to obtain the forecast of an ARIMA process. The estimation method allows us to calculate predicted ranges of error or confidence intervals (ignored in some automatic programs). As usual the only (potentially) valid test of the forecasts and of the confidence intervals is an *ex ante* test using fresh data.

Trend analysis in ARIMA models

The statistical information contained in an ARMA model typically extends only a small period into the future, after which the forecast eventually becomes either horizontal or, in the case of some IMA elements, fixed into a rigid trend. The latter may be unrealistic since no trend lasts for ever. (Note that the IMA process itself is expected to change its trend in future — it is simply that at forecasting time we have no indication what the future trend changes will be.) Box and Jenkins also allowed for a rigid polynomial trend to be imposed additionally on an ARIMA model. (They call the trend element gamma — see equation 13.13 in the Appendix.) The longer-term forecasting performance of a Box Jenkins ARIMA model (an ARMA with integration) may be dominated either by an imposed trend, or by the implicit trend of an IMA process, or by the data changes used to reach an ARMA model with normally distributed errors. These changes can include differencing and/or transforming the raw data (e.g. by taking logarithms or powers). A model of the first difference of the logarithm may in effect be an exponential growth curve.

Other methods for time series: classical decomposition

ARIMA models assume that every time series behaves a little like a mechanical system driven by random shocks. Future behaviour will be driven by future shocks (unforecastable, and hence assumed to be at their average value of zero), plus the amount of 'memory' the system has for past shocks, shown in its dynamic behaviour over time. Past shocks have already happened, but may have to be estimated indirectly, through smoothing, etc. In contrast, Classical Decomposition of time series (a much older method) assumes that the time series is the total effect of a completely rigid mechanical process. Random shocks are added, but in no way deflect the future pattern, which is driven by time like the hands of a watch. The assumed time pattern usually consists of a straight line (trend) plus or minus a yearly seasonal pattern, plus or minus a much longer 'cyclical' pattern (e.g. the rise and fall of the five- to six-year 'business cycle'), with random noise added on top.

Like many ideas in forecasting, classical decomposition is attractive (even common sense) to some, but in fact it has no rigorously developed theoretical base to explain how it should be used in forecasting, or even why it should be any good in forecasting the future at all, as opposed to 'fitting' some past data set *ex post*. The latter it is almost sure to do well, since it has so many variables. In fact, one of the central ideas in the classical decomposition model, the cyclical component, is explicitly rejected from ARIMA modelling. ARIMA analysis shows that GNP can be well forecast (or simulated) as a random walk with a trend. No 'cycles' enter either the simulation or the forecasting of this ARIMA model — it is only with hindsight that we can separate the actual or simulated GNP into periods of rising GNP and periods of falling GNP. Identifying GNP 'cycles' or turning-points as they happen is notoriously difficult in the real economy: it is comparable to watching a cloud appear past the edge of a building — the first part of a cloud to appear may chance to resemble something, say a lion's head, but this does not mean the rest of the cloud will resemble the lion's body. Only when the whole cloud is visible (and past) can we decide with hindsight what its total shape is and what it most resembled. 'Business cycles' have very little more forecasting power than the lion's head, although they can always be fitted impressively *ex post* by classical decomposition.

In a similar way the fixed linear trend assumed by classical decomposition simply does not exist in many ARIMA and ARARMA models — in most ARI models *all* trends are curved, dying to zero, while in many IMA processes there is no trend at all, the forecast being horizontal after a few steps ahead.

Other methods for time series: Bayesian

We have mentioned the problem of unusual extreme observations or 'outliers'. The ideal time series assumed in the mathematical theories of Brown, Box and Jenkins, Parzen and others (and even in classical decomposition) contain no outliers, but real-life data often contain outliers, for reasons such as holidays, strikes, physical accidents, consumer panics and so on.

Harrison and Stevens (1971, 1976) are among the few workers who have explicitly tried to model outliers, and have given the name 'Bayesian' to their forecasting system. They have also tried to model sharp discontinuities of level or trend. These occur in selling situations (e.g. if a new safety law makes a product compulsory, or if a major customer takes business elsewhere). Neither outliers nor discontinuities are well handled by most other forecasting methods. The Bayesian statistics used in the Harrison—Stevens model can also be applied to situations of a 'one off' nature where there is no past history (such as a new fashion style), but where managers have some prior forecast of what may happen, and can also estimate (based on comparable experience) how reliable or unreliable their forecast probably is.

Harrison and Stevens use exponential smoothing with a trend as their basic model, and constantly model four different 'states' that the system may possibly be in:

1. Normal — it is correct to update gently both the trend and level.
2. Outlier — to be ignored: no change in level or trend.
3. Big change in level — update level rapidly.
4. Big change in trend — update trend rapidly.

State space methods and the Kalman Filter are used to update each of these four models continually, and an approximate method of Bayesian statistics is used to 'sit in judgement' on the four models and decide which is closest to the truth. A weighted combination of the four models forms the final forecast and confidence interval. The system can in effect 'learn' about its environment and can express its (changing) degree of uncertainty more accurately than most other methods.

The Bayesian method, like many others, is intuitively appealing, but has little explicit theory of how data points are generated and does not quite live up to its promise. In a world of outliers and sharp discontinuities the Bayesian method must 'catch up' after these events faster than most others, but it cannot ever foresee them. The practical question is: how often do the exceptions arise, how big is the actual performance improvement when they do arise, and how well or poorly does the Bayesian system perform under 'normal' conditions? Under normal conditions the Bayesian method is 'overfitting' the data, as it uses far more parameters than its basic model of exponential smoothing with trend (which itself is not optimal for all series or all lead times). In fact the time series properties of the Bayesian model are not fully understood. The evidence from 'forecasting competitions', in which different methods are applied by different experts to forecast the same data (these are not conclusive tests of forecasting quality, see Jenkins 1982) is slightly disappointing. It seems that the Bayesian method performs a little less well than ARIMA, exponential smoothing or even the random walk (Fildes 1987).

However, an important advantage of the Bayesian method is that it computes far more accurate confidence intervals for its forecasts than most others. In an uncertain world the expected error of a forecast can be a more important fact than the forecast itself, and usually needs action by a higher level of management (e.g. to set an inventory policy, or to decide on the size of a new factory, are risk decisions, and these must be taken by higher-level managers than those who merely execute the inventory policy or build the factory). Therefore in special 'discontinuity filled' situations Bayesian forecasting may have a useful role.

Others methods for time series: adaptive methods

The value of the exponential smoothing constant, alpha, can be set to fit a particular past run of data *ex post* (to give, say the best one-step-ahead 'forecast'). This alpha value may not give the best *ex ante* forecasting performance on a further run of new data. Intuitively, it may seem obvious (within the subjective world of mathematical forecasters and/or their customers), that alpha should be increased sometimes, for example if we encounter discontinuities, or extreme forecasting errors. If we can devise an automatic way to recognize discontinuities themselves (which is what Bayesian forecasting does), or merely to recognize simple patterns in the forecasting errors, then the value of alpha could become automatically 'adaptive', which is effectively the case in Bayesian forecasting.

Several methods have been suggested, including the methods of Trigg and Leach (1967) and the adaptive smoothing of Makridakis and Wheelwright (1977). These methods contain little or no statistical theory as to how discontinuities arise or how one should respond to them. As so often in forecasting, a combination of commonsense appeal and no statistical theory proves disappointing in practice. There is the usual risk of 'overfitting' because the adaptive model is more complex. The builders of adaptive models often demonstrate them on a data set that exemplifies their favourite problem, rather than on the true general run of data (e.g. the test data may overstate the frequency of step changes). The performance of such adaptive models has been disappointing in practice, and *ad hoc* modifications are often needed, which usually take them closer to fixed-coefficient exponential smoothing. Fixed-coefficient exponential smoothing has often outperformed adaptive models in forecasting competitions, but such tests are not conclusive.

Seasonality

Seasonality is a bigger problem than it seems, as it carries a big risk of over fitting. It is usual to assume that the actual observation consists of some true deseasonalized level, with a seasonal factor either added to it or multiplied by it (in a logarithmic model of course, if we add a seasonal factor to the log this is equivalent to a percentage change in the observation, and the statistical error behaviour also becomes multiplicative and slightly biased). The seasonal factor can be estimated as a dummy variable by regression, but this gives a huge problem of overfitting. Suppose we have monthly data for two years (a luxury in many business settings). Even a simple exponential smoothing model will now contain thirteen parameters (alpha plus the twelve seasonal factors), so there are less than two data points per parameter, and our estimates of all the coefficients will be unreliable. Exponentially smoothing the seasonal factors, as recommended by Brown and by Holt and Winters, also risks overfitting, as each fresh data point now has to update an extra (seasonal) coefficient.

Of course, some economic variables do have long runs of history, so that we can safely try to deseasonalize them, but even here caution is needed, as tests have shown that officially deseasonalized data may still contain autocorrelation, sometimes in the form of 'reverse seasonality' where the original pattern has been overcompensated for. It may therefore be wise to avoid deseasonalized data, as there is a loss of statistical information when we estimate the seasonality, which may not be apparent. Of course, a deseasonalizing method that is 'fitted' to a single run of data *ex post* — even if not overfitted — is unlikely to produce exactly zero seasonal autocorrelation in any other *ex ante* run of the same variable. We therefore need seasonal models which will not lead to overfitting — they are called 'parsimonious', because they generate many seasonal effects with as few coefficients as possible. An early idea of Brown's (1967) was to assume that the seasonal pattern is a sine curve. Having decided the phase of the curve (i.e. when the seasonal peak comes) it is only necessary to estimate one coefficient, the amplitude (how big the swings are) in order to get, say, twelve monthly coefficients. More complex patterns (e.g. with multiple peaks) can be achieved by adding a very few more sine waves of higher frequencies, each one needing only one coefficient (its amplitude). A pattern using three sine waves would need only three coefficients, so a two-year run of monthly data would provide a tolerable six data points per coefficient (if alpha is also to be fitted).

An even more parsimonious approach is by Box and Jenkins (1976), who suggest 'seasonal differencing'. This means we subtract from each value the corresponding value last year. In effect we are forecasting not the variable itself but the difference from the corresponding value last year, which forms the starting point of the forecast (see equations 13.14 and 13.15 in the Appendix). There are several ways of implementing seasonal differencing, and as usual the specification of the variables in important; for example, a logarithmic specification means that if we take seasonal differences we are modelling each actual as a *multiple* of the previous year's actual, with implications of exponential growth or decline.

Seasonal differencing is more efficient than sine curves. We need more than a year of data in order to get the first seasonally differenced data point (we can scarcely begin to analyse seasonality with less), but we can then start to estimate other coefficients (e.g. alpha), however complex the fixed seasonality. So twenty-four monthly observations would leave us twelve differenced data points, with which we could estimate alpha. For longer runs of data the advantage of seasonal differencing is greater: forty-eight months of data would give us barely four points to estimate alpha if we used monthly seasonal dummy variables (assuming all thirteen coefficients place an equal strain on the data), but we would have twelve points for alpha if we used three sine curves, and thirty-six points for alpha if we used seasonal differencing.

However, all these methods share an assumption that is often false, namely that each month this year is exactly comparable to the same month last year. This is often untrue. Sales, shipments and production often vary with the number of working days in the month (not the same in all three cases), and these, driven by the public and private holidays of firms, their suppliers and international customers, vary from one year to the next. It is therefore important to check for working-day seasonality, and adjust for it as needed. Officially deseasonalized data should be used with caution, as the act of deseasonalizing may suppress this effect and there may be other problems.

Seasonal differencing should always be considered (the differenced data should be graphed to look for patterns and outliers) but may not always be ideal. Box and Jenkins (1976) have suggested a more complex version of seasonal differencing, in which each month can have a potentially different year-on-year growth trend, updated from year to year. A special form of this is said to be equivalent to Holt−Winters exponential smoothing, which contains exponentially smoothed seasonal coefficients. This very general seasonal method clearly carries a risk of overfitting in small data sets (equation 13.15). If only a short run of data is available (e.g. for a new item) it may be best to assume plausible fixed values for the seasonal coefficients rather than wasting the information content of the data to estimate or to smooth seasonal coefficients. If an item has less than a full year of history we cannot yet do seasonal differencing, but it may be valid to assume that it has the same seasonal pattern as comparable items for which we have a longer history. If so, fixed seasonal coefficients taken from other items can be used to deseasonalize even during the first few months.

Miscellaneous other problems and methods in extrapolation forecasting

Important problems include 'style goods' whose sales will only be made in a single season, such as fashion clothing. Various methods will be found in Fildes *et al.* (1981 and 1984), and see also Oliver (1987). Related problems are to predict the cumulative sales of part-work publications using the early stages of the decay curve, and also to predict the cumulative response rate to surveys, advertisements and mailings.

There may be a need to predict the cumulative future demand for spares of an obsolete product ('all time stocks'). A well-known method of longer-term forecasting is the 'trend curve', including various saturation curves. Learning curves may also need to be forecast (Howell 1981). Models may be needed of market share, where market shares are constrained to sum to one. Most of the above problems are indexed in Fildes *et al.* (1981 and 1984).

Comparative accuracy of extrapolation methods

This is well reviewed by Fildes (1987). Several forecasting competitions have been conducted in recent years, and despite criticisms by Jenkins (1982) and others they clearly have something to teach us.

There seems to be no clear winner. Simple exponential smoothing and ARIMA are often among the better methods, but with the random walk not very far behind. Exponential smoothing with a trend can be the best method for short lead times but is very bad for longer lead times (e.g. two years). There have been encouraging results from some very different methods which all assume that trends will eventually die away — see Parzen (1982), Gardner and McKenzie (1989) and Schnaars (1986). Other well-known methods are on average inferior to those mentioned, but may do well in special circumstances. On balance Fildes seems to conclude that there is a strong risk of 'overfitting' forecasting models: a model which performs best over an *ex post* fitting period, or even over a later *ex ante* testing period, can sometimes perform extremely badly on subsequent data.

It is probably best to choose a forecasting model based on its average *ex ante* forecasting performance across a very large sample of relevant time series, and using a range of different '*ex ante*' testing periods, to avoid atypical testing results. We must then accept that the chosen model may still perform badly when it encounters future 'atypical' periods of data. Many large-scale industrial forecasting problems, notably inventory control, offer the opportunity to do precisely this sort of large-scale testing on hundreds or thousands of data series, with the chance that the average costs of forecast error will thereby be minimised.

Leading indicator (or transfer function or ARMAX) models

The ARIMA time series models of Box and Jenkins have been extended to include independent variables, or so-called 'leading indicators' — see Box and Jenkins (1976), Granger and Newbold (1979), Jenkins and McLeod (1983). These models have been called 'transfer function' models, because different time patterns of the input variables produce different effects on the output, and in this they resemble the transfer function models used in engineering, on which they are based. For example, the suspension system of a car is a transfer function, which transforms violent road and wheel fluctuations into gentler passenger fluctuations, but one identical road (input) may produce different passenger fluctuations when driven at different speeds: ranging from violent pitching or heavy vibration, to no great disturbance to the passengers. In contrast, an audio amplifier has a transfer function which transforms gentle electrical input fluctuations into violent mechanical fluctuations of the output speakers, but it may be designed to transform towards zero some input fluctuations which are not needed (inaudible high frequencies) or which could be damaging (fluctuations caused by switching on, or radio interference).

Transfer function models are also called ARMAX (ARMA models with e[X]planatory variables). The behaviour of the dependent variable is supposed to be driven by two influences: random distrubances, which produce complex delayed effects exactly as in an ARMA model, and independent variables, each of which also produces complex delayed effects through an ARMA like process, but driven by successive values of the independent variable instead of successive random distrubances. The dependent variable may be driven by the combined past values of the independent both in their exponentially smoothed (MA) and 'as observed' (AR) forms. A price has to be paid for this extreme richness of potential relationships, namely that ARMAX models, although they try to be parsimonious (use few coefficients), require a lot of data both to *identify* them correctly (i.e. to decide how many times to difference the data, and what are the orders of the different ARMA processes for noise and for each independent variable) and to *estimate* the coefficients.

In practice it is not often possible to identify more than one or two independent variables (Jenkins and McLeod 1983), and even for non-seasonal data large samples are needed: if there are two ARMA processes (for one independent variable plus random noise) which are suspected to be of orders up to (2, 2) there are eight parameters to estimate, and it would be a brave forecaster who would select between such a rich range of potential dynamic relationships using as few as say eighty data points (recall that the single parameter of the IBM stock price model was mis-estimated by 10 per cent from 100 data points: errors as large as this may possibly impair the accuracy of the forecast, and may, or may not, damage the payoff from a specific decision based on the forecast).

Transfer function models are also called 'leading indicator' models. The 'leading' part of the name signals that an ARMAX model can capture relationships between the dependent and, potentially, *all* past values of the independent (it does not use the value of the independent that coincides with the dependent, since this is not knowable when forecasting). The 'indicator' part acknowledges that one independent variable cannot usually be the *only* causal driver of the dependent: it merely contains information. A rationale for this approach is that real-life independents are often highly intercorrelated, and 'real' causal relationships are often impossible to disentangle. So it may be better to locate a leading indicator that contains *most* information, and model its actual independent forecasting power in a statistically accurate way, and then model the residual impact of all the omitted variables as a realistically dynamic ARMA error term. This is done in preference to building a conventional causal regression model, which will include many potential independents, but will not estimate what their separate and time dependent impacts are, and will not usually model the impact of any unknown or omitted effects, in the form of a carefully modelled error term.

Selecting potential leading indicators and choosing between them

Each different forecasting problem suggests possible leading indicator variables; for example, GNP, the order book, new car registrations, sales by (not to) customers, consumer inventories, and so on. Particular functional specifications may seem likely or unlikely (e.g. putting the variables in logarithmic form implies that the effect of the indicator is multiplicative, maybe with increasing or diminishing effects of scale). The problem of deciding whether to include a leading indicator, and if so which, is complicated as usual by the risk of overfitting. In any finite data set if we add an independent variable (and hence perhaps four extra parameters — depending on the ARMA structure of its influence) we are almost certain to improve the model's *ex post* fit to the past data. The only valid test is 'whether the enlarged model gives better forecasts for data other than that to which it was statistically fitted (*ex ante* test).

Causal models

In contrast to ARMAX models, which are built by searching for the few 'best' statistical relationships, causal models typically begin with a large set of independent variables, which by economic theory or intuition might exert some influence (e.g. price, population, Gross National Product, share of advertising voice, relative quality, etc.). Their effect is often jointly estimated statistically by multiple regression of some kind (see Wood and Fildes 1976, or basic statistics texts for introductions to multiple regression).

The central problem with most causal models is that they are built to explain the past rather than to forecast the future, so they usually relate the dependent variable to the values of the 'causal' variables *at the same time*. Thus even if the dependent variable is perfectly fitted (and not overfitted) to, say, four causal variables, this gives us the problem of forecasting the four causal variables instead of the dependent variable. Fortunately, some potential independents, such as GNP, are fairly easy to forecast, but others, such as interest and exchange rates, are not. All this is in addition to the usual problem of overfitting. A causal model that has a 'good' *ex post* fit to a small data set (high R^2) may be worthless for forecasting — the fitted coefficients may not fit fresh (*ex ante*) values of the dependent and the independent, and even if they do they might still be useless for a 'forecast', when the values of the independent are not yet known. Most econometric practice (and even some of its precept) has little to say about this problem. It is still common to see econometric articles referring to 'forecast' values of a dependent variable, when a regression model has merely been fitted *ex post* to a small data set.

Single equation models

The most common type of causal model is a 'single equation', which has the forecast variable on one side and the potential causal variables on the other. The equation is usually estimated by multiple regression.

Functional specification

There are many different ways to specify any causal (or indeed time series) model, all of which have different theoretical implications. For example we can use the variable itself, or the first difference of the variable (latest value minus previous value), or use logarithms, or first differences of logarithms, or other transformations of some or all of the variables. Using logarithms can lead to a much more orderly data set, but when the forecasts of the logarithm are converted back into forecasts of the raw variable, using data other than that used to fit the model (*ex ante* test), there may be little or no improvement in accuracy. Using logarithms leads to a different theoretical specification. This may sometimes be better, but could imply implausible or nonsense relationships between the variables.

A case study of specification choice
An example of specification choice arose when a firm tried to study the effect of advertising in getting recruits. The independent variable was the intensity of advertising, and the dependent variable was the length of time it took to fill each job. Hundreds of data points were available from local offices.

At first sight the relationship was unexpected: there was a positive correlation between the intensity of advertising and the length of time it took to fill the job — as if more advertising actually delayed the arrival of recruits! The reason was that some offices were in prosperous areas, and so found it hard to obtain staff; for them the delay in finding recruits caused more advertising, and not *vice versa*. A specification was finally chosen that used the first difference of the logarithm of both variables. This may seem obscure, but it had simple theoretical advantages. By taking first differences we were looking at the effect of *changing* the advertising policy in any one area. The first difference of the logarithm is the *multiplicative* change — in effect the percentage change — so we were also controlling for the different sizes of the offices, and their different general levels of both advertising and recruiting.

It would have been possible to produce the above effects in a non-logarithmic (linear) model, but this would still have been unsatisfactory, since a linear model has a constant term, which implies that there will be some recruiting even with no advertising, and the response to advertising in such a model is implausibly linear: a tenfold change in advertising would produce a tenfold change in recruitment. The statistical error behaviour of the linear model was also unsatisfactory. The logarithmic model produced in contrast a very plausible shape for the response curve to advertising, namely 'diminishing returns': great reductions in advertising produce great reductions in recruiting, but beyond a certain point, great increases in advertising produce almost no extra recruitment. Statistical errors were orderly. This information was used along with cost data to suggest an overall change in advertising intensity for the firm (in fact a substantial increase). The constant term in the logarithmic model has no implications, plausible or implausible, about what happens when there is zero advertising, as there is no log of zero (and so the effect of zero advertising cannot be predicted at all). This limitation can be important, but it happened not to matter for this particular decision problem.

Estimating a single-equation model

The most widely used estimation method is multiple regression by Ordinary Least Squares. This may not be appropriate if the errors are not normally distributed, or are serially correlated over time (autocorrelated), or have differing variances (heteroscedasticity), or if the 'single equation' is actually part of a larger simultaneous system of equations (see next section). These problems occupy much of the space in econometric textbooks. Their impact on forecasting is discussed below.

Non-normal errors may be due to individual outliers (which should always be checked for and specially treated, either by deletion or interpolation), or there may be a basically non-normal distribution of errors. The latter is sometimes easy to correct by a transformation (such as the logarithm) provided the logarithm exists and will lead to theoretically acceptable relationships, but when this is not the case, so-called 'robust' methods of estimation may help.

Heteroscedasticity can often be reduced by a logarithmic or other transformation. Otherwise Generalized Least Squares may be used. It may not affect accuracy much in *ex ante* work, but confidence intervals will be wrong.

Autocorrelation is normally due to specification error, for example seasonality that has been ignored, a curved trend ignored, or an ignored dynamic behaviour of the dependent variable (as in ARIMA models) or dynamic lagged effects of the independent variables (as in transfer function or ARMAX models), or the effects (lagged or not) of independent variables that have been omitted altogether. It matters in *ex ante* work.

Modelling strategies of time series and causal modellers

Both ARMAX (engineering) and causal (econometric) modellers agree that an ideal model would contain all the correctly lagged effects of all the relevant independent variables. Many dependent variables ought then to show no independent dynamics (autocorrelation) of their own, but if they did so, ARMA models would be fitted to the error terms. ARMAX and causal modellers have different policies for approaching this (usually unattainable) ideal. ARMAX modellers, as we have seen, work within an ultimately engineering tradition, to produce rich and accurate models of a relationship with perhaps only one independent variable, and then use statistically powerful methods to measure and model any remaining unexplained dynamics of the dependent. They strive to avoid overfitting, at the cost of having an incomplete or implausible understanding of 'causal' effects. Econometric modellers cheerfully overfit in the interests of getting a more complete (but perhaps unreliable) *ex post* 'causal' explanation of the past.

The general practice (not precept) of econometrics is to ignore the autocorrelation problem whenever possible, by making weak tests for autocorrelation or none, and sometimes by ignoring positive autocorrelation test results. The most common response to autocorrelation, if there is one, is to look for extra independent variables. There is, however, a growing tradition among econometricians of modelling lagged relationships, often using methods which are special cases of the transfer function model, such as the so-called 'distributed lag'. Data shortages mean that these models must be identified (i.e. selected) on a fairly arbitrary basis. Sometimes arbitrary assumptions about the nature of lagged effects can be defended, if they imply plausible assumptions about individual's economic behaviour, for example the 'rational expectation' model. However, by estimating an incorrectly identified specification one can make significant practical and theoretical errors.

Multicollinearity

Another standing problem of multiple regression is multicollinearity, which is when the independent variables are highly correlated with each other. This is common with economic variables, which often have a shared time trend due to a shared external cause or to mutual causation. Multicollinearity does not make ordinary least squares (OLS) a statistically unsound method of estimation (the only technical problem is that if two of the independent variables are *perfectly* correlated OLS is impossible even to compute). The problem is that the effects of the correlated independent variables are impossible to separate. OLS 'shares out' the total effect of, say, two correlated independent variables in a fairly unpredictable way, and reports itself very unconfident about the answer, by reporting wide confidence intervals for both coefficients.

If *variables* are *positively* correlated their *coefficients* will be *negatively* correlated. For example, one variable may be given a large coefficient and the second a small, or *vice versa*, or both variables may be given a roughly equal share of the total effect. These and other possible allocations are all almost equally good fits, and the choice made by OLS is very sensitive to small sampling variations in the data. It is even possible for one of two positively correlated variables to be given a *negative* effect; for example, the equation may imply that rising population increases sales, but rising GNP slightly reduces sales. Corresponding effects happen if more than two independents are correlated, or if the correlation is negative instead of positive. In all cases the individual coefficients are highly uncertain, but are all intercorrelated, and OLS can only make confident statements about the 'supervariable' which the correlated variables effectively represent.

These effects make it difficult to build causal explanations, but may not much matter for forecasting as long as the multicollinearity holds constant. A forecasting problem arises if and when the multicollinearity breaks down and the variables move in different ways for the first time. The best that can be done for forecasting (and perhaps for causal analysis) may be to impose prior information, based on the theory of the problem, in order to select from the many 'almost equally likely' solutions one which is either most plausible (perhaps equal effects for both variables), or least risky in its effects on the decision to be taken using the forecast.

Other treatments for multicollinearity
There are various ways to force a regression to produce smaller confidence intervals for the coefficients. If two variables are *perfectly* correlated it is essential to drop one of them, and safe to do so if they are effectively the same variable (e.g. temperature reported in both Celsius and Fahrenheit). However, it may or may not be safe to delete one of two variables that are not theoretically identical (e.g. GNP and population) — in this case we are merely closing our eyes to the uncertainty that exists, by making it impossible for the program to report it, and we are also discarding any slight extra predictive power the deleted variable may have. Our forecasting problems if and when the multicollinearity breaks down will be just as great.

Other treatments exist. For example, Ridge Regression is a method of importing prior information to the calculation in order to give coefficient estimates which are biased but more precise. Principal Components Regression abandons the original variables entirely, and works with slightly simplified versions of a smaller number of 'supervariables' that they seem to represent. Principal Components Regression should probably not be used unless there is a very large and collinear data set which cannot be dealt with otherwise. This is because the simplified Principal Components discard a certain amount of information, and are themselves greatly subject to overfitting. Neither of these problems will show up in *ex post* tests. A variant of Principal Components known as Canonical. Correlation (using a single dependent variable) may be (slightly) less unsatisfactory.

Perhaps the best method, when applicable, is to take the difference of each of the variables, since this will remove any collinearity due to shared time trends and/or shared causes. This may lead to lower *ex post* R^2 and to larger *ex post* confidence intervals for the coefficients, but to better *ex ante* forecasts. There are arguments for and against differencing, which should be done with thought.

It is interesting to note that univariate Time Series Analysis itself was invented to deal with a multicollinearity problem, namely that many variables are multicollinear with their own past. Since many past values of an industrial variable are almost sure to be similar to each other, it would be overfitting to use all (or many) of these multicollinear values as independent variables in a regression, but equally dangerous to use too few, or the wrong few, for fitting. Time series methods such as ARIMA and ARMAX first use differencing to remove shared or unshared trends, the very method which we have just recommended as a way to reduce multicollinearity, and then try to build parsimonious models that use the smallest number of genuinely independent (i.e. non-multicollinear) variables.

Simultaneous system models

A special case of causal model is those many problems in business or macroeconomics which involve not one causal equation but several, which must simultaneously hold true. a microeconomic example might be cigarette sales, which are partly determined by advertising (a so-called behavioural equation defines this effect). However, advertising itself in many industries is partly set as a percentage of sales. A second behavioural equation defines this effect, and both equations must be simultaneously true. Statistical error terms are assumed in both equations.

In macroeconomics the best-known example of the same effect is the determination of national income. The size of people's incomes (earned as producers or employees) decides the amount they will consume — hence making them customers for that amount (first behavioural equation), but the amount they consume (as customers) decides what they will pay out to each other and hence what they receive as income (as producers and employees) and this is described in a second equation. Again both equations must hold true simultaneously.

It is possible to rearrange the algebra of a simultaneous system, so as to isolate the variable we want to explain on the left hand side of a single equation, with all other variables on the right hand side (the special circumstances when this is possible or useful to do are defined by something called the 'identification problem'). This rearranged form is called the 'reduced form' of the system, and we can use it to isolate any of the variables as if it were a dependent variable in one single equation — subject of course to the identification problem. Unfortunately, a reduced-form single equation is *not* an equation on which we can correctly use normal multiple regression (OLS). Statistical problems arise because the algebraic rearrangement of the variables has also distorted the statistical error terms, and the estimated coefficients based on OLS will be biased and inconsistent (i.e. the coefficient estimates would not be correct even if the sample size approached infinity, and standard errors are understated). This problem is often called 'simultaneous system bias' — more logically we might call it 'reduced form bias'.

Econometrics texts contain many methods for partly or completely curing simultaneous system bias (their names include Full Information Maximum Likelihood, Three Stage Least Squares and many others). These methods are ponderous and of little value in small or noisy data sets, and an approximate method called Two Stage Least Squares (which can be implemented easily using an OLS package) seems to achieve an adequate *ex post* result, at least, in many causal system models. It is regrettable that many published macroeconomic models do not make even this concession to the simultaneous system problem, but use OLS, thereby mis-estimating the coefficients and exaggerating even more the *ex post* fit of the model.

It may be that in some *ex ante* forecasting problems the overall uncertainty is large enough to dwarf the relative advantage of even Two Stage Least Squares, and in this case OLS may be acceptable as an approximate way to estimate a reduced form single equation. As always, its accuracy should be measured in *ex ante* tests, since the *ex post* calculated OLS confidence intervals are certain to be understated. This will be so even if the true *ex ante* confidence intervals of the OLS coefficients (and their forecasts) are similar to those of better estimators.

Specification error

Causal modellers, whether they use a single-equation or simultaneous system, face the problem of which variables to include. A blind search for statistically 'significant' variables can be misleading, and significance levels themselves can be seriously distorted if one uses stepwise or other consecutive or conditional search procedures. Specification error tests have been devised to check various assumptions about the variables, the functional specification and the error terms, but they are by no means comprehensive, or powerful in small data sets. It seems essential to include all the independent variables that prior theory regards as important, even if the regression must be constrained to force them in. Fildes (1987, pp. 560−2) offers a useful review. It seems there is no best sequence for searching for a simplified model, and a different sequence of tests can lead to a different final choice of model.

Conclusion: practical recommendations

The chapter closes with some practical recommendations based on the literature summarized.

Evaluate the accuracy of a forecast by its economic impact on the decision to be taken

The Brown and Box−Jenkins forecasting models for the IBM share price, mentioned above, did not differ much in accuracy. However, if the decision problem was when to buy and sell IBM stock options, *both* models would have lost all the users' money. If the decision was to buy and sell IBM stock itself, the money would have been lost more slowly.

Use the decision problem to interpret R^2

In the job recruitment case study discussed above, R^2 for the final model was very small at 0.12 but was highly significant (*ex post* fit). This meant that the model made a bad job of predicting the effects of changing advertising in any one office, but did it mean that the model was economically useless?

An *ex ante* test on fresh data confirmed the model's coefficients and its low R^2. If the decision problem was (or could be made to be) to set the advertising policy for *all* offices, then the model could be used to predict a small average impact for all offices with high precision, and with considerable economic benefit.

Incidentally, it would have been useless to try out the recommended new policy on a small sample of offices, because of the low predictive power for individual offices: it was calculated that a sample of at least fifty offices was needed to test the average effect of the new policy.

Understand the importance of forecast error

The estimated error of a forecast is often much more important than the forecast itself. Forecast errors are often disappointingly large, and the difference between the best and the next best method may only reduce the error itself from say 100 units to 85. If so, the better forecast may leave the nature of the management problems unchanged.

Usually junior managers have to act as if forecasts are certain ('we will make a batch of 2,000 units'), but it is senior managers who set the policies which recognize and respond to the risks in the forecasts, for example tactically they may hold safety stocks of product, money, staff or machine capacity, or strategically they may decide to build a factory larger or smaller than a base forecast suggests, or they may renegotiate the fixed and variable parts of financial and other contracts in order to produce a desired match between operating risks (from the assets of the business) and financial risks (from its liabilities).

The form and accuracy of error distributions will be the major input needed for such decisions (e.g. if you have an error distribution that is normal in the logarithm, always work out the meaning and economic impact of the same distribution transformed back out of logarithms).

Analyse the hidden assumptions in specifications

Use algebraic analysis, together with prior knowledge of the problem area, to evaluate possible specifications. Are there hidden assumptions such as exponential growth? What happens if any of the variables takes values which are zero, close to zero or very large? Does the model imply diminishing returns, increasing returns or neutral returns? What are the interaction effects of variables (e.g. addition of logarithms means multiplication of the variables)? Are these assumptions plausible or implausible for this problem? Do they have material impacts at the values of the variables which you are likely to use?

Specifications using the first difference and/or the logarithm are often theoretically or statistically attractive, but sometimes they have a zero or adverse impact on *ex ante* forecasting accuracy (e.g. they may be oversensitive to outliers). They cannot directly handle events such as zero or negative values, which are sometimes practically important.

Avoid overfitting

Box and Jenkins recommend using at least fifty points to fit even a univariate ARIMA model. Overfitting can be a danger if you have less than thirty points per parameter, and is a near certainty if you have less than five. If you are forced to use sparse data, fit only models which are simple. Vet the calculated coefficients against common sense, prior knowledge and relevant theory. Use *ex ante* testing if you can. Remember the random walk does surprisingly well in short-term, or even long-term, *ex ante* forecasting. Also check your estimated coefficients for any sensitive impacts they may have on forecast accuracy, or the economics of the decision. Do not use coefficients or models that clearly risk instability or severe economic loss (e.g. if a small data set is equally well fitted *ex post* by exponential smoothing and by a strongly negative autocorrelation model, exponential smoothing is probably the safer choice for *ex ante* work).

In small samples the likelihood functions are often flat and confidence intervals are wide, which means that you can impose a wide range of values for any one coefficient without changing the fit to your *ex post* sample very much. At best this may help you to avoid instability, and at worst you are not likely to damage *ex ante* forecast accuracy very much. But you *must* correctly maintain any strong estimated correlation of the coefficients. It is deadly to violate a joint confidence interval if the variables are strongly multicollinear, since the estimated coefficients *must* then be correlated; for example, if two variables are highly positively correlated, you may force either coefficient to be large, but the other must then be small (you will get this effect if you drop one of the variables entirely). Alternatively, you can force both the coefficients to be positive and equal in their effect, but you then have little flexibility as to how large that effect is.

Beware of outliers

A single outlier can dominate an extrapolation or causal model: it can create correlation or autocorrelation when there is none in the rest of the sample, or destroy it where it otherwise exists. Always graph the data in whatever transformation you are using (logarithm, first difference, seasonal difference, etc.) to check for outliers or other unusual patterns.

Beware of *ex post* fitting and high R^2

Remember that a high R^2 (or even high adjusted R^2) in a small *ex post* sample may be worthless, while a low but significant R^2 in a large sample may be economically useful. Beware of unconscious bias in the data sets you use to test special model features. Do you have enough data to know whether your data are typical? If not, you are in the risk business, and should pay more attention to *measuring* your *ex ante* errors than slightly *reducing* your *ex post* errors.

Use simple seasonal models

Always check for working-day seasonality (also use it to help to understand outliers such as strikes). Avoid 'overfitting' due to estimating or updating the seasonal coefficients from limited data. Prior deseasonalizing to zero autocorrelation may destroy some of the information content, and some of the statistical 'degrees of freedom' (significance), of your data. It may be better to use either fixed seasonal models based on prior knowledge, or seasonal differencing.

Use prior knowledge

Simple causal models can be highly useful *ex ante*. Be willing to force important variables into the equation with plausible coefficients, even if they are not 'statistically significant'. Exploit the widths of the confidence intervals to do this (but never violate a highly significant joint confidence interval, if the variables are multicollinear, as the estimated coefficients must then be correlated).

Manage your own subjectivity

Avoid overinterpreting (or underinterpreting) evidence. Don't stay wedded to your first guess. Don't assume one or two high values start a boom, or one low value starts a recession. An insignificant result is what it says, whether you like it or you don't — insignificant, and no indication of the next value. Have the courage to realize that in any trend turning-points are inevitable — but are almost always unforecastable in size and timing.

Avoid the seduction of complex and elaborate methods, or methods that appeal to your own particular (high or low) educational background. Avoid conscious and unconscious bias in the data sets you use to test and select models.

Know your own biases. What do you stand to gain or lose from acting on (or even announcing) a particular forecast? How much of that gain or loss is uncertain? Decide how you will deal with the uncertainty — inside or outside the forecast? by hedging or insurance? by portfolio balancing? by stockholding? by politics or negotiation? What evidence would it take to persuade you that your forecast was wrong? Are you planning to look for that evidence, now or in the future?

Manage the subjectivity of others

How does the other person compare with you in prior knowledge, in understanding or confidence with regard to: the general problem, the data, the methods and the results? Fifteen minutes spent experimenting with the method may teach both sides more than twenty four hours arguing over the results. Would a simplified method be easier for the other side to understand and trust even if slightly less accurate?

Can you reach agreement on assumptions, methods, objectives, base forecast, degree of uncertainty in the forecast, sources of uncertainty, possible ways of dealing with it? Can you agree about the costs of error, the sources of error, the degree of risk being taken, the value to be put on uncertainties or delays in costs and benefits? (The answer is almost always no.) If not, can you agree about where you differ, and what the economic impact of the disagreement could be?

Who will 'own' the uncertainty, gains and losses if things go right? What if things go wrong? Who will have the power to declare *ex post* that forecasts were wrong or decisions were unacceptable? What is those people's present level of understanding and beliefs? What actions will be in their self-interest in the possible futures you have identified?

Decide whether your next action should be to elaborate your forecasting method; or to improve your data; or to remeasure *ex ante* errors; or to improve the education of yourself or the other side; or to investigate the economics of your decision problem; or to negotiate new perceptions of the possible actions, possible outcomes, their impacts and their values?

Good forecasting — and even if your forecasts are bad — good decision-making!

Appendix: key equations

A moving average (of past observations) of order p is defined as M_p where x_t is the observation at time t

$$M_p(x_t) = (x_{t-1} + x_{t-2} + x_{t-3} \cdots x_{t-p})/p \qquad (13.1)$$

The exponentially smoothed value of x at time t (which is used as the forecast for time $t + 1$) is S_t where

$$S_t = \alpha x_t + (1 - \alpha)S_{t-1} \qquad (13.2)$$

Equivalently

$$S_t = S_{t-1} + \alpha e_t \qquad (13.3)$$

(where e_t is the forecast error given by $x_t - S_{t-1}$)

$$Y_t(k) = S_t + kT_t \qquad (13.4)$$

where $Y_t(k)$ is the forecast made at time t of the value of x_{t+k} and:

$$S_t = \alpha x_t + (1 - \alpha)(S_{t-1} + T_{t-1}) \tag{13.5}$$

$$T_t = \gamma(S_t - S_{t-1}) + (1 - \gamma)T_{t-1} \tag{13.6}$$

Notes on the backshift operator B

The backshift operator B reduces the subscript of x by one, i.e. it transfers attention to the previous value. It is an economical way to write relationships between values spaced in time, as it can be made to act algebraically on itself and on variables, e.g. as follows:

$Bx_t = x_{t-1}$

$B^2x_t = B(Bx_t) = Bx_{t-1} = x_{t-2}$

$B^dx_t = x_{t-d}$

$(1-B)x_t = x_t - Bx_t = x_t - x_{t-1}$ (first difference of x)

$(1-B)^2x_t = (1-2B+B^2)x_t = x_t - 2Bx_t + B^2x_t$

$= x_t - 2x_{t-1} + x_{t-2}$ (second difference of x)

Define a polynomial ϕ_p in B:

$$\phi_p(B) = (1 \times B^0 + \phi_1B^1 + \phi_2B^2 + \phi_3B^3 \ldots + \phi_pB^p)$$

therefore:

$$\phi_p(B)x_t = (1 + \phi_1B^1 + \phi_2B^2 + \phi_3B^3 \ldots + \phi_pB^p)x_t$$

$$= x_t + \phi_1x_{t-1} + \phi_2x_{t-2} + \phi_3x_{t-3} \ldots + \phi_px_{t-p}$$

i.e. $\phi_p(B)x_t$ is simply a weighted combination of x_t and the p preceding values of x. If we similarly define a polynomial $\theta_q(B)$ then $\theta_q(B)a_t$ is a weighted combination of a_t and the q preceding values of a.

$$(1-B^{12})x_t = x_t - B^{12}x_t = x_t - x_{t-12}$$

(seasonal differencing of x at 12-period gap)

The general form of seasonal differencing of x at a gap of s is $(1-B^s)x_t$ using s = 4, 12, 52 for quarterly, monthly, weekly data respectively with annual cycles, and s = 7 (or 5, 6, etc.) for daily data with a weekly cycle.

Box—Jenkins Autoregressive process (AR):

$$\phi_p(B)x_t = a_t \tag{13.7}$$

where a_t is 'white noise', i.e. a normally distributed random variable whose mean is zero and variance constant.

[For example $x_t = \phi_1x_{t-1} + \phi_2x_{t-2} + a_t$ can be written as

$$(1 - \phi_1 B + \phi_2 B^2)x_t = a_t]$$

Box–Jenkins Moving Average process (MA):

$$x_t = \theta_q(B)a_t \tag{13.8}$$

[For example $x_t = a_t + \theta_1 a_{t-1}$ can be written as $x_t = (1 + \theta_1 B)a_t$. This makes x_t a moving average of unobservable noise events a, rather than of observed values of x as in equation 13.1.]

Box–Jenkins Autoregressive Moving Average process (ARMA) of order (p, q)

$$x_t + \phi_1 x_{t-1} + \phi_2 x_{t-2} \ldots \phi_p x_{t-p} = a_t + \theta_1 a_{t-1} + \theta_2 a_{t-2} \ldots \theta_p a_{t-p}$$

which is written in shorthand as

$$\phi_p(B)x_t = \theta_q(B)a_t \tag{13.9}$$

Box–Jenkins Autoregressive Integrated Moving-Average process (ARIMA) of order (p, d, q)

$$\phi_p(B)(1-B)^d x_t = \theta_q(B)a_t \tag{13.10}$$

Box–Jenkins Autoregressive Integrated process (ARI) integrated d times, of order (p, d)

$$\phi_p(B)(1-B)^d x_t = a_t \tag{13.11}$$

For example, if X_t is the cumulative (integrated) value at time t of an AR process of order 2 which generates Y_t as follows:

$$Y_t + \phi_1 Y_{t-1} + \phi_2 Y_{t-2} = a_t$$

then

$$X_t = Y_t + X_{t-1} \text{ and } Y_t = X_t - X_{t-1} = (1-B)X_t$$

therefore

$$(1-B)X_t + \phi_1 BX_t + \phi_2 B^2(1-B)X_t = a_t$$

is an ARI of order (2, 1) which means that

$$X_t - (1 - \phi_1)X_{t-1} + (\phi_2 - \phi_1)X_{t-2} - \phi_2 X_{t-3} = a_t$$

Box–Jenkins Integrated Moving-Average process (IMA); of order (d, q)

$$(1-B)^d x_t = \theta_q(B)a_t \tag{13.12}$$

The Box–Jenkins Autoregressive Integrated Moving-Average process (ARIMA) is the combination of equations 13.11 and 13.12 given by 13.10.

Box–Jenkins Autoregressive Integrated Moving-Average process (ARIMA) with superimposed fixed trend γ (producing a polynomial trend in x of order d):

$$\phi_p(B)(1-B)^d x_t = \gamma + \theta_q(B) a_t \qquad (13.13)$$

Simplified form of Box–Jenkins ARIMA process without a fixed trend, operating on variable x ·seasonally differenced at gap s:

$$\phi_p(B)(1-B)^d(1-B^s) x_t = \theta_q(B) a_t \qquad (13.14)$$

Generalized seasonal form of Box–Jenkins ARIMA process without fixed trend, having statistical structure both between adjacent months (ϕ_p and θ_q) and across several successive years at seasonal gap s ($\Phi_P(B^s)$ and $\Theta_Q(B^s)$) which implies slowly changing seasonal patterns, evolving in a forecastable way from year to year:

$$\phi_p(B)\ \Phi_P(B^s)(1-B)^d(1-B^s)^D x_t = \theta_q(B)\ \Theta_Q(B^s) a_t \qquad (13.15)$$

References and further reading

Box, G.E.P. and G. Jenkins (1976) *Time Series Analysis Forecasting and Control*, 2nd edn, San Francisco: Holden Day.

Brown, R.G. (1967) *Smoothing, Forecasting and Prediction of Discrete Time Series*, New York: Rhinehart & Winston.

Cleary, J.P. and H. Levenbach (1982) *The Professional Forecaster*, Belmont, Calif.: Lifetime Learning Publications.

Fildes, R. (1985) 'Quantitative forecasting — the state of the art: econometric models', *Journal of the Operational Research Society*, vol. 36, pp. 549–80.

Fildes, R. (1987) 'Recent developments in time series forecasting', unpublished working paper, Manchester Business School, Manchester.

Fildes, R. and D. Dews (1984) 'A bibliography of business and economic forecasting (first supplement)', Manchester Business School working paper, Manchester.

Fildes, R., D. Dews, and S. Howell (1981) *A Bibliography of Business and Economic Forecasting*, Farnborough: Gower.

Gardner, E.S. and E. McKenzie (1988) 'Model identification in exponential smoothing', *Journal of the Operational Research Society*, vol. 39, pp. 863–7.

Granger, C.W.J. and P. Newbold (1979) *Forecasting Economic Time Series*, New York: Academic Press.

Harrison, R.J. and C.F. Stevens (1971) 'A Bayesian approach to short-term forecasting', *Operational Research Quarterly*, vol. 22, pp. 341–62.

Harrison, R.J. and C.F. Stevens (1976) 'Bayesian forecasting; with discussion', *Journal of the Royal Statistical Society*, vol. 38, pp. 205–47.

Harvey, A.C. (1981) *The Econometric Analysis of Time Series*, Oxford: Philip Allan.

Harvey, A.C. (1984) 'A unified view of statistical forecasting procedures; with discussion', *Journal of Forecasting*, vol. 3, pp. 245–75.

Howell, S.D. (1981) 'Learning and experience curves: a review', *Managerial Finance*, vol. 7, pp. 26–8.

Intrigilator, M.D. (1987) *Economic Models, Techniques and Applications*, Amsterdam: North Holland.

Jenkins, G.M. (1982) 'Some practical aspects of forecasting in organizations', *Journal of Forecasting*, vol. 1, pp. 3–21.

Jenkins, G.M. and G. McLeod (eds) (1983) *Case Studies in Time Series Analysis*, Lancaster: GJP Publications.

Judge, G.G., W.E. Griffiths, C.R. Hill, H. Lütkerphol and T. Lee (1980) *The Theory and Practice of Econometrics*, New York: John Wiley.

Levenbach, H. and J.P. Cleary (1982) *The Beginning Forecaster*, Belmont, Calif.: Lifetime Learning Publications.

Lewandowski, R. (1982) 'Sales forecasting by FORSYS', *Journal of Forecasting*, vol. 1, pp. 205–14.

Makridakis, S. and S.C. Wheelwright (1977) 'Adaptive filtering: an integrated autoregressive moving average filter for time series forecasting', *Operational Research Quarterly*, vol. 28, pp. 425–37.

Oliver, R. (1987) 'Bayesian forecasting with stable seasonal patterns', *Journal of Business and Economic Statistics*, vol. 5, pp. 77–85.

Parzen, E. (1982) 'ARARMA models for time series analysis and forecasting', *Journal of Forecasting*, vol. 1, pp. 67–82.

Schnaars, S.P. (1986) A comparison of extrapolation models on yearly sales forecasts', *International Journal of Forecasting*, vol. 2, pp. 71–85.

Trigg, D.W. and A.G. Leach (1967) 'Exponential smoothing with an adaptive response rate', *Operational Research Quarterly*, vol. 18, pp. 53–9.

Wood, D. and R. Fildes (1976) *Forecasting for Business: Methods and Applications*, London: Longman.

Chapter 14

Information technology and the changing role of management accountants

M. KING, R.A. LEE, J.A. PIPER and J. WHITTAKER

Anyone involved with leading organizations over the past decade has witnessed a new culture emerging in which managers have become increasingly able, proactive and innovative. This change provides the backcloth against which we will examine the relationship between information technology (IT) and developments in management accounting. We then explore the implications of IT for the role of the management accountant. It is apparent from the research underlying this chapter that IT and the new culture create opportunities and pressures for the management accountant.

Some reasons why this area of study is currently dynamic are:

1. Smaller, more powerful machines with increased storage capacity which are capable of handling sophisticated modelling packages are rapidly becoming available. The advent of remote work stations in the form of lap-top computers are increasing the flexibility of systems. Alongside these developments the costs of data-processing have significantly declined in recent years and further decreases are anticipated. (Processing costs have declined from $200,000 per million instructions in 1969 to $2,500 in 1980.)

2. The advances in technology referred to above have increased the type and quantity of financial and non-financial data collection and its diffusion within organizations. The traditional view of management accounting as the core of an organization's information system is being challenged and the boundaries of management accounting are being questioned. This raises the problem of how management accountants should respond. Should management accounting be concerned with primarily financial data or should it encompass the totality of the management information system?

3. The traditional role of the management accountant is being questioned both by themselves and other managers. Some are seen as 'scorekeepers', others as 'controllers' and others as 'providers of management information'. Many managers who were content to receive routine reports are now demanding

specific information or help with decision-making. Many who were prepared to be controlled by management accountants are now demanding to be treated as customers.

4. The three factors referred to above are closely interrelated and they are located in a complex web of dynamic organizational processes. For example, IT developments within a particular organization and their impact upon the management accounting function will be influenced by social and political considerations. A powerful financial controller may initiate IT developments to extend the domain of management accounting within the organization, while a weak or inexperienced one may witness the contraction of their function as other managers develop skills possessed by the accountants.

Developments in information technology

Towards the end of the middle ages the development of printing ushered in a revolution in information technology. Many would argue that a bigger revolution was started by the development of electronic computers in the 1940s. However, this second revolution was hampered by technological constraints. In the 1970s progress in the design and application of micro-processors helped bring together two distinct but interrelated elements of IT: computing and telecommunications. This encouraged developments in programming, which made computing accessible to an increasing range of non-specialists. The 1980s has seen a major growth in computing. In many organizations most managers have access to computing power, often at their finger tips on their desk. This trend will undoubtedly continue until nearly all accountants and managers have a computer on their desk linked to a central computer. This spread will be fuelled by further developments in telecommunications and computing.

As shown in Figure 14.1, telecommunications and computing impact on a number of interrelated data management activities, the main elements of which are data capture, data storage, data-processing and data retrieval. These activities have always been important to organizations and were undertaken by various laborious methods prior to electronic computing. However, major advances in IT have transformed the costs and benefits of these activities. Calculations, which twenty years ago would have taken a clerk hours, if not days, to complete, can now be achieved in seconds with a few key depressions on a personal computer. Micro-processor developments have enabled the accountant and managers to have the computing power of an army of clerks on their desks. Programming developments have enabled them to harness this power without specialist training often with little more than a few hours practice. Advances in telecommunications have not only enhanced instantaneous verbal communication, but they have also enabled high-speed, reliable, lower-cost data transmission over long distances. Further advances in telecommunications technology will continue to change the costs and benefits of long-distance data transmission.

In order to understand the impact of IT developments on management accountants, it is necessary to examine Figure 14.1 in more detail and to consider how the changes in the data management activities have been manifest in office automation and computer-based information systems.

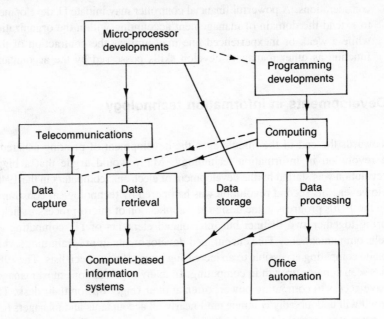

Figure 14.1 A classification of IT developments

Data capture

Advances in telecommunication and computing allow more data to be captured at an earlier stage and at remote locations. The electronic scanning of bar codes can be used in many industries to track raw materials, work in progress and finished products. Such systems are most evident in retailing where the use of Electronic Point of Sale (EPOS) equipment has significantly increased productivity. In the manufacturing industry much data can now be captured as each operation is completed, either being entered by the operator or being captured automatically by computer-controlled machines. Some data is captured by hand-held devices, which are then remotely interrogated by distant computers. In other situations central computers ring round remote locations in the middle of the night to collect data recorded during the day. In the office, routine data can be captured by typing in simple responses to standard forms on screens and professionals often find it more convenient to enter their own data using simple packages on personal computers.

Data storage

Technological advances have enabled increasingly large amounts of data to be stored in a readily accessible form. This has led to the growth of large central databases. Alongside the hardware improvement there have been programming developments which have facilitated the management of these databases. Theoretical developments paved the way to a more flexible approach to structuring databases. Programming concepts such as data dictionaries have led to standard ways of developing databases which can be linked together. At the local level, desk-top micro-computers with large working memories and impressive permanent storage on hard discs now enable increasingly sophisticated and fast applications. The development of networks has facilitated the rapid transference of data between local desk-top storage and the large central databases.

Data-processing

Perhaps the most apparent change is the stand-alone desk-top micro-computer or personal computer (PC). Once micro-processors had been developed so that the data on a normal screen could be virtually instantly modified, manipulated and redisplayed, then PCs were born. They were given commercial life by the rapid development of user-friendly and effective software for word-processing and spreadsheet applications. During the 1980s further micro-processor developments have improved the speed and capacity of PCs and developments in hard discs have greatly simplified storage. Also programming developments have brought applications packages which a novice can use and experts can admire.

Similar developments have been taking place with larger systems. Mini-computers are now available which can serve the needs of a small department. No special environment is needed and the systems are run within departments without the need for specialist computing staff or links to any other part of the organization. However, the opportunity for creating links has increased and the cost of processing power of large systems has been dramatically reduced. The processing power to manipulate very large company-wide databases is now readily available. Perhaps even more importantly, there has been significant improvements in the programming tools available to develop large systems. A key concept has been the separation of specific applications (such as order-processing or payroll) from the central database or databases. The databases are treated separately with an emphasis on reliability, consistency and compatibility. A variety of applications can be developed which rely on these databases. New languages, often referred to as fourth-generation programming languages, have emerged which enable the rapid development of such applications. These languages increase the productivity of programmers and can also be used by non-specialist programmers to develop their own applications.

Data retrieval

This has been affected by developments in telecommunications, micro-processors and programming. On-line enquiry facilities from remote locations to central databases are now available on a more cost-effective basis. The use of fourth-generation report-writing languages means that the design and creation of management reports is not only cheaper technologically, but it is being deskilled and productivity is continually improving. Advances in local area networks have enabled managers to retrieve data from the centre and then manipulate it on their own PCs. Further developments in PC packages and printers have facilitated the retrieval and display of information in attractive formats with graphical displays and high-quality printing. Perhaps the most significant implication for management is that data can be retrieved at a remote site almost instantaneously without any intermediary. So a branch manager can make an on-line enquiry about a customer's account or order status, without needing to contact any accountant, clerk or other worker. In fact, one branch manager may be able to check on another branch's stock so that a customer's requirements can be met quickly. Such systems mean that all the organization's operations are 'visible' to those with appropriate access to the system.

Returning to Figure 14.1, it will be seen that the changes in the data management activities have manifest themselves through developments in office automation and computer-based information systems. The spread of PCs in the 1980s started with word-processing and spreadsheet uses, and these continue to be the major applications. Word-processing facilities have become easier to use, quicker and more flexible, with ever more attractive output, now merging into desk-top publishing. Spreadsheets stabilized in a standard form in the mid-1980s but many managers have now incorporated database and financial modelling packages on their PCs. The trend to stand-alone micro-computers in office automation is now being replaced by the desire to link the micro-computers together and to central databases. This will allow a freer flow of information between departments and will encourage the use of electronic mail in organizations.

In the case of computer-based information systems, the developments in the early 1980s led to different departments buying and running their own small systems independently of the central systems. However, there is now a realization of the importance of linking all of the systems together and the concept of one or more central systems maintaining key databases, which other systems supply and interrogate, is becoming accepted. The next logical step of linking organizations has already begun with suppliers and customers being plugged into electronic data interchange systems. These allow customers to call off items from suppliers directly, and in return the payment can be made automatically over the system.

This description of IT developments may read rather like a computer sales presentation. The reality is that while much is technologically feasible for management information systems, in practice its achievement is difficult within specific organization situations. Problems occur because the technological developments in information technology have evolved in a discontinuous and diffuse manner. In particular:

1. new breakthroughs are often initially unreliable and unpredictable;
2. there are disparate and discontinuous rates of change in the costs of developments after they have entered the market;
3. there often needs to be a breakthrough in several related technological areas and a confluence of their cost/benefits.

A good illustration of the need for these elements to synchronize before a beneficial application occurs is EPOS systems for retailing. This required computing, telecommunications and scanners to be integrated in a reliable and cost-effective manner. Organizations are also constrained by their existing less flexible IT.

It is very difficult for managers and accountants who are not confident with the technology to be informed and knowledgeable about relevant developments and their implications for business, and to be aware of the significance of the timing of the introduction of IT developments. Developments in IT present the management accountant with both opportunities and threats, and can provide a basis for developing their strengths and overcoming or further exposing their weaknesses.

Management accounting: a perspective

There is a growing and rich literature in management accounting, which employs a wide variety of perspectives. Management accounting is not a coherent discipline or body of knowledge: it relies on various disparate disciplines, for example sociology, information sciences, psychology and statistics. This chapter employs a perspective which focuses upon the management of the organization and the enhancement of organization performance. To this end the approach of Chandler (1962) is used, whereby organizations are seen as objective seeking through the effective matching of strategy, structure and systems, as shown in Figure 14.2. This approach has the advantage of being structured and rational. It is also prescriptive but was derived from empirical study.

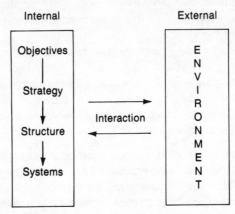

Figure 14.2 Elements of the strategy/structure process

From this perspective objectives are the ends pursued, strategy is the means, structure is the mechanism through which strategy is achieved, and systems provide the flow of information and other resources to enable the overall process to operate. The internal elements need to be consistent and to interact with the environment if the organization is to be effective. For example, if the objective is to double market share in six months, then the organization may formulate a strategy involving a range of production and marketing improvements. In order to bring about the improvements it may have to change structural aspects of the organization such as the tasks people perform, their location, their authority, their reporting relationships and so on. Having done this it will then need to redesign the systems governing flows of information, money, people and other resources. It will also need to create a control system providing information monitoring performance against the objectives so that corrective action can be taken if necessary. Once the organization has made the *strategic decision* and it has begun to implement the necessary changes, it then needs to carry out the day-to-day work leading towards the objective. This requires *operational decisions* and activity. To convert strategy into operation requires an intermediate level of decisions which Anthony *et al.* (1984) call *management decisions*.

In essence, 'strategic' decisions are concerned with the direction of the organization as a unit. They tend to be long term and involve complex deliberations concerning the nature and balance of resources within organizational activities. 'Management' decisions are concerned with the control of people and other resources so that strategic objectives and plans can be achieved. 'Operational' decisions are concerned with the day-to-day steering of activities. These levels of decision-making are also distinguishable by reference to the type of information they employ; information for strategic decisions being based primarily upon soft, outward-looking data, while at the other end of the spectrum, operational decisions rely primarily on information derived from hard, inward-looking data. There is no question that the management accountant can potentially be involved at every stage and level, but this is not always the case.

Simon *et al.* (1954) argued that accounting has three major functions:

1. Score-keeping: 'How well are we doing?'
2. Attention-directing: 'Which problems should I look into?'
3. Problem-solving: 'Which alternative should I choose?'

In Figure 14.3 the classification systems of Anthony *et al.* and Chandler have been combined into a matrix whereby management accounting and its developments can be discussed. In each cell of the matrix an example of the relevant type of management accounting activity is provided.

Management accounting has traditionally focused upon score-keeping, attention-directing and problem-solving, at the operational and management decision levels. Kaplan (1984) concludes that most major developments in management accounting were complete by the first quarter of this century: 'it is clear that the organizational form and reporting and evaluation systems for virtually all modern enterprises had evolved in General Motors by 1923 — 60 years ago.' (p. 399) As a result, Kaplan has questioned the appropriateness of traditional management accounting within the current economic and organizational environment.

Increasing managerial awareness of strategic aspects of management is, however, beginning to impact management accounting (see Ch. 5 in this volume). Traditionally the management accountant has been perceived as a scorekeeper functioning at the operational level.

Accountants have, to varying degress, extended their role into other cells within Figure 14.3 from the top left-hand cell, moving both down and to the right, and the majority now operate at the management level. Expansion into the management level implies a more forward-looking and holistic orientation.

As already illustrated, the organization structure is the mechanism through which activity takes place in the effort to fulfil strategies and to achieve objectives. The formal structure is referred to as the management planning and control system (MPCS). This outlines areas of responsibility, authority levels and reward structures (see Anthony *et al.* 1984). The formal organization systems that support the MPCS are the management information systems (MIS)

Orientation/ decision level Activity	Operational	Management	Strategic
Score-keeping	E.g. historical control management accounts	E.g. budgetary planning and control reports	E.g. strategic financial management concerned with evaluating strategic progress
Attention- directing	E.g. monitoring of production costs	E.g. variance analysis and exception reporting	E.g. strategic management accounting concerned with ascertaining competitors' costs
Problem- solving	E.g. pricing decisions (cost plus)	E.g. capital investment appraisal	E.g. strategic financial management concerned with evaluating acquisitions and disposals

Figure 14.3 Management accounting activity and orientation

— a subset of which is the financial information system (FIS). A schematic illustration of these relationships is presented in Figure 14.4.

In many people's minds, including accounting practitioners, the terms MIS and FIS are synonymous. MIS is often equated with a computerized information system. As the FIS has traditionally been the most developed and influential information system within organizations, the MIS has often been seen as nothing more than a technologically advanced FIS.

Many organizations have long-established information systems, particularly at the operational level, operated and controlled by various functional areas of management, to control the use of resources. For example, production has systems concerned with planning, scheduling and loading and distribution has systems concerned with fleet maintenance, replacement, and so on. All of these systems form part of the total MIS.

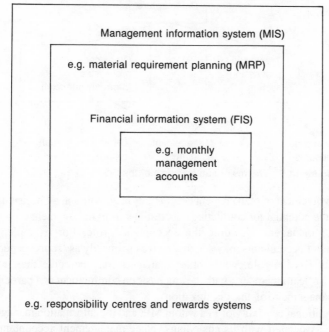

Management planning and control systems (MPCS)

Management information system (MIS)

e.g. material requirement planning (MRP)

Financial information system (FIS)

e.g. monthly management accounts

e.g. responsibility centres and rewards systems

Figure 14.4 The hierarchy of formal information systems

While the sub-systems operated by other functional specialists may provide data for the FIS, the FIS is itself a sub-system of MIS. The major elements of the FIS are illustrated in Figure 14.5. It is primarily associated with the capture and processing of financial data. A major element of the FIS is the transaction processing system, which is used to construct conventional financial and management accounts. While these two statements are primarily driven by the transactions processing systems, their compilation also relies upon data from other sources. For instance, data provided by the production sub-system may well be coupled with the costing system located in the FIS, to provide figures for management accounts as well as other more detailed management reports on production performance.

IT developments and the management accountant

Having outlined the management accounting activity and its orientation (see Figure 14.3) and the location and elements of the FIS (see Figures 14.4 and 14.5), we can now examine how IT has affected the management accountant's role with respect to the FIS.

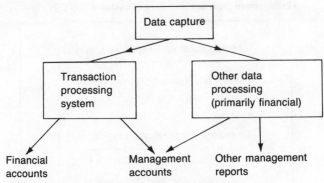

Figure 14.5 The major sub-elements of the FIS

The involvement of management accountants in activities at all decision levels presents the potential for conflicting expectations from management accountants and other managers regarding the accountants' role. For example, some management accountants may see themselves primarily as 'scorekeepers', an essentially passive role, while other managers may perceive their role as 'adviser' or 'team member', with the emphasis on commitment and participation in the management of the organization.

The traditional centrality of FIS within MIS and the information management expertise associated with its custodians, place management accountants in a privileged position within the MIS hierarchy. IT developments present them with an opportunity to exploit their position and to become custodians of an organization's IT resource. Potentially they could develop a broader role for themselves within the organization, that of information manager. But the adoption of a broader role enabling them to extend their influence across all information activities in the organization may give rise to heightened conflict with other managers. Alternatively, if they assume the passive role of customers of a separate IT department their influence may diminish and their role be reduced to, or remain as, that of 'scorekeeper'. The alternatives present significant opportunities and threats for management accountants.

Score-keeping

Computerized systems offer considerable potential for improvements ranging from the comprehensiveness of data to the timeliness of reporting. Electronic data capture can result in increased data collection at increased speed with a reduction in manpower. Remote terminals can be used to enter data, reducing the duplication of effort in manual systems. Disaggregation of data becomes easier, potentially quickening response times to queries. The time taken to produce management accounts and reports should reduce and the use of graphics should improve the quality of reporting. Another major advance in score-keeping using IT may be achieved through 'integrated information systems'. Such systems link the FIS with other functional sub-systems within the MIS. For instance, the FIS may be linked to materials requirement planning (MRP) systems in the production area. Thus data from one function can be processed and manipulated by another function. If these potential benefits are realized, one may expect a marked improvement in the productivity and service provided by management accountants in the score-keeping area.

Attention directing

IT developments present the opportunity for improvements in the quality and timeliness of information. A richer basis for analysis is provided by increased levels of data which are more interrelated and more accessible. In addition, IT can be used for automated signalling, that is automated exception reports, and to provide management reports that highlight trends or variances. The question arises as to whether these potential benefits are being exploited by management. One might expect this area of activity to be on the increase if increased score-keeping productivity has released some of the management accountant's time.

Problem-solving

It is anticipated that lower cost, more user-friendly IT, especially in the form of personal computers (PCs), will be used by management accountants to handle problem-solving situations, for example analysis of a capital investment proposal or the financial viability of marketing plans. It is possible, however, that the same medium, PCs, may be used by other functional areas to perform these same problem-solving tasks for themselves. If this is the case, will management accountants become more concerned with problem-solving at the strategic level? Given more user-friendly software packages and improved communication links with large databases, the sophistication of the problem-solving activities at the strategic level have the potential to increase.

Some preliminary observations from research into management accounting and IT

The remainder of this chapter examines some preliminary observations from ongoing research into the relationship between IT changes and management accounting. The observations focus on four issues:

1. What impact have IT developments had on the score-keeping aspects of management accounting?
2. What impact have IT developments had on the attention directing aspects of management accounting?
3. What impact have IT developments had on the problem-solving aspects of management accounting?
4. What impact have IT developments had on the working relationship between management accountants and other managers?

Score-keeping

Score-keeping is the activity that has received the greatest attention in terms of IT. It includes both the production of management and financial accounts and budgets. While commentators and vendors of IT refer to the creation of integrated information systems there is limited evidence of their current use. Only two of the sixteen companies studied had moved to computer-based systems which integrated financial processes or had introduced or were contemplating introducing integrated management information systems. All of these examples of IT being used to integrate information systems lay in the distribution, mineral extraction and retailing sectors. In the manufacturing sector some organizations were planning to achieve integration while the others have not even considered this option. An inference is that integration may be more difficult in the manufacturing sector. This state of affairs raises the question of why current practice is so far behind what is technically feasible. One factor is the inertia that is created by the long-established and fragmented systems that exist. Fragmentation may lead to systems which are computerized to different degrees and also non-compatible computer systems.

Another possible cause of the lack of integration is the observed tendency of a significant number of management accountants to use IT developments to computerize existing score-keeping systems rather than to use them as an opportunity to redesign the existing systems. Those companies that were subsidiaries had a tendency to computerize their score-keeping systems so that they could produce the information packages required by head office more rapidly.

Below are our general observations on the impact of computerization on accounting systems and the benefits of using IT for the scorekeeping system.

1. There is evidence of improved labour productivity at all levels of the process, for example data capture, processing, storage and retrieval.
2. Monthly management accounts can often be produced more rapidly, although they are usually produced in the same format. (Note in this regard the above comments about subsidiary companies.)

3. Disaggregation of information and response to enquiries are enhanced.

To summarize, the impact upon score-keeping systems of computerization is fragmented, variable across organizations, and in many cases it is concerned with computerizing existing operational and management systems with some potential benefits in terms of productivity, timeliness and disaggregation. On the other hand, in the distribution, extraction and retailing case studies, there had been significant progress towards integrated information systems. In manufacturing, our evidence suggests much slower progress.

Attention-directing

In the companies researched we found few examples of IT being used to enhance attention-directing, and even where the facility is available there was little evidence of it being used. In addition, the management accountants did not seem to be spending more time on this area. This appears to be because the score-keeping productivity gains were primarily at the junior and clerical levels.

Attention-directing falls into two distinct areas: first, the use of IT to produce management reports which highlight exceptions or trends automatically (a simple example would be the use of bold type for all variances over a certain percentage); second, the release of management accountants' time from more mundane score-keeping which could be used on the interpretive and analytical aspects.

In general, the research findings to date do not identify developments in either of these areas. While the IT facilities to enhance attention-directing in reports are available, the IT tends to be used to produce conventional reports. It is not clear whether this was due to a lack of interest by management accountants in this innovation or whether the users of the management information did not require the potential service. Given the developments to date in expert systems, complex exception reporting systems could be developed.

Furthermore, while we found increases in score-keeping productivity, this did not create more time for management accountants to undertake more attention-directing activities. While they tended to claim a desire to do this, coping with the introduction of IT and the increasing pressures for better and faster score-keeping appeared to be more pressing issues on the management accountants' current agenda.

Problem-solving

In the companies studied there was varying use by management accountants of PCs in general and for problem-solving specifically. In one case PCs were banned by the chief executive in the belief that their introduction would result in the proliferation of duplicate and incompatible databases.

Nevertheless, there was some evidence of PCs being used for problem-solving analyses and subsequent report generation. In a few cases the PCs were linked to the main computer processing facility. When this took place there was evidence of management accountants using the facility and being satisfied with it. This appeared to be so because they could obtain specific analyses without being dependent upon a computer services department. Interestingly, in one case study site which had this facility, the older management accountants felt that their contemporaries spent too much time using the newer PC facilities.

While the management accountant is using IT to aid problem-solving, we will demonstrate in the next section that the end-users are not always satisfied with the results.

The role of the management accountant

We will refer to the recipients of management accounting information as end-users. End-users can be classified into those who are of equal or senior status to the management accountant in the organizational hierarchy and those who are more junior.

In general we found management accountants to be more orientated to meeting the information needs of senior managers. There was widespread dissatisfaction amongst all end-users about the service which they receive from management accountants, but not surprisingly in view of the greater attention they receive, this was lowest amongst senior managers. Dissatisfaction was least prevalent in those companies which had fully introduced integrated management information systems.

Many end-users see themselves as customers of the management accountants, whereas management accountants often do not share this perspective, seeing themselves more as 'watchdogs', overseeing the activities of end-users. To illustrate the point a specific example will be used. In a large consumer goods company the marketing manager asked the management accountants for certain management accounting information. The management accountants responded by stating that they could not meet the request as they were too busy compiling routine reports for senior management. The marketing manager's response was that he still needed the information, so he established his own independent marketing management accounting information system. About two years later the management accountants expressed concern and anxiety about what the marketing manager had done. While IT developments create opportunities to fulfil information needs, they also create threats to the management accountant. Opportunities not taken may be lost for good.

The preliminary case study findings indicate that there are three distinct situations with regard to the provision of IT:

1. where the management accountant is responsible for the management accounting activities and has control of the IT to produce the management accounting information;
2. as above, except that the management accountant is responsible for the management of all or a significant part of the company's IT activity, not just that concerned with management accounting;
3. where the management accountant receives the IT service for the production of the management accounting information from a separate responsibility centre.

When managment accountants received an IT service from another responsibility centre, they tended to express dissatisfaction in similar terms to other end-users. However, there were also management accountants who expressed increasing satisfaction with the service they are receiving. This was often because they had obtained direct access to the computing service and because of intelligent terminals and/or PCs linked to the main systems. They could access data and in a user-friendly system could produce new reports or modify reports and perform analysis. Their increased satisfaction with the service appeared to be because they could now achieve these tasks without being dependent upon the IT department.

End-users' dissatisfaction, which appears to exist whether the management accountants control the IT or not, is studied below in more detail. As one might expect, there were several explanations:

1. The end-users of management accounting and/or IT services were not customers in the true sense of the word. They did not pay for the information service that they received. There is a propensity, when receiving an important service which is free, to expect and demand a high-quality service. In the research case studies there was little evidence of end-users being given the choice of receiving a 'better' service level but having to pay for this out of their own budget.

2. Remembering that the end-users who expressed most dissatisfaction were middle-line managers, there was evidence that they were under increasing managerial pressure. One reason for this was that the environment in which they were operating had become increasingly hostile. In addition, efforts by senior managers to improve score-keeping through IT had resulted in more information for hierarchical control, which had increased insecurity amongst middle managers and had led to more questioning of their activities.

3. Given that the ownership and control of information is a major source of power in organizations, there will be a tendency, especially if the formal information is available without cost to the end-user, for the providers to

be put under pressure to deliver increasing amounts, more rapidly and in different formats. By this argument some dissatisfaction may be seen as politically motivated.

4. There is a phenomenon in organizations of managers wishing to be 'over-informed' — not necessarily because information is power, but because there is a cultural value in 'being informed'. Not to know, even if this is reasonable and/or rational, is seen as a political source of failure and has negative connotations.

5. Another potential reason for dissatisfaction of end-users is that the controllers of the IT derive power from this control. The introduction of IT therefore changes the status quo in favour of the group controlling it.

The above only starts what should be an important debate about the future role of the management accountant. Changes in IT appear likely to add urgency to the need for such a debate.

Summary

In the preceding sections the following salient points have been made:

1. The focus and breadth of management accounting as a body of knowledge is changing and the boundaries are being expanded away from the traditional base of score-keeping.
2. There continues to be a rapid advance of IT, and this opens up new opportunities for management accounting and more broadly based information management.
3. The creation and operation of management information systems is not predominantly a technical issue, but is also heavily dependent upon people operating in complex contexts.
4. The current practice of management accounting and information management is widely divergent, but is significantly below what is technically, and possibly financially, feasible.
5. In general, the end-users of information systems expressed dissatisfaction with the service that they were receiving even when additional IT is introduced into the organization.
6. All of the above factors raise major questions about what the role of the management accountant is and should be.

References

Anthony, R.N., J. Dearden, and N.M. Bedford (1984) *Management Control Systems*, Homewood, Ill.: R.D. Irwin.

Bromwich, M. and A.G. Hopwood (1986) *Research and Current Issues in Management Accounting*, London: Pitman.

Chandler, A.D. (1962) *Strategy and Structure*, Cambridge, Mass.: MIT Press.

Kaplan, R.S. (1984) 'The evolution of management accounting', *The Accounting Review*, July, pp. 390–418.

Simon, H.A. (1966) *The New Science of Management Decision*, London: Harper & Row.

Simon, H.A., H. Gwetzkow, G. Kozmetsky, and G. Tyndall (1954) *Centralisation v Decentralisation in Organising the Controllers Department*, New York: Controllership Foundation.

Index